11/07

VIZ GRAPHIC NOVEL

THE RETURN OF LUM * URUSEI YATSURA™
LUM
IN THE SUN

STORY & ART BY
RUMIKO TAKAHASHI

CONTENTS

This volume contains the monthly series THE RETURN OF LUM * URUSEI YATSURA #1 through #6 and the first half of #7 in their entirety.

**STORY AND ART BY
RUMIKO TAKAHASHI**

English Adaptation/Gerard Jones & Mari Morimoto
Touch-Up Art & Lettering/Wayne Truman
Cover Design/Viz Graphics
Editor/Annette Roman

Editor-in-Chief/Hyoe Narita
Publisher/Seiji Horibuchi
Director of Sales & Marketing/Dallas Middaugh
Marketing Manager/Renée Solberg
Sales Representative/Mike Roberson

Printed in Canada

Published by Viz Communications, Inc.
P.O. BOX 77010 • San Francisco, CA 94107

10 9 8 7 6 5 4 3 2
First printing, April 1996
Second printing, November 2001

PART ONE
THE DEVIL'S RUN

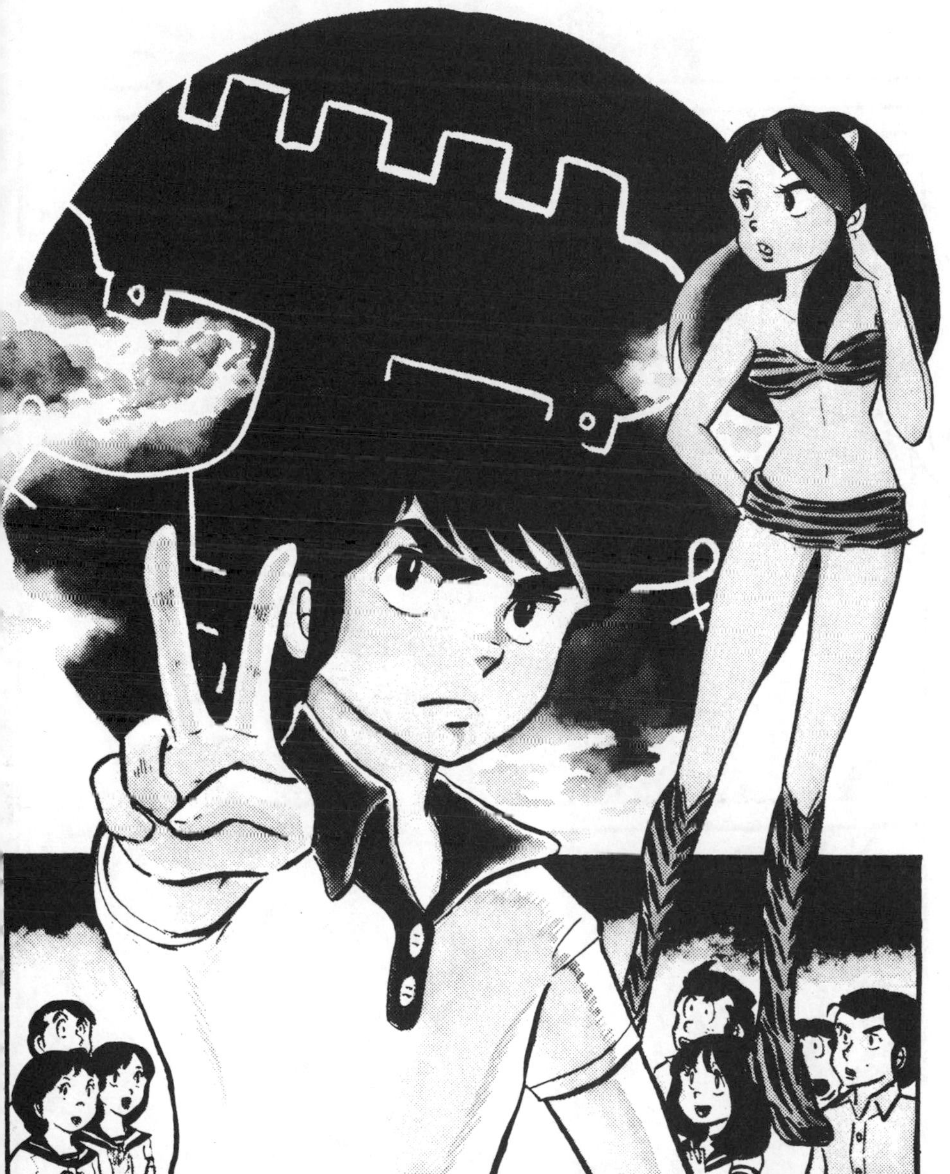

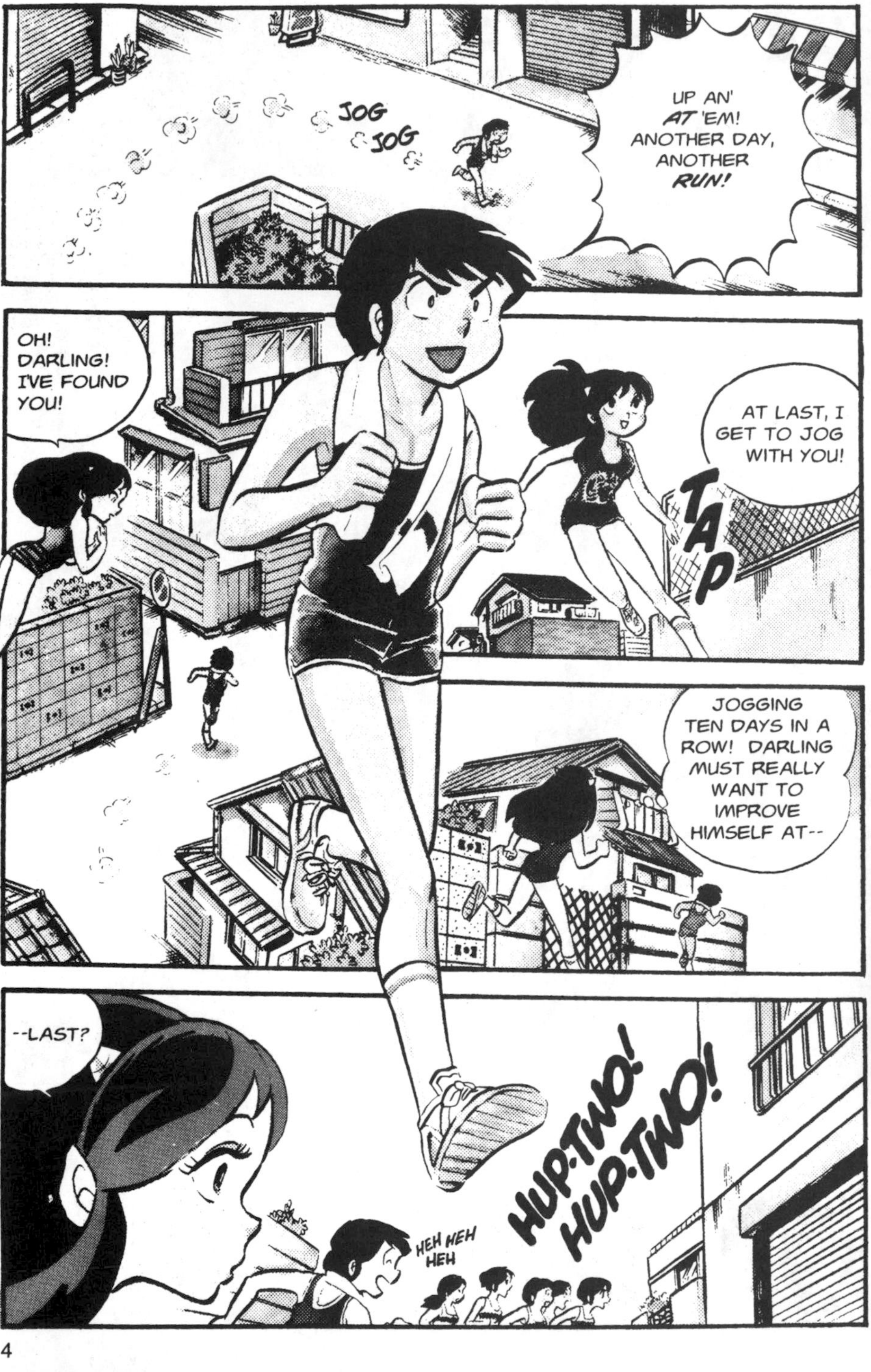
JOG JOG
UP AN' AT 'EM! ANOTHER DAY, ANOTHER RUN!
OH! DARLING! I'VE FOUND YOU!
AT LAST, I GET TO JOG WITH YOU!
TAP
JOGGING TEN DAYS IN A ROW! DARLING MUST REALLY WANT TO IMPROVE HIMSELF AT--
--LAST?
HEH HEH HEH
HUP-TWO! HUP-TWO!

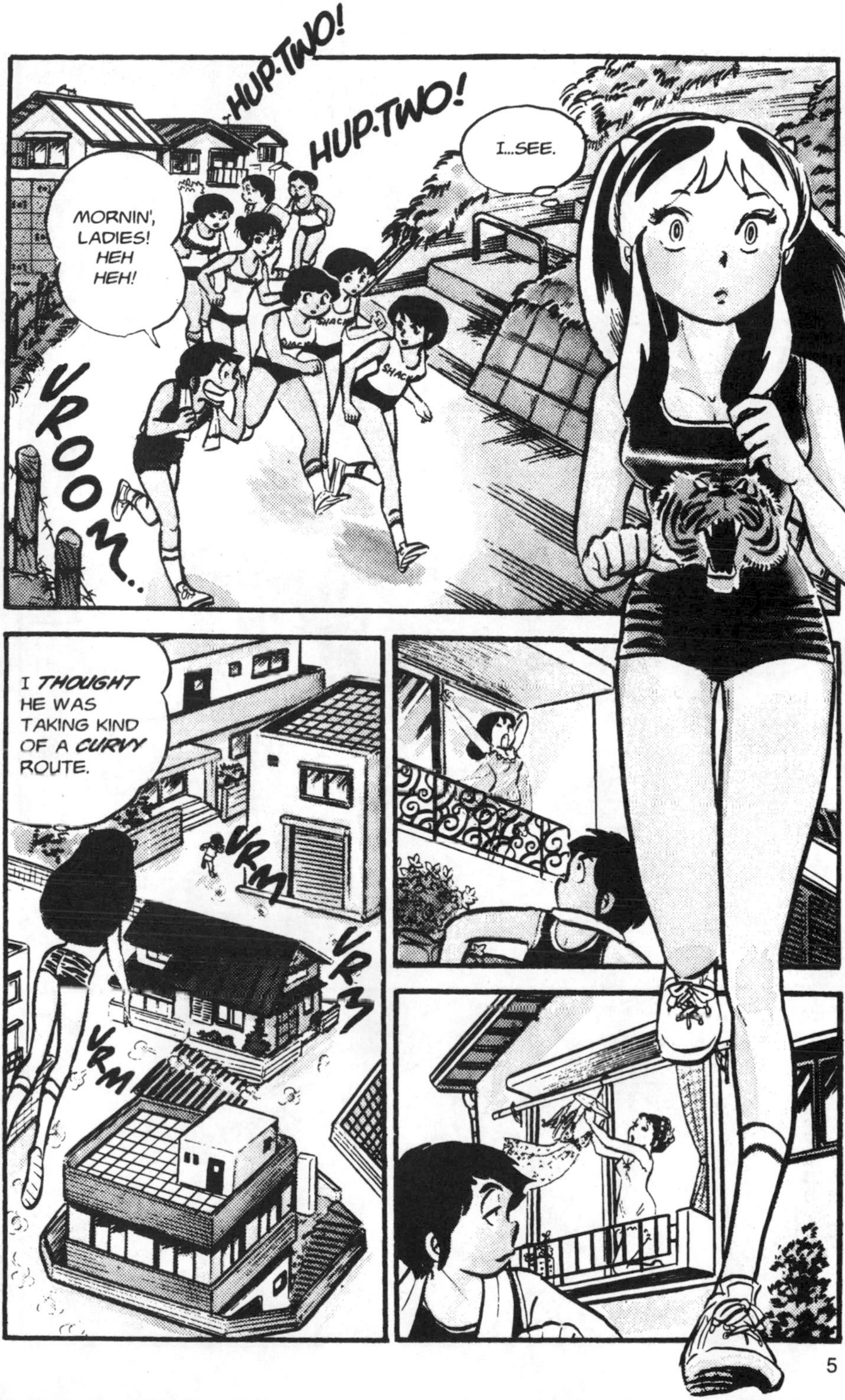
HUP-TWO!
HUP-TWO!
MORNIN', LADIES! HEH HEH!
VROOOM...
I...SEE.
I *THOUGHT* HE WAS TAKING KIND OF A *CURVY* ROUTE.
VRM
VRM
VRM
VRM

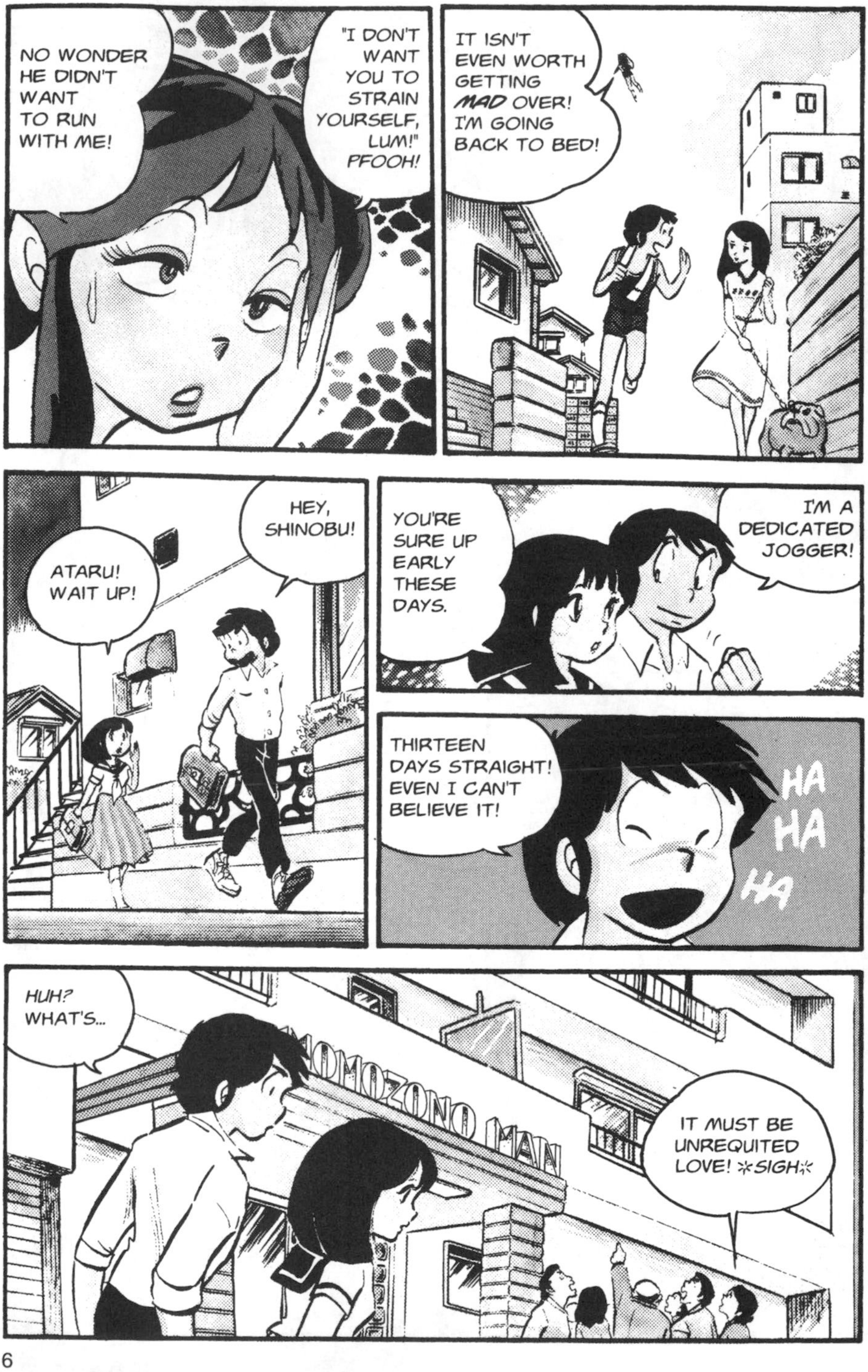
NO WONDER HE DIDN'T WANT TO RUN WITH ME!
"I DON'T WANT YOU TO STRAIN YOURSELF, LUM!" PFOOH!
IT ISN'T EVEN WORTH GETTING MAD OVER! I'M GOING BACK TO BED!
ATARU! WAIT UP!
HEY, SHINOBU!
YOU'RE SURE UP EARLY THESE DAYS.
I'M A DEDICATED JOGGER!
THIRTEEN DAYS STRAIGHT! EVEN I CAN'T BELIEVE IT!
HA HA HA
HUH? WHAT'S...
MOMOZONO MAN
IT MUST BE UNREQUITED LOVE! ✲SIGH✲

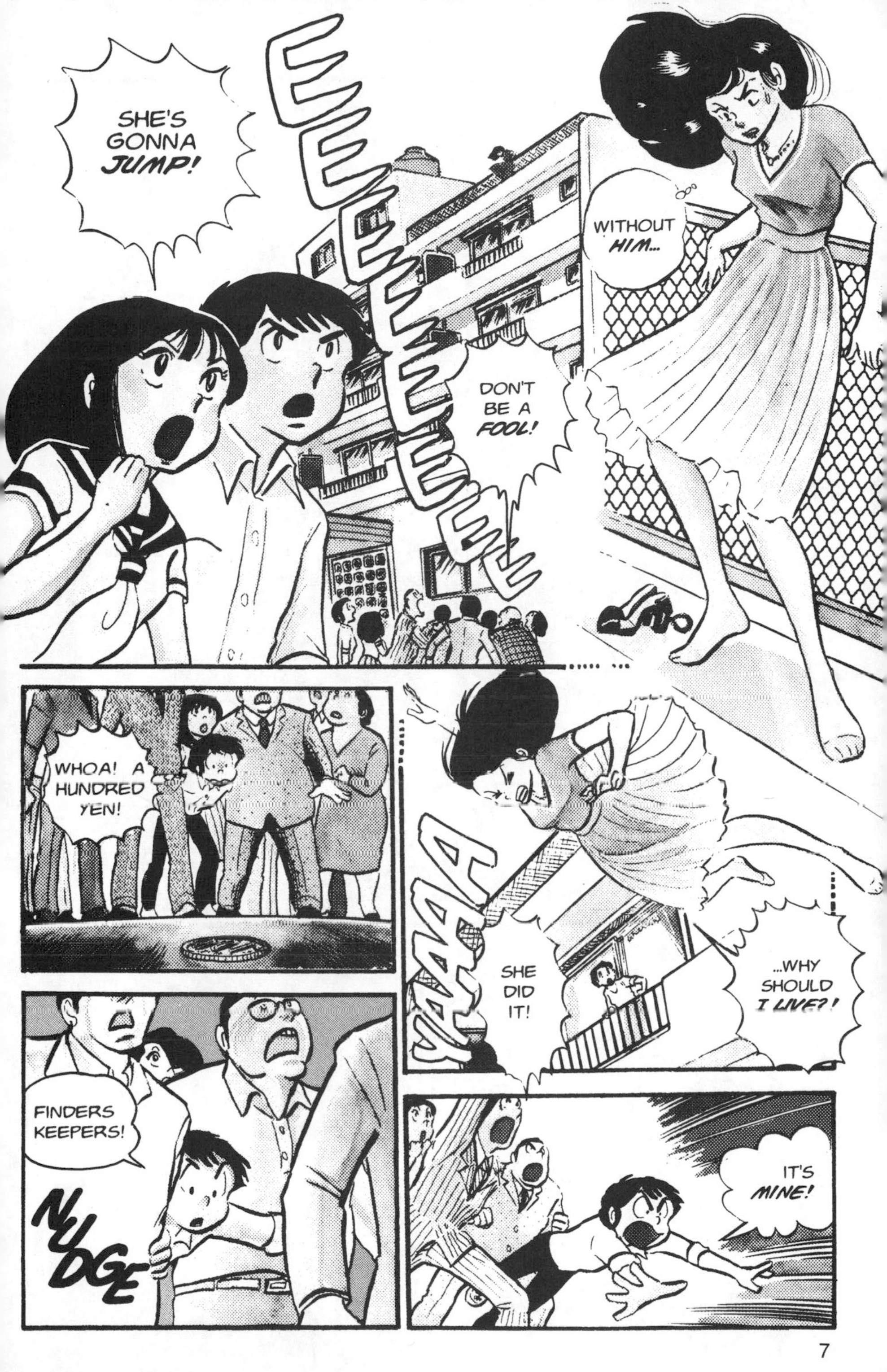
SHE'S GONNA JUMP!
EEEEEEEEEE
WITHOUT HIM...
DON'T BE A FOOL!
WHOA! A HUNDRED YEN!
FINDERS KEEPERS!
NUDGE
HAAAA
SHE DID IT!
...WHY SHOULD I LIVE?!
IT'S MINE!

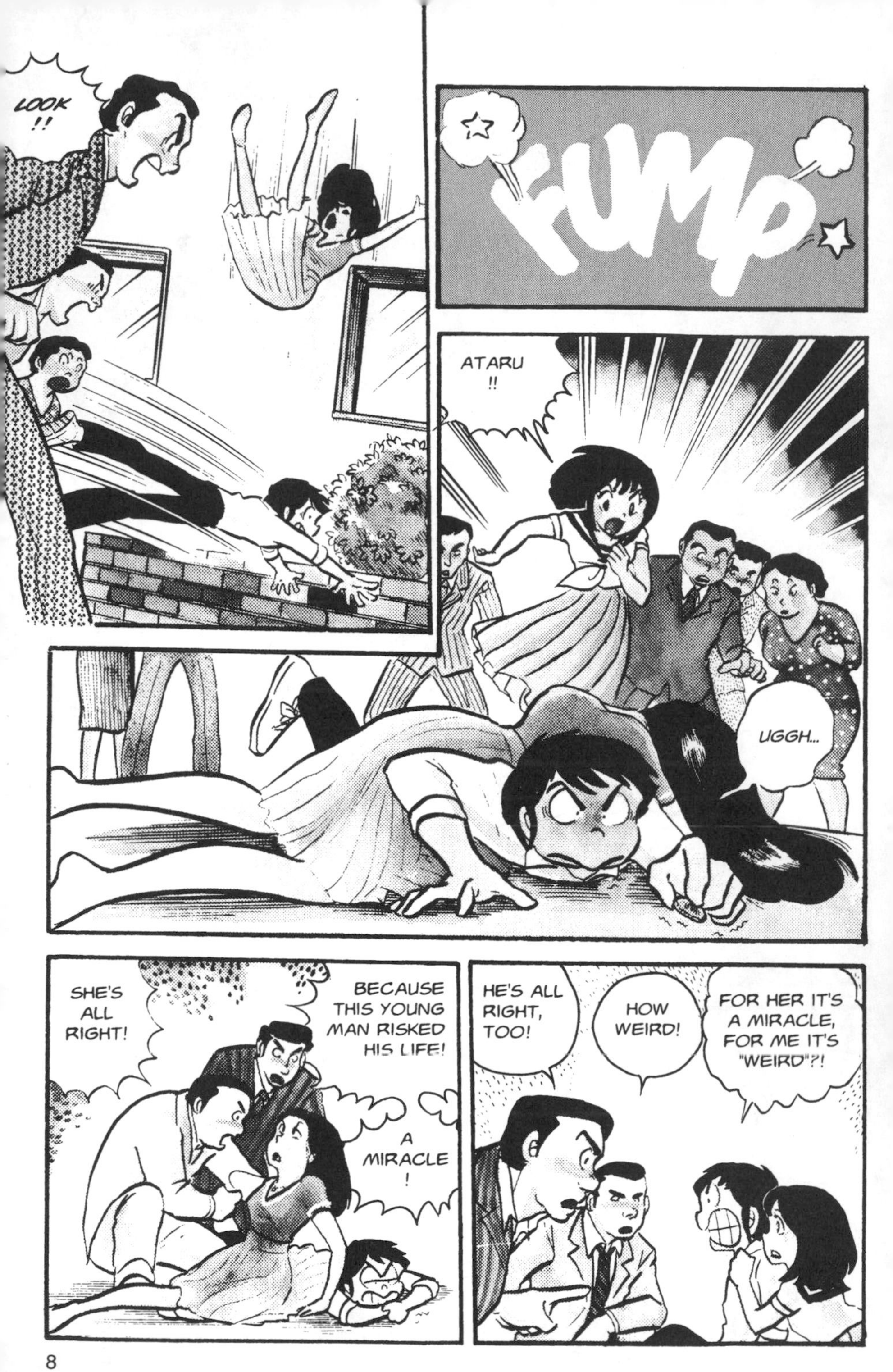
LOOK !!
FUMP
ATARU !!
UGGH...
SHE'S ALL RIGHT!
BECAUSE THIS YOUNG MAN RISKED HIS LIFE!
A MIRACLE !
HE'S ALL RIGHT, TOO!
HOW WEIRD!
FOR HER IT'S A MIRACLE, FOR ME IT'S "WEIRD"?!

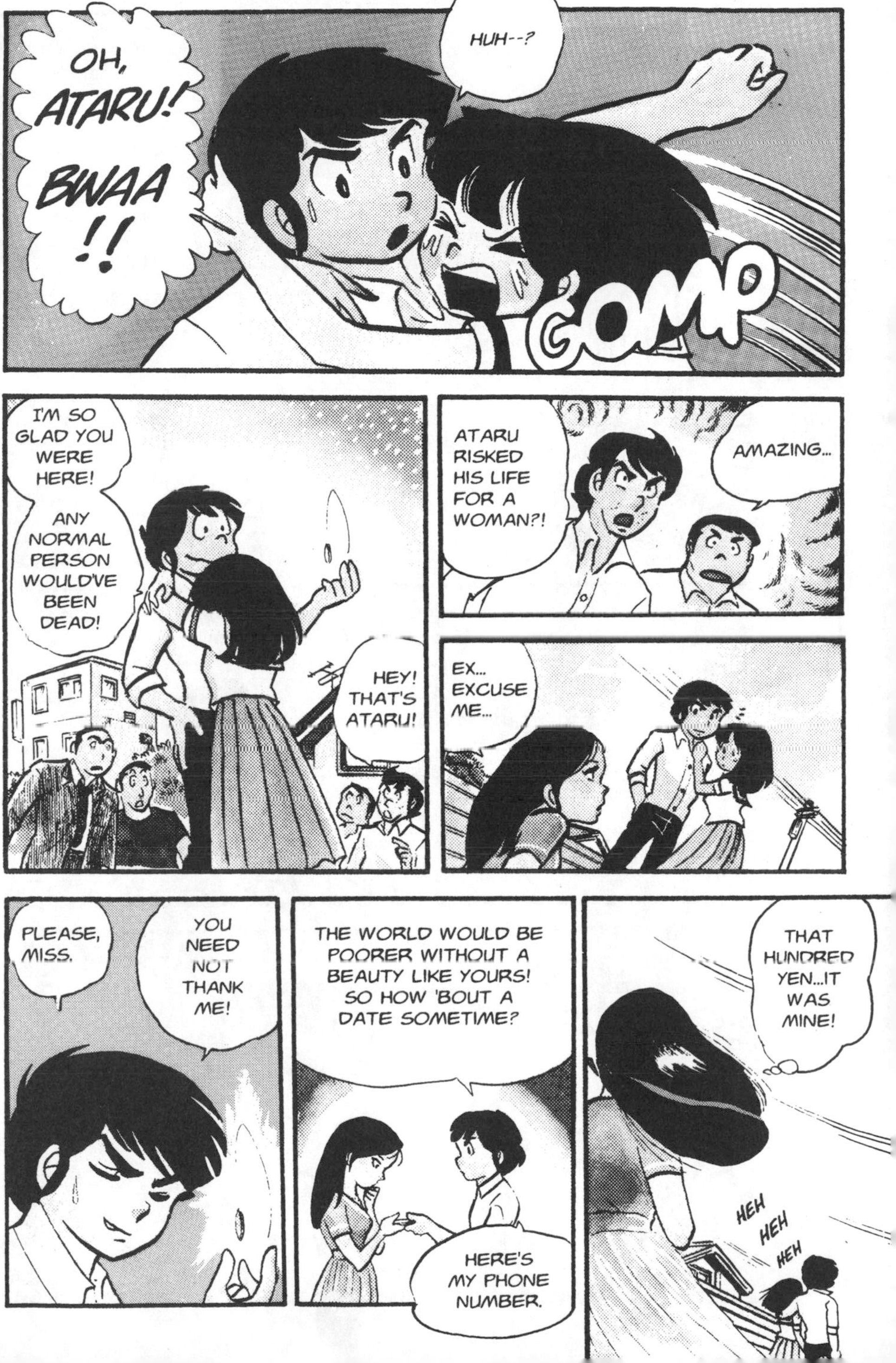
OH, ATARU! BWAA!!
HUH--?
GOMP
I'M SO GLAD YOU WERE HERE!
ANY NORMAL PERSON WOULD'VE BEEN DEAD!
HEY! THAT'S ATARU!
ATARU RISKED HIS LIFE FOR A WOMAN?!
AMAZING...
EX... EXCUSE ME...
PLEASE, MISS.
YOU NEED NOT THANK ME!
THE WORLD WOULD BE POORER WITHOUT A BEAUTY LIKE YOURS! SO HOW 'BOUT A DATE SOMETIME?
HERE'S MY PHONE NUMBER.
THAT HUNDRED YEN...IT WAS MINE!
HEH HEH HEH

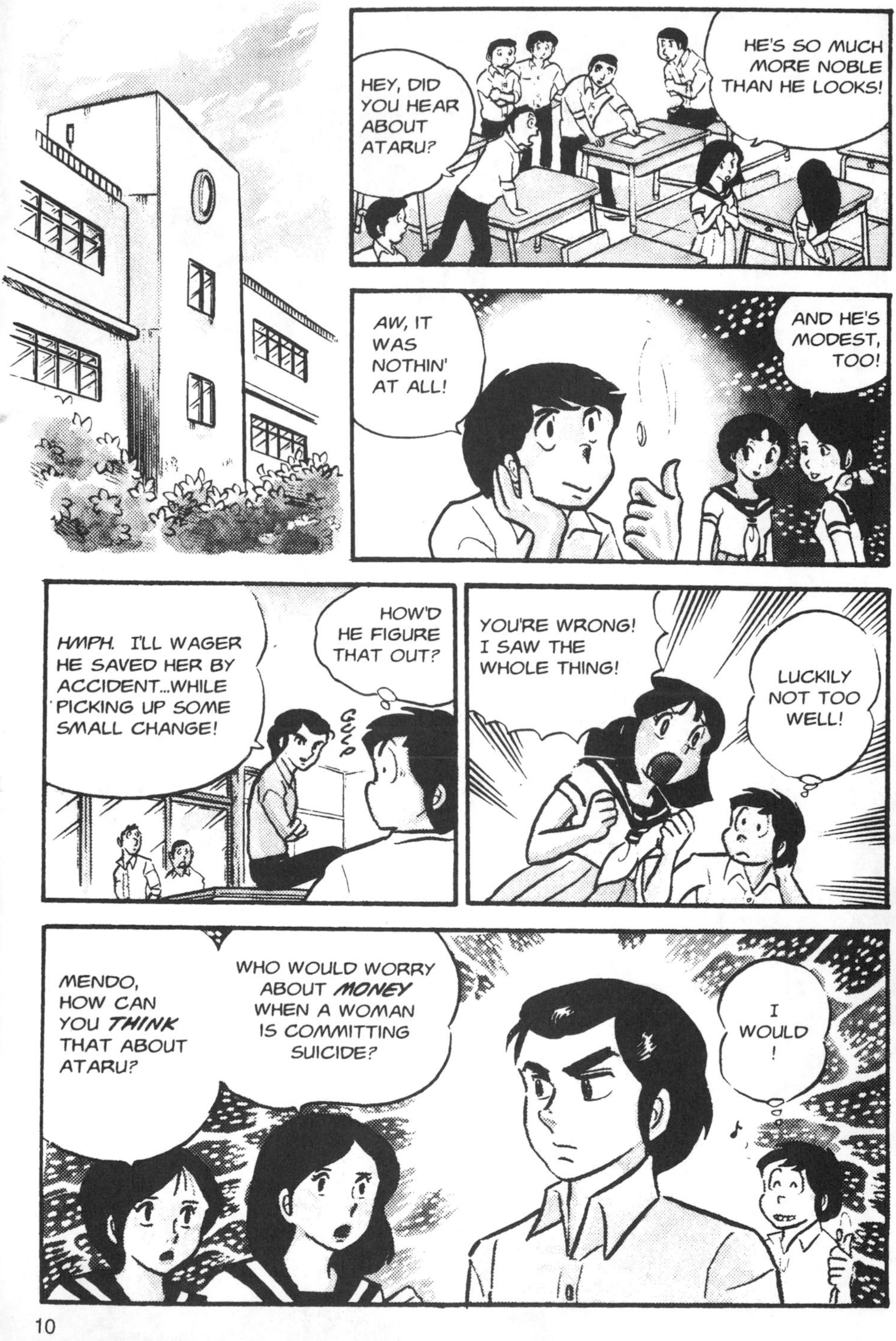
HEY, DID YOU HEAR ABOUT ATARU?
HE'S SO MUCH MORE NOBLE THAN HE LOOKS!
AW, IT WAS NOTHIN' AT ALL!
AND HE'S MODEST, TOO!
HMPH. I'LL WAGER HE SAVED HER BY ACCIDENT...WHILE PICKING UP SOME SMALL CHANGE!
HOW'D HE FIGURE THAT OUT?
GULP
YOU'RE WRONG! I SAW THE WHOLE THING!
LUCKILY NOT TOO WELL!
MENDO, HOW CAN YOU THINK THAT ABOUT ATARU?
WHO WOULD WORRY ABOUT MONEY WHEN A WOMAN IS COMMITTING SUICIDE?
I WOULD!

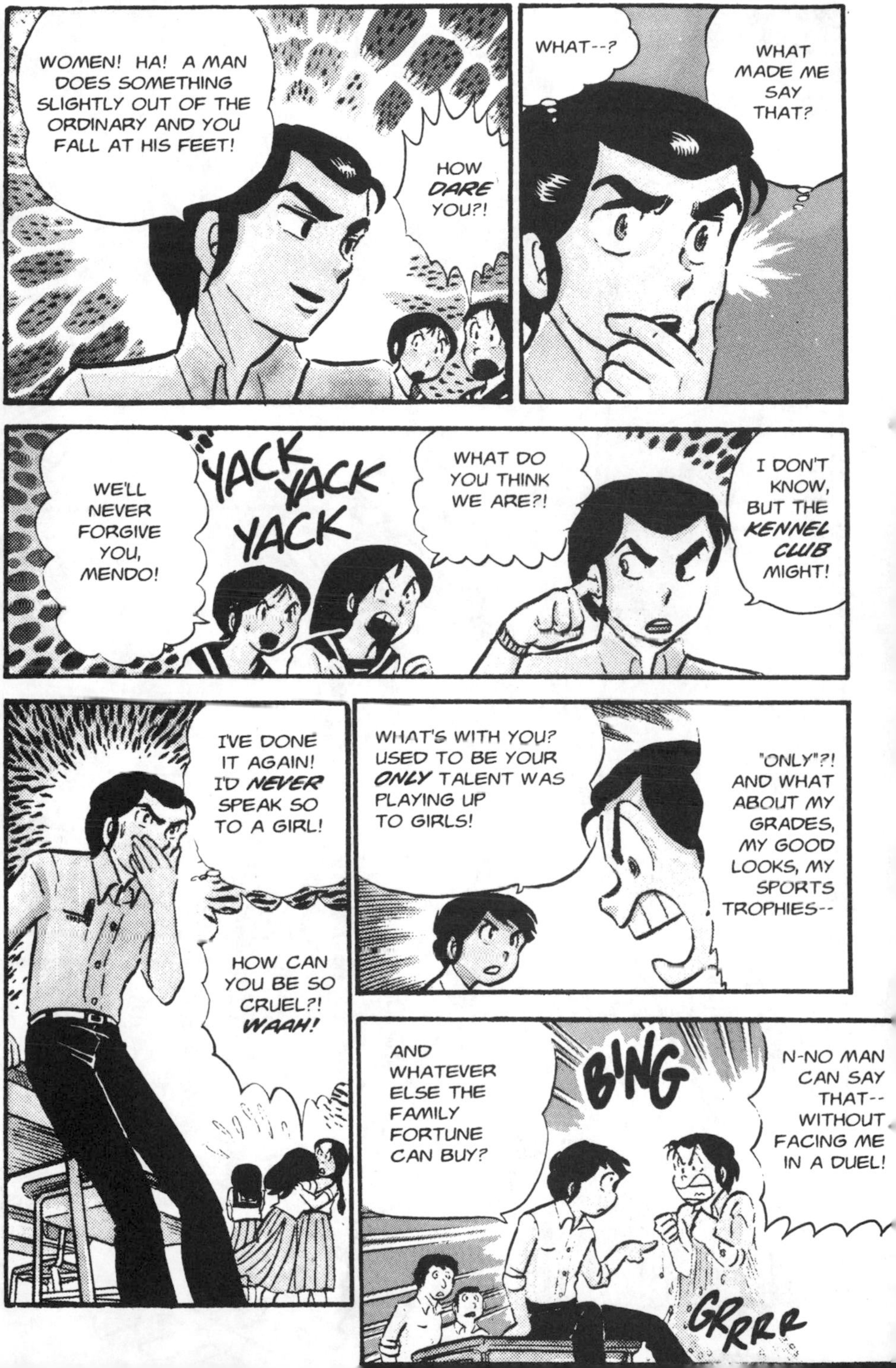
WOMEN! HA! A MAN DOES SOMETHING SLIGHTLY OUT OF THE ORDINARY AND YOU FALL AT HIS FEET!
HOW DARE YOU?!
WHAT--?
WHAT MADE ME SAY THAT?
WE'LL NEVER FORGIVE YOU, MENDO!
YACK YACK YACK
WHAT DO YOU THINK WE ARE?!
I DON'T KNOW, BUT THE KENNEL CLUB MIGHT!
I'VE DONE IT AGAIN! I'D NEVER SPEAK SO TO A GIRL!
HOW CAN YOU BE SO CRUEL?! WAAH!
WHAT'S WITH YOU? USED TO BE YOUR ONLY TALENT WAS PLAYING UP TO GIRLS!
"ONLY"?! AND WHAT ABOUT MY GRADES, MY GOOD LOOKS, MY SPORTS TROPHIES--
AND WHATEVER ELSE THE FAMILY FORTUNE CAN BUY?
BING
N-NO MAN CAN SAY THAT-- WITHOUT FACING ME IN A DUEL!
GRRRR

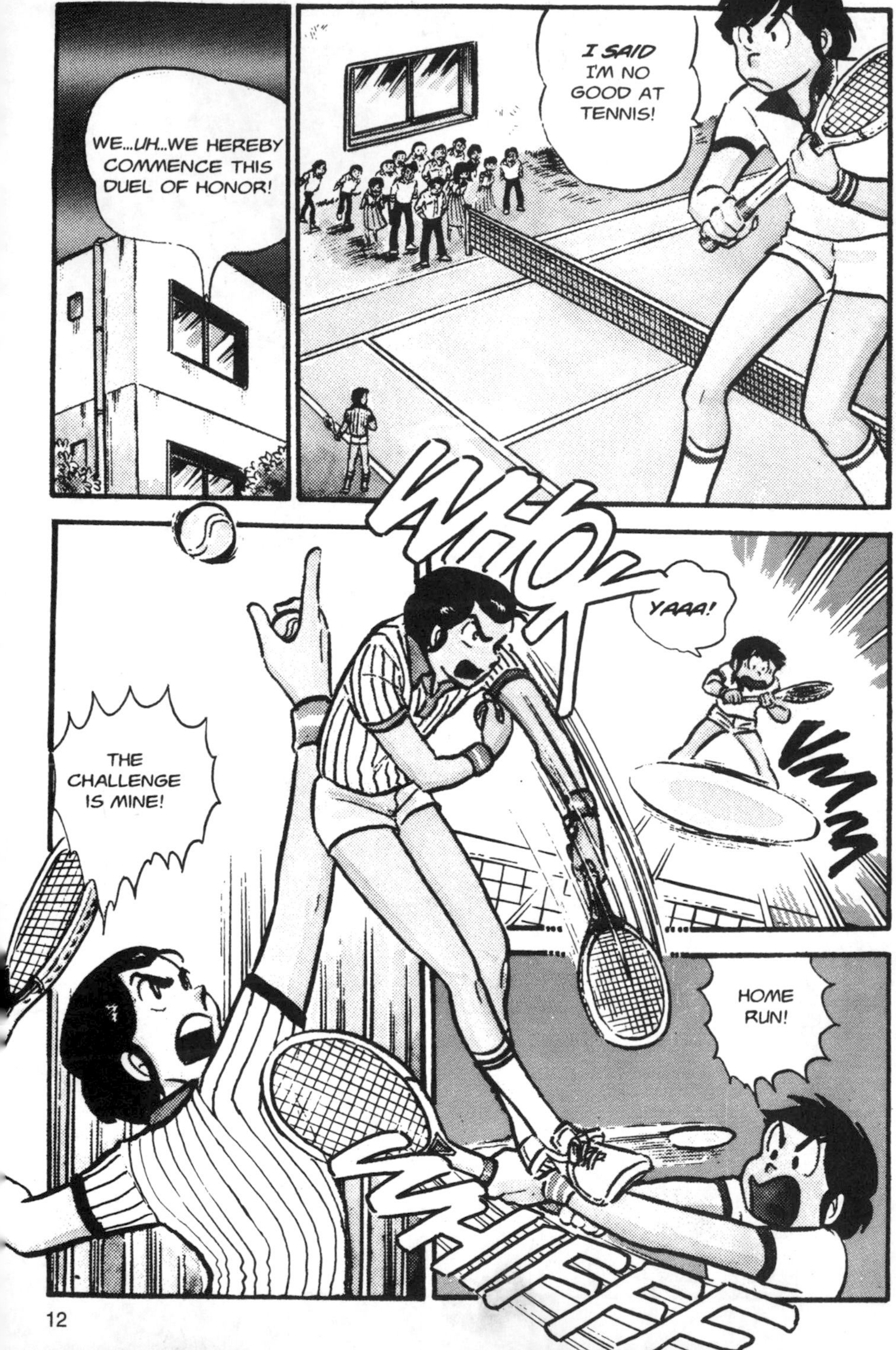
WE...UH...WE HEREBY COMMENCE THIS DUEL OF HONOR!
I SAID I'M NO GOOD AT TENNIS!
THE CHALLENGE IS MINE!
WHOK
YAAA!
VMMM
HOME RUN!
WHIFFF

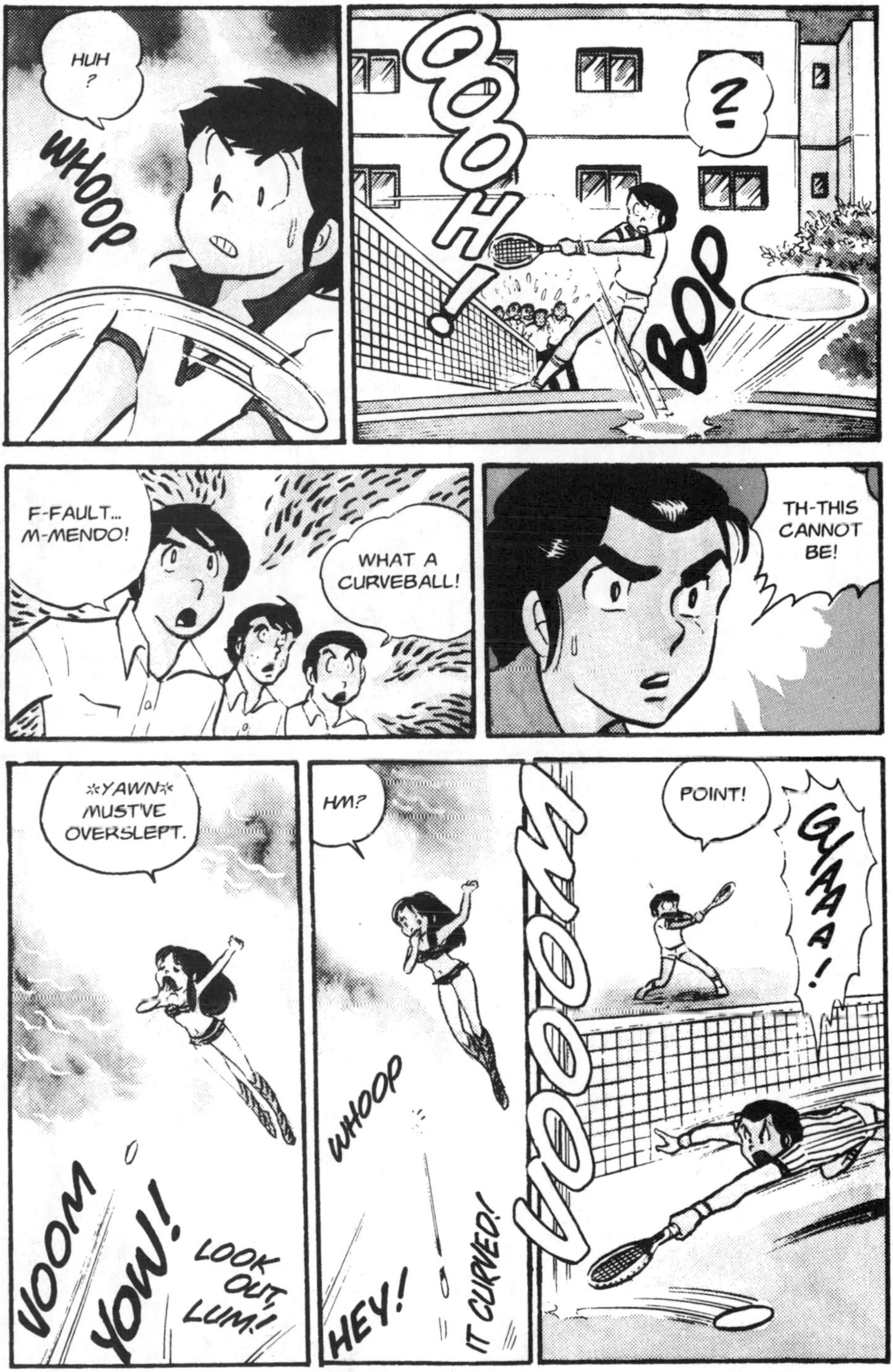
HUH?
WHOOP
OOOH!
?!
BOP
F-FAULT... M-MENDO!
WHAT A CURVEBALL!
TH-THIS CANNOT BE!
YAWN MUST'VE OVERSLEPT.
VOOM
YOW!
LOOK OUT, LUM!
HM?
WHOOP
HEY!
IT CURVED!
VOOOOM
POINT!
GYAAAA!

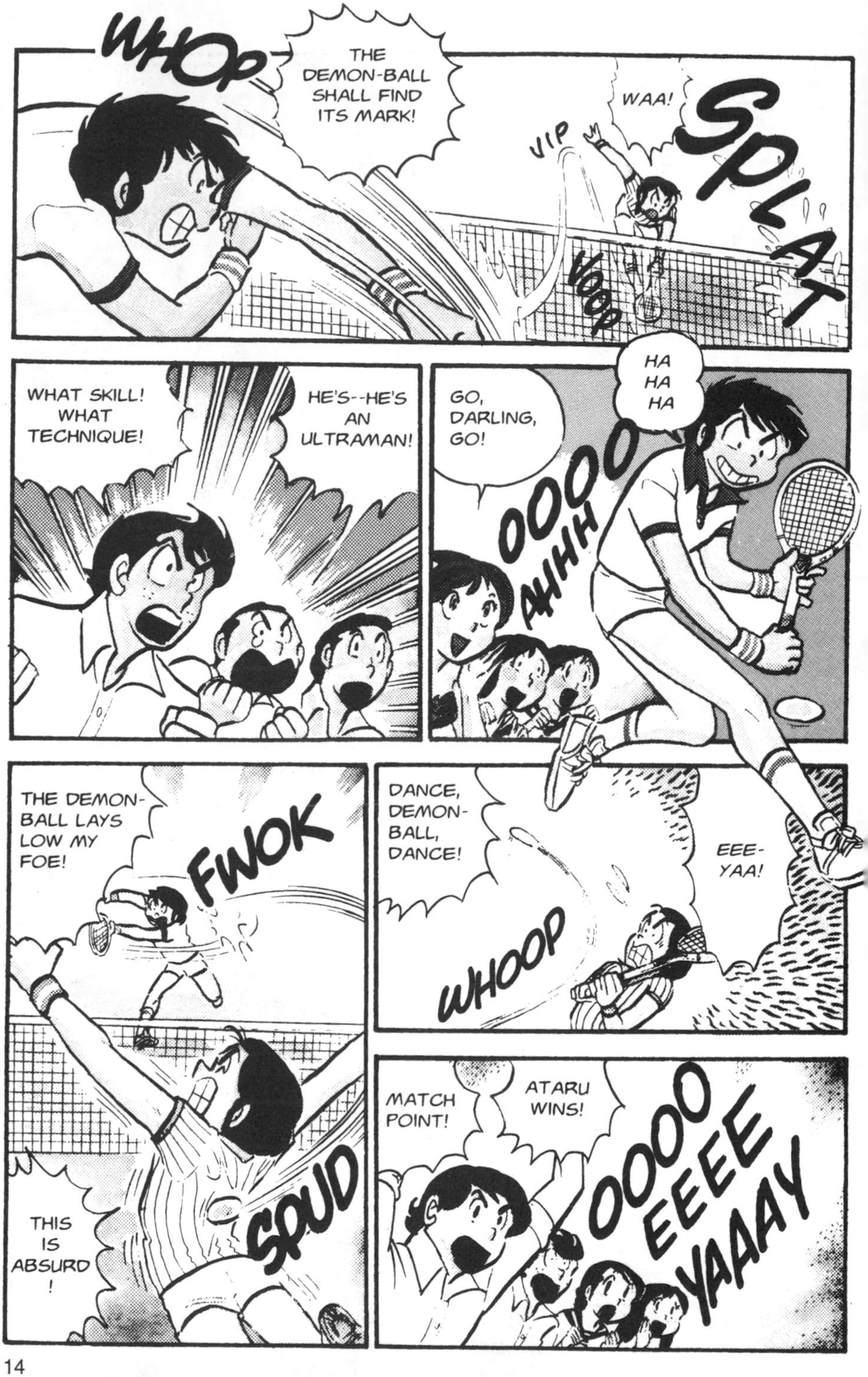
WHOP
THE DEMON-BALL SHALL FIND ITS MARK!
WAA!
SPLAT
VIP
VOOP
WHAT SKILL! WHAT TECHNIQUE!
HE'S--HE'S AN ULTRAMAN!
GO, DARLING, GO!
HA HA HA
OOOOO AHHH
THE DEMON-BALL LAYS LOW MY FOE!
FWOK
THIS IS ABSURD!
SPUD
DANCE, DEMON-BALL, DANCE!
EEE-YAA!
WHOOP
MATCH POINT!
ATARU WINS!
OOOO EEEE YAAAY

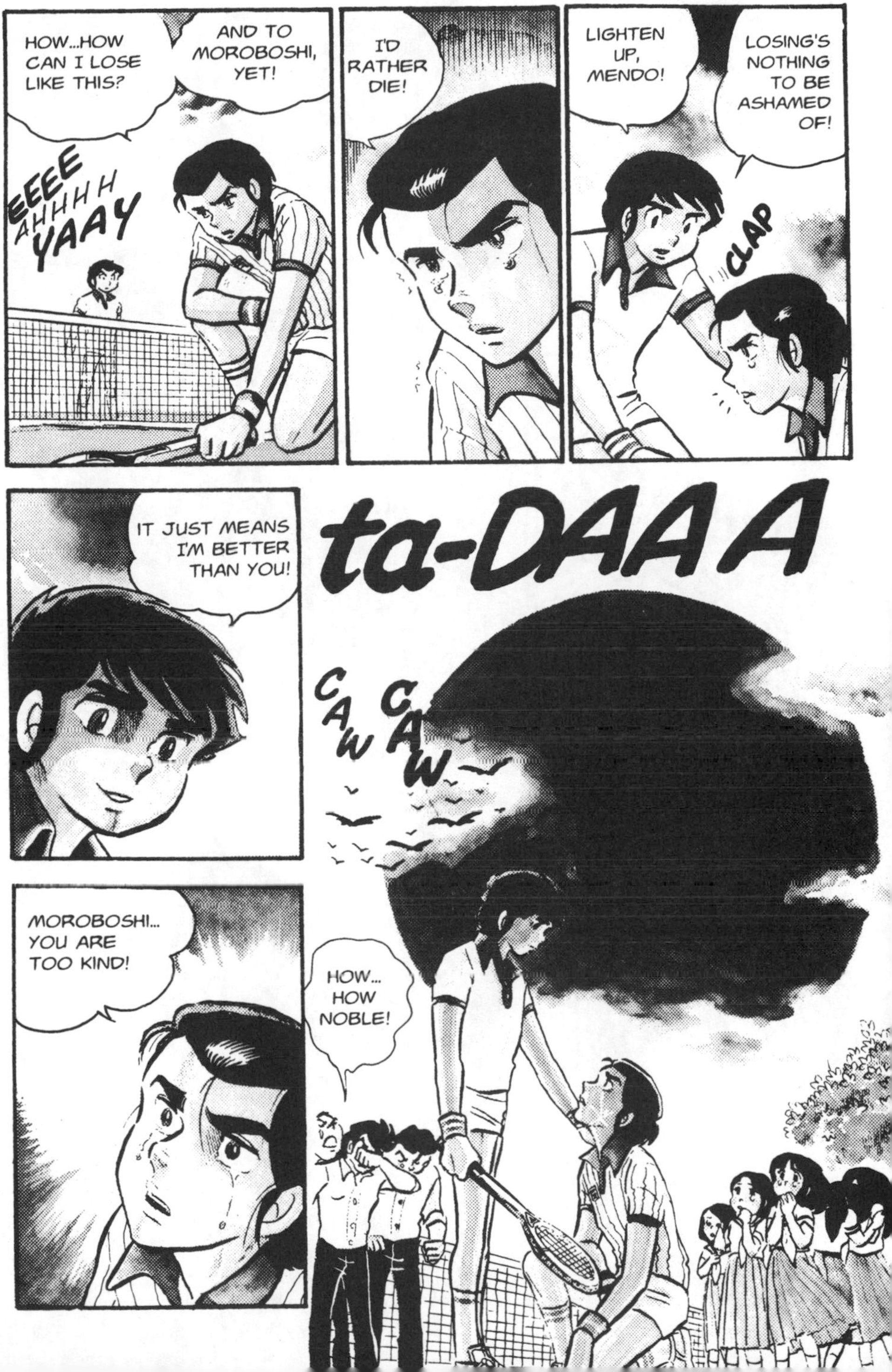
HOW...HOW CAN I LOSE LIKE THIS?
AND TO MOROBOSHI, YET!
EEEE AHHHHH YAAY
I'D RATHER DIE!
LIGHTEN UP, MENDO!
LOSING'S NOTHING TO BE ASHAMED OF!
CLAP
IT JUST MEANS I'M BETTER THAN YOU!
ta-DAAAA
CAW CAW
MOROBOSHI... YOU ARE TOO KIND!
HOW... HOW NOBLE!

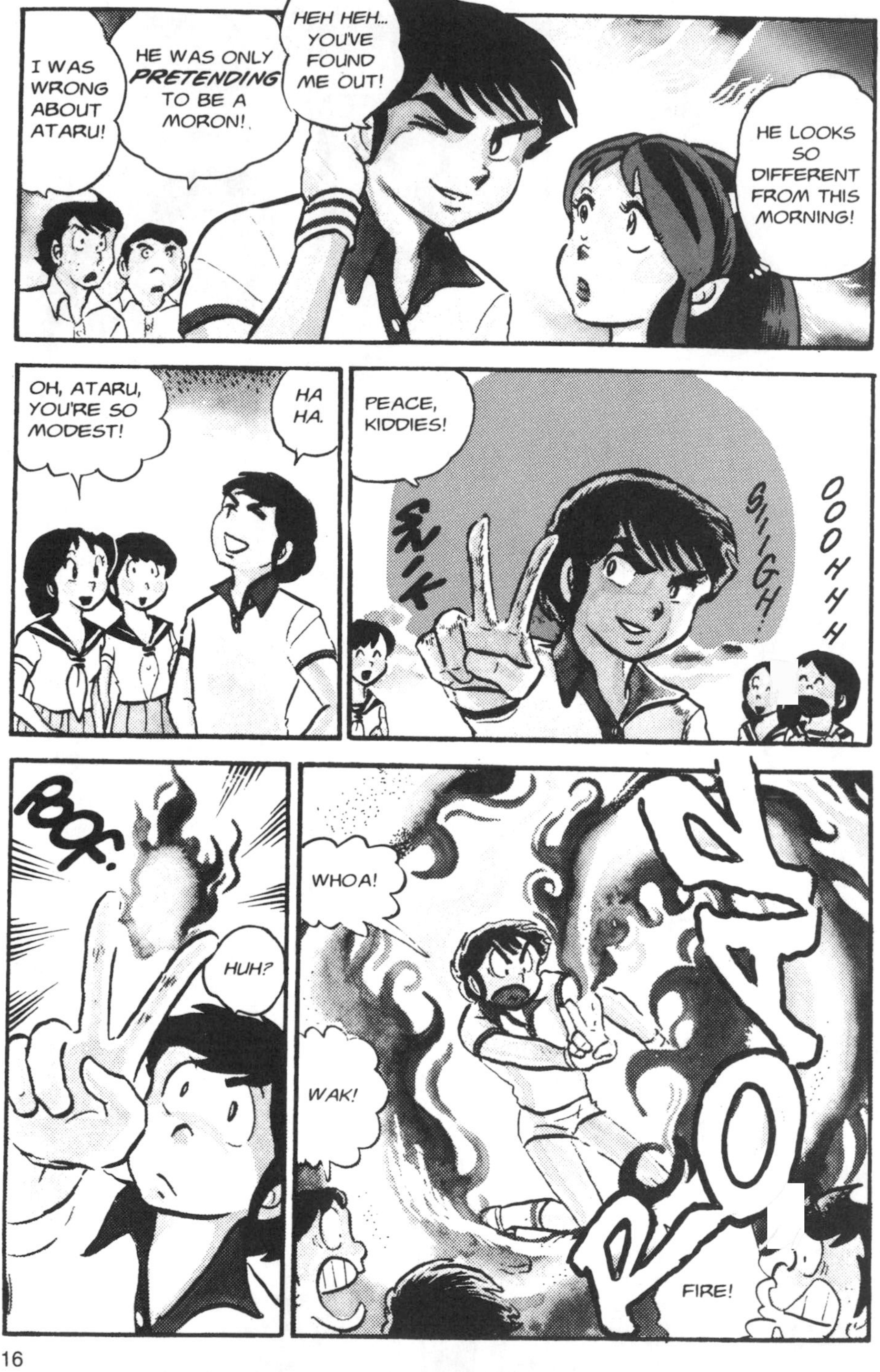
I WAS WRONG ABOUT ATARU!
HE WAS ONLY PRETENDING TO BE A MORON!
HEH HEH... YOU'VE FOUND ME OUT!
HE LOOKS SO DIFFERENT FROM THIS MORNING!
OH, ATARU, YOU'RE SO MODEST!
HA HA.
PEACE, KIDDIES!
SIIGH...
OOOHHHH
POOF!
HUH?
WHOA!
WAK!
ROAR
FIRE!

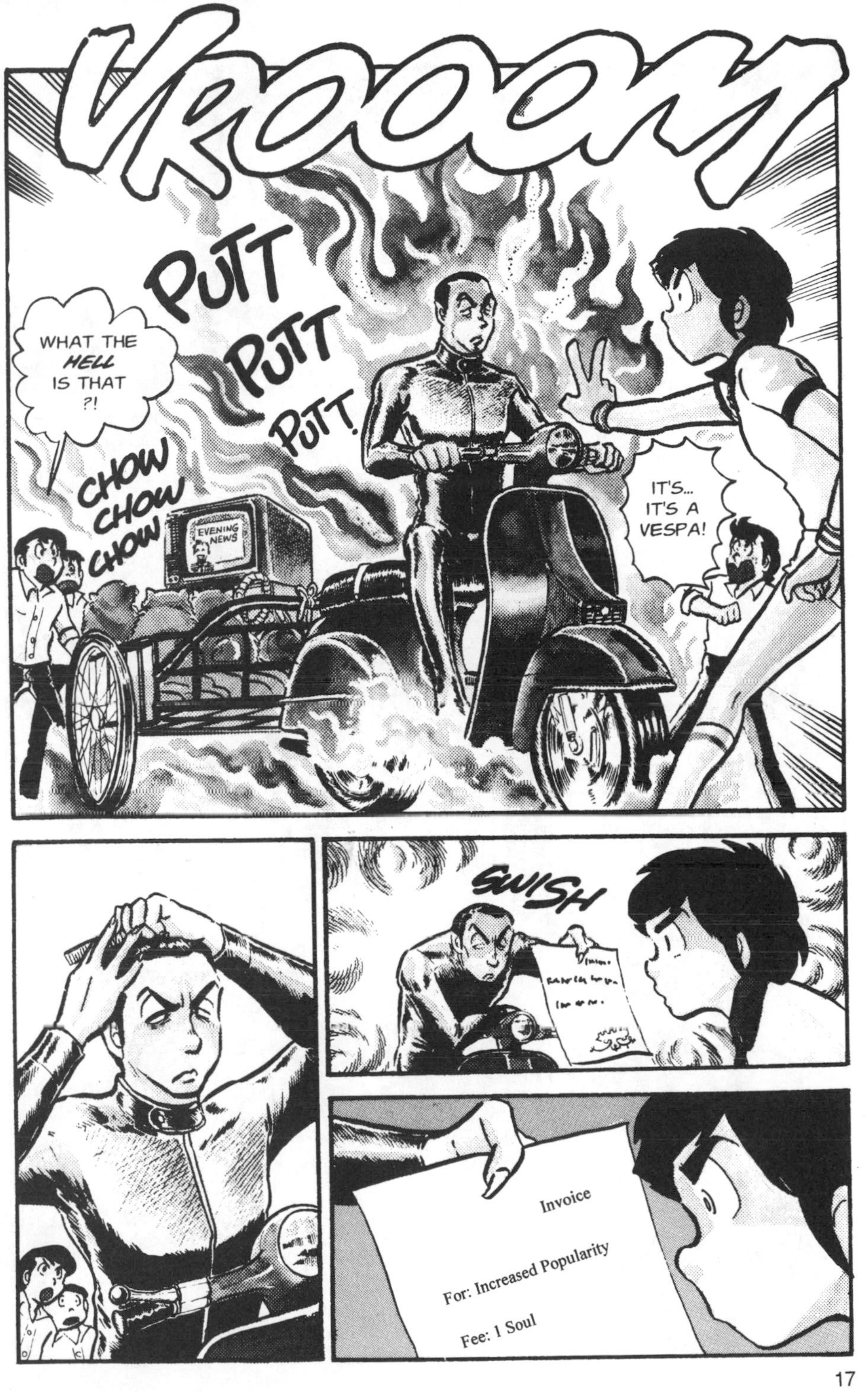
VROOOM
WHAT THE HELL IS THAT ?!
PUTT PUTT PUTT!
CHOW CHOW CHOW
EVENING NEWS
IT'S... IT'S A VESPA!
SWISH
Invoice
For: Increased Popularity
Fee: 1 Soul

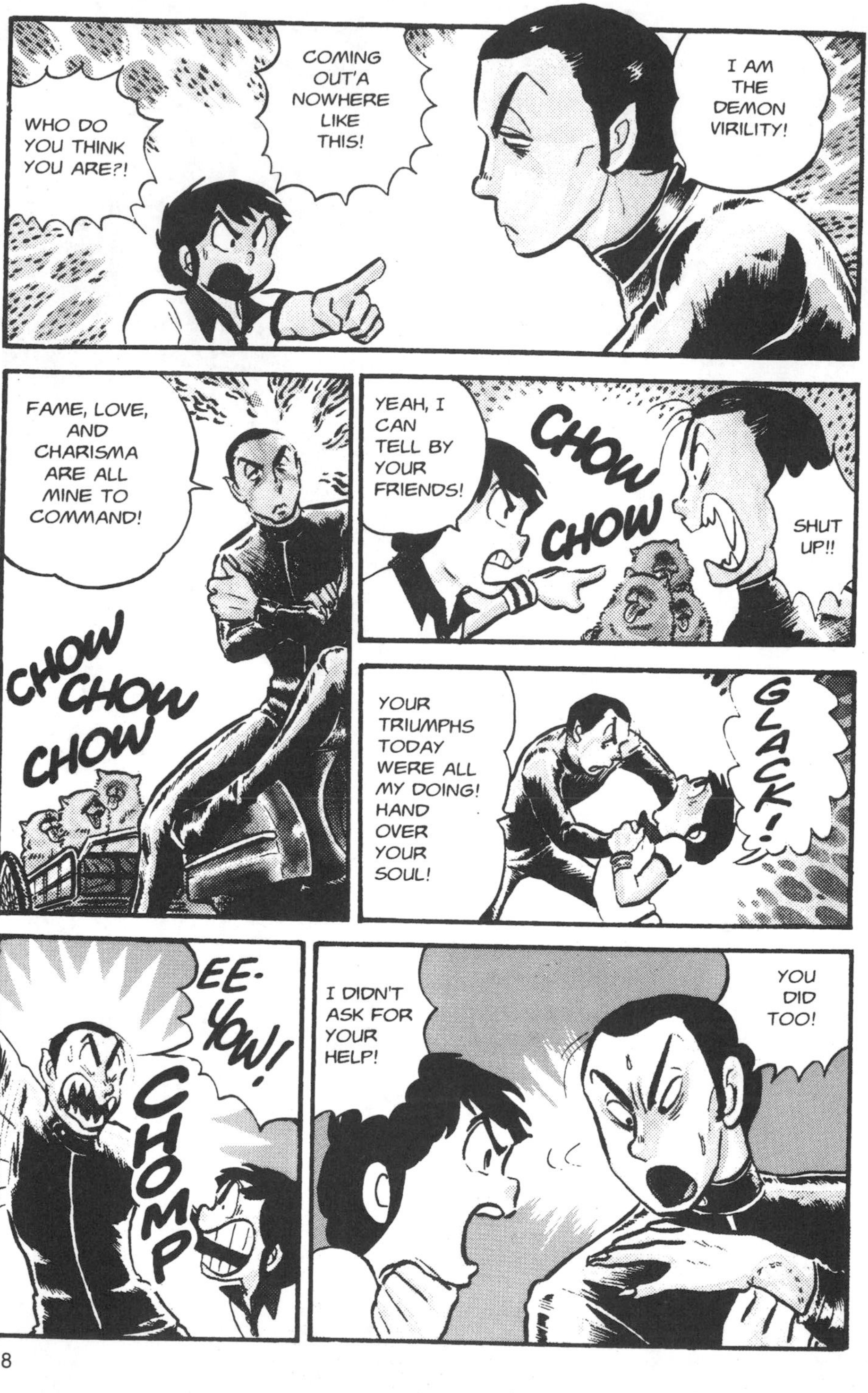
WHO DO YOU THINK YOU ARE?!
COMING OUT'A NOWHERE LIKE THIS!
I AM THE DEMON VIRILITY!
FAME, LOVE, AND CHARISMA ARE ALL MINE TO COMMAND!
CHOW CHOW CHOW
YEAH, I CAN TELL BY YOUR FRIENDS!
CHOW CHOW
SHUT UP!!
YOUR TRIUMPHS TODAY WERE ALL MY DOING! HAND OVER YOUR SOUL!
GLACK!
EE-YOW!
CHOMP
I DIDN'T ASK FOR YOUR HELP!
YOU DID TOO!

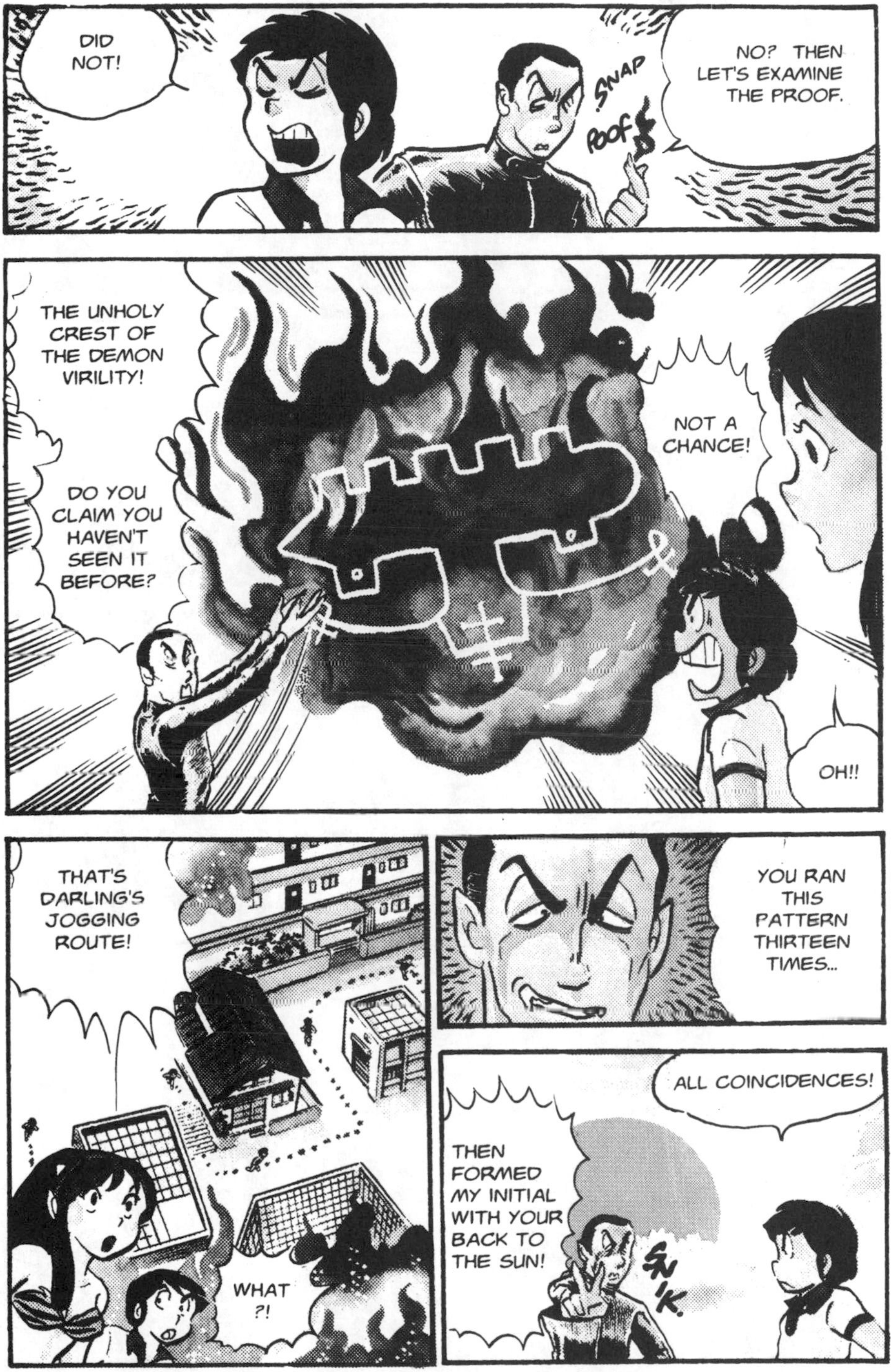
DID NOT!
SNAP
POOF
NO? THEN LET'S EXAMINE THE PROOF.
THE UNHOLY CREST OF THE DEMON VIRILITY!
DO YOU CLAIM YOU HAVEN'T SEEN IT BEFORE?
NOT A CHANCE!
OH!!
THAT'S DARLING'S JOGGING ROUTE!
WHAT ?!
YOU RAN THIS PATTERN THIRTEEN TIMES...
ALL COINCIDENCES!
THEN FORMED MY INITIAL WITH YOUR BACK TO THE SUN!
SNIK.

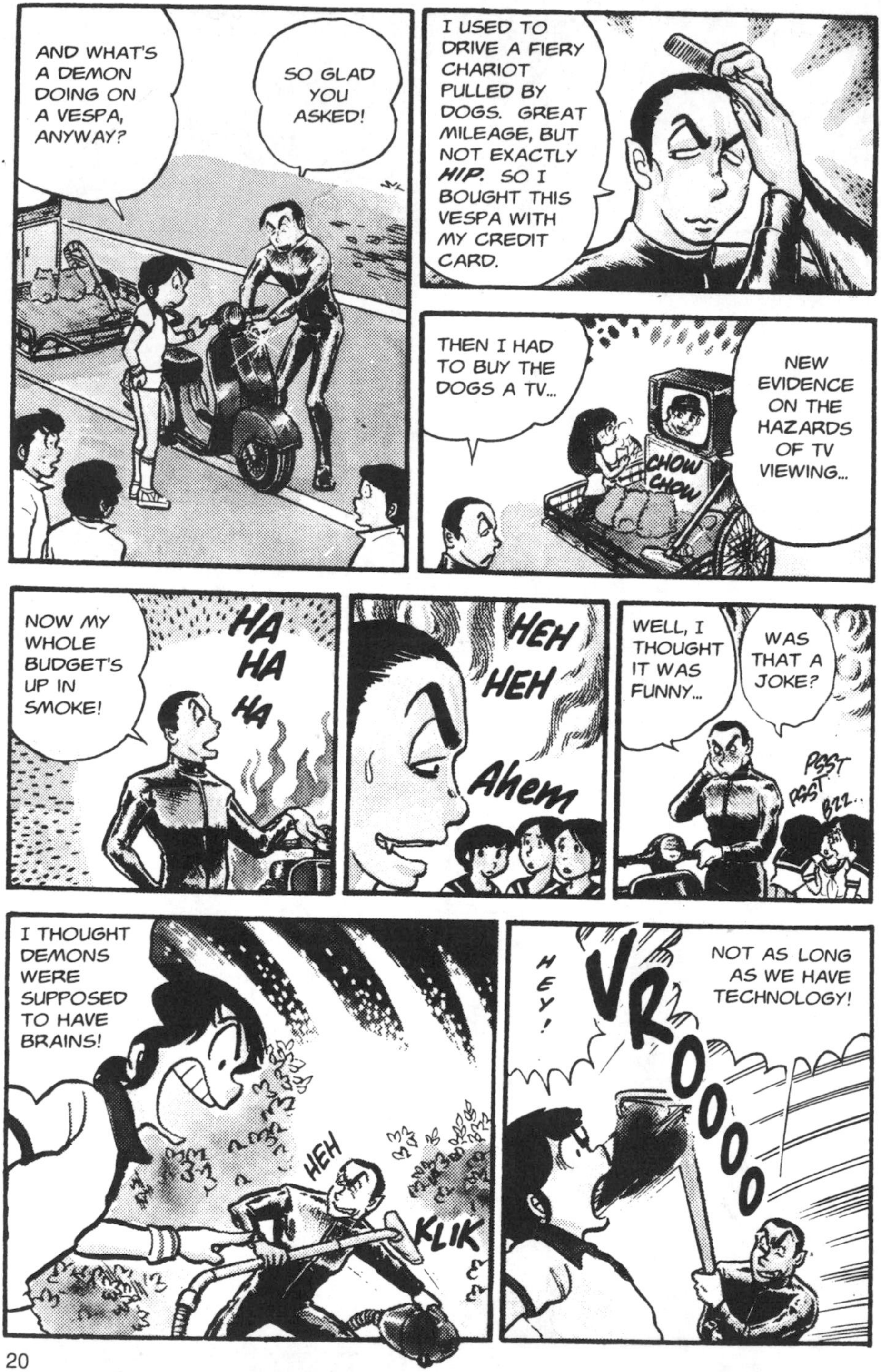
AND WHAT'S A DEMON DOING ON A VESPA, ANYWAY?
SO GLAD YOU ASKED!
I USED TO DRIVE A FIERY CHARIOT PULLED BY DOGS. GREAT MILEAGE, BUT NOT EXACTLY HIP. SO I BOUGHT THIS VESPA WITH MY CREDIT CARD.
THEN I HAD TO BUY THE DOGS A TV...
NEW EVIDENCE ON THE HAZARDS OF TV VIEWING...
CHOW CHOW
NOW MY WHOLE BUDGET'S UP IN SMOKE!
HA HA HA
HEH HEH
Ahem
WELL, I THOUGHT IT WAS FUNNY...
WAS THAT A JOKE?
PSST PSST BZZ..
I THOUGHT DEMONS WERE SUPPOSED TO HAVE BRAINS!
HEH
KLIK
HEY!
VROOOOO
NOT AS LONG AS WE HAVE TECHNOLOGY!

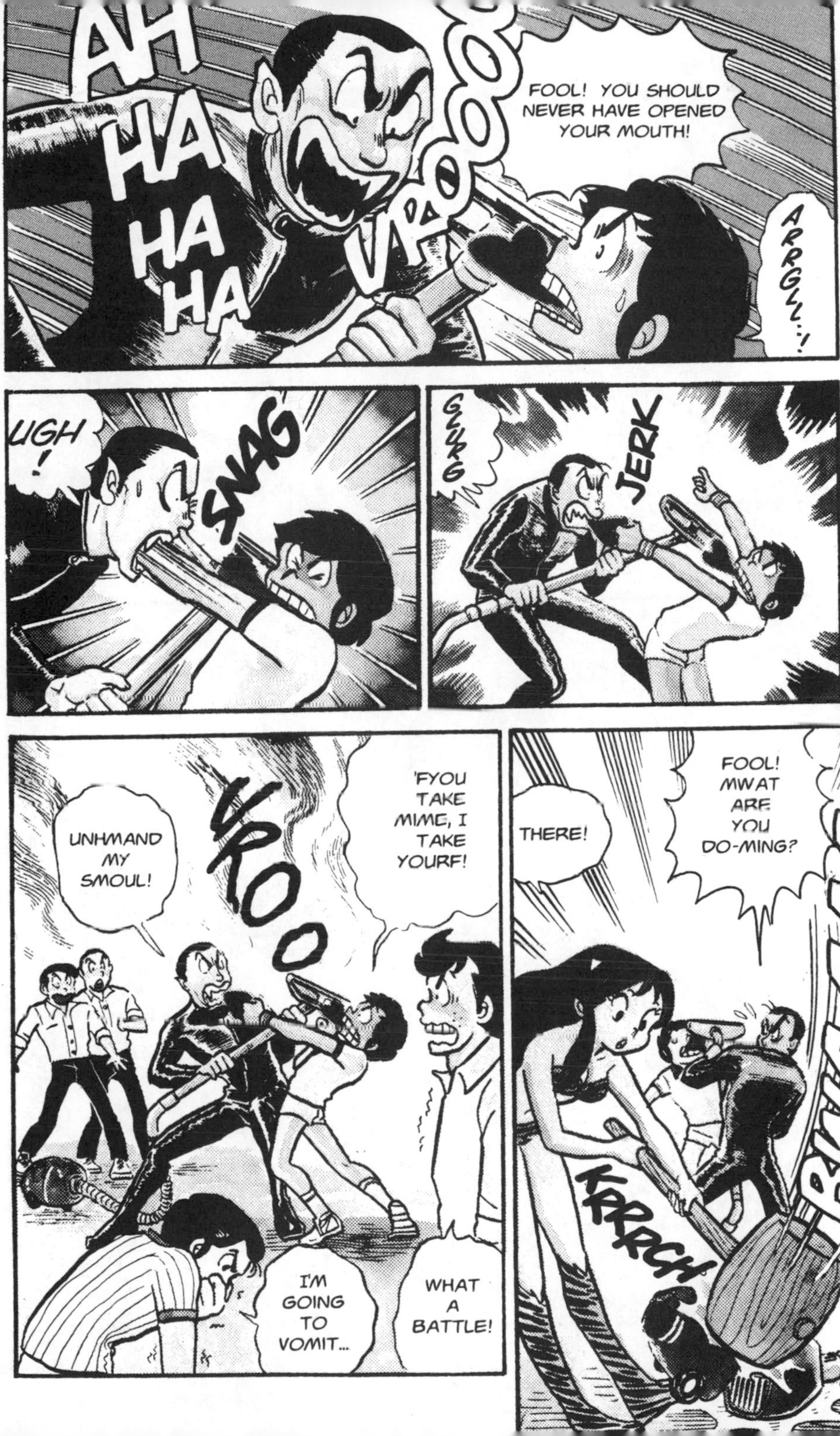

AH HA HA HA HA
VROOOOOO
FOOL! YOU SHOULD NEVER HAVE OPENED YOUR MOUTH!
ARRGLL..!
UGH!
SNAG
GLURG
JERK
UNHMAND MY SMOUL!
VROOO
'FYOU TAKE MIME, I TAKE YOURF!
I'M GOING TO VOMIT...
WHAT A BATTLE!
THERE!
FOOL! MWAT ARE YOU DO-MING?
BWAM
KRRRCH

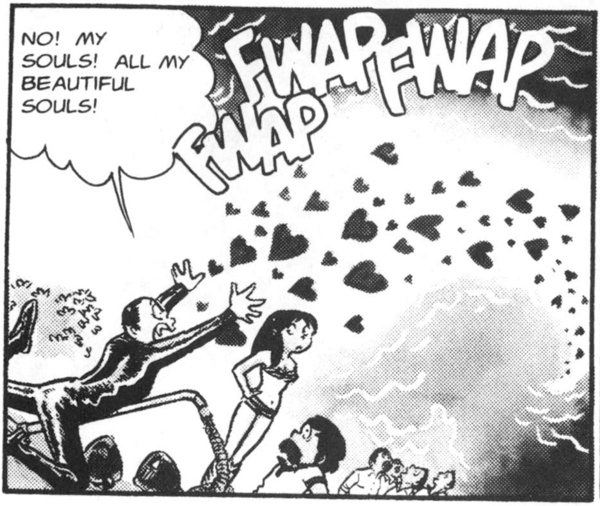
NO! MY SOULS! ALL MY BEAUTIFUL SOULS!
FWAP FWAP FWAP

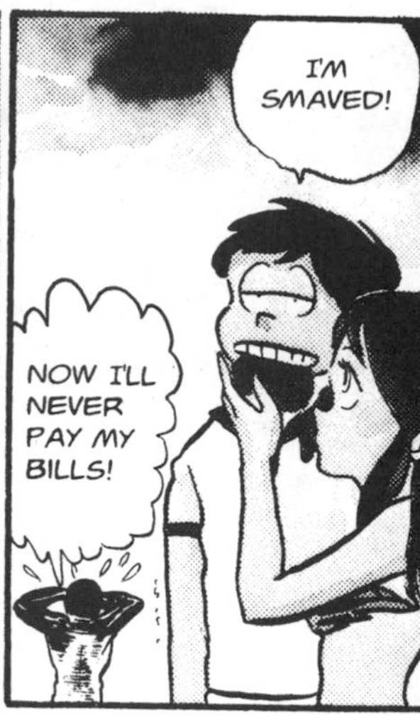
I'M SMAVED!
NOW I'LL NEVER PAY MY BILLS!

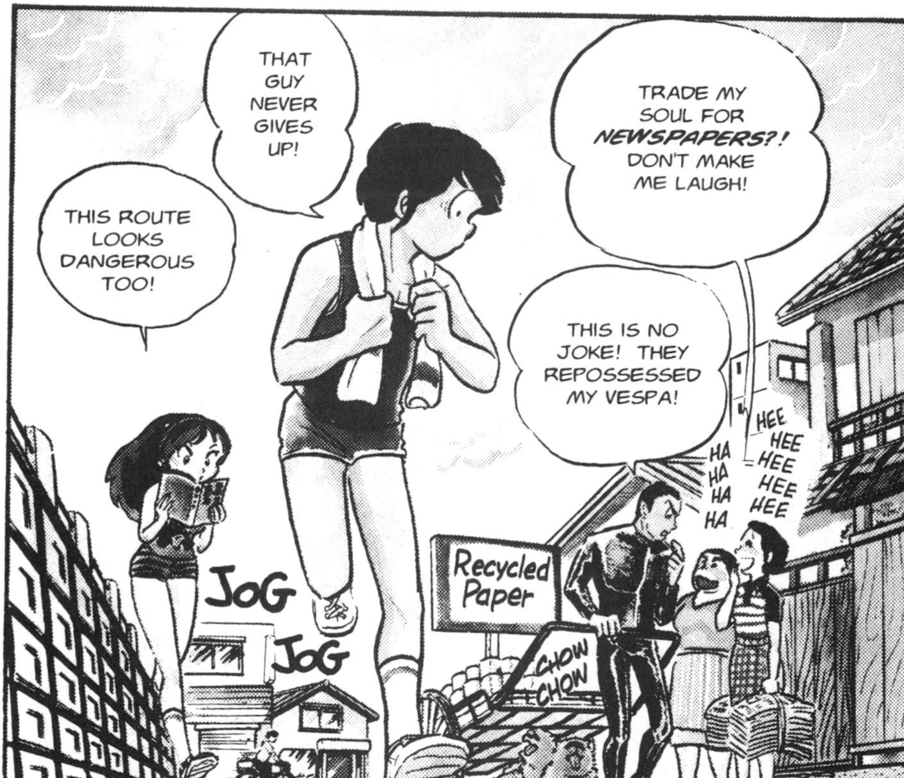
THAT GUY NEVER GIVES UP!
THIS ROUTE LOOKS DANGEROUS TOO!
TRADE MY SOUL FOR ***NEWSPAPERS?!*** DON'T MAKE ME LAUGH!
THIS IS NO JOKE! THEY REPOSSESSED MY VESPA!
HEE HEE HEE HEE HEE
HA HA HA HA
JOG
JOG
Recycled Paper
CHOW CHOW

PART TWO
STAR-CROSSED

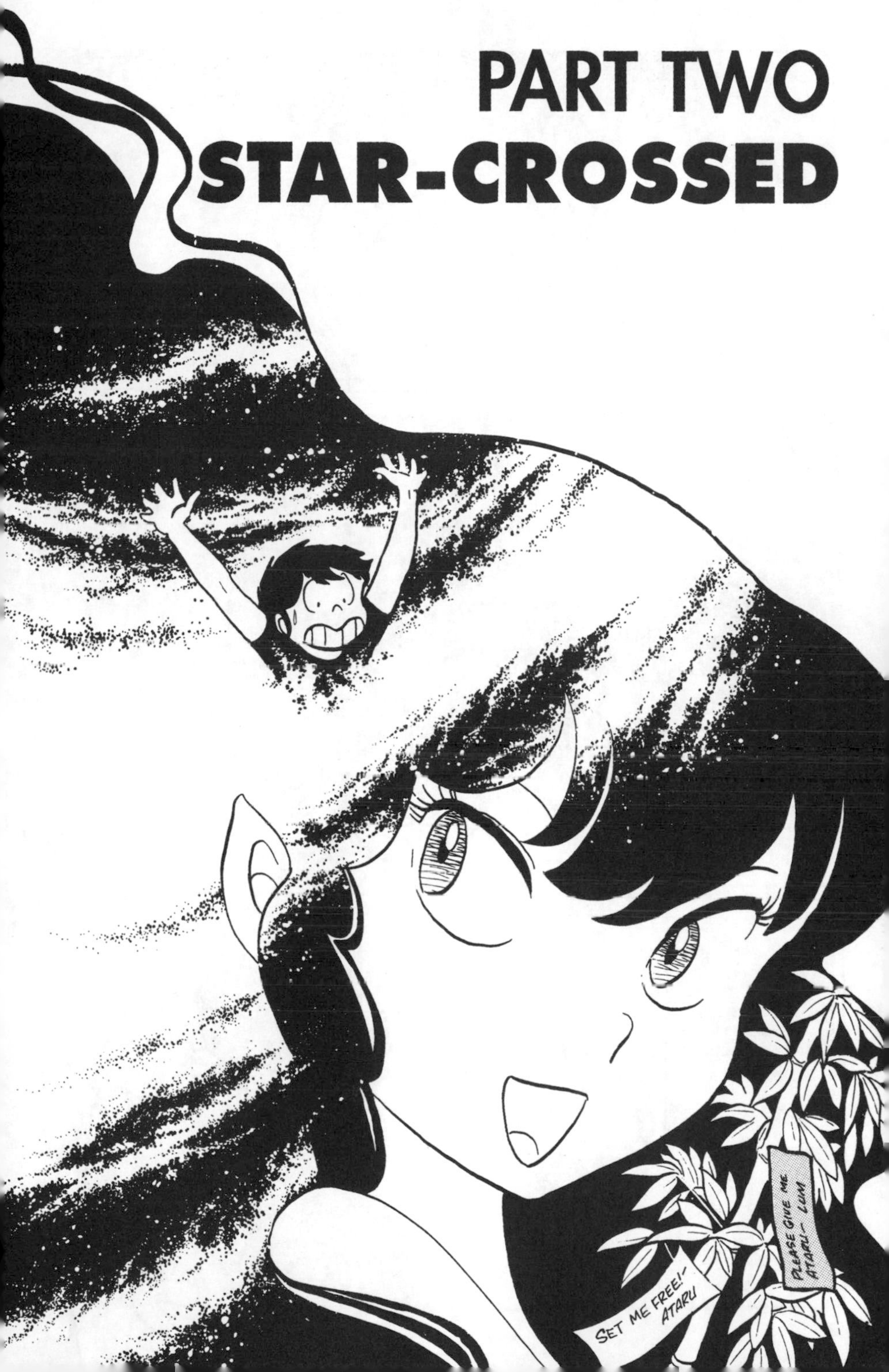
SET ME FREE! - ATARU
PLEASE GIVE ME ATARU - LUM

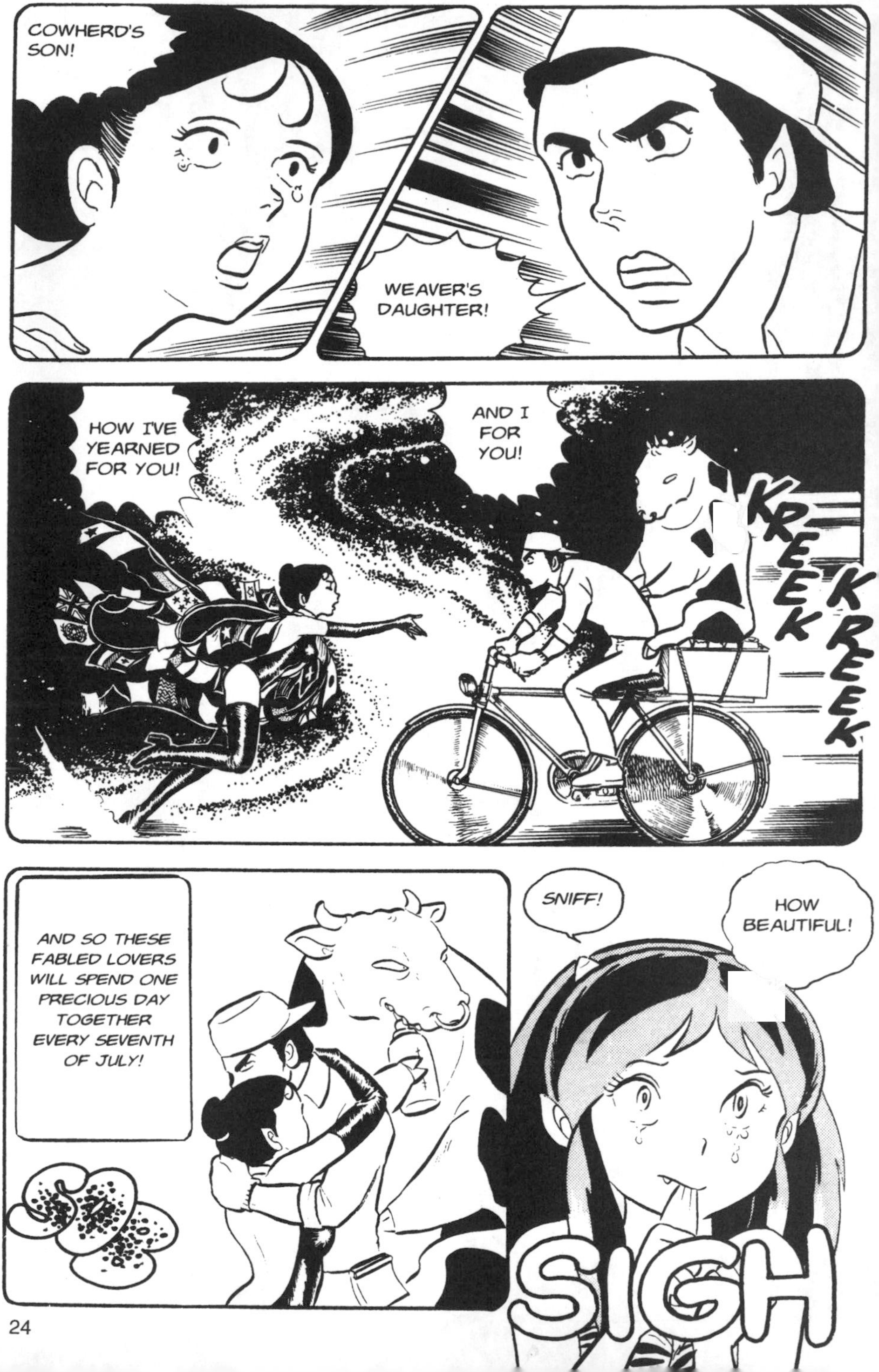
COWHERD'S SON!
WEAVER'S DAUGHTER!
HOW I'VE YEARNED FOR YOU!
AND I FOR YOU!
KREEK KREEK
KREEK KREEK
AND SO THESE FABLED LOVERS WILL SPEND ONE PRECIOUS DAY TOGETHER EVERY SEVENTH OF JULY!
SNIFF!
HOW BEAUTIFUL!
SIGH

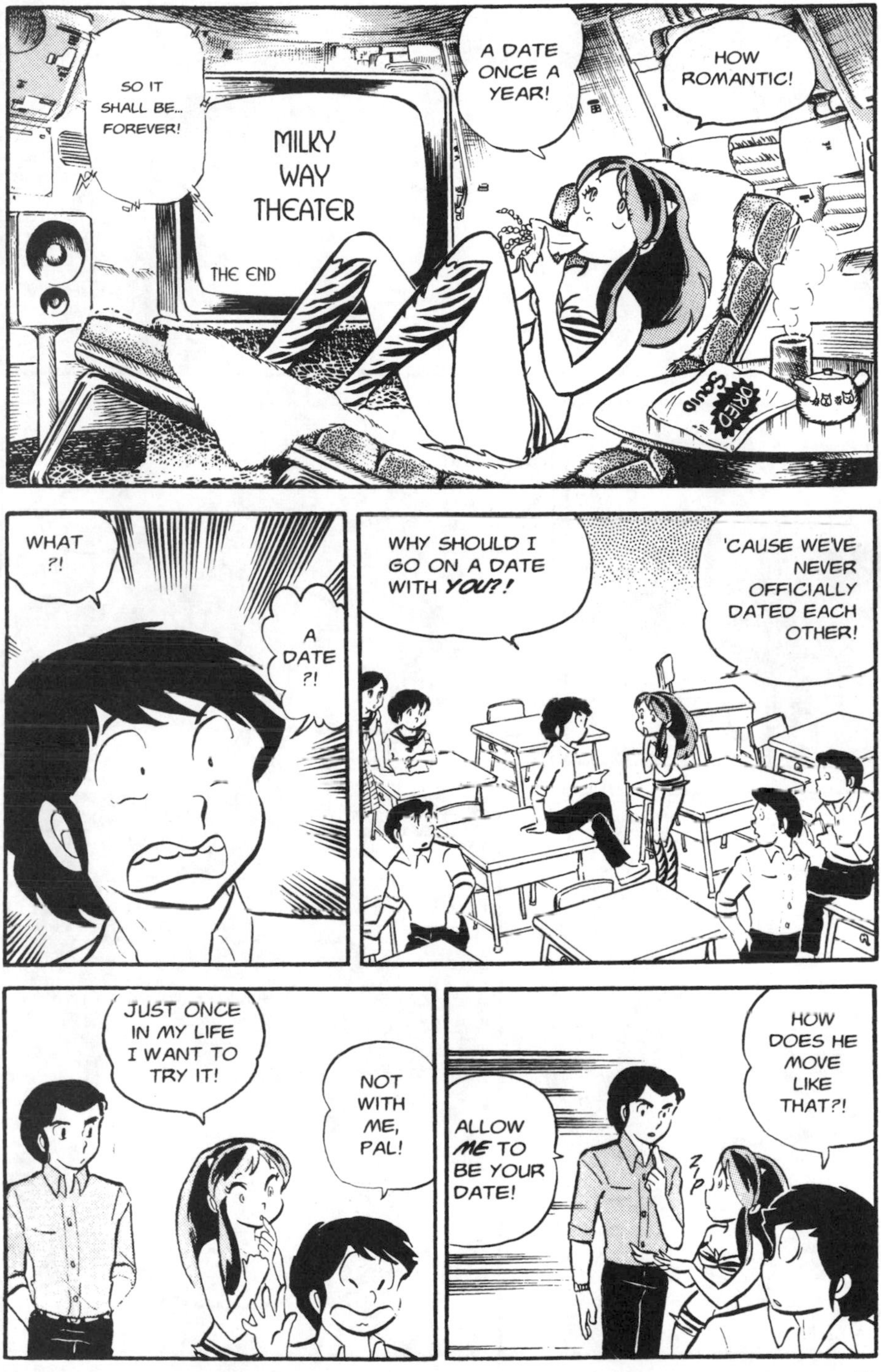
SO IT SHALL BE... FOREVER!
MILKY WAY THEATER
THE END
A DATE ONCE A YEAR!
HOW ROMANTIC!
DRIED SQUID
WHAT ?!
A DATE ?!
WHY SHOULD I GO ON A DATE WITH YOU?!
'CAUSE WE'VE NEVER OFFICIALLY DATED EACH OTHER!
JUST ONCE IN MY LIFE I WANT TO TRY IT!
NOT WITH ME, PAL!
ALLOW ME TO BE YOUR DATE!
ZIP
HOW DOES HE MOVE LIKE THAT?!

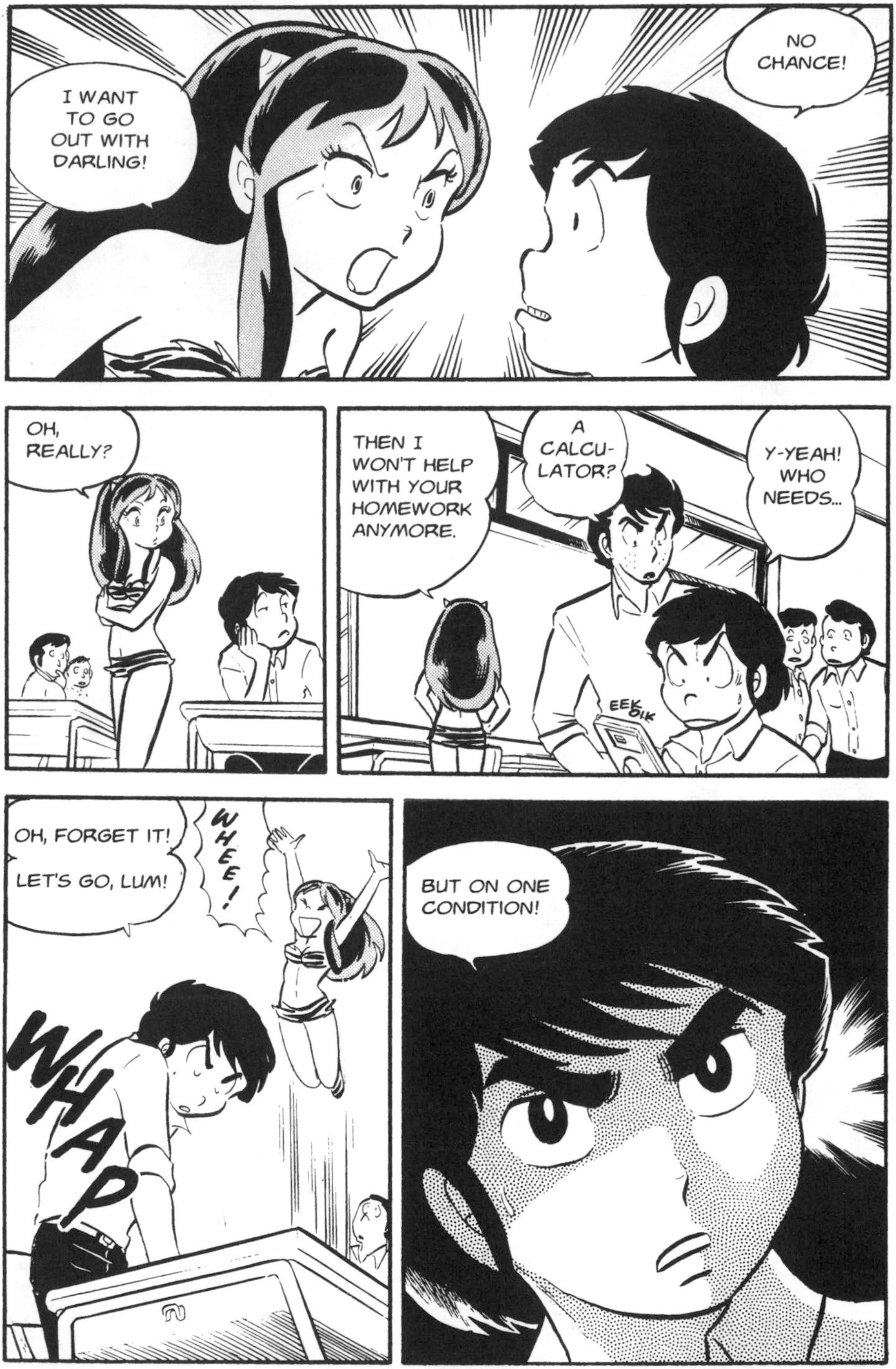
I WANT TO GO OUT WITH DARLING!
NO CHANCE!
OH, REALLY?
THEN I WON'T HELP WITH YOUR HOMEWORK ANYMORE.
A CALCULATOR?
Y-YEAH! WHO NEEDS...
EEK OIK
OH, FORGET IT!
LET'S GO, LUM!
WHEE!
WHAP!
BUT ON ONE CONDITION!

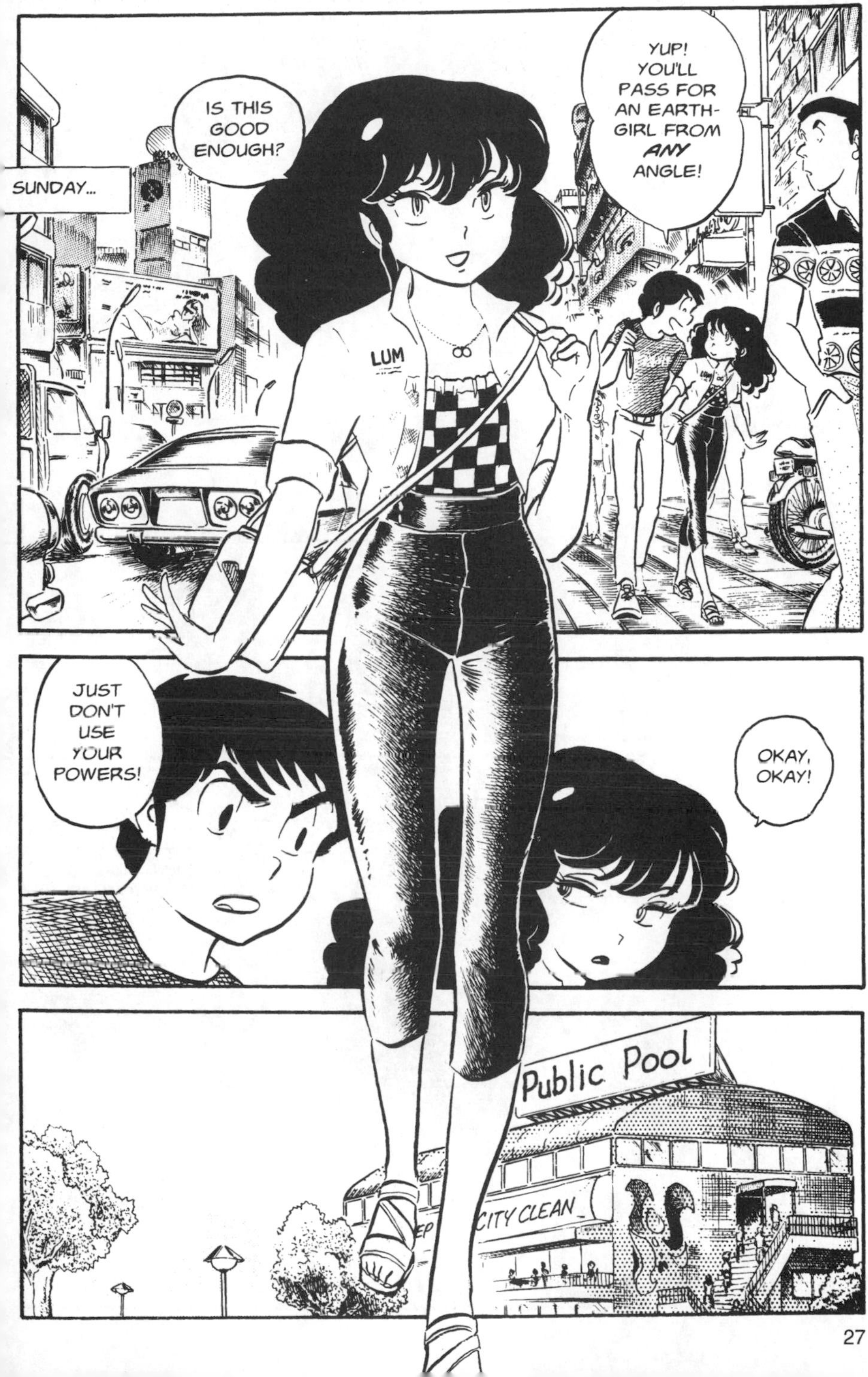
SUNDAY...
IS THIS GOOD ENOUGH?
YUP! YOU'LL PASS FOR AN EARTH-GIRL FROM ANY ANGLE!
LUM
JUST DON'T USE YOUR POWERS!
OKAY, OKAY!
Public Pool
CITY CLEAN

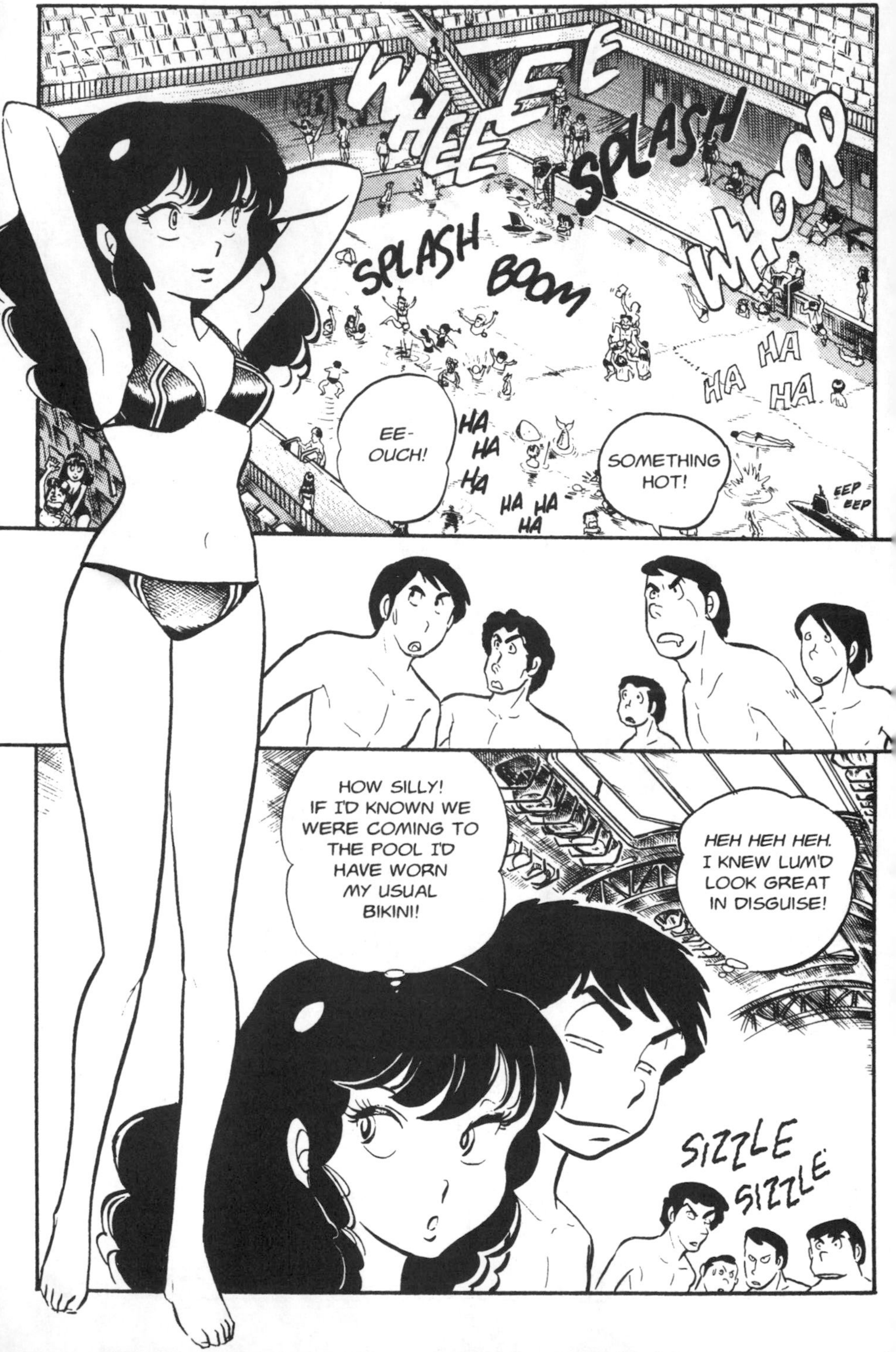
WHEEE
E-E-E
SPLASH
WHOOP
SPLASH
BOOM
HA HA HA
EE-OUCH!
HA HA HA
HA HA HA
SOMETHING HOT!
EEP EEP
HOW SILLY! IF I'D KNOWN WE WERE COMING TO THE POOL I'D HAVE WORN MY USUAL BIKINI!
HEH HEH HEH. I KNEW LUM'D LOOK GREAT IN DISGUISE!
SIZZLE SIZZLE

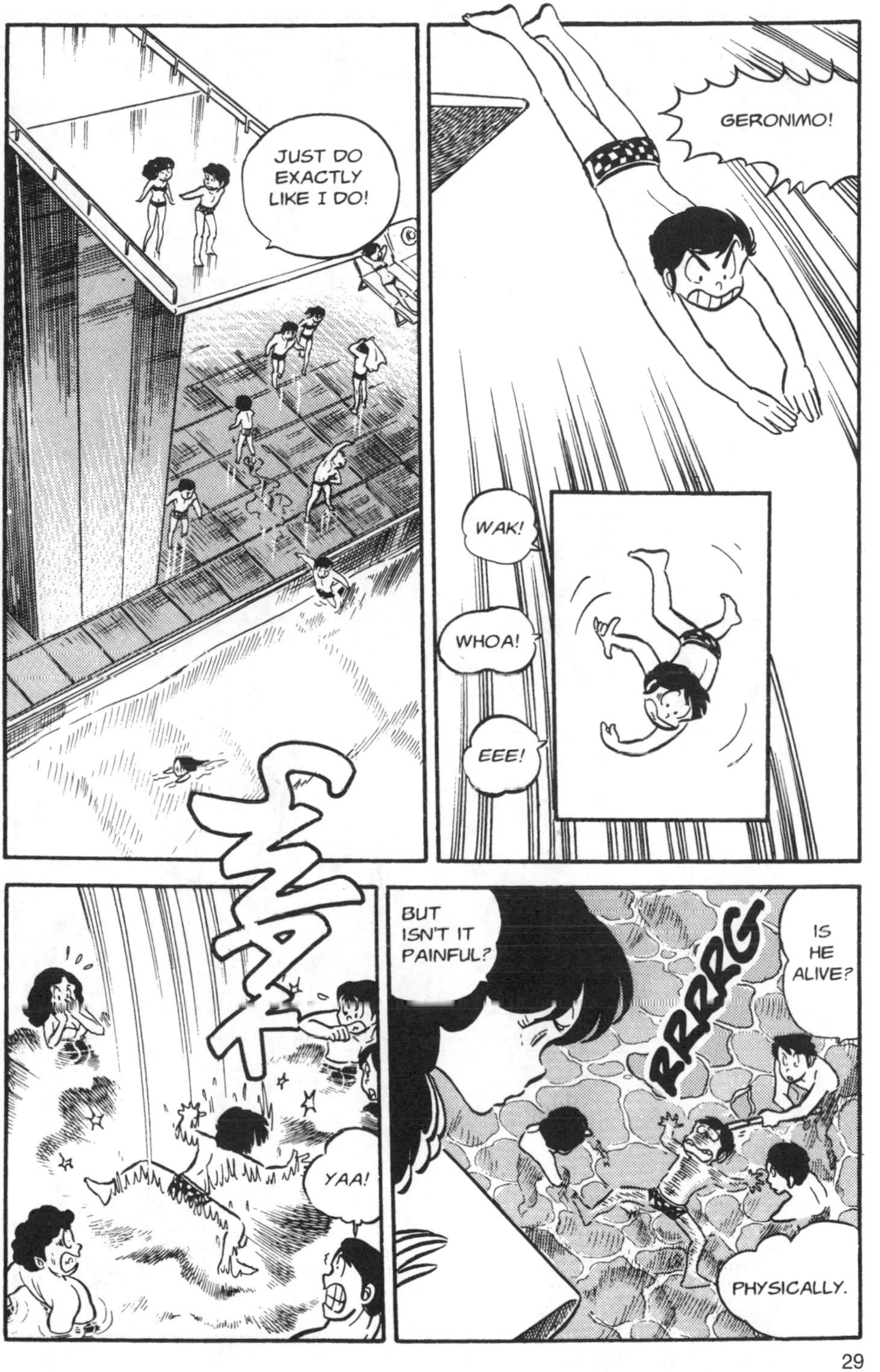

JUST DO EXACTLY LIKE I DO!
GERONIMO!
WAK!
WHOA!
EEE!
SMAT
YAA!
BUT ISN'T IT PAINFUL?
RRRRG
IS HE ALIVE?
PHYSICALLY.

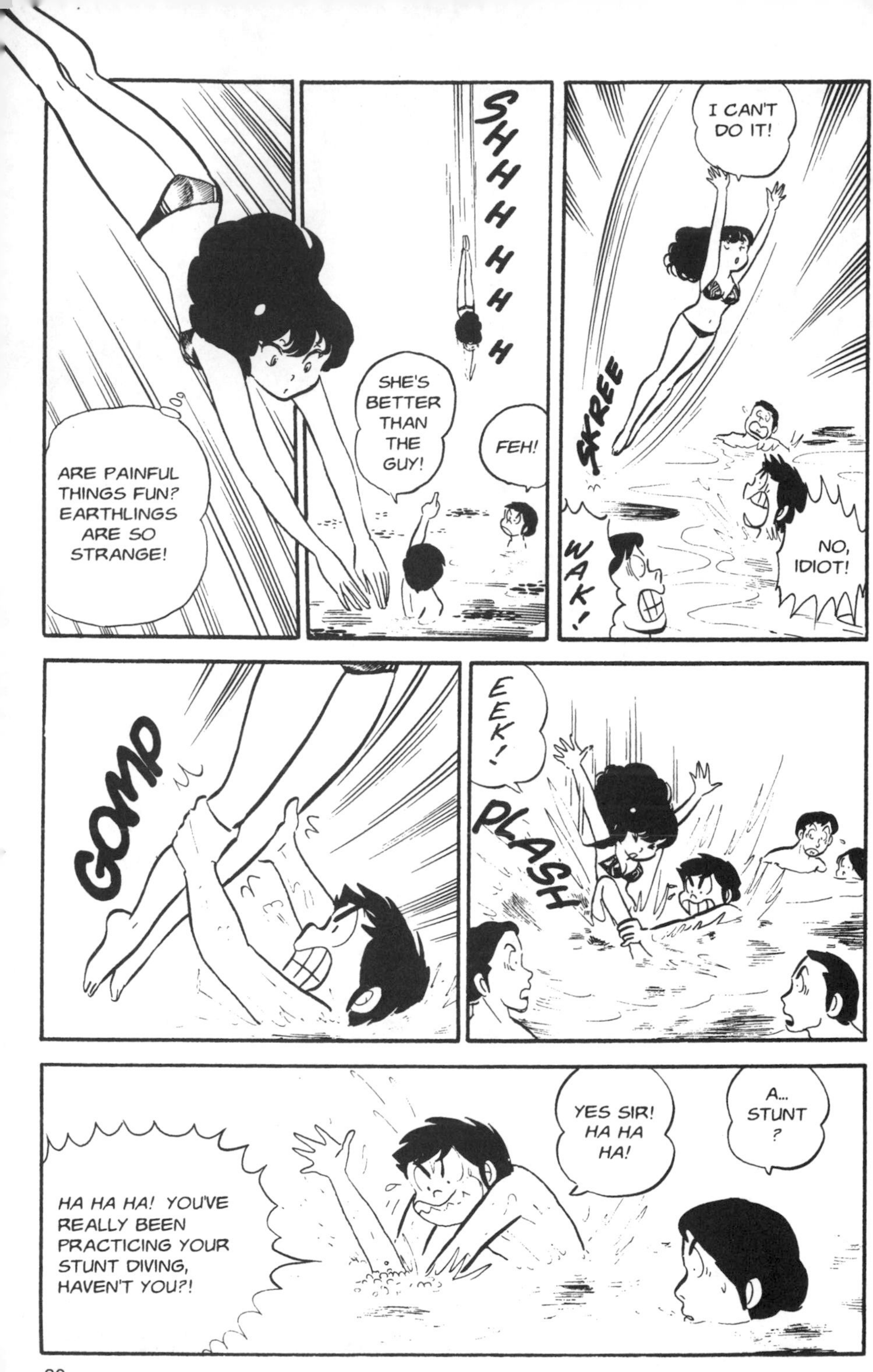
ARE PAINFUL THINGS FUN? EARTHLINGS ARE SO STRANGE!
SHHHHHHHH
SHE'S BETTER THAN THE GUY!
FEH!
I CAN'T DO IT!
SKREE
WAK!
NO, IDIOT!
GOMP
EEK!
PLASH
HA HA HA! YOU'VE REALLY BEEN PRACTICING YOUR STUNT DIVING, HAVEN'T YOU?!
YES SIR! HA HA HA!
A... STUNT ?

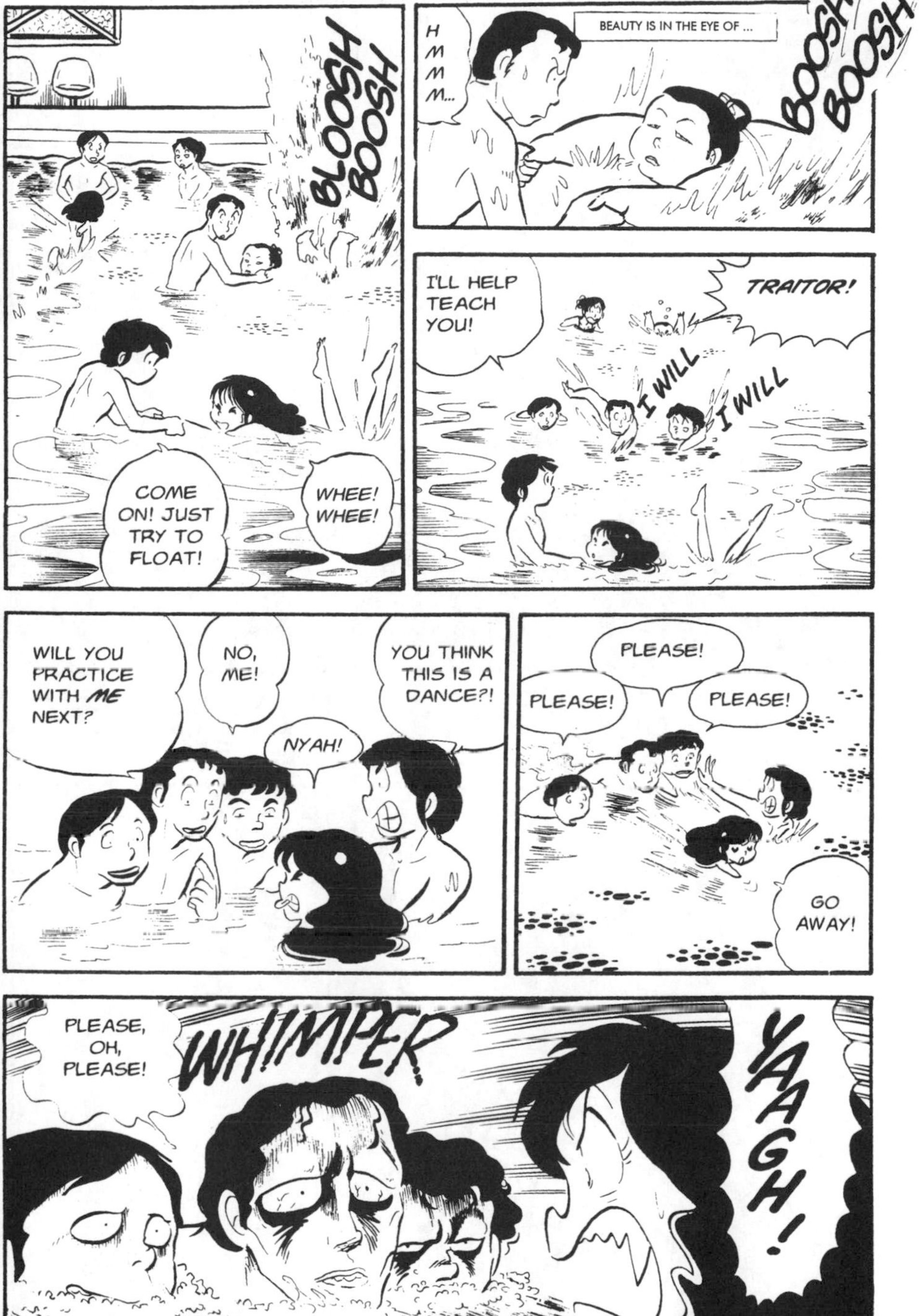

BLOOSH BOOSH
COME ON! JUST TRY TO FLOAT!
WHEE! WHEE!
BEAUTY IS IN THE EYE OF ...
HMMM...
BOOSH BOOSH
I'LL HELP TEACH YOU!
TRAITOR!
I WILL
I WILL
WILL YOU PRACTICE WITH *ME* NEXT?
NO, ME!
NYAH!
YOU THINK THIS IS A DANCE?!
PLEASE!
PLEASE!
PLEASE!
GO AWAY!
PLEASE, OH, PLEASE!
WHIMPER
YAAGH!

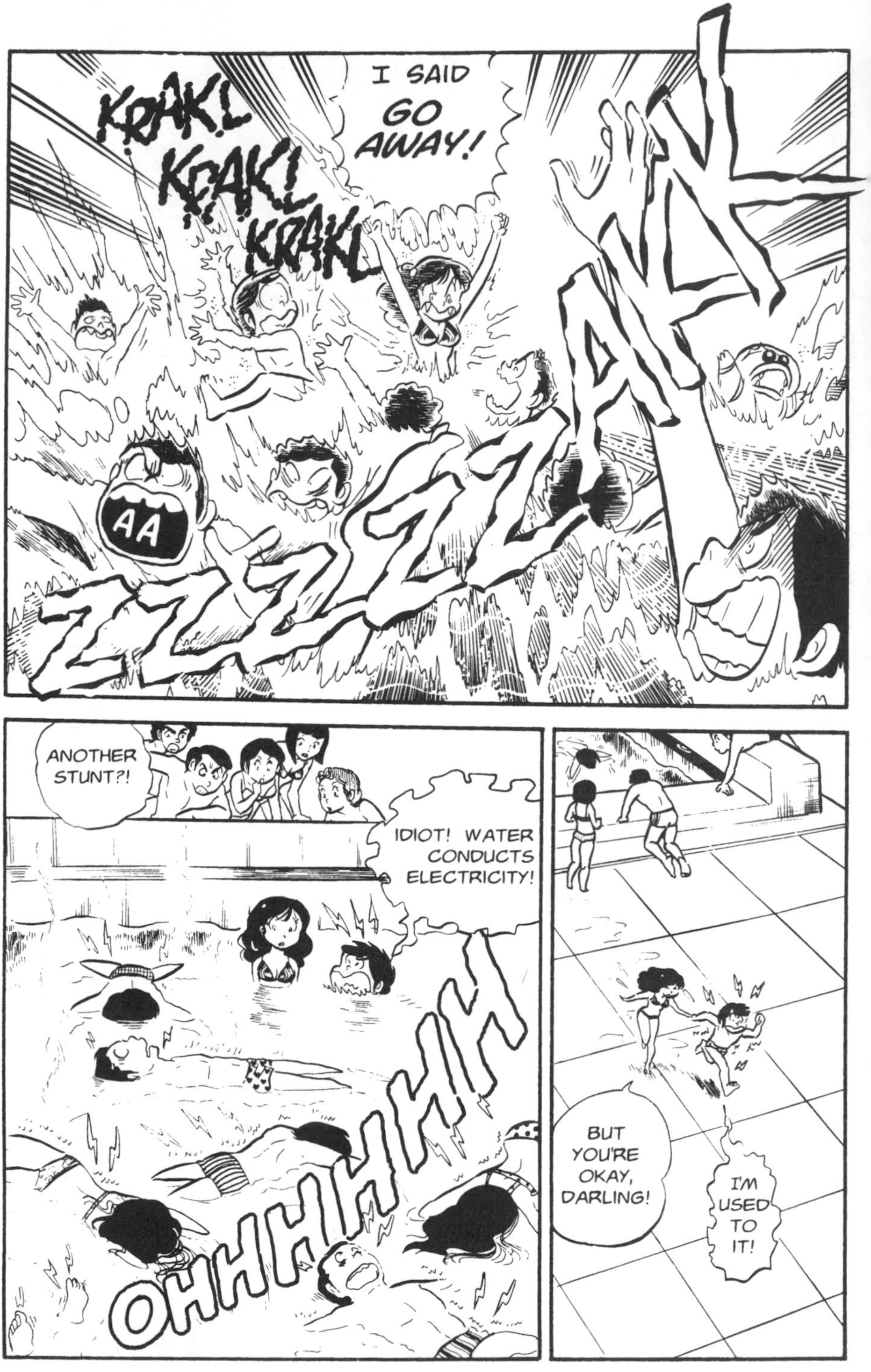
KRAK! KRAK! KRAK!
I SAID GO AWAY!
AA
ANOTHER STUNT?!
IDIOT! WATER CONDUCTS ELECTRICITY!
BUT YOU'RE OKAY, DARLING!
I'M USED TO IT!

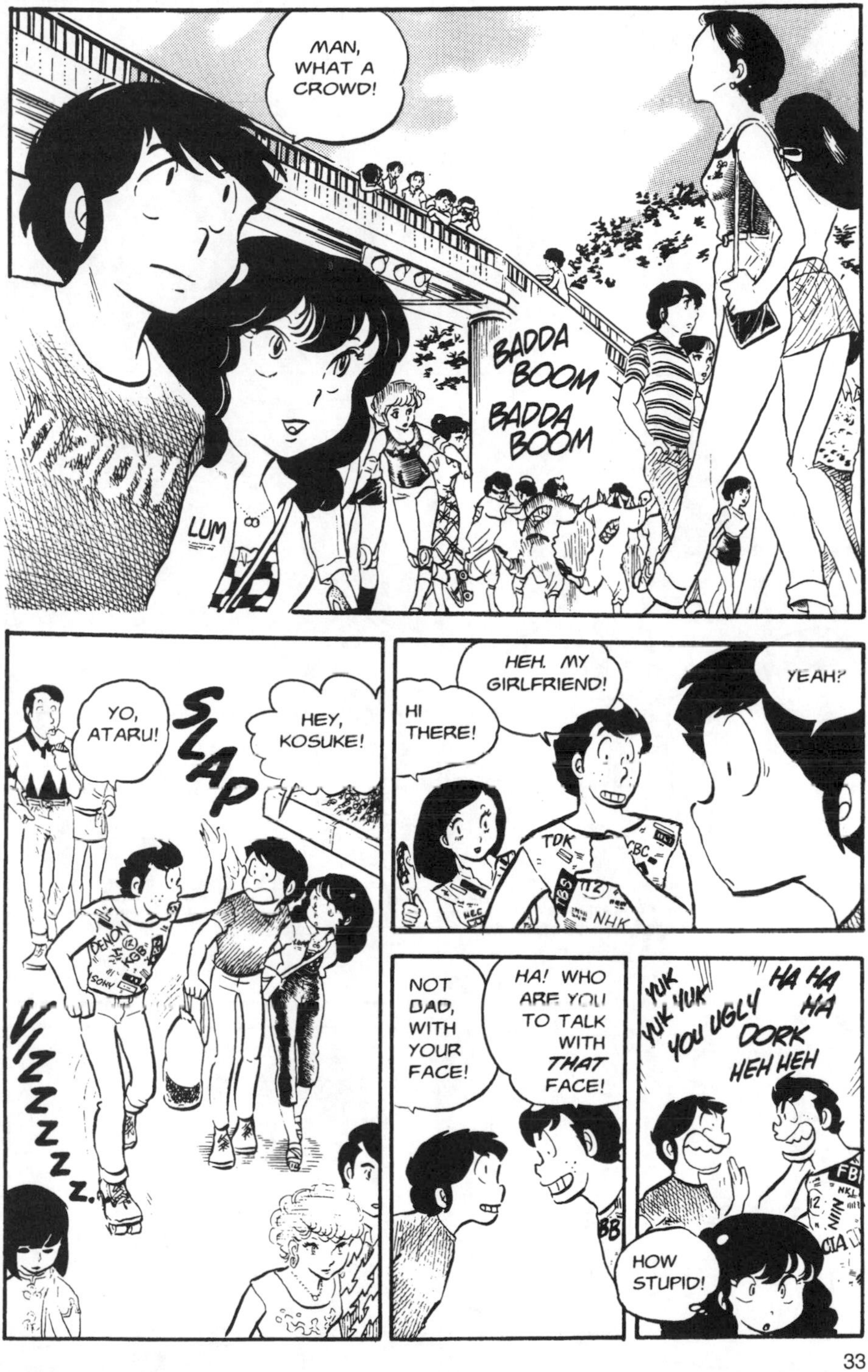
MAN, WHAT A CROWD!
BADDA BOOM BADDA BOOM
LUM
YO, ATARU!
SLAP
HEY, KOSUKE!
VIZZZZZZ.
HI THERE!
HEH. MY GIRLFRIEND!
YEAH?
NOT BAD, WITH YOUR FACE!
HA! WHO ARE YOU TO TALK WITH *THAT* FACE!
YUK YUK YUK
YOU UGLY
HA HA HA
DORK
HEH HEH
HOW STUPID!

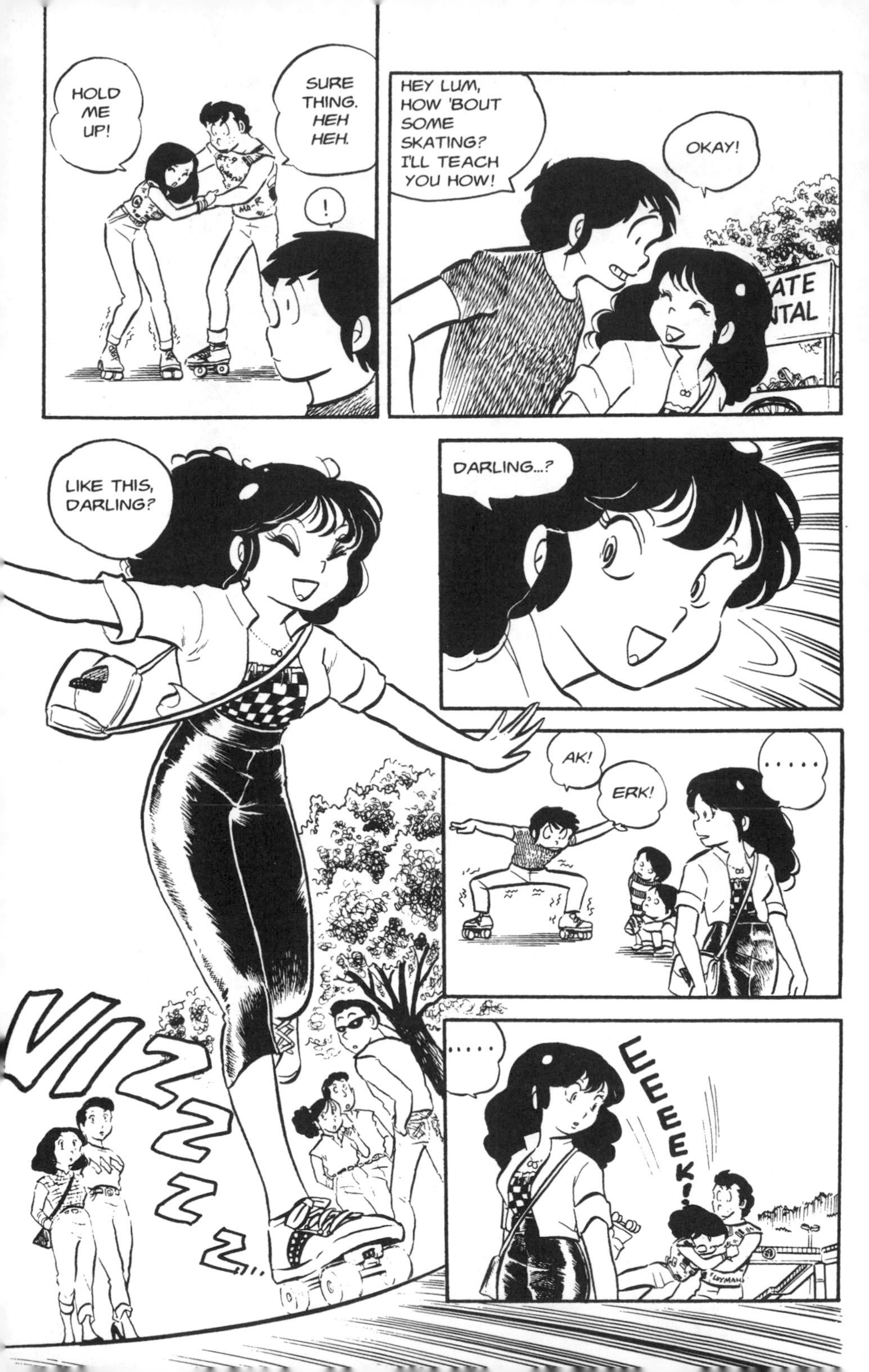
HOLD ME UP!
SURE THING. HEH HEH.
!
HEY LUM, HOW 'BOUT SOME SKATING? I'LL TEACH YOU HOW!
OKAY!
LIKE THIS, DARLING?
VIZZZZZ...
DARLING...?
AK!
ERK!
.....
.....
EEEEEK!

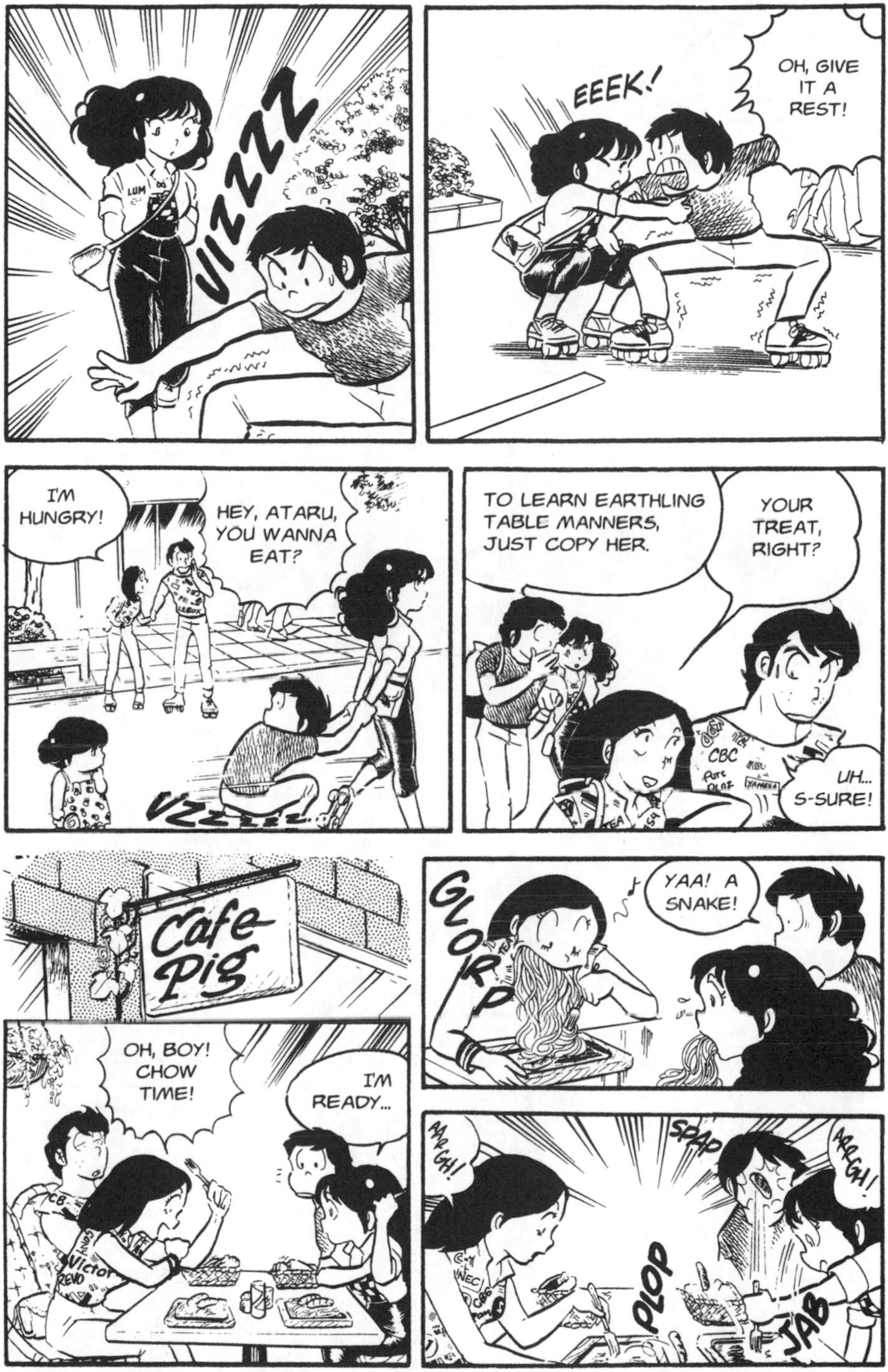
VIZZZZ
EEEK!
OH, GIVE IT A REST!
I'M HUNGRY!
HEY, ATARU, YOU WANNA EAT?
VZZZZZ
TO LEARN EARTHLING TABLE MANNERS, JUST COPY HER.
YOUR TREAT, RIGHT?
UH... S-SURE!
Cafe Pig
OH, BOY! CHOW TIME!
I'M READY...
GLORP
YAA! A SNAKE!
AARGH!
SPAP
ARRGH!
PLOP
JAB

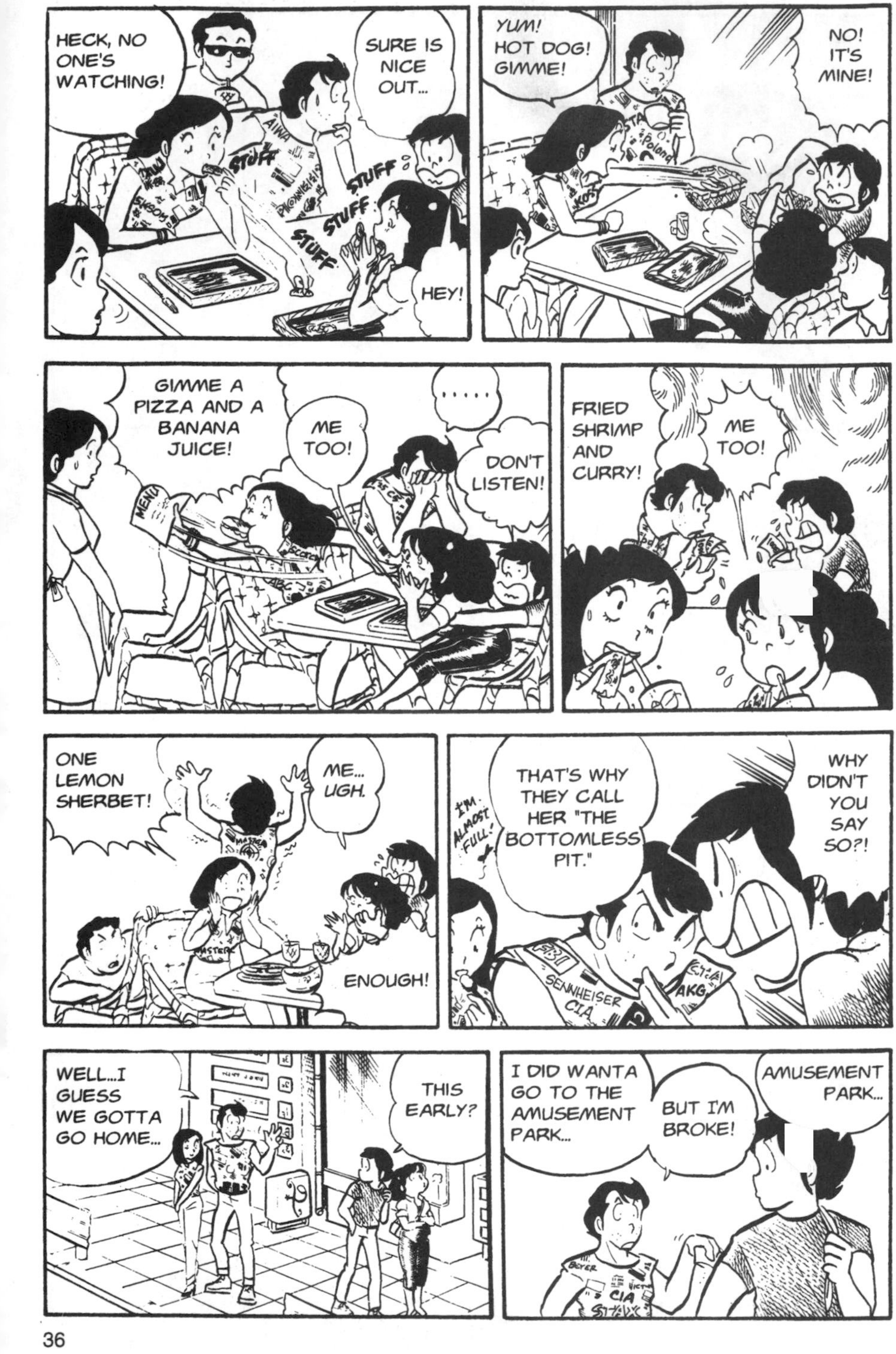
HECK, NO ONE'S WATCHING!
SURE IS NICE OUT...
STUFF
STUFF
STUFF
STUFF
HEY!
YUM! HOT DOG! GIMME!
NO! IT'S MINE!
GIMME A PIZZA AND A BANANA JUICE!
.....
ME TOO!
DON'T LISTEN!
FRIED SHRIMP AND CURRY!
ME TOO!
ONE LEMON SHERBET!
ME... UGH.
ENOUGH!
I'M ALMOST FULL!
THAT'S WHY THEY CALL HER "THE BOTTOMLESS PIT."
WHY DIDN'T YOU SAY SO?!
WELL...I GUESS WE GOTTA GO HOME...
THIS EARLY?
I DID WANTA GO TO THE AMUSEMENT PARK...
BUT I'M BROKE!
AMUSEMENT PARK...

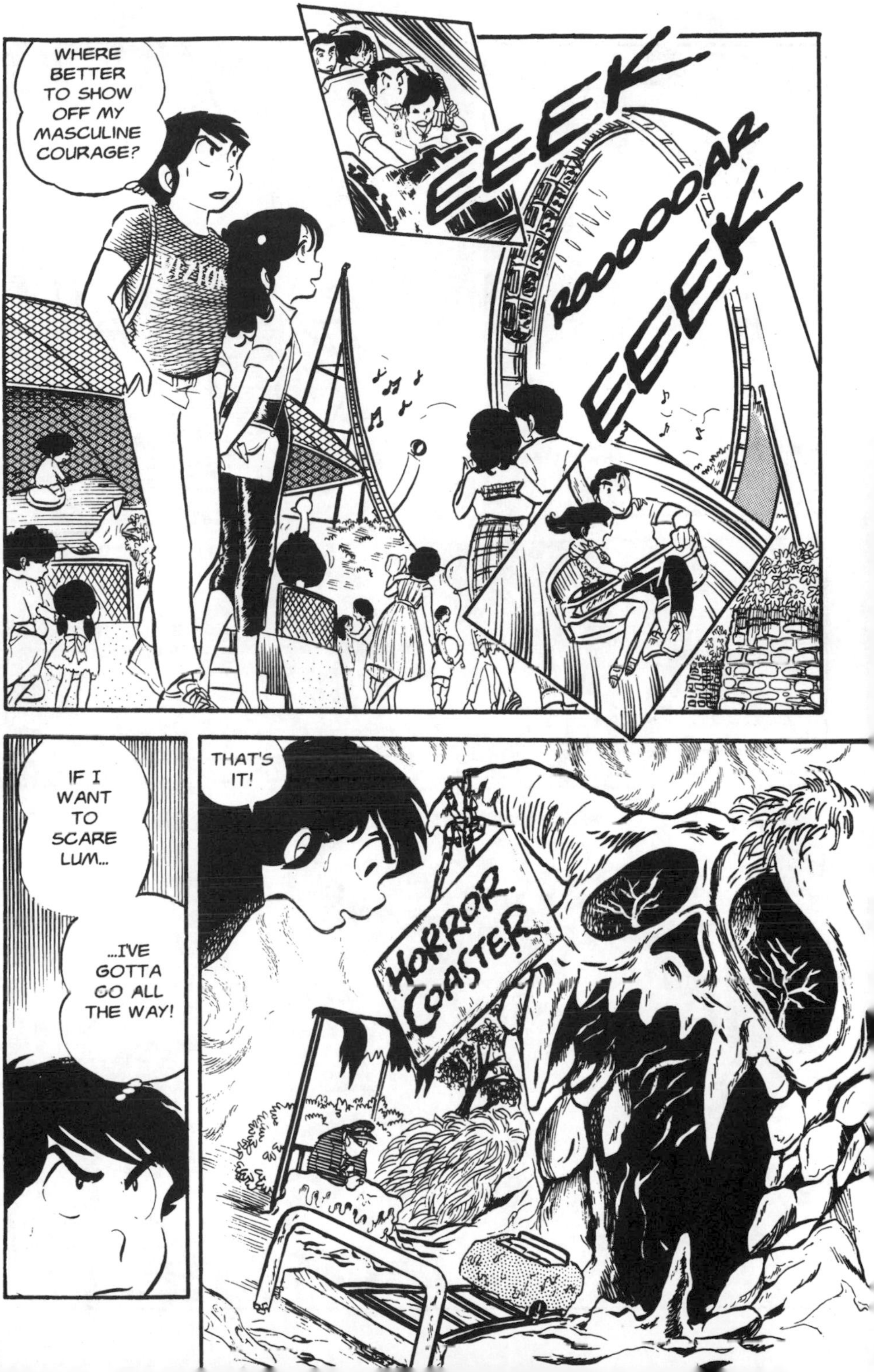
WHERE BETTER TO SHOW OFF MY MASCULINE COURAGE?
EEEEK
ROOOOOOAR
EEEEK
IF I WANT TO SCARE LUM...
...I'VE GOTTA GO ALL THE WAY!
THAT'S IT!
HORROR COASTER

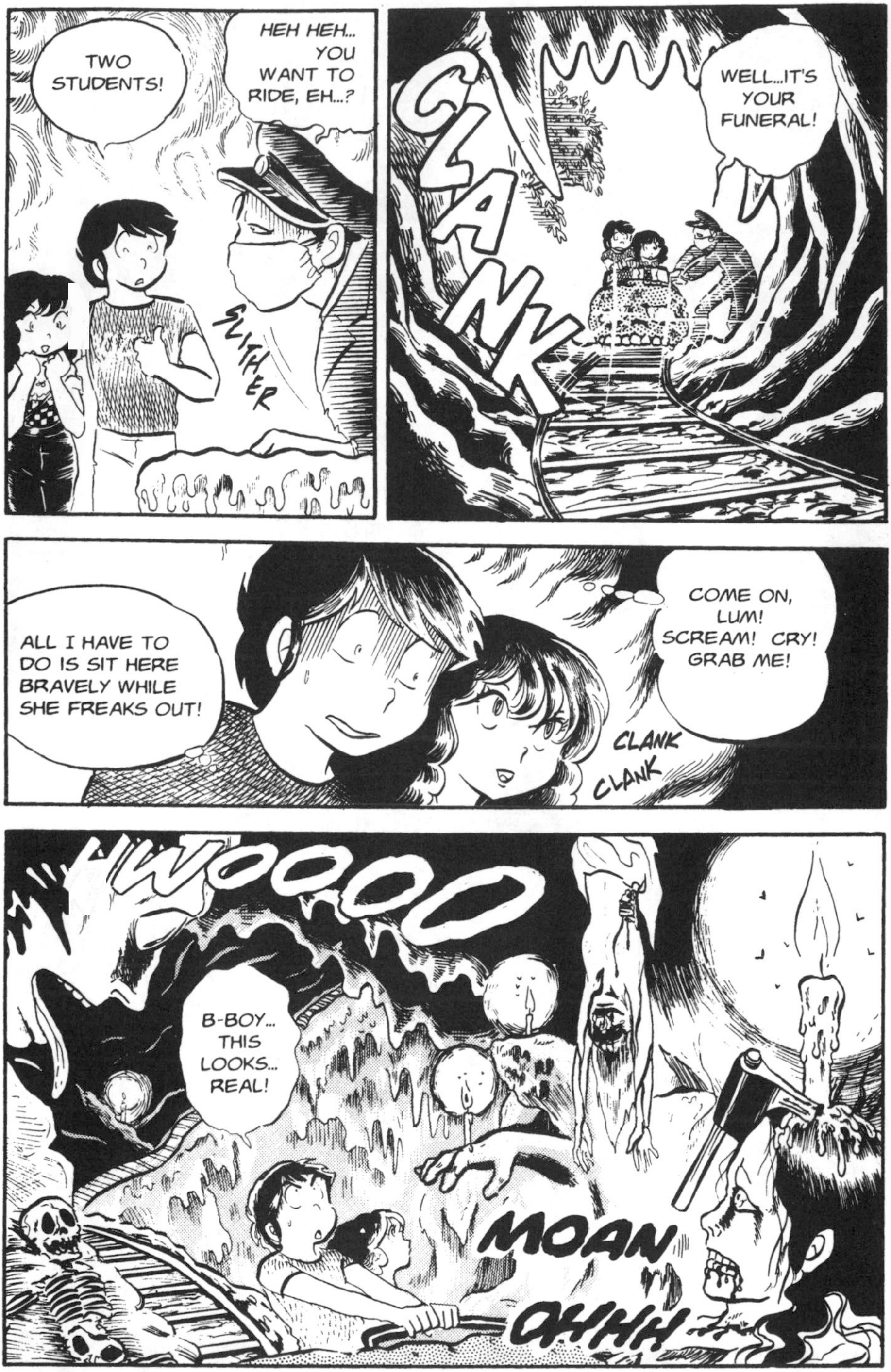
TWO STUDENTS!
HEH HEH... YOU WANT TO RIDE, EH...?
SLITHER
CLANK
WELL...IT'S YOUR FUNERAL!
ALL I HAVE TO DO IS SIT HERE BRAVELY WHILE SHE FREAKS OUT!
COME ON, LUM! SCREAM! CRY! GRAB ME!
CLANK
CLANK
WOOOOO
B-BOY... THIS LOOKS... REAL!
MOAN
OHHH

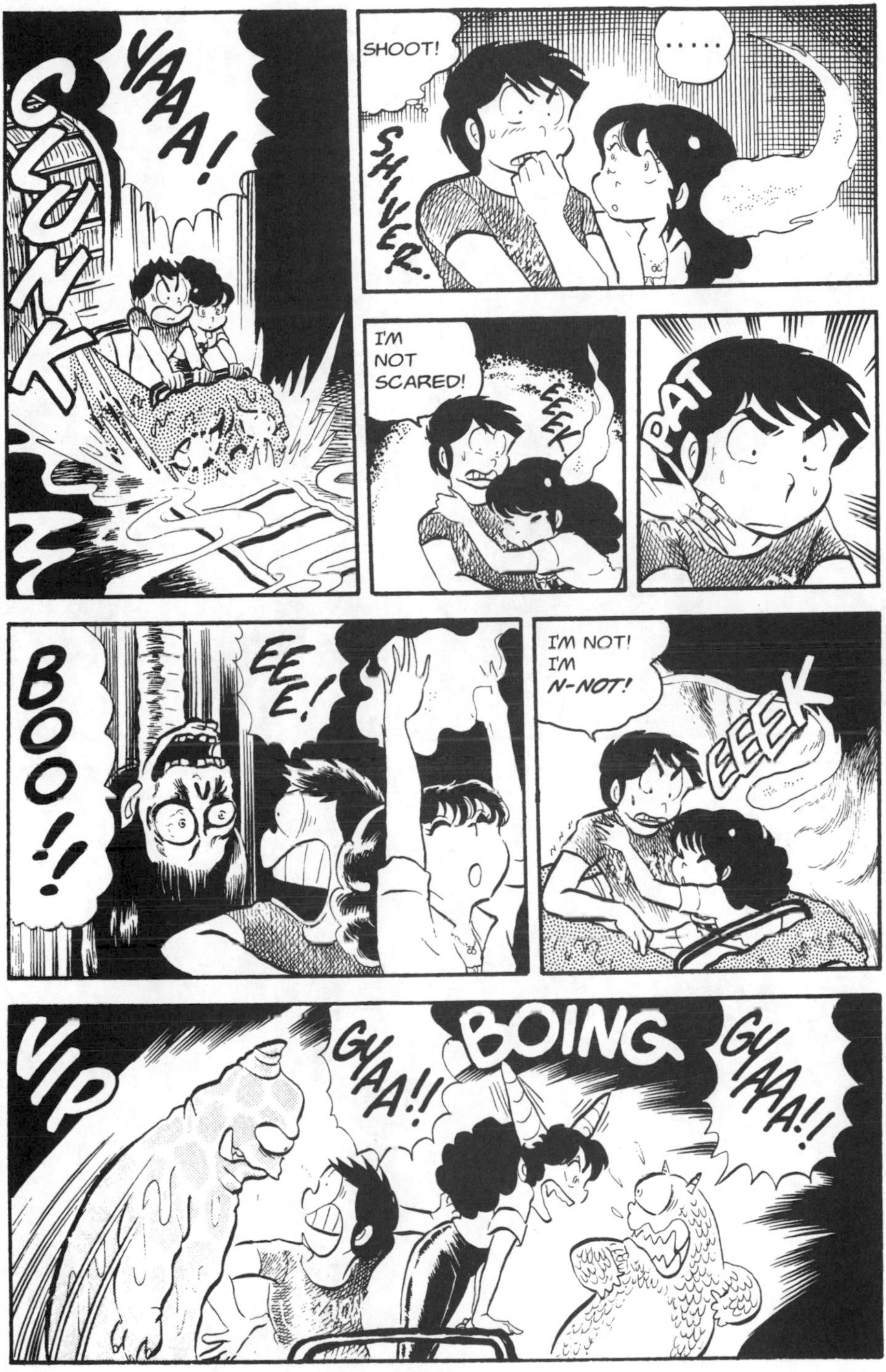
YAAAA!
CLUNK
SHOOT!
......
SHIVER..
I'M NOT SCARED!
EEEK
PAT
BOO!!
EEEE!
I'M NOT! I'M N-NOT!
EEEK
EEEK
VIP
GYAA!!
BOING
GYAAA!!

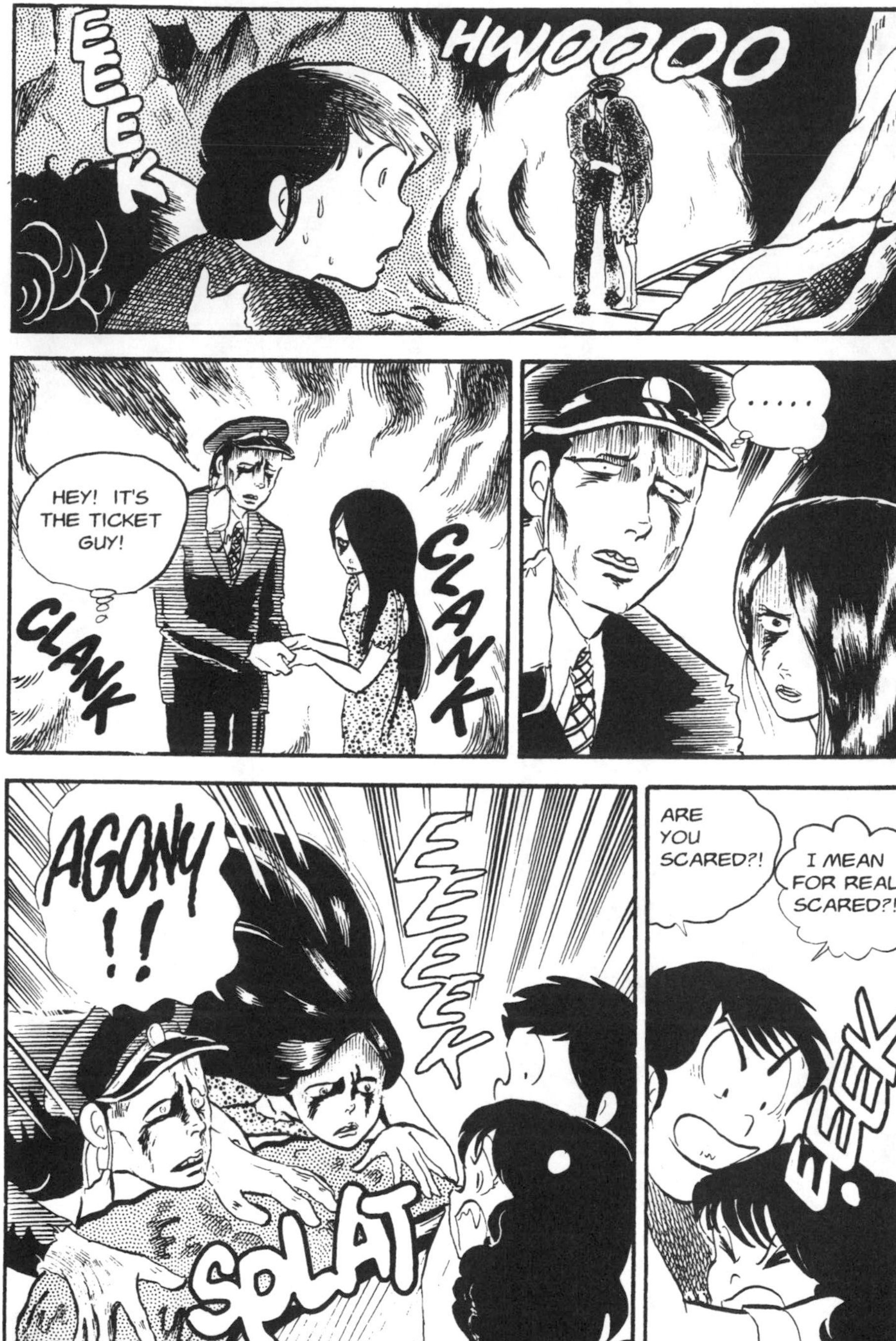

EEEEK
HWOOOOO
HEY! IT'S THE TICKET GUY!
CLANK
CLANK
.....
AGONY !!
EEEEEK
SPLAT
ARE YOU SCARED?!
I MEAN FOR REAL SCARED?!
EEEEK

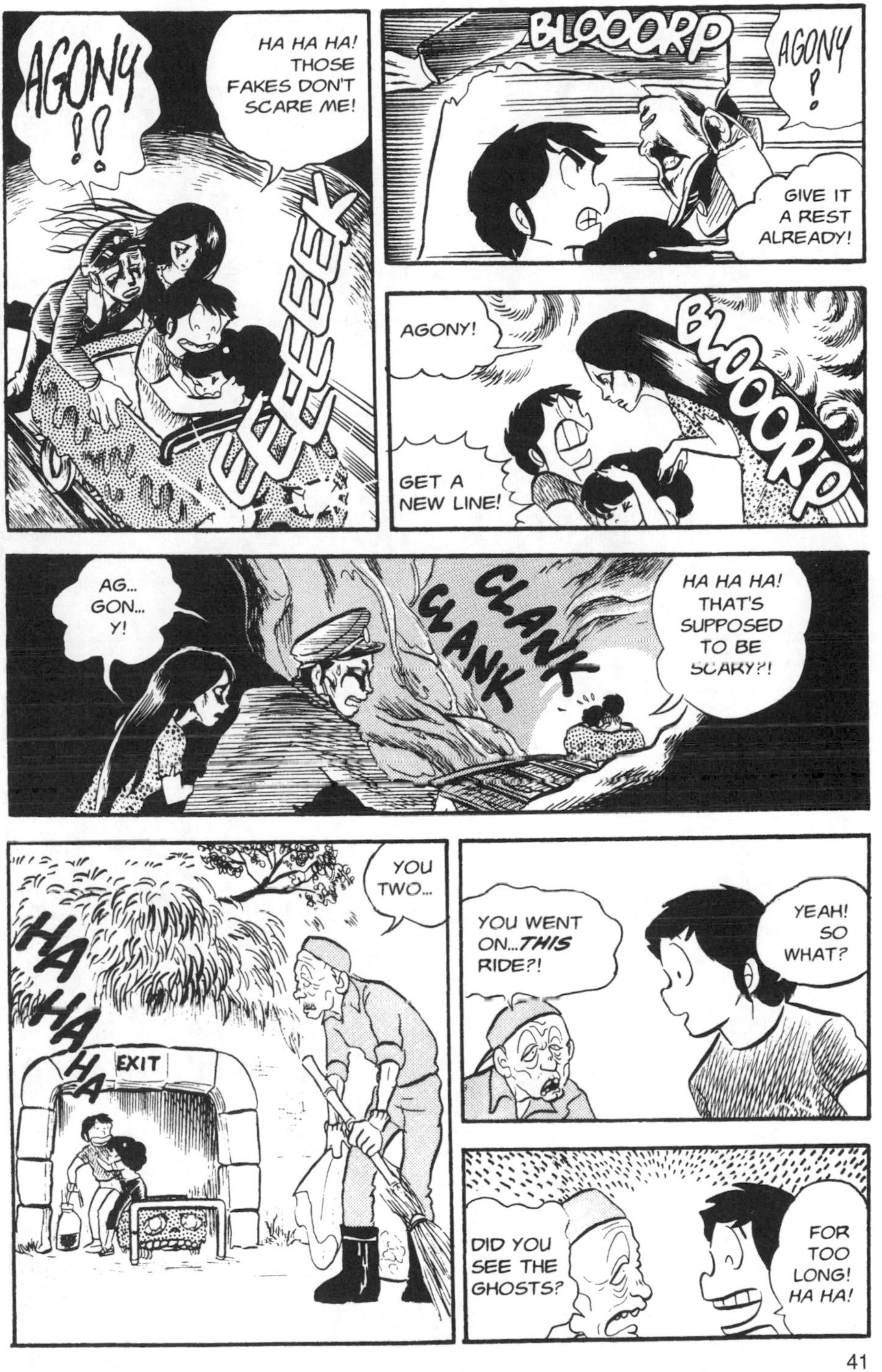
AGONY !!
HA HA HA! THOSE FAKES DON'T SCARE ME!
EEEEEEK
BLOOORP
AGONY?
GIVE IT A REST ALREADY!
AGONY!
BLOOORP
GET A NEW LINE!
AG... GON... Y!
CLANK CLANK
HA HA HA! THAT'S SUPPOSED TO BE SCARY?!
YOU TWO...
HA HA HA HA
EXIT
YOU WENT ON...*THIS* RIDE?!
YEAH! SO WHAT?
DID YOU SEE THE GHOSTS?
FOR TOO LONG! HA HA!

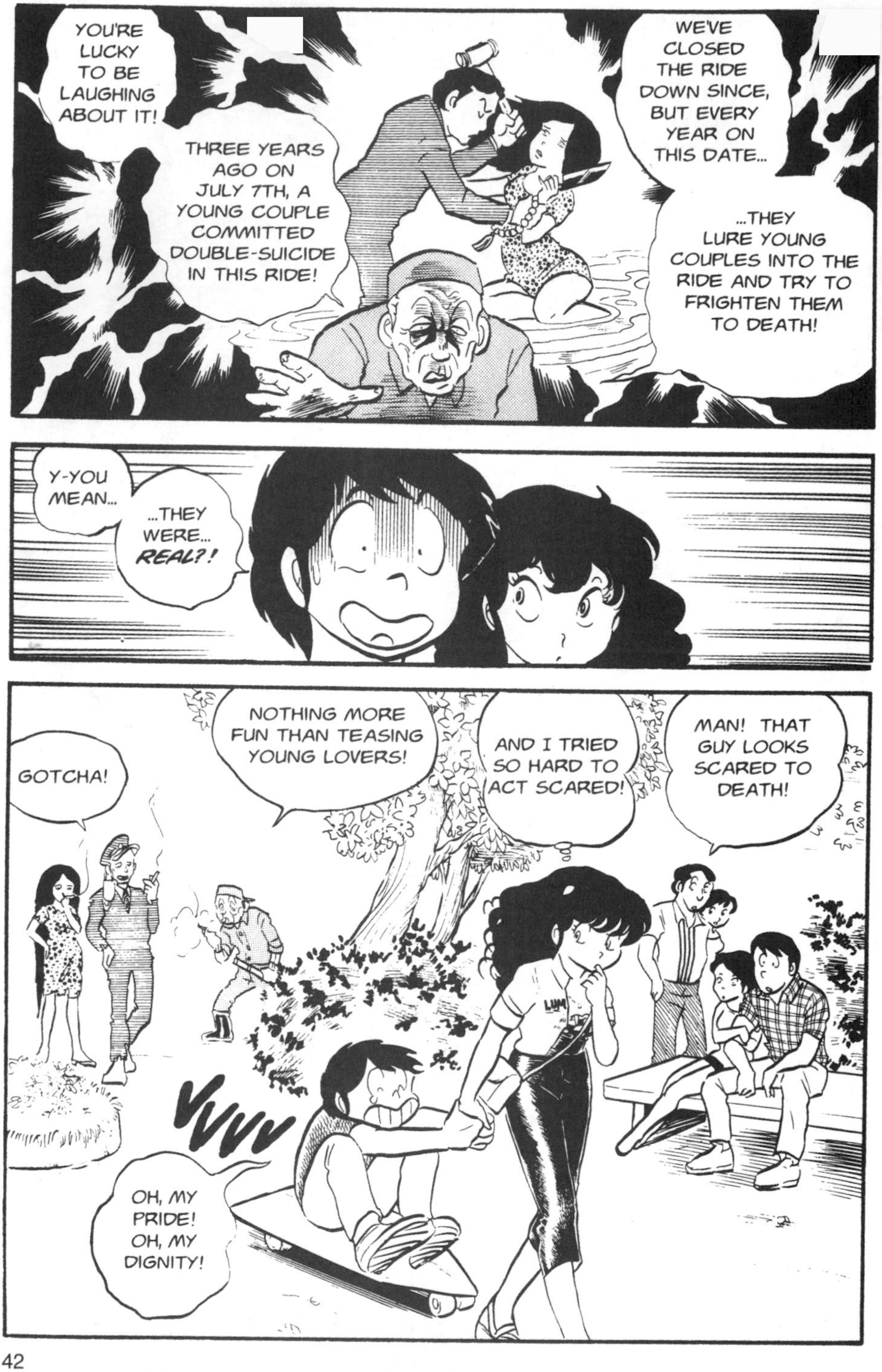
YOU'RE LUCKY TO BE LAUGHING ABOUT IT!
THREE YEARS AGO ON JULY 7TH, A YOUNG COUPLE COMMITTED DOUBLE-SUICIDE IN THIS RIDE!
WE'VE CLOSED THE RIDE DOWN SINCE, BUT EVERY YEAR ON THIS DATE...
...THEY LURE YOUNG COUPLES INTO THE RIDE AND TRY TO FRIGHTEN THEM TO DEATH!
Y-YOU MEAN...
...THEY WERE... *REAL?!*
GOTCHA!
NOTHING MORE FUN THAN TEASING YOUNG LOVERS!
AND I TRIED SO HARD TO ACT SCARED!
MAN! THAT GUY LOOKS SCARED TO DEATH!
VVVV
OH, MY PRIDE! OH, MY DIGNITY!

PART THREE
NURSERY TALES

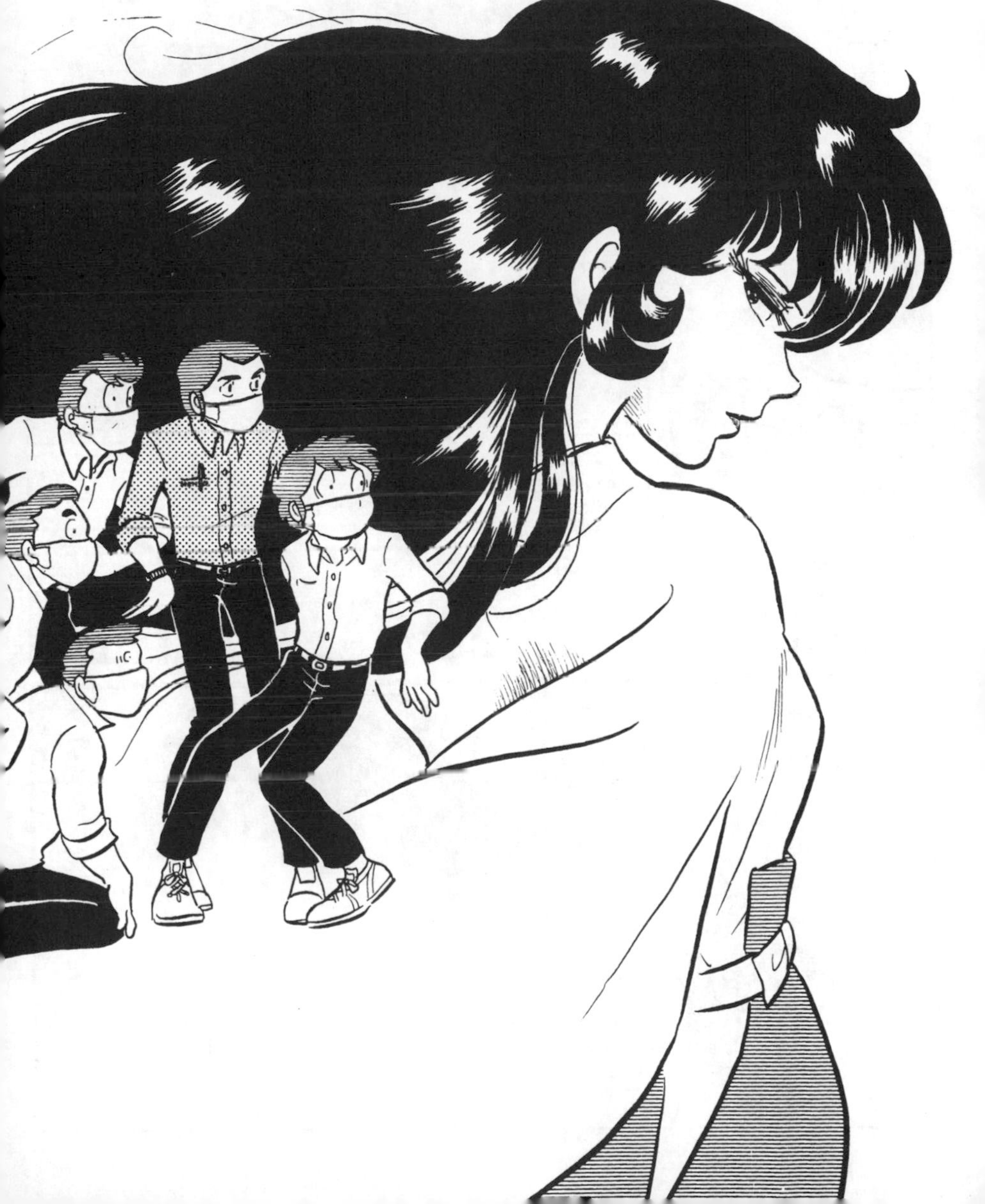

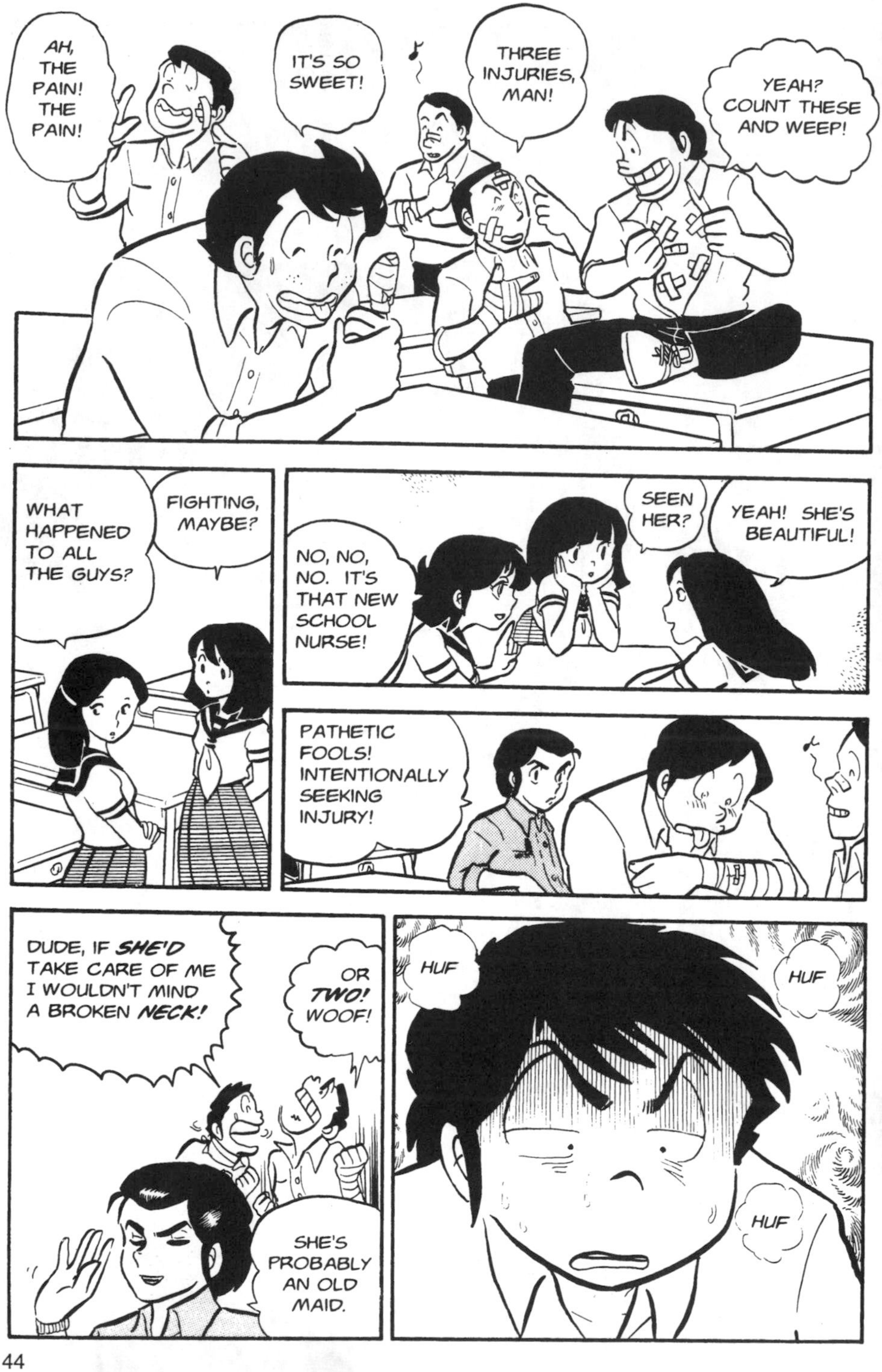
AH, THE PAIN! THE PAIN!
IT'S SO SWEET!
THREE INJURIES, MAN!
YEAH? COUNT THESE AND WEEP!
WHAT HAPPENED TO ALL THE GUYS?
FIGHTING, MAYBE?
NO, NO, NO. IT'S THAT NEW SCHOOL NURSE!
SEEN HER?
YEAH! SHE'S BEAUTIFUL!
PATHETIC FOOLS! INTENTIONALLY SEEKING INJURY!
DUDE, IF ***SHE'D*** TAKE CARE OF ME I WOULDN'T MIND A BROKEN ***NECK!***
OR ***TWO!*** WOOF!
SHE'S PROBABLY AN OLD MAID.
HUF
HUF
HUF

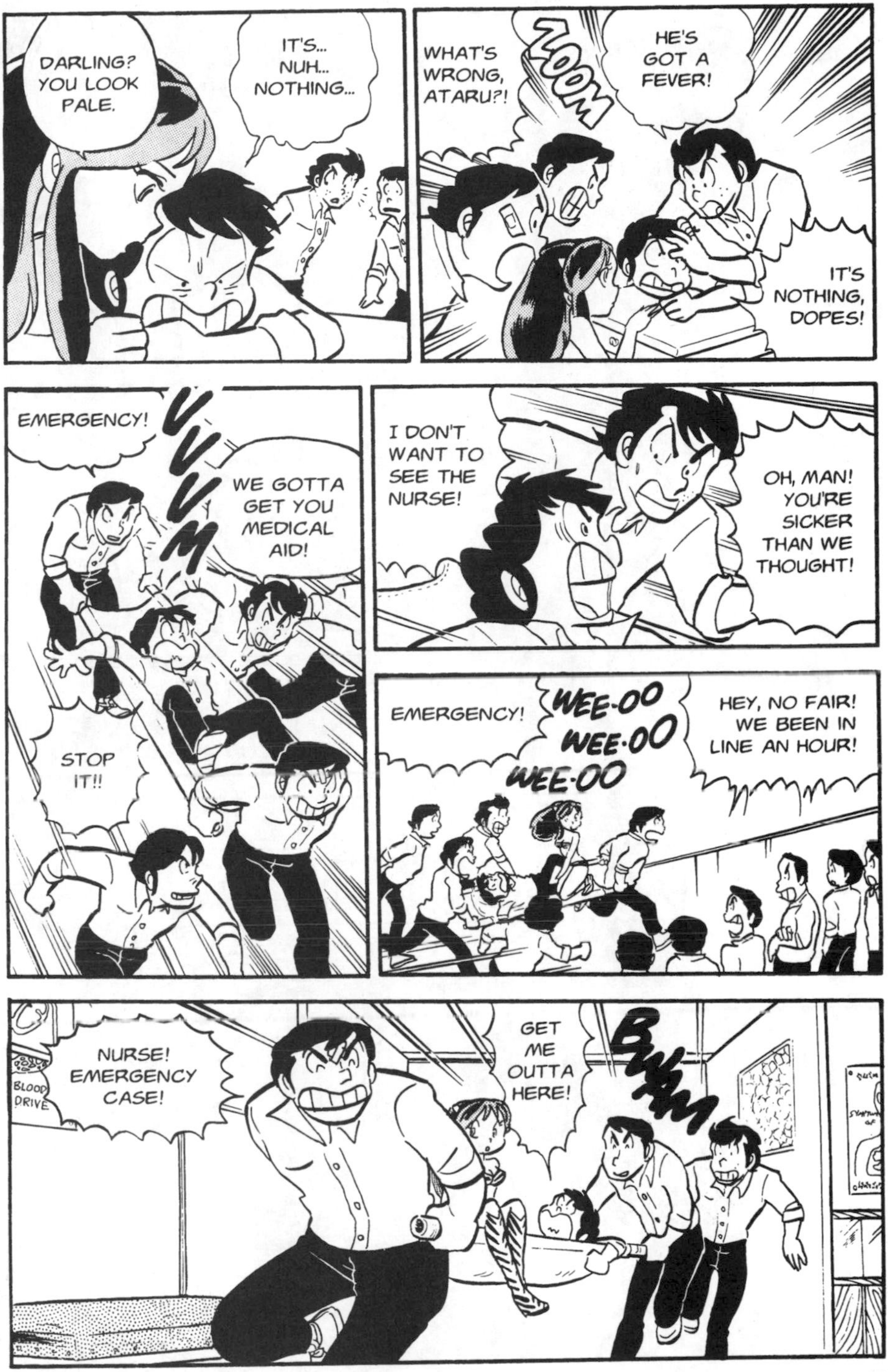
DARLING? YOU LOOK PALE.
IT'S... NUH... NOTHING...
WHAT'S WRONG, ATARU?!
ZOOM
HE'S GOT A FEVER!
IT'S NOTHING, DOPES!
EMERGENCY!
VUUUM
WE GOTTA GET YOU MEDICAL AID!
STOP IT!!
I DON'T WANT TO SEE THE NURSE!
OH, MAN! YOU'RE SICKER THAN WE THOUGHT!
EMERGENCY!
WEE-OO
WEE-OO
WEE-OO
HEY, NO FAIR! WE BEEN IN LINE AN HOUR!
BLOOD DRIVE
NURSE! EMERGENCY CASE!
GET ME OUTTA HERE!
BWAM

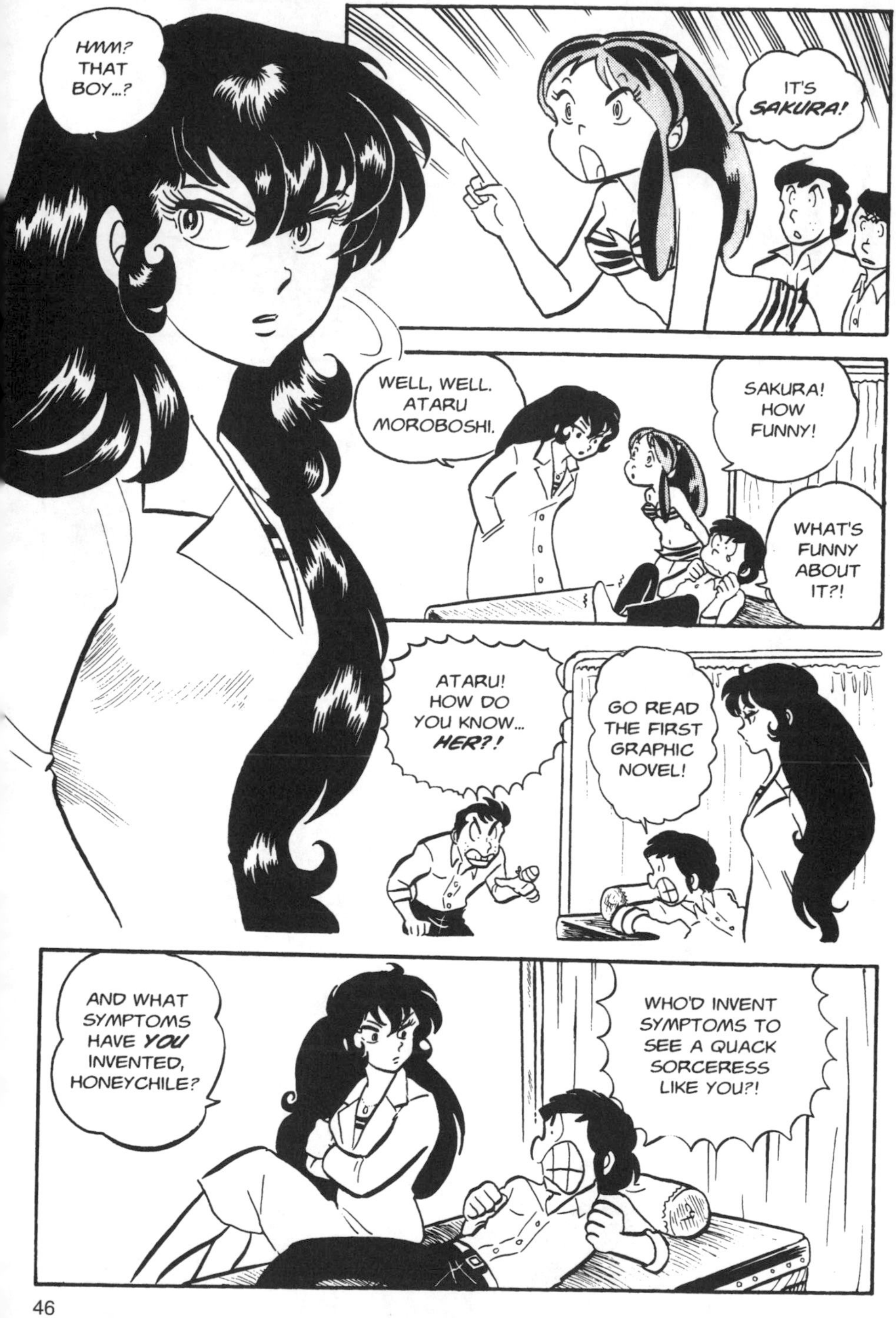
HMM? THAT BOY...?
IT'S SAKURA!
WELL, WELL. ATARU MOROBOSHI.
SAKURA! HOW FUNNY!
WHAT'S FUNNY ABOUT IT?!
ATARU! HOW DO YOU KNOW... HER?!
GO READ THE FIRST GRAPHIC NOVEL!
AND WHAT SYMPTOMS HAVE YOU INVENTED, HONEYCHILE?
WHO'D INVENT SYMPTOMS TO SEE A QUACK SORCERESS LIKE YOU?!

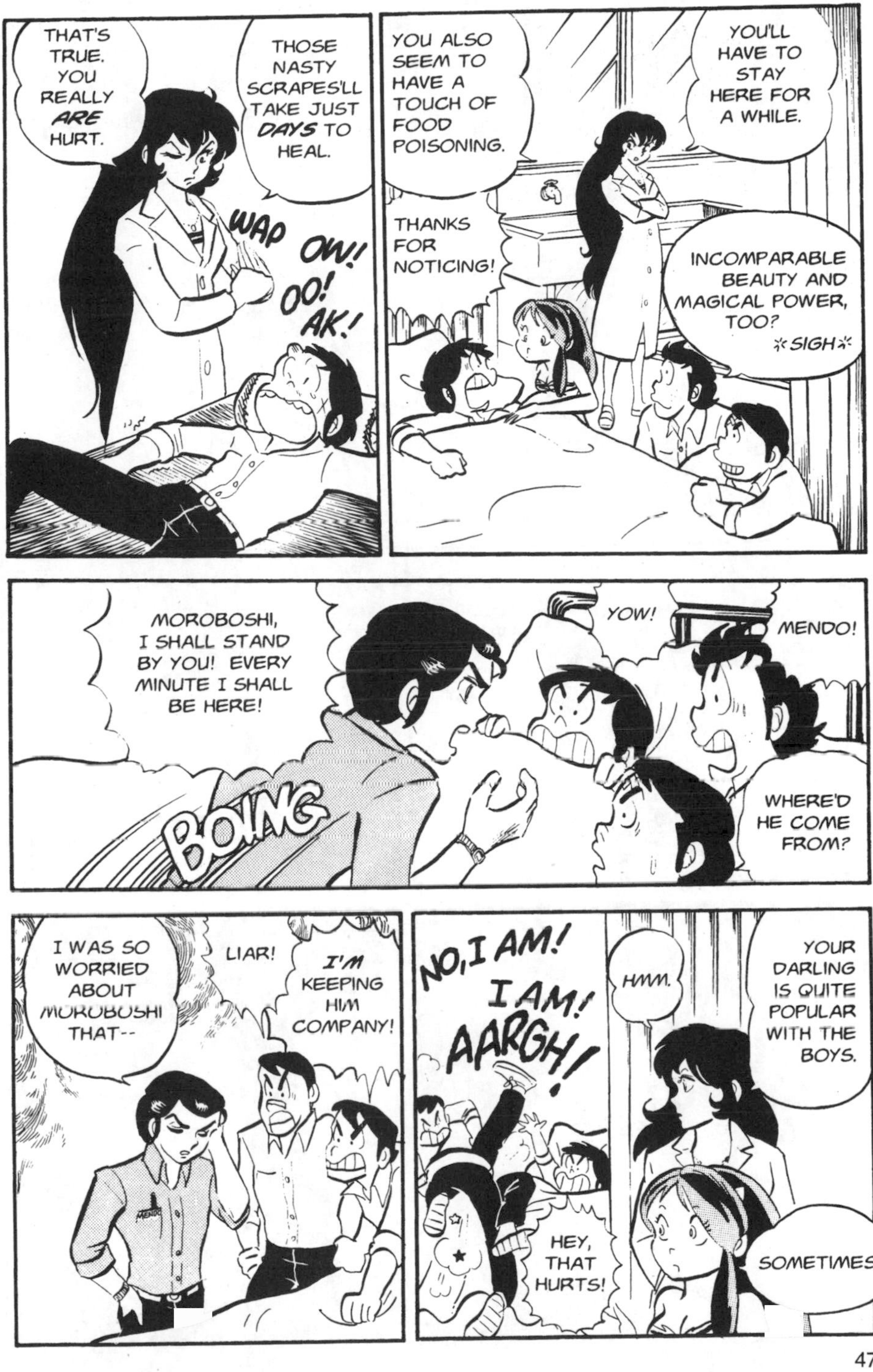
THAT'S TRUE. YOU REALLY ARE HURT.
THOSE NASTY SCRAPES'LL TAKE JUST DAYS TO HEAL.
WAP
OW!
OO!
AK!
YOU ALSO SEEM TO HAVE A TOUCH OF FOOD POISONING.
THANKS FOR NOTICING!
YOU'LL HAVE TO STAY HERE FOR A WHILE.
INCOMPARABLE BEAUTY AND MAGICAL POWER, TOO?
SIGH
MOROBOSHI, I SHALL STAND BY YOU! EVERY MINUTE I SHALL BE HERE!
BOING
YOW!
MENDO!
WHERE'D HE COME FROM?
I WAS SO WORRIED ABOUT MOROBOSHI THAT--
LIAR!
I'M KEEPING HIM COMPANY!
MENDO
NO, I AM!
I AM!
AARGH!
HEY, THAT HURTS!
HMM.
YOUR DARLING IS QUITE POPULAR WITH THE BOYS.
SOMETIMES...

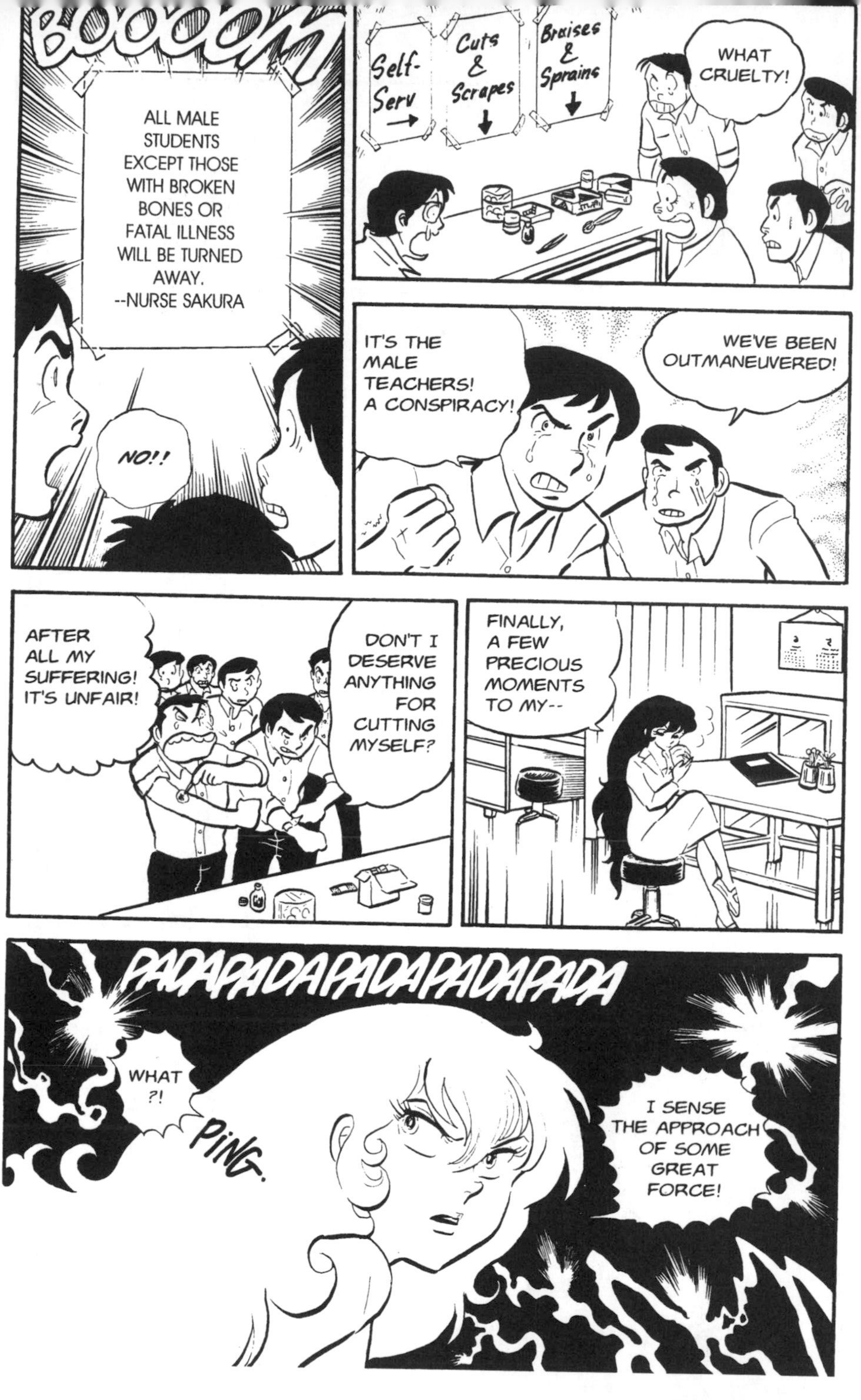
BOOOOOM
ALL MALE STUDENTS EXCEPT THOSE WITH BROKEN BONES OR FATAL ILLNESS WILL BE TURNED AWAY. --NURSE SAKURA
NO!!
Self-Serv
Cuts & Scrapes
Bruises & Sprains
WHAT CRUELTY!
IT'S THE MALE TEACHERS! A CONSPIRACY!
WE'VE BEEN OUTMANEUVERED!
AFTER ALL MY SUFFERING! IT'S UNFAIR!
DON'T I DESERVE ANYTHING FOR CUTTING MYSELF?
FINALLY, A FEW PRECIOUS MOMENTS TO MY--
PADAPADAPADAPADAPADAPADA
WHAT ?!
PING
I SENSE THE APPROACH OF SOME GREAT FORCE!

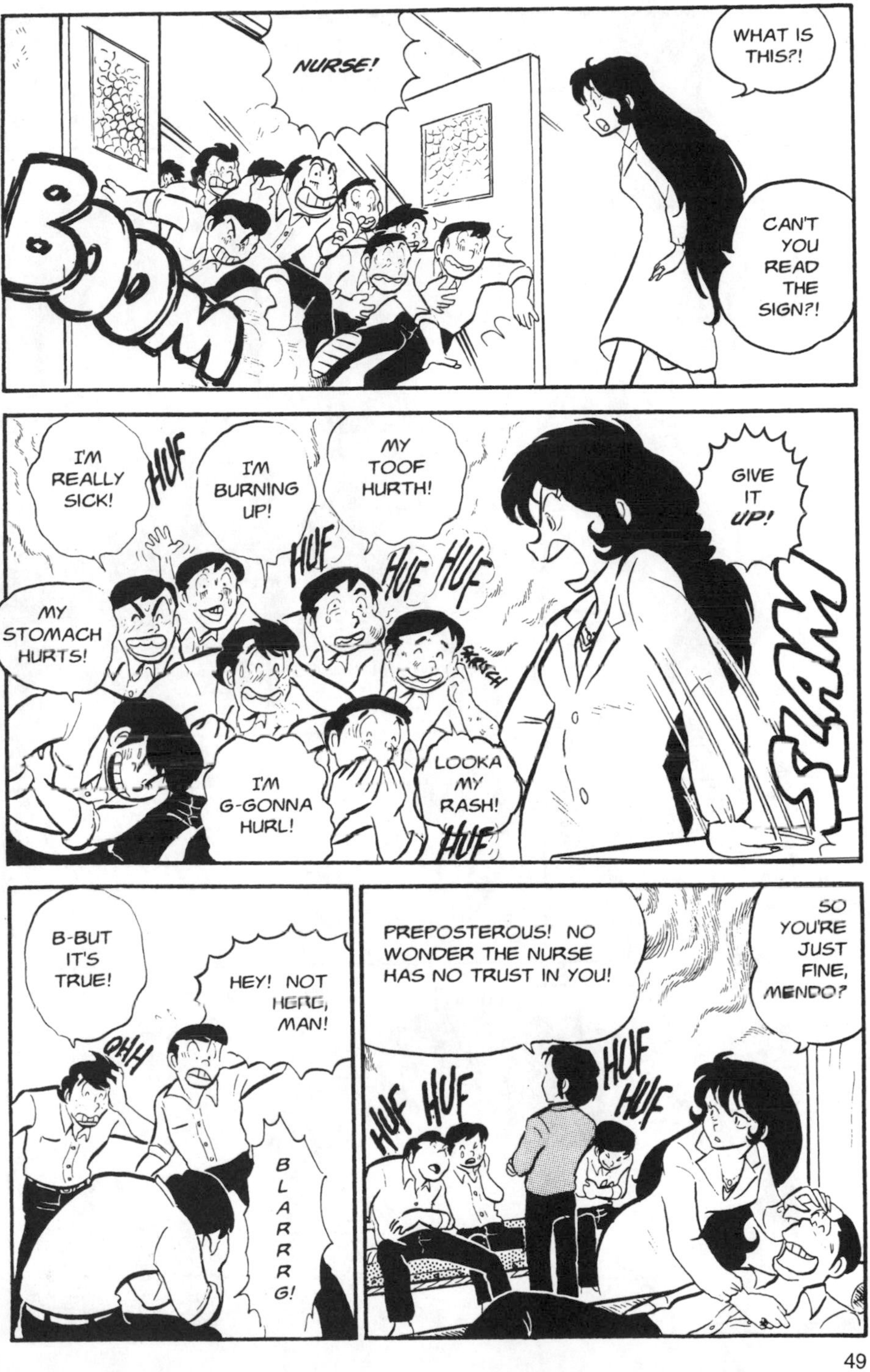

NURSE!
BOOM
WHAT IS THIS?!
CAN'T YOU READ THE SIGN?!
I'M REALLY SICK!
HUF
I'M BURNING UP!
MY TOOF HURTH!
HUF
HUF HUF
GIVE IT UP!
MY STOMACH HURTS!
I'M G-GONNA HURL!
LOOKA MY RASH!
HUF
SLAM
B-BUT IT'S TRUE!
HEY! NOT HERE, MAN!
OHH
BLARRRG!
PREPOSTEROUS! NO WONDER THE NURSE HAS NO TRUST IN YOU!
SO YOU'RE JUST FINE, MENDO?
HUF HUF
HUF HUF

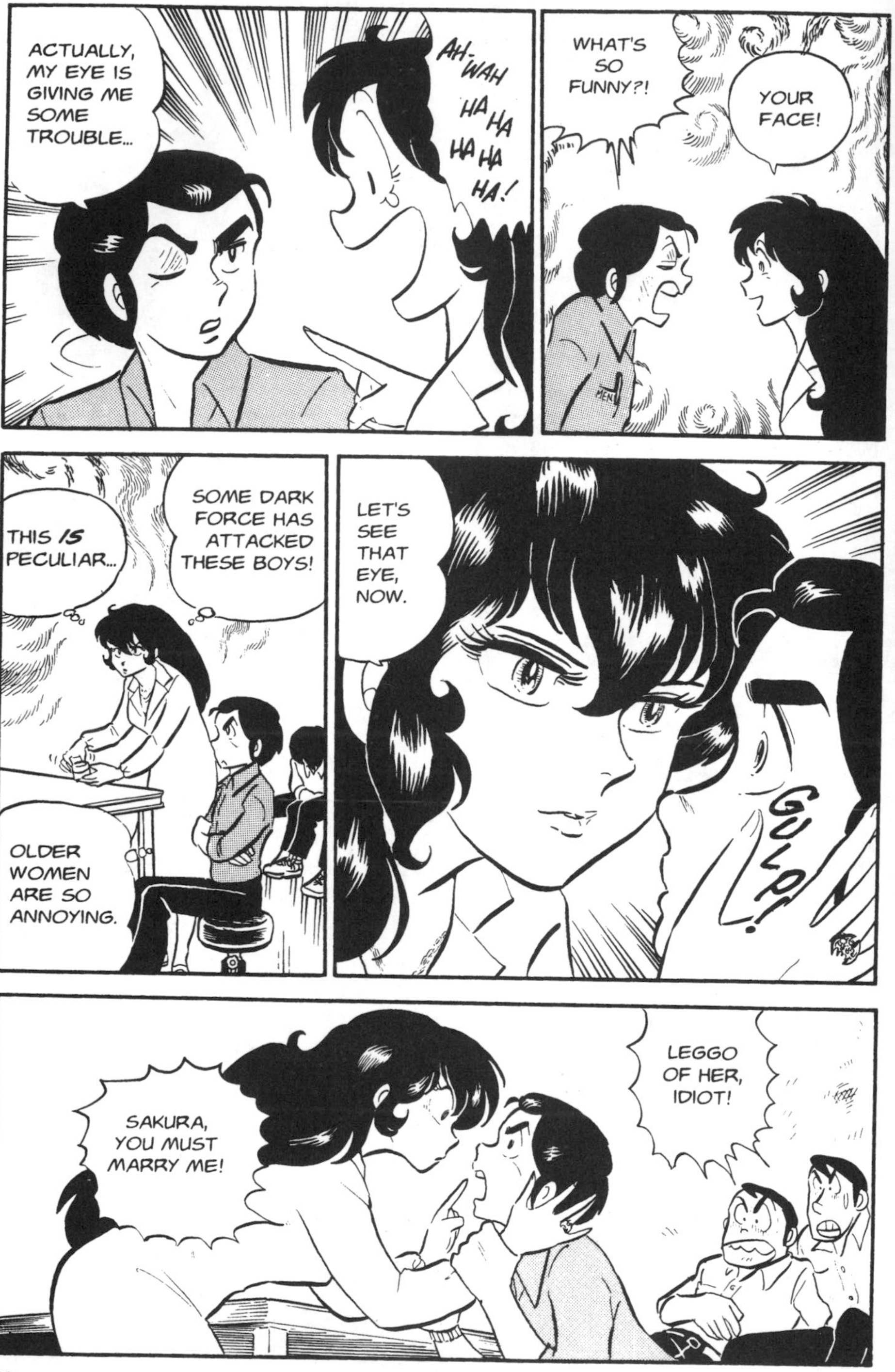
ACTUALLY, MY EYE IS GIVING ME SOME TROUBLE...
AH-WAH HA HA HA HA HA!
WHAT'S SO FUNNY?!
YOUR FACE!
THIS *IS* PECULIAR...
SOME DARK FORCE HAS ATTACKED THESE BOYS!
OLDER WOMEN ARE SO ANNOYING.
LET'S SEE THAT EYE, NOW.
GULP!
SAKURA, YOU MUST MARRY ME!
LEGGO OF HER, IDIOT!

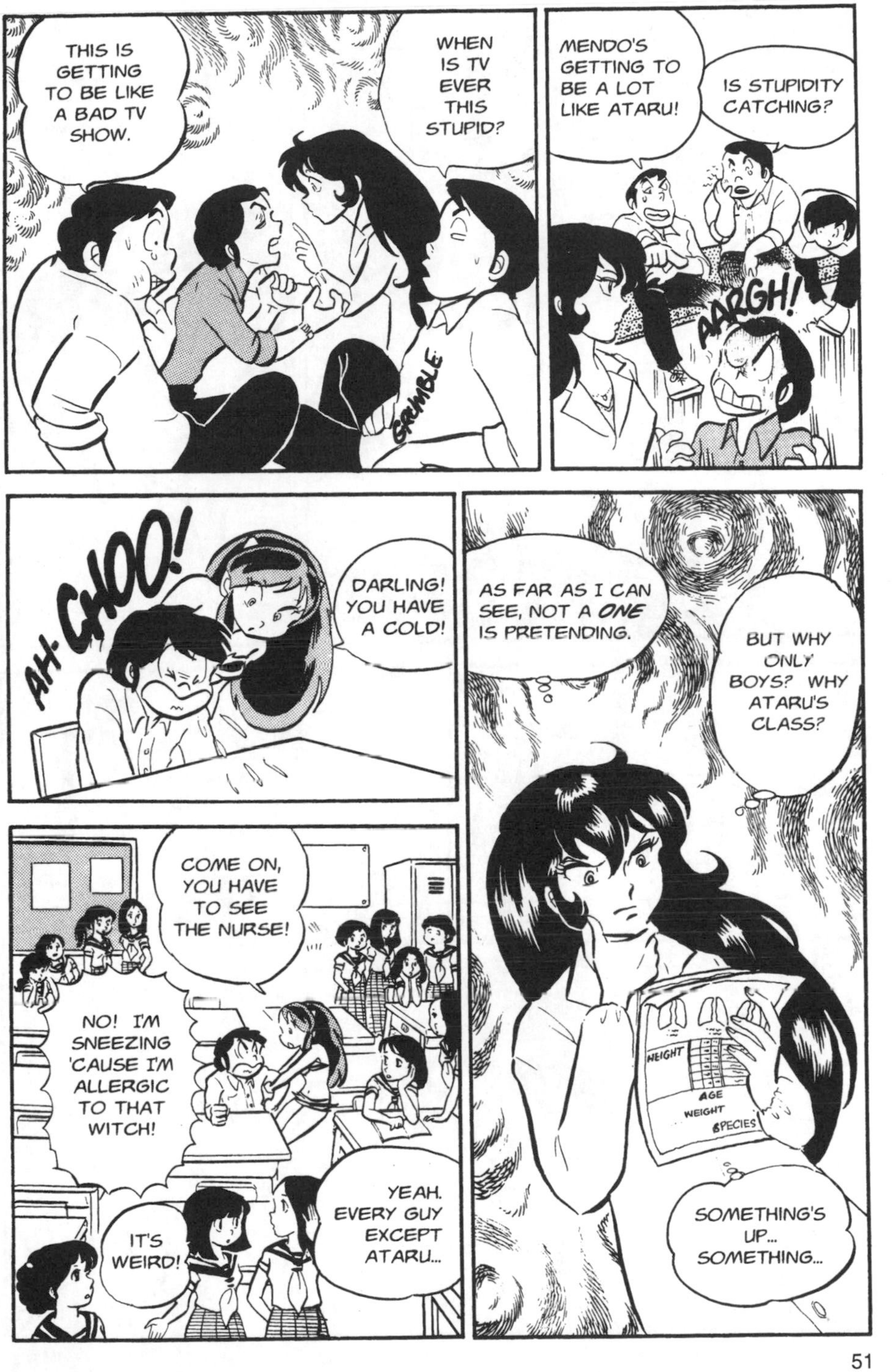
THIS IS GETTING TO BE LIKE A BAD TV SHOW.
WHEN IS TV EVER THIS STUPID?
GRUMBLE
MENDO'S GETTING TO BE A LOT LIKE ATARU!
IS STUPIDITY CATCHING?
AARGH!
AH-CHOO!
DARLING! YOU HAVE A COLD!
COME ON, YOU HAVE TO SEE THE NURSE!
NO! I'M SNEEZING 'CAUSE I'M ALLERGIC TO THAT WITCH!
IT'S WEIRD!
YEAH. EVERY GUY EXCEPT ATARU...
AS FAR AS I CAN SEE, NOT A *ONE* IS PRETENDING.
BUT WHY ONLY BOYS? WHY ATARU'S CLASS?
WEIGHT
AGE
WEIGHT
SPECIES
SOMETHING'S UP... SOMETHING...

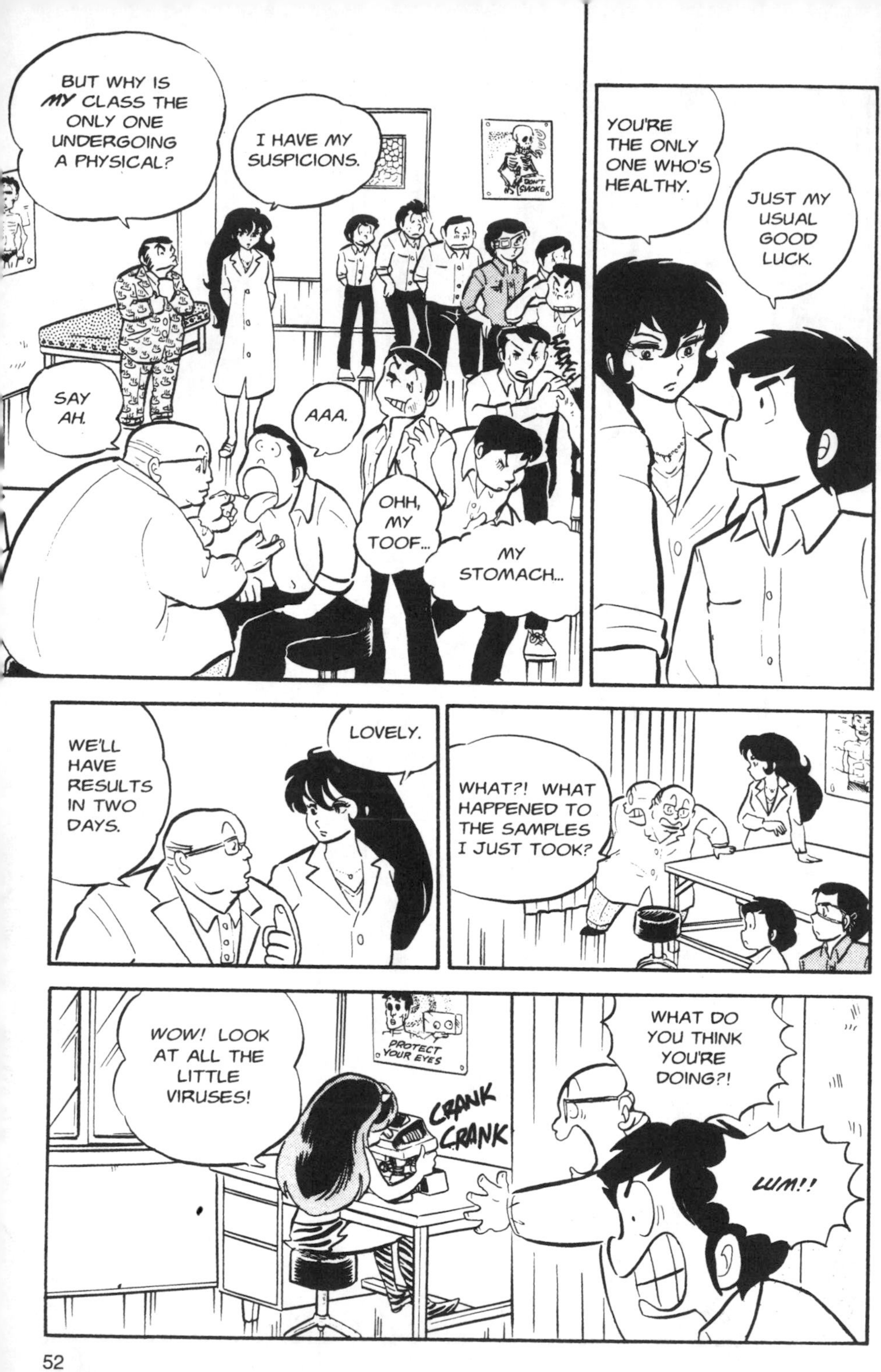
BUT WHY IS MY CLASS THE ONLY ONE UNDERGOING A PHYSICAL?
I HAVE MY SUSPICIONS.
DON'T SMOKE
SAY AH.
AAA.
OHH, MY TOOF...
MY STOMACH...
YOU'RE THE ONLY ONE WHO'S HEALTHY.
JUST MY USUAL GOOD LUCK.
WE'LL HAVE RESULTS IN TWO DAYS.
LOVELY.
WHAT?! WHAT HAPPENED TO THE SAMPLES I JUST TOOK?
WOW! LOOK AT ALL THE LITTLE VIRUSES!
PROTECT YOUR EYES
CRANK CRANK
WHAT DO YOU THINK YOU'RE DOING?!
LUM!!

I WON'T HAVE YOU PLAYING WITH THAT!

BUT WHAT IF DARLING'S SICK?

STEP ASIDE, PLEASE.

I'M A DOCTOR!

FOOEY!

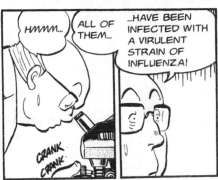

HMMM...

ALL OF THEM...

...HAVE BEEN INFECTED WITH A VIRULENT STRAIN OF INFLUENZA!

CRANK CRANK

HOW DOES THE FLU GIVE ME ATHLETE'S FOOT?

OR RHEUMA-TISM?

OR A RASH?

ARITCH

OR EVERY-THING ELSE?!

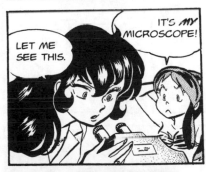

LET ME SEE THIS.

IT'S *MY* MICROSCOPE!

?

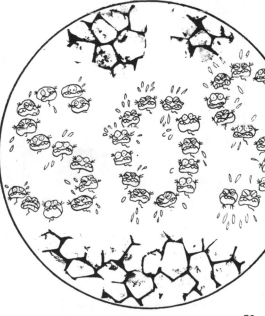

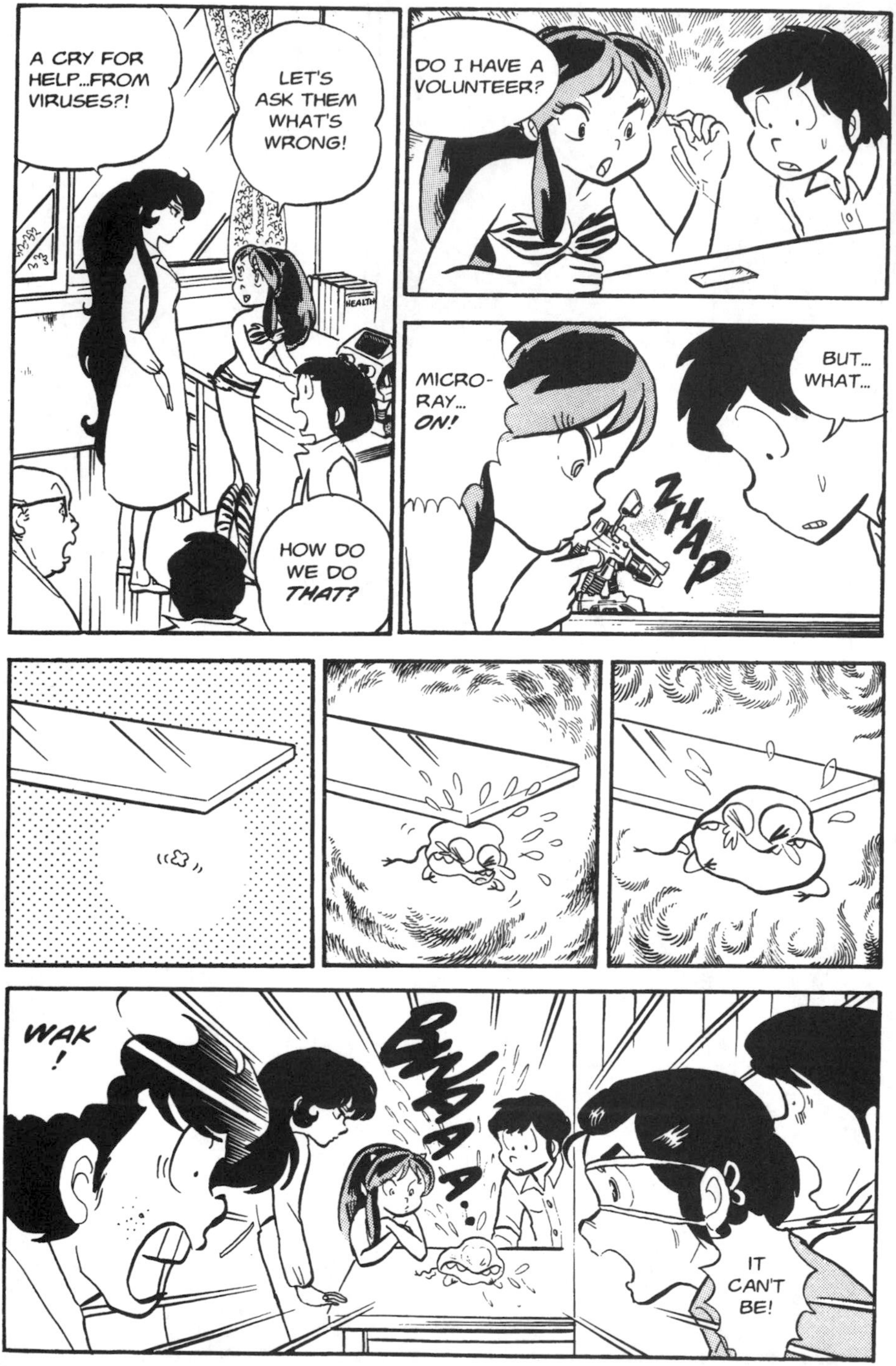

A CRY FOR HELP...FROM VIRUSES?!
LET'S ASK THEM WHAT'S WRONG!
HOW DO WE DO *THAT?*
DO I HAVE A VOLUNTEER?
MICRO-RAY... *ON!*
BUT... WHAT...
ZHAP
WAK!
BWAAAA..
IT CAN'T BE!

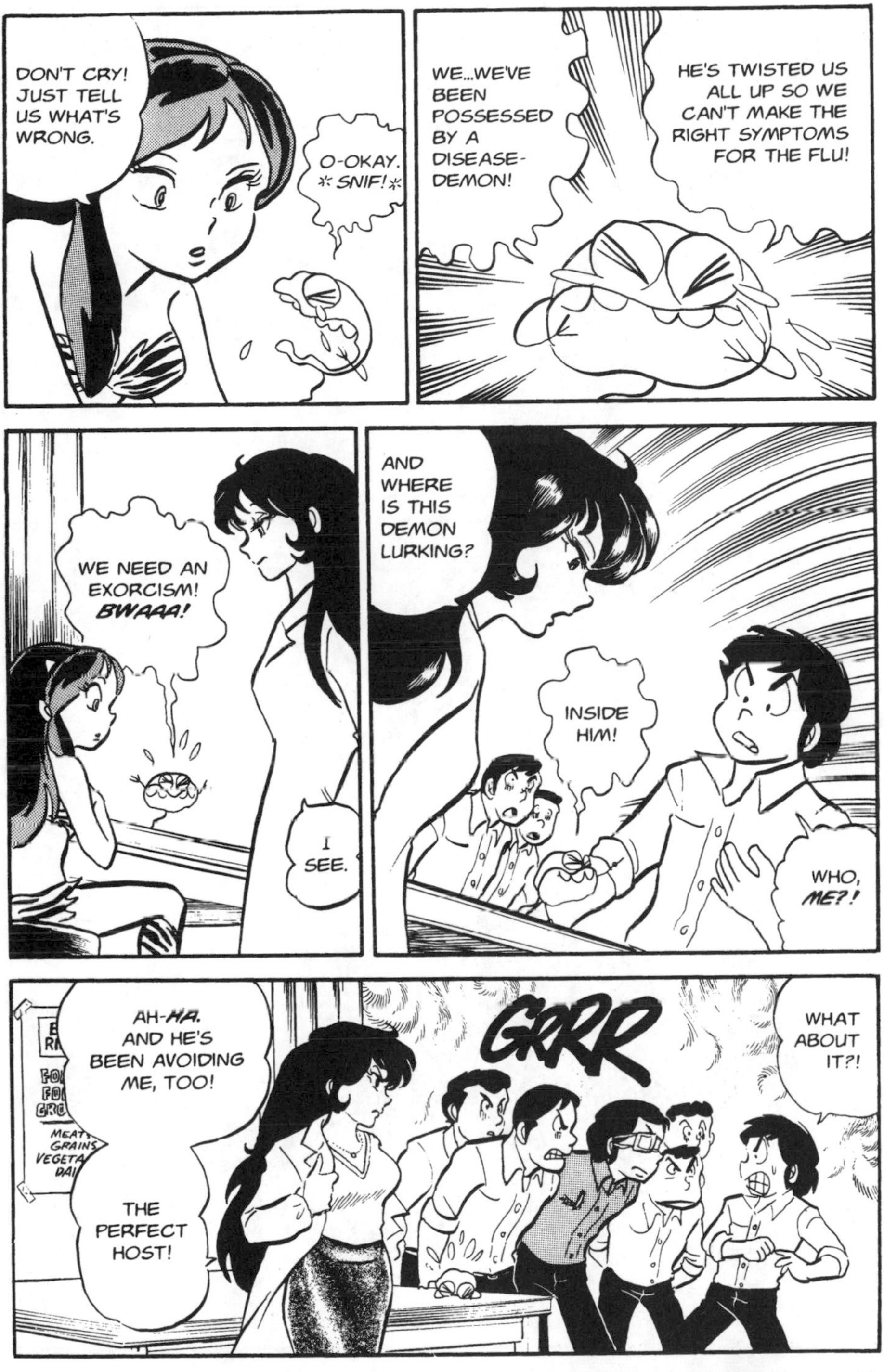
DON'T CRY! JUST TELL US WHAT'S WRONG.
O-OKAY. *SNIF!*
WE...WE'VE BEEN POSSESSED BY A DISEASE-DEMON!
HE'S TWISTED US ALL UP SO WE CAN'T MAKE THE RIGHT SYMPTOMS FOR THE FLU!
WE NEED AN EXORCISM! BWAAA!
I SEE.
AND WHERE IS THIS DEMON LURKING?
INSIDE HIM!
WHO, ME?!
AH-HA. AND HE'S BEEN AVOIDING ME, TOO!
THE PERFECT HOST!
GRRR
WHAT ABOUT IT?!

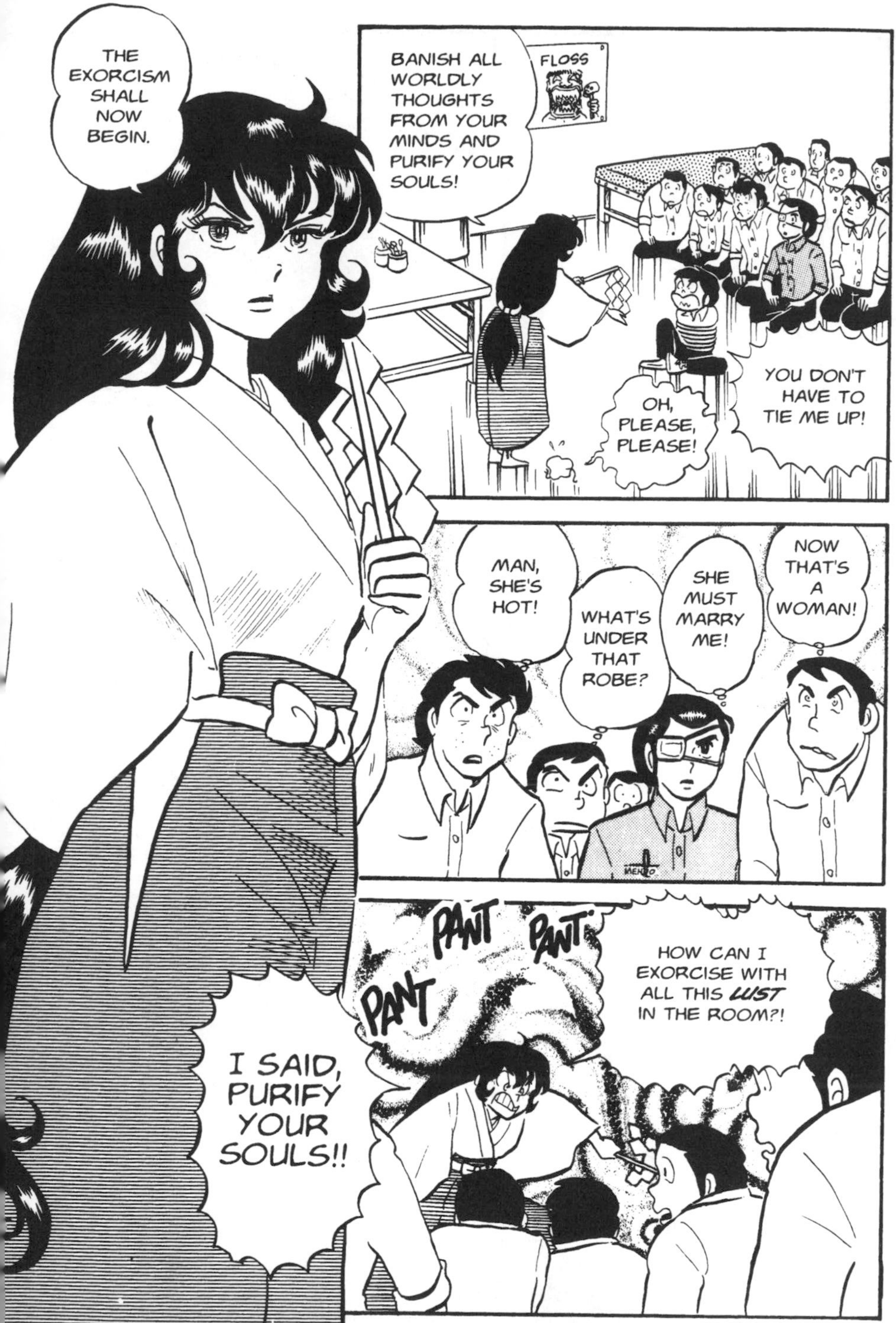
THE EXORCISM SHALL NOW BEGIN.
BANISH ALL WORLDLY THOUGHTS FROM YOUR MINDS AND PURIFY YOUR SOULS!
FLOSS
OH, PLEASE, PLEASE!
YOU DON'T HAVE TO TIE ME UP!
MAN, SHE'S HOT!
WHAT'S UNDER THAT ROBE?
SHE MUST MARRY ME!
NOW THAT'S A WOMAN!
PANT
PANT
PANT
HOW CAN I EXORCISE WITH ALL THIS *LUST* IN THE ROOM?!
I SAID, PURIFY YOUR SOULS!!

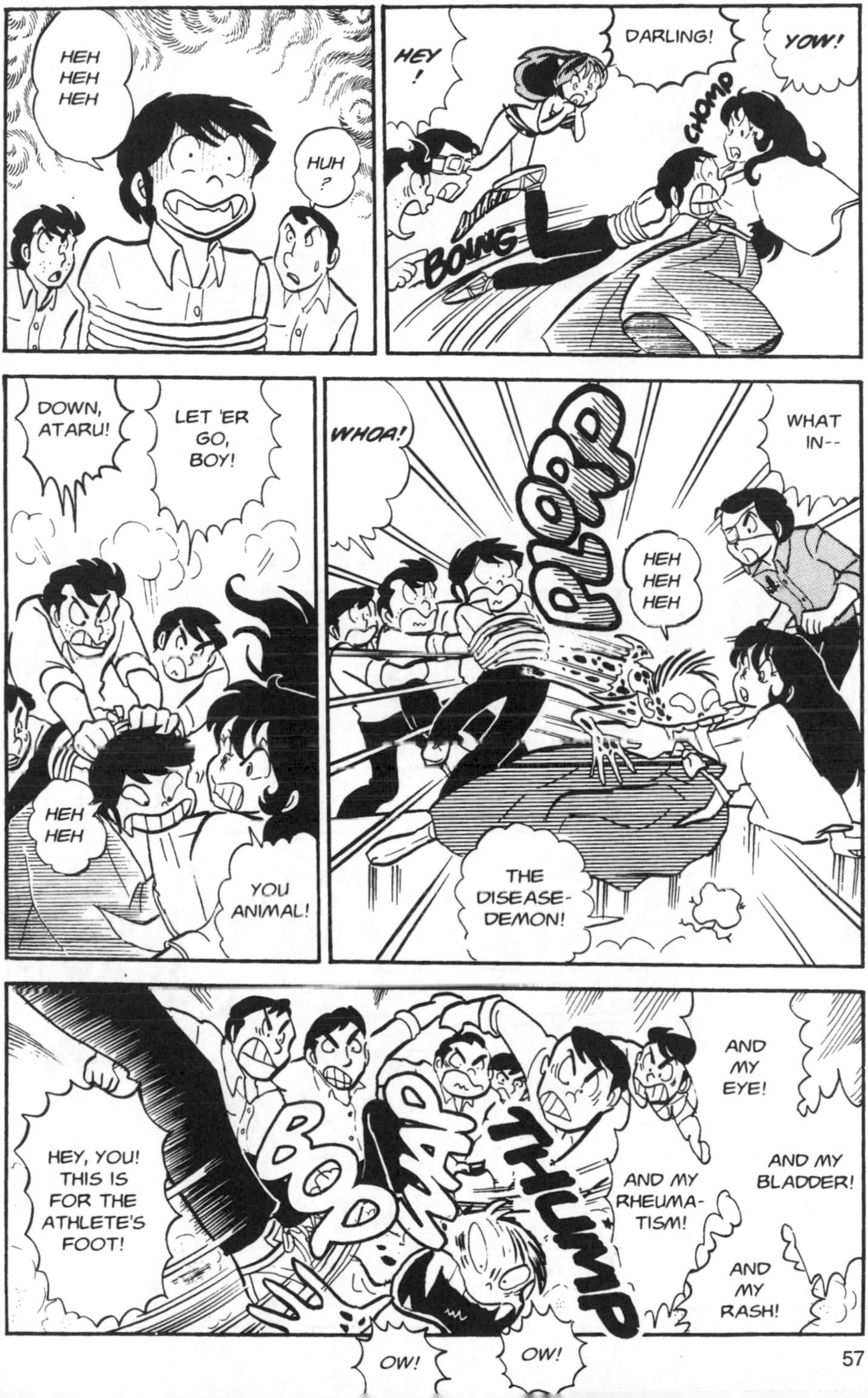
HEH HEH HEH
HUH?
HEY!
DARLING!
YOW!
CHOMP
BOING
DOWN, ATARU!
LET 'ER GO, BOY!
HEH HEH
YOU ANIMAL!
WHOA!
PLOOP
WHAT IN--
HEH HEH HEH
THE DISEASE-DEMON!
HEY, YOU! THIS IS FOR THE ATHLETE'S FOOT!
BOP
WHAP
THUMP
AND MY RHEUMATISM!
AND MY EYE!
AND MY BLADDER!
AND MY RASH!
OW!
OW!

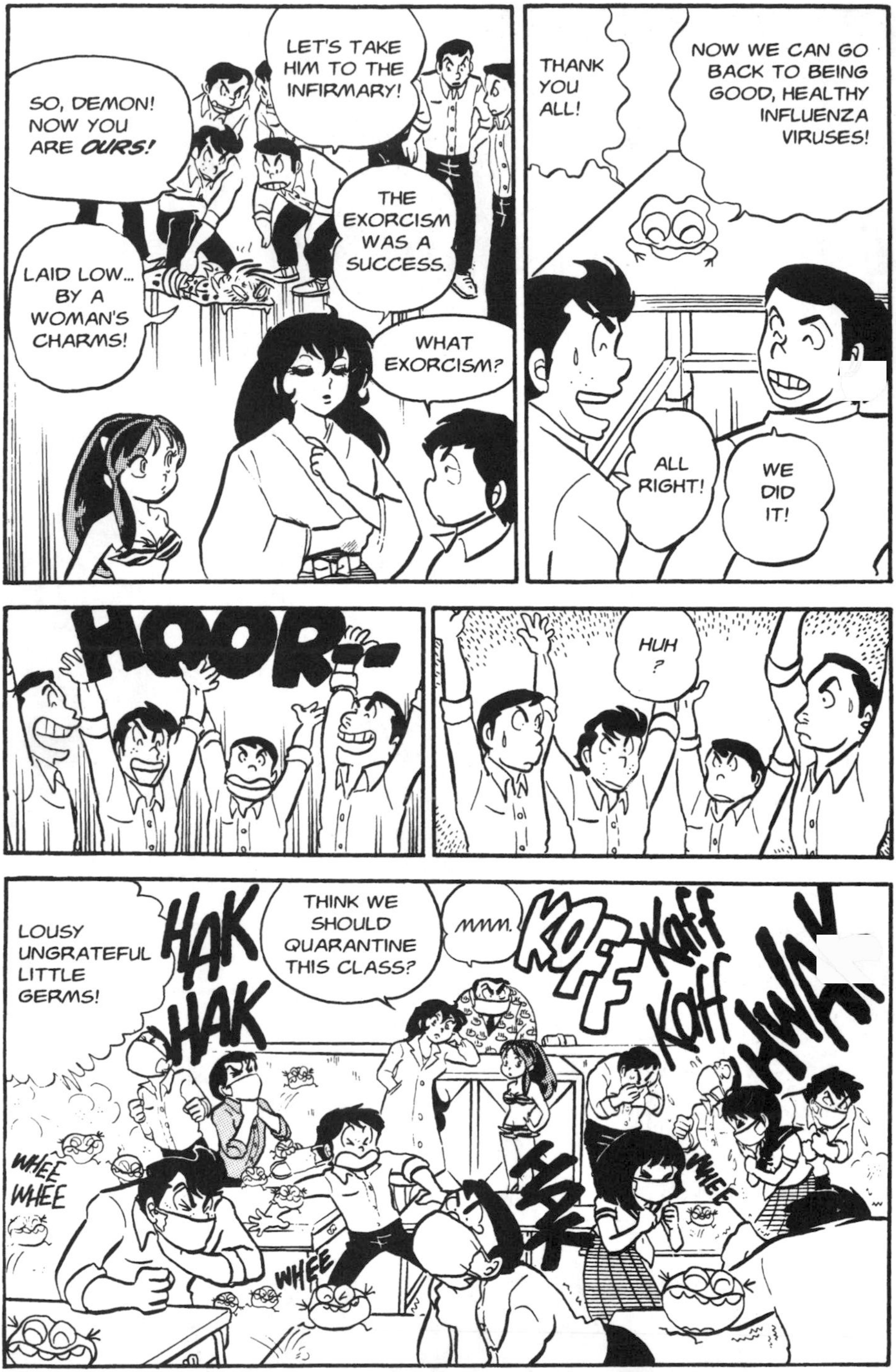
SO, DEMON! NOW YOU ARE *OURS!*
LET'S TAKE HIM TO THE INFIRMARY!
LAID LOW... BY A WOMAN'S CHARMS!
THE EXORCISM WAS A SUCCESS.
WHAT EXORCISM?
THANK YOU ALL!
NOW WE CAN GO BACK TO BEING GOOD, HEALTHY INFLUENZA VIRUSES!
ALL RIGHT!
WE DID IT!
HOOR--
HUH?
LOUSY UNGRATEFUL LITTLE GERMS!
HAK HAK
THINK WE SHOULD QUARANTINE THIS CLASS?
MMM.
KOFF KAFF KOFF
WHEE WHEE
HAK
WHEE
WHEE

PART FOUR
RAINDROPS KEEP FALLIN'

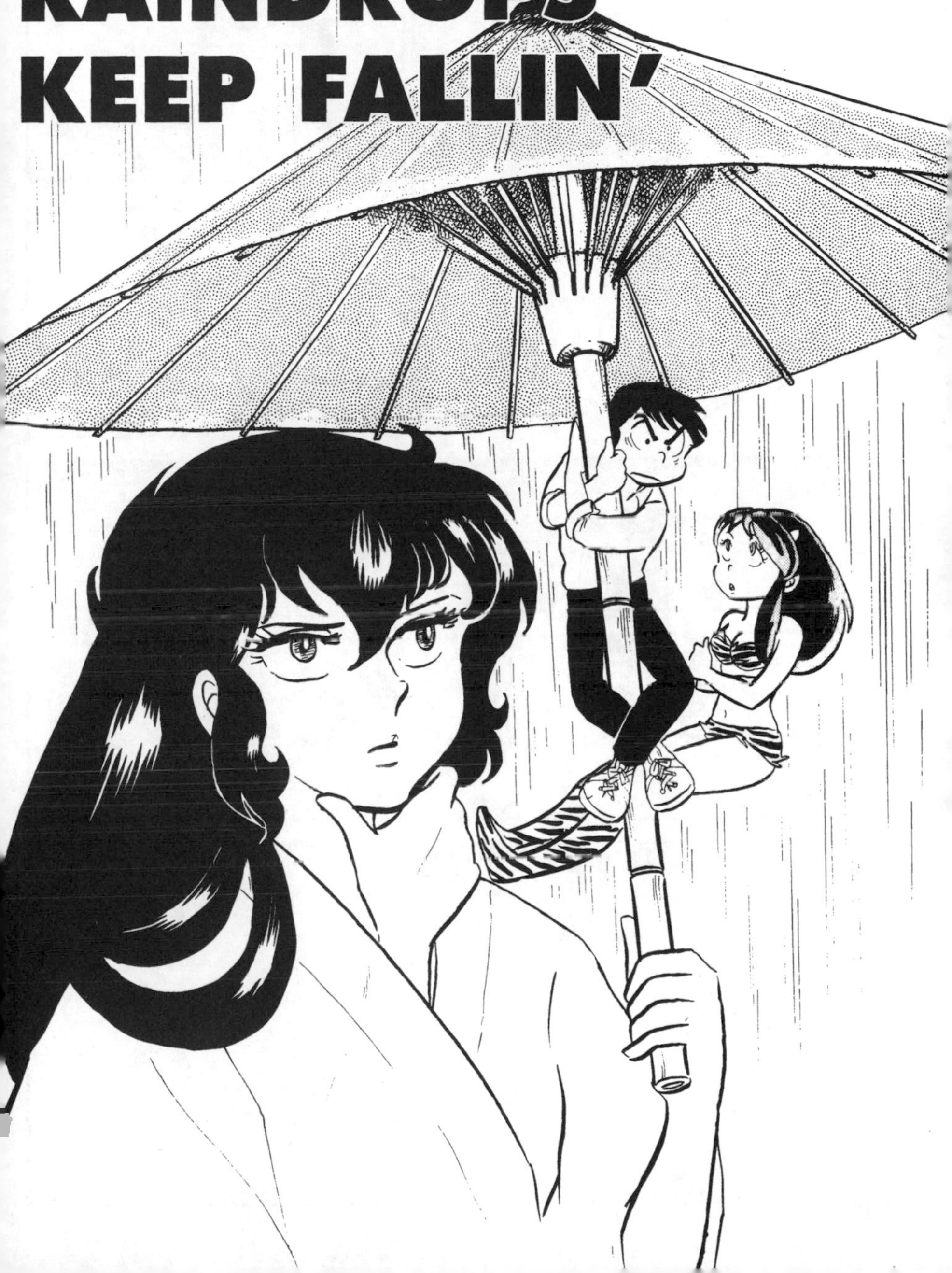

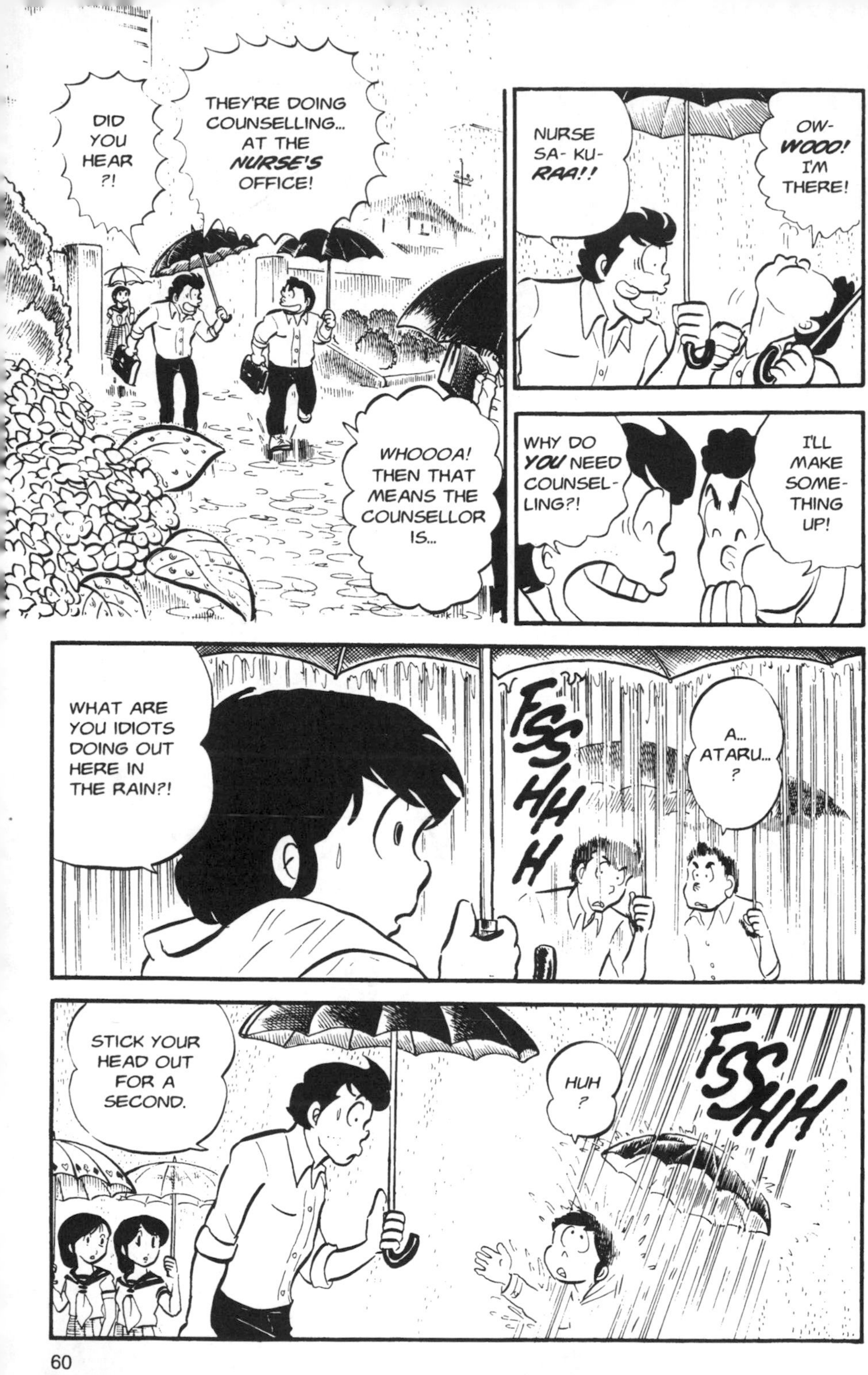
DID YOU HEAR ?!
THEY'RE DOING COUNSELLING... AT THE *NURSE'S* OFFICE!
WHOOOA! THEN THAT MEANS THE COUNSELLOR IS...
NURSE SA- KU- *RAA!!*
OW- *WOOO!* I'M THERE!
WHY DO *YOU* NEED COUNSEL- LING?!
I'LL MAKE SOME- THING UP!
WHAT ARE YOU IDIOTS DOING OUT HERE IN THE RAIN?!
FSSHHH
A... ATARU... ?
STICK YOUR HEAD OUT FOR A SECOND.
HUH ?
FSSHH

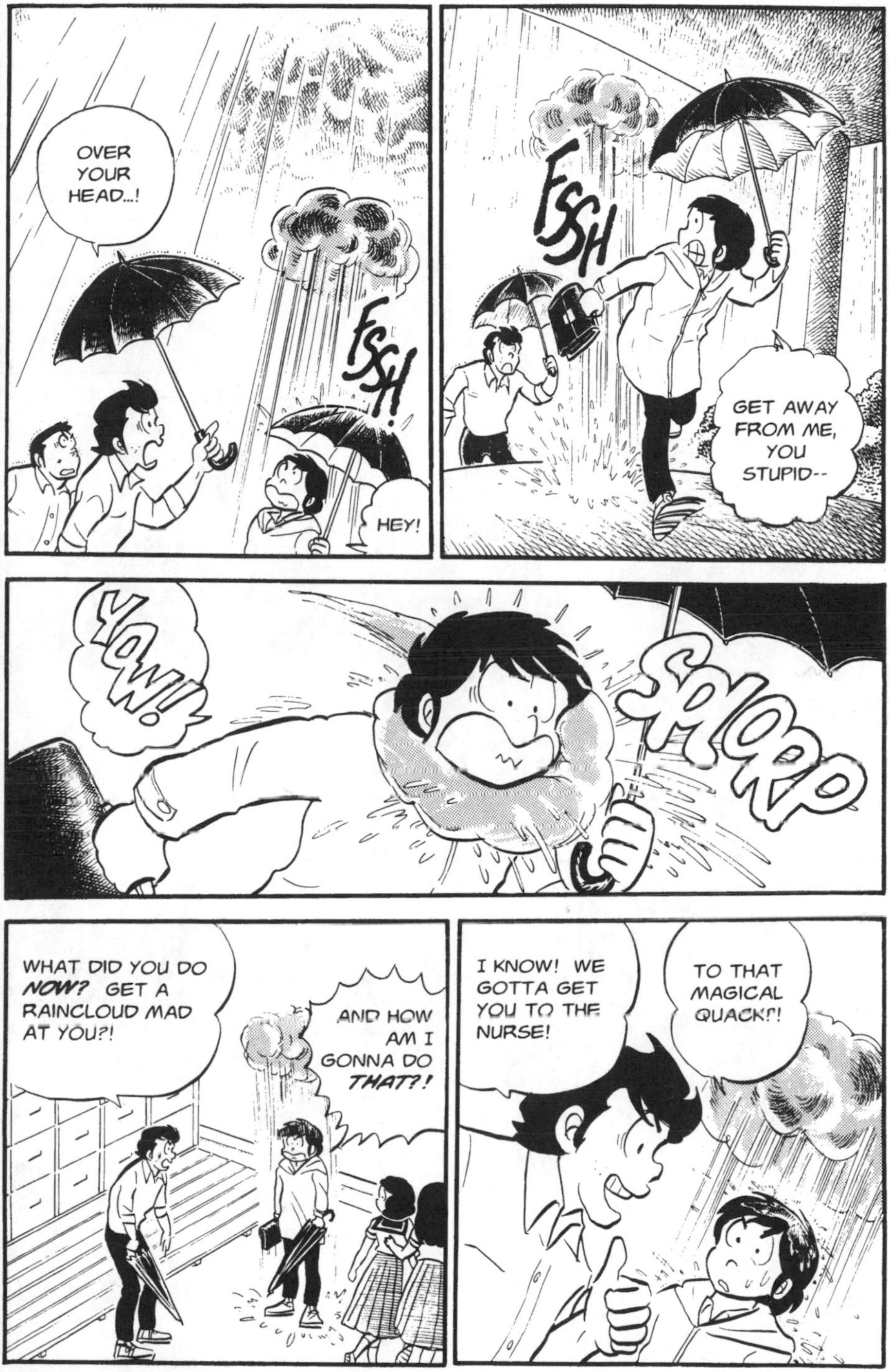
OVER YOUR HEAD...!
FSSH!
HEY!
FSSH
GET AWAY FROM ME, YOU STUPID--
YOW!!
SPLORP
WHAT DID YOU DO *NOW?* GET A RAINCLOUD MAD AT YOU?!
AND HOW AM I GONNA DO *THAT?!*
I KNOW! WE GOTTA GET YOU TO THE NURSE!
TO THAT MAGICAL QUACK?!

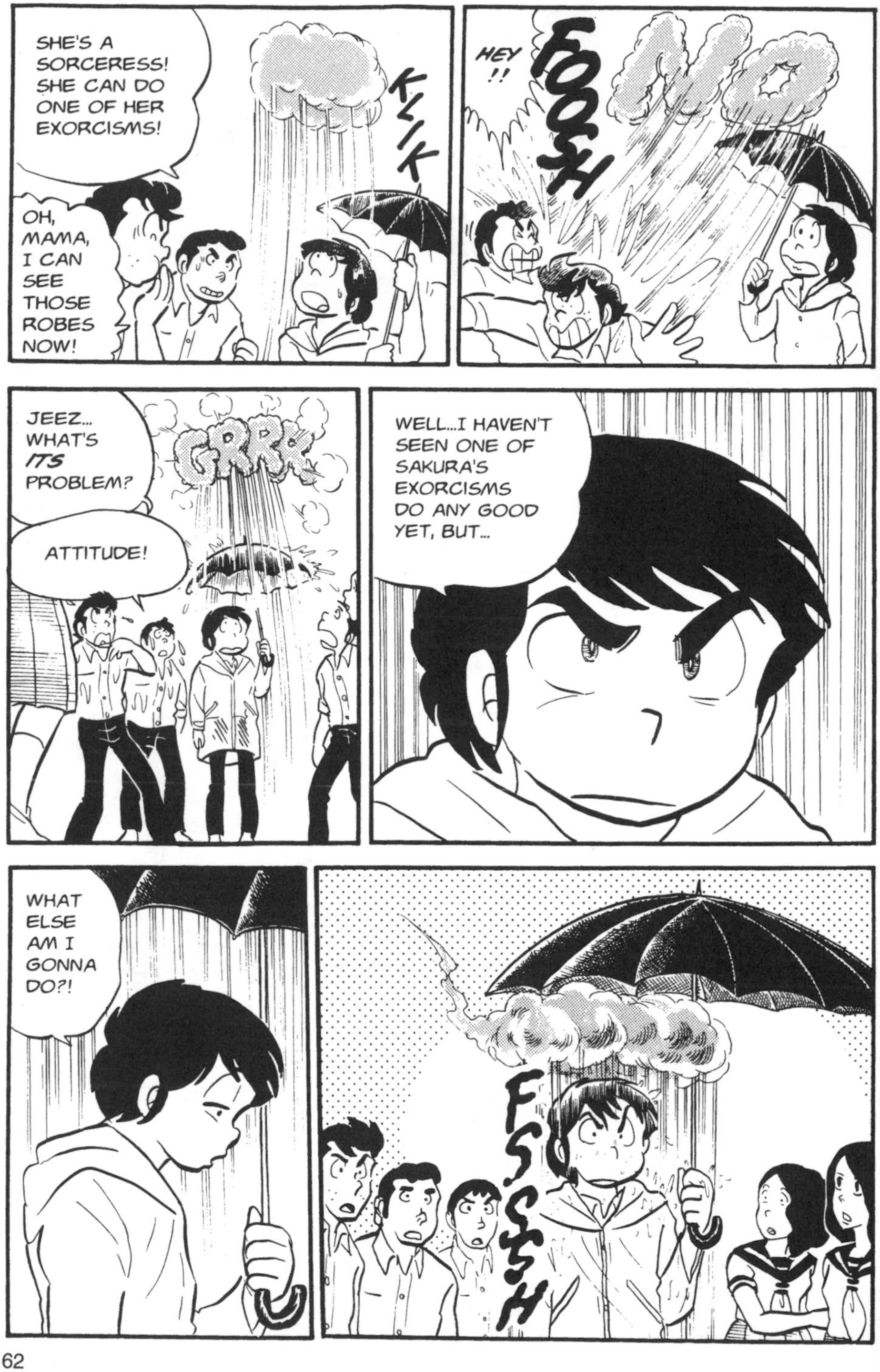
SHE'S A SORCERESS! SHE CAN DO ONE OF HER EXORCISMS!
OH, MAMA, I CAN SEE THOSE ROBES NOW!
KLIK
HEY !!
FOOOSH
JEEZ... WHAT'S ITS PROBLEM?
GRRR
ATTITUDE!
WELL...I HAVEN'T SEEN ONE OF SAKURA'S EXORCISMS DO ANY GOOD YET, BUT...
WHAT ELSE AM I GONNA DO?!
FSSSH

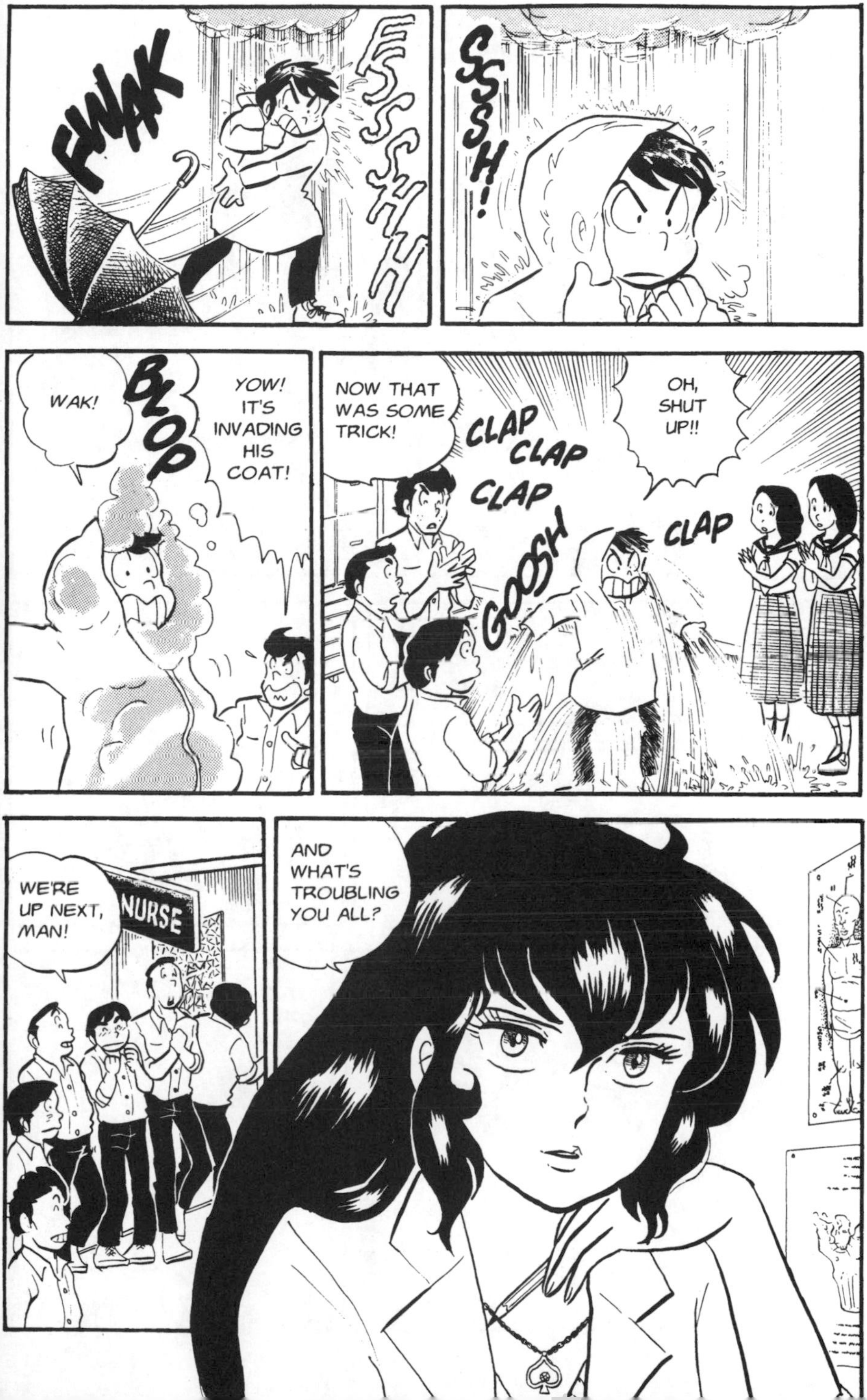
FWAK
FSSSHH
SSSH!
WAK!
BLOOP
YOW! IT'S INVADING HIS COAT!
NOW THAT WAS SOME TRICK!
CLAP CLAP CLAP
GOOSH
CLAP
OH, SHUT UP!!
WE'RE UP NEXT, MAN!
NURSE
AND WHAT'S TROUBLING YOU ALL?

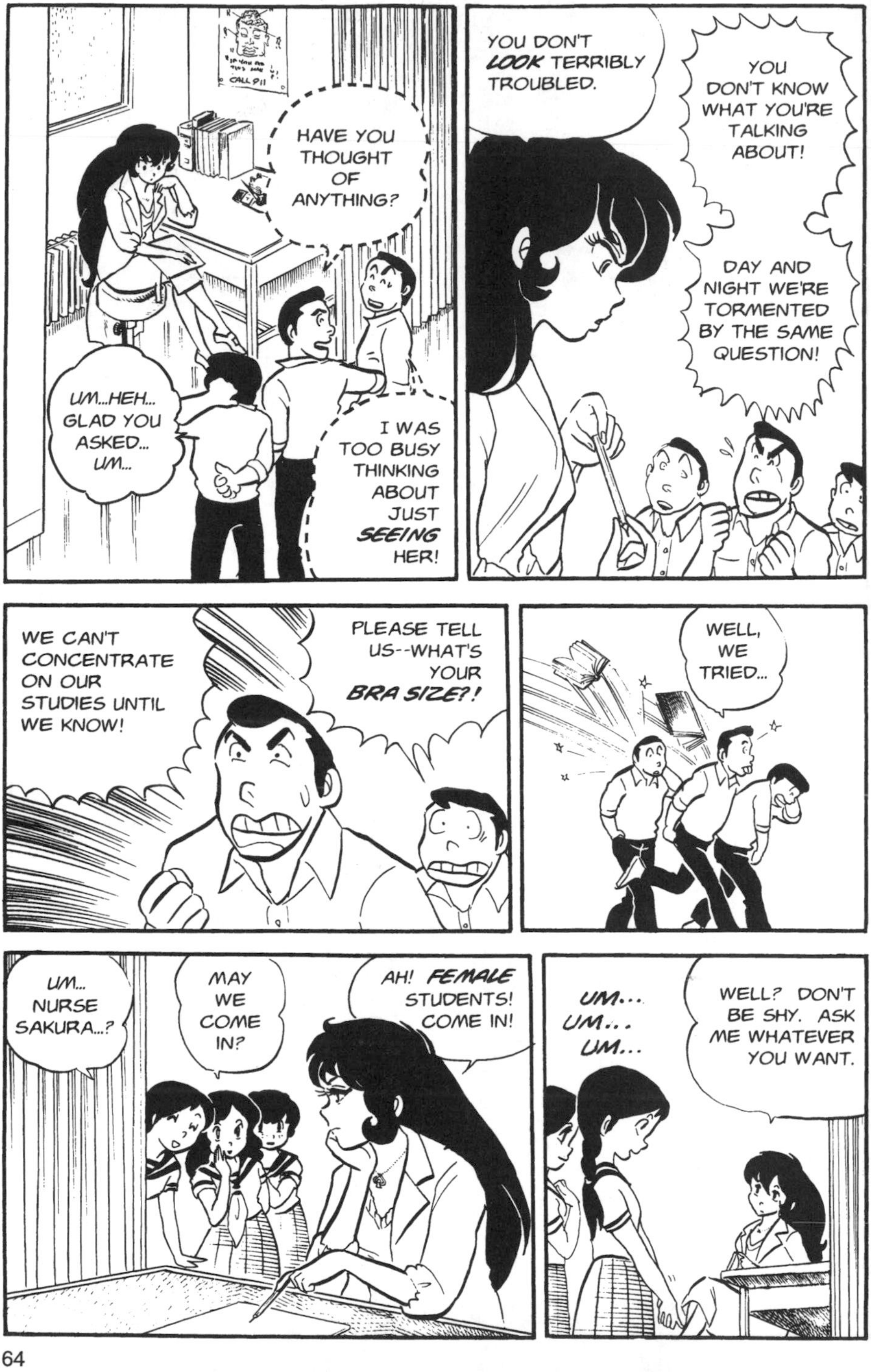
CALL 911
HAVE YOU THOUGHT OF ANYTHING?
UM...HEH... GLAD YOU ASKED... UM...
I WAS TOO BUSY THINKING ABOUT JUST SEEING HER!
YOU DON'T LOOK TERRIBLY TROUBLED.
YOU DON'T KNOW WHAT YOU'RE TALKING ABOUT!
DAY AND NIGHT WE'RE TORMENTED BY THE SAME QUESTION!
WE CAN'T CONCENTRATE ON OUR STUDIES UNTIL WE KNOW!
PLEASE TELL US--WHAT'S YOUR BRA SIZE?!
WELL, WE TRIED...
UM... NURSE SAKURA...?
MAY WE COME IN?
AH! FEMALE STUDENTS! COME IN!
UM... UM... UM...
WELL? DON'T BE SHY. ASK ME WHATEVER YOU WANT.

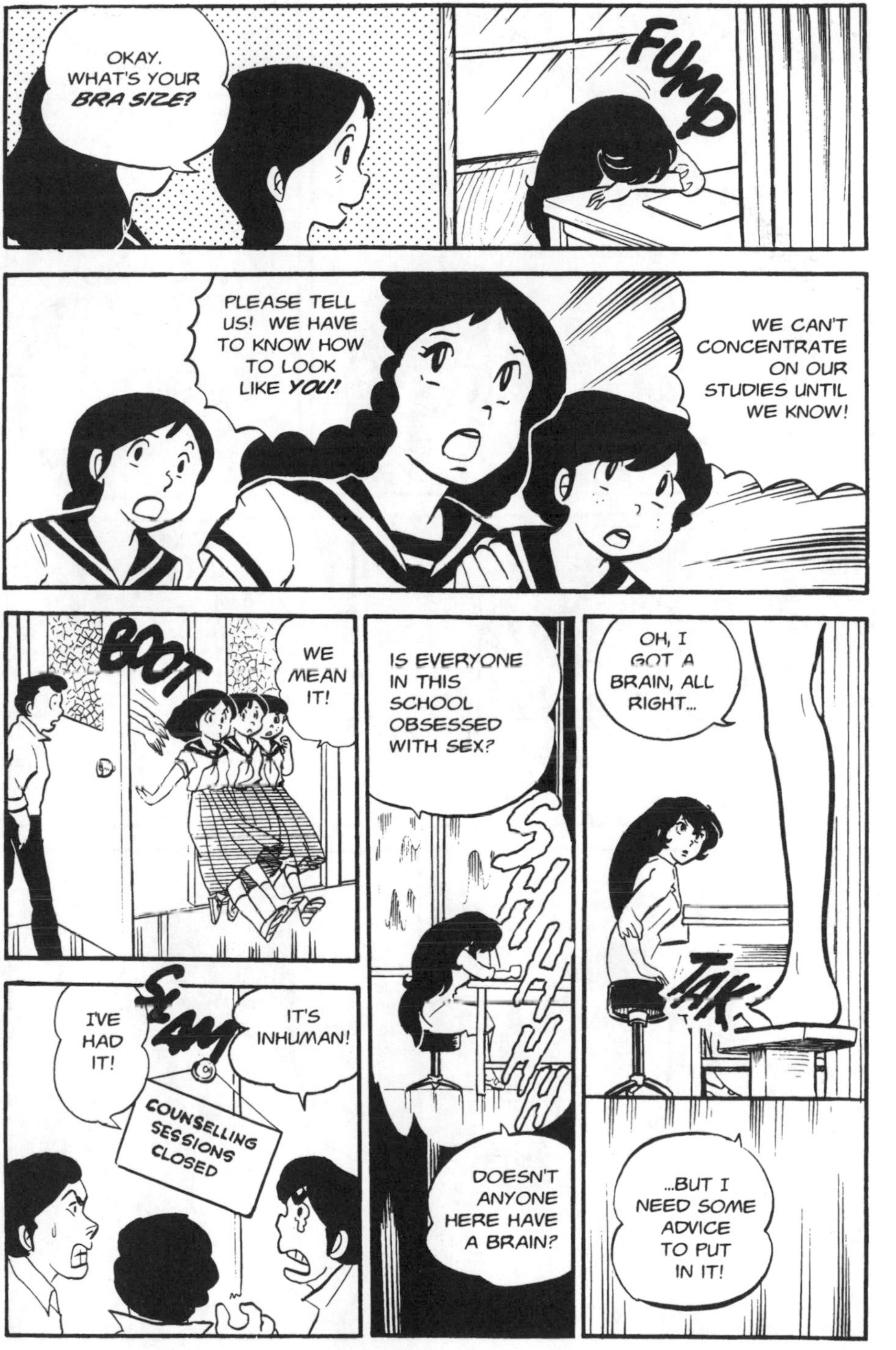

OKAY. WHAT'S YOUR *BRA SIZE?*
FUMP
PLEASE TELL US! WE HAVE TO KNOW HOW TO LOOK LIKE *YOU!*
WE CAN'T CONCENTRATE ON OUR STUDIES UNTIL WE KNOW!
BOOT
WE MEAN IT!
IVE HAD IT!
SLAM
IT'S INHUMAN!
COUNSELLING SESSIONS CLOSED
IS EVERYONE IN THIS SCHOOL OBSESSED WITH SEX?
SHHHHH
DOESN'T ANYONE HERE HAVE A BRAIN?
OH, I GOT A BRAIN, ALL RIGHT...
TAK
...BUT I NEED SOME ADVICE TO PUT IN IT!

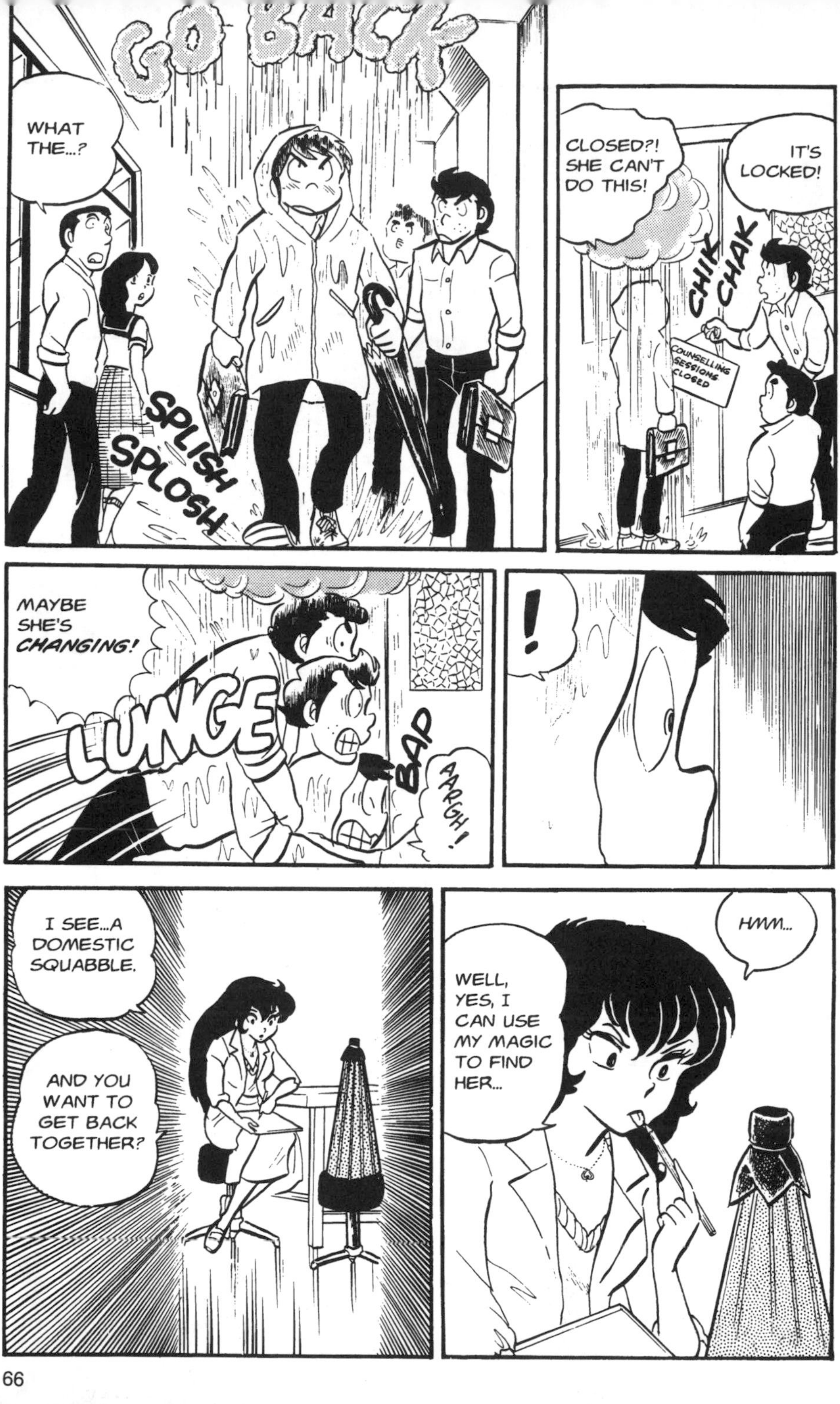
GO BACK
WHAT THE...?
SPLISH SPLOSH
CLOSED?! SHE CAN'T DO THIS!
IT'S LOCKED!
CHIK CHAK
COUNSELLING SESSIONS CLOSED
MAYBE SHE'S CHANGING!
LUNGE
BAP
AARGH!
!
I SEE...A DOMESTIC SQUABBLE.
AND YOU WANT TO GET BACK TOGETHER?
HMM...
WELL, YES, I CAN USE MY MAGIC TO FIND HER...

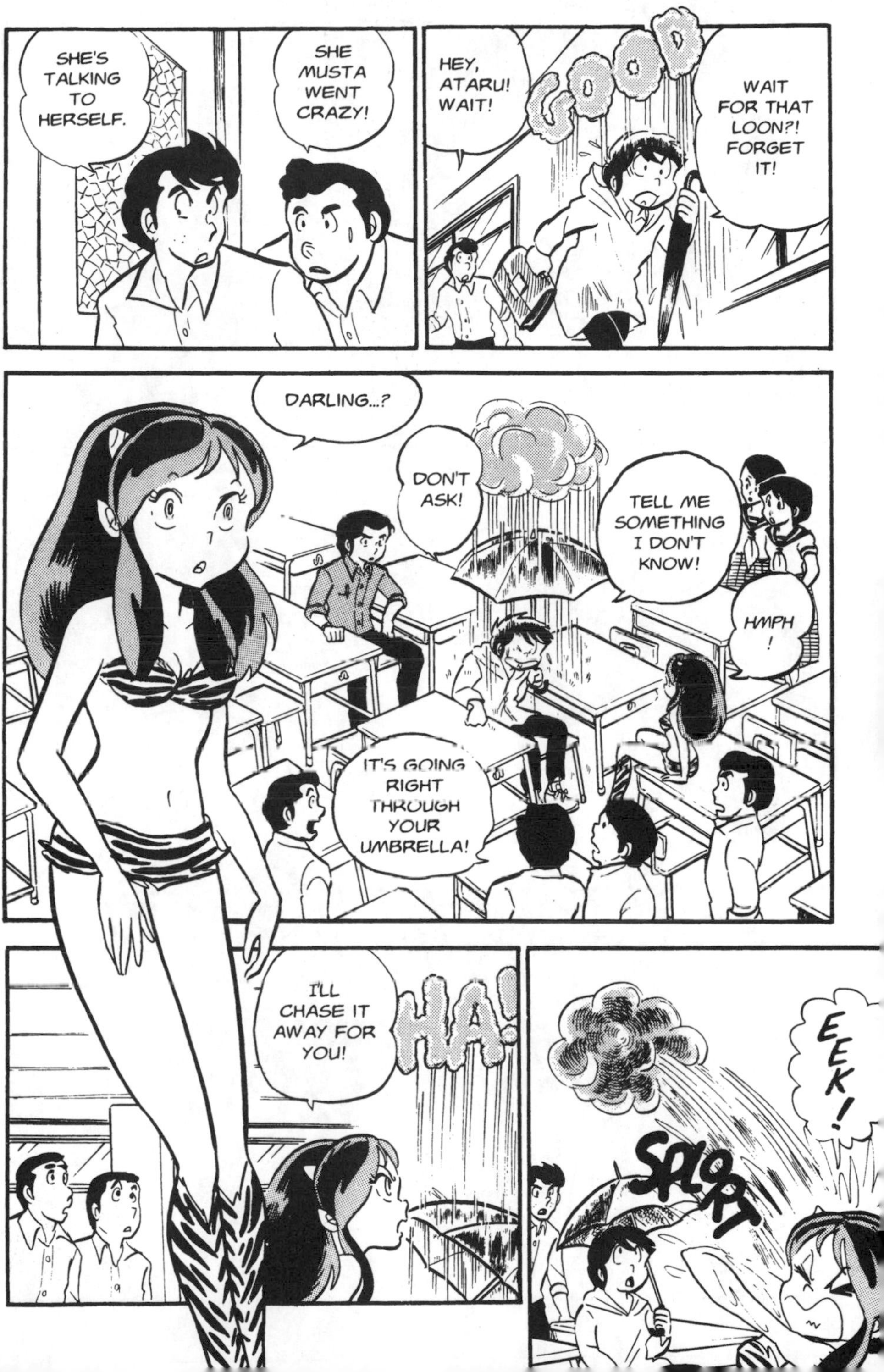
SHE'S TALKING TO HERSELF.
SHE MUSTA WENT CRAZY!
HEY, ATARU! WAIT!
GOOD
WAIT FOR THAT LOON?! FORGET IT!
DARLING...?
DON'T ASK!
TELL ME SOMETHING I DON'T KNOW!
HMPH!
IT'S GOING RIGHT THROUGH YOUR UMBRELLA!
I'LL CHASE IT AWAY FOR YOU!
HA!
EEK!
SPLORT

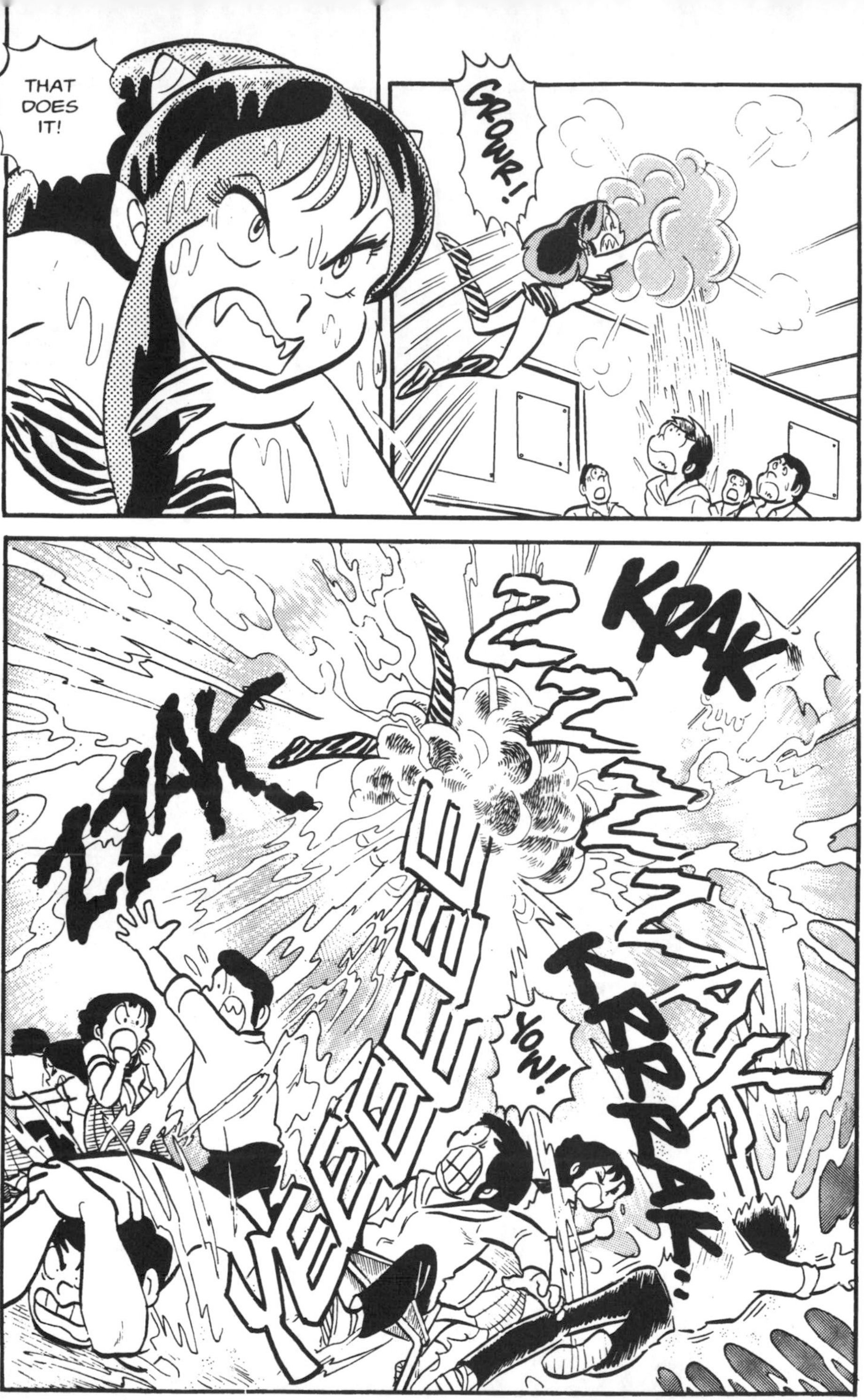
THAT DOES IT!
GROWR!
ZZAK
KRAK
YEEEEEEE
YOW!
KRRRAK!!

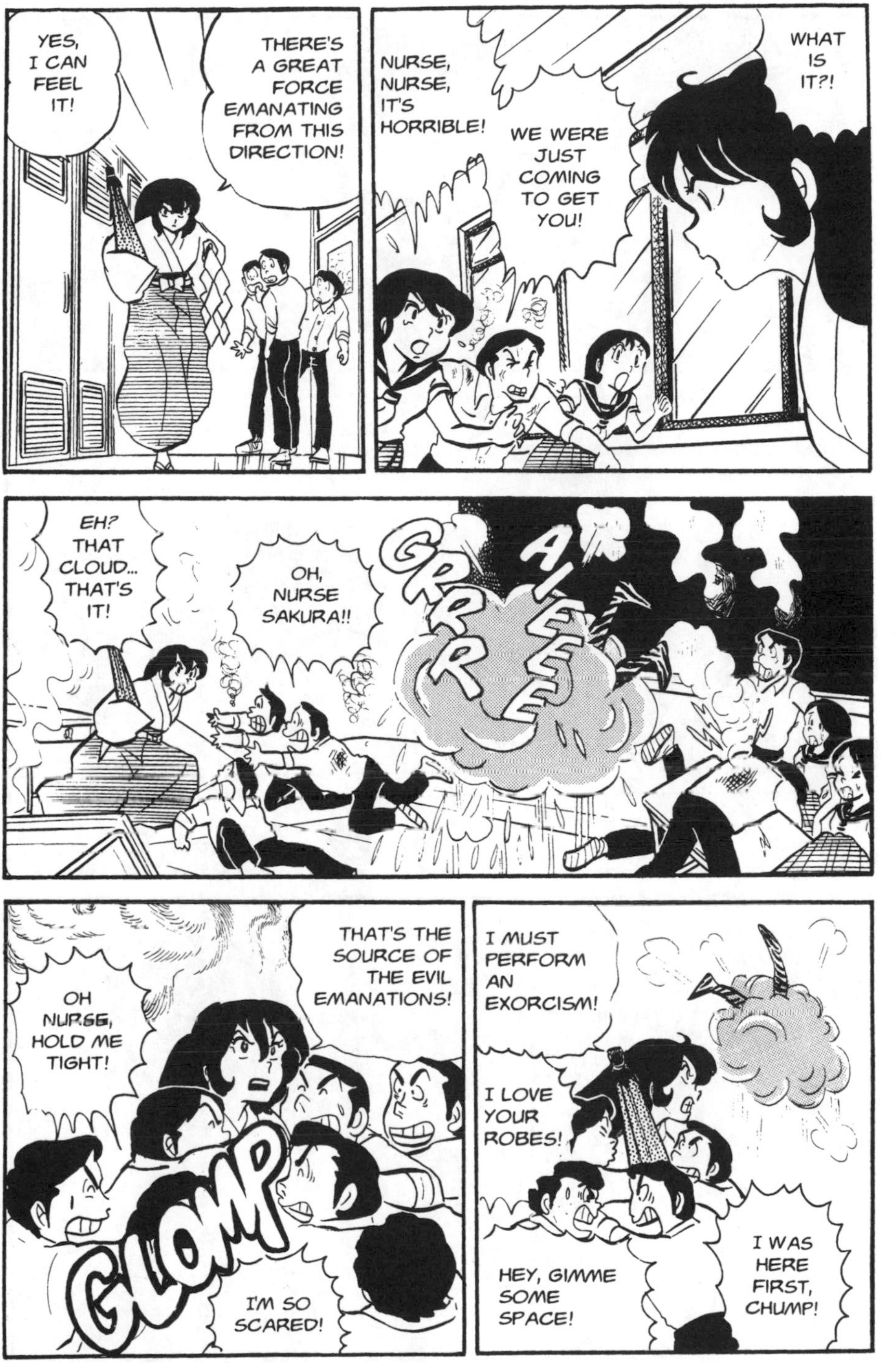
YES, I CAN FEEL IT!
THERE'S A GREAT FORCE EMANATING FROM THIS DIRECTION!
NURSE, NURSE, IT'S HORRIBLE!
WE WERE JUST COMING TO GET YOU!
WHAT IS IT?!
EH? THAT CLOUD... THAT'S IT!
OH, NURSE SAKURA!!
GRRR
AIEEEE
OH NURSE, HOLD ME TIGHT!
THAT'S THE SOURCE OF THE EVIL EMANATIONS!
GLOMP
I'M SO SCARED!
I MUST PERFORM AN EXORCISM!
I LOVE YOUR ROBES!
HEY, GIMME SOME SPACE!
I WAS HERE FIRST, CHUMP!

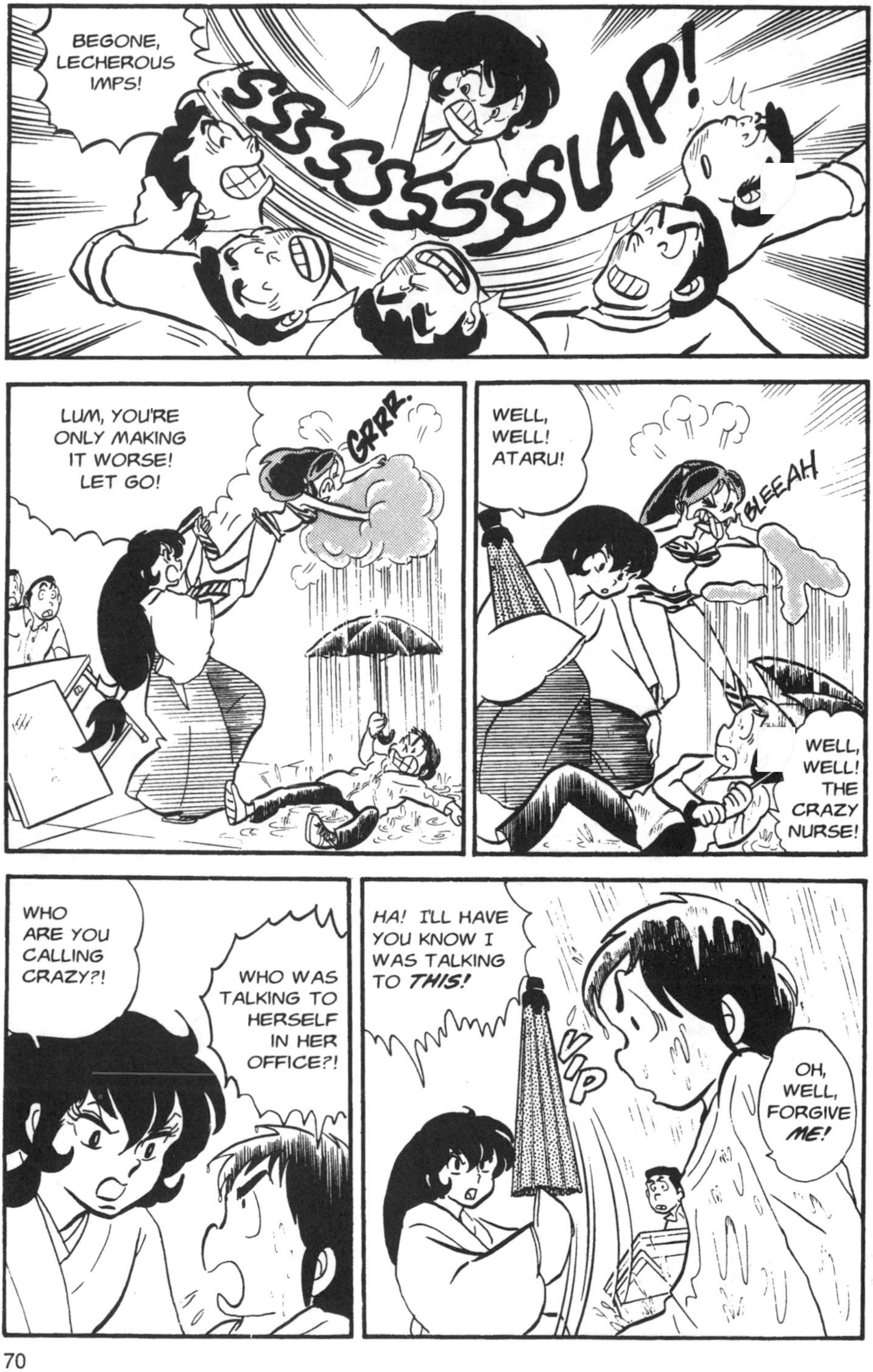
BEGONE, LECHEROUS IMPS!
SSSSSSSSLAP!
LUM, YOU'RE ONLY MAKING IT WORSE! LET GO!
GRRR.
WELL, WELL! ATARU!
BLEEAH
WELL, WELL! THE CRAZY NURSE!
WHO ARE YOU CALLING CRAZY?!
WHO WAS TALKING TO HERSELF IN HER OFFICE?!
HA! I'LL HAVE YOU KNOW I WAS TALKING TO *THIS!*
VIP
OH, WELL, FORGIVE *ME!*

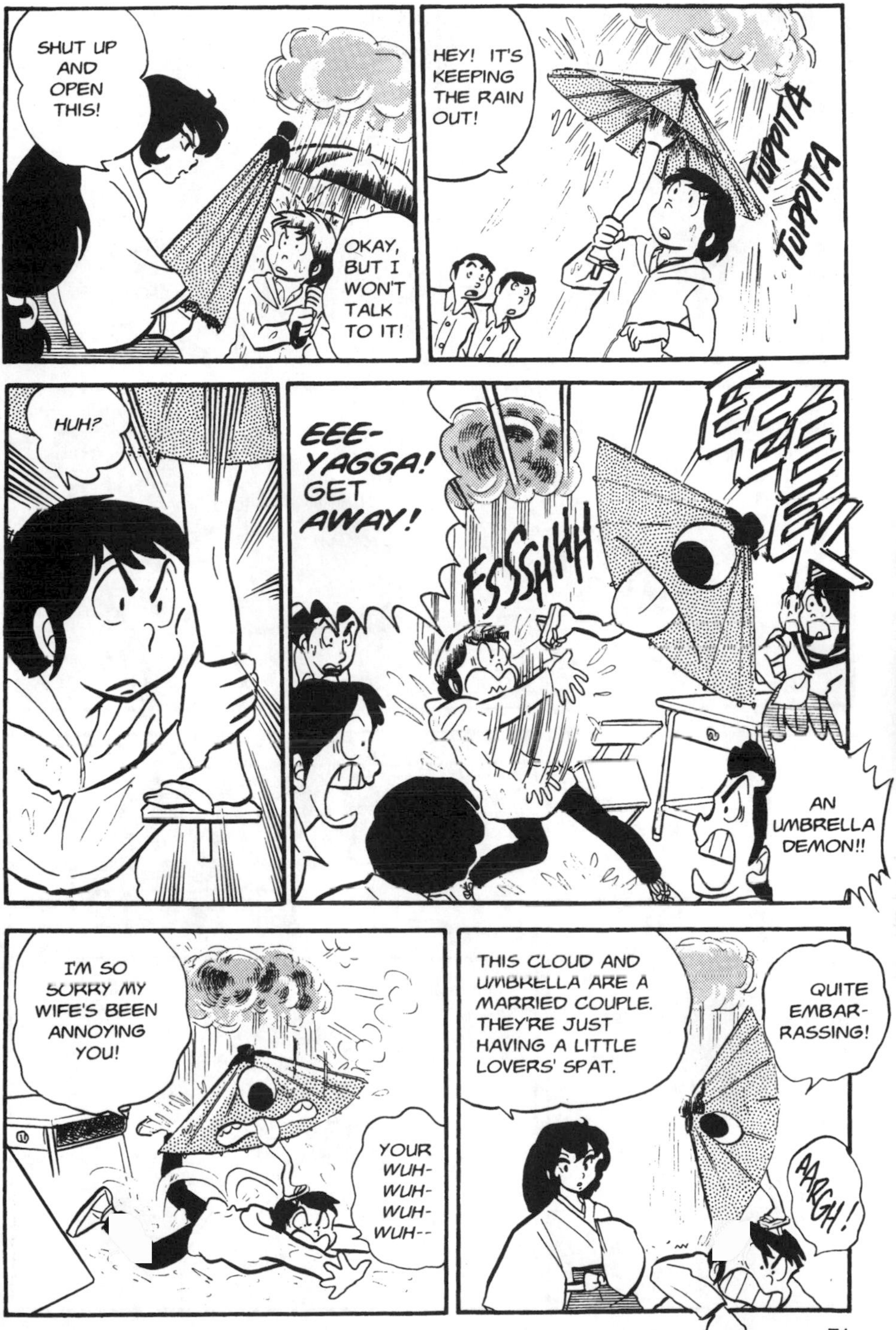
SHUT UP AND OPEN THIS!
OKAY, BUT I WON'T TALK TO IT!
HEY! IT'S KEEPING THE RAIN OUT!
TUPPITA TUPPITA
HUH?
EEE-YAGGA! GET AWAY!
FSSSHHH
AN UMBRELLA DEMON!!
I'M SO SORRY MY WIFE'S BEEN ANNOYING YOU!
YOUR WUH-WUH-WUH-WUH--
THIS CLOUD AND UMBRELLA ARE A MARRIED COUPLE. THEY'RE JUST HAVING A LITTLE LOVERS' SPAT.
QUITE EMBARRASSING!
AARGH!

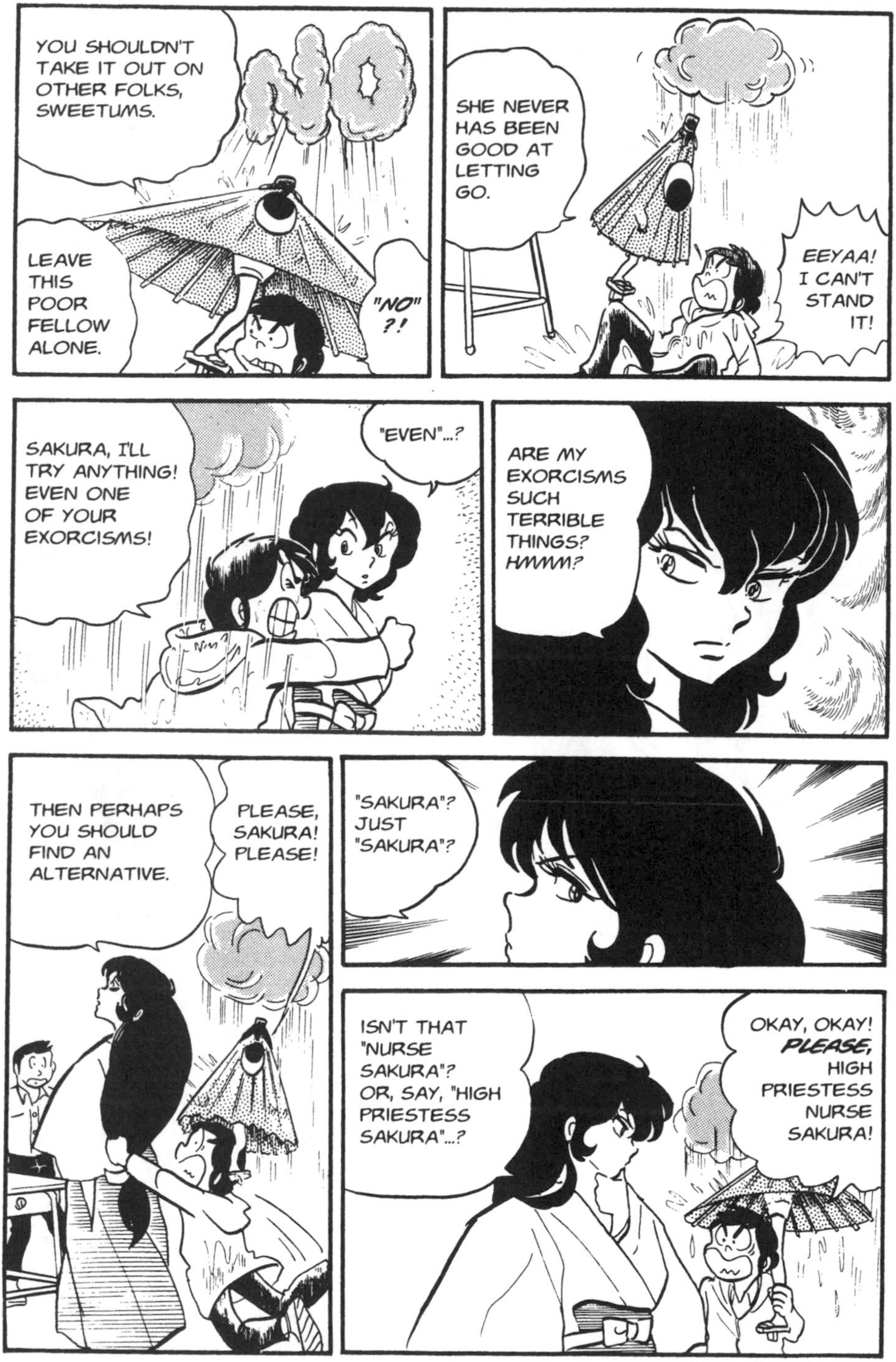
YOU SHOULDN'T TAKE IT OUT ON OTHER FOLKS, SWEETUMS.
NO
LEAVE THIS POOR FELLOW ALONE.
"NO" ?!
SHE NEVER HAS BEEN GOOD AT LETTING GO.
EEYAA! I CAN'T STAND IT!
SAKURA, I'LL TRY ANYTHING! EVEN ONE OF YOUR EXORCISMS!
"EVEN"...?
ARE MY EXORCISMS SUCH TERRIBLE THINGS? HMMM?
THEN PERHAPS YOU SHOULD FIND AN ALTERNATIVE.
PLEASE, SAKURA! PLEASE!
"SAKURA"? JUST "SAKURA"?
ISN'T THAT "NURSE SAKURA"? OR, SAY, "HIGH PRIESTESS SAKURA"...?
OKAY, OKAY! ***PLEASE,*** HIGH PRIESTESS NURSE SAKURA!

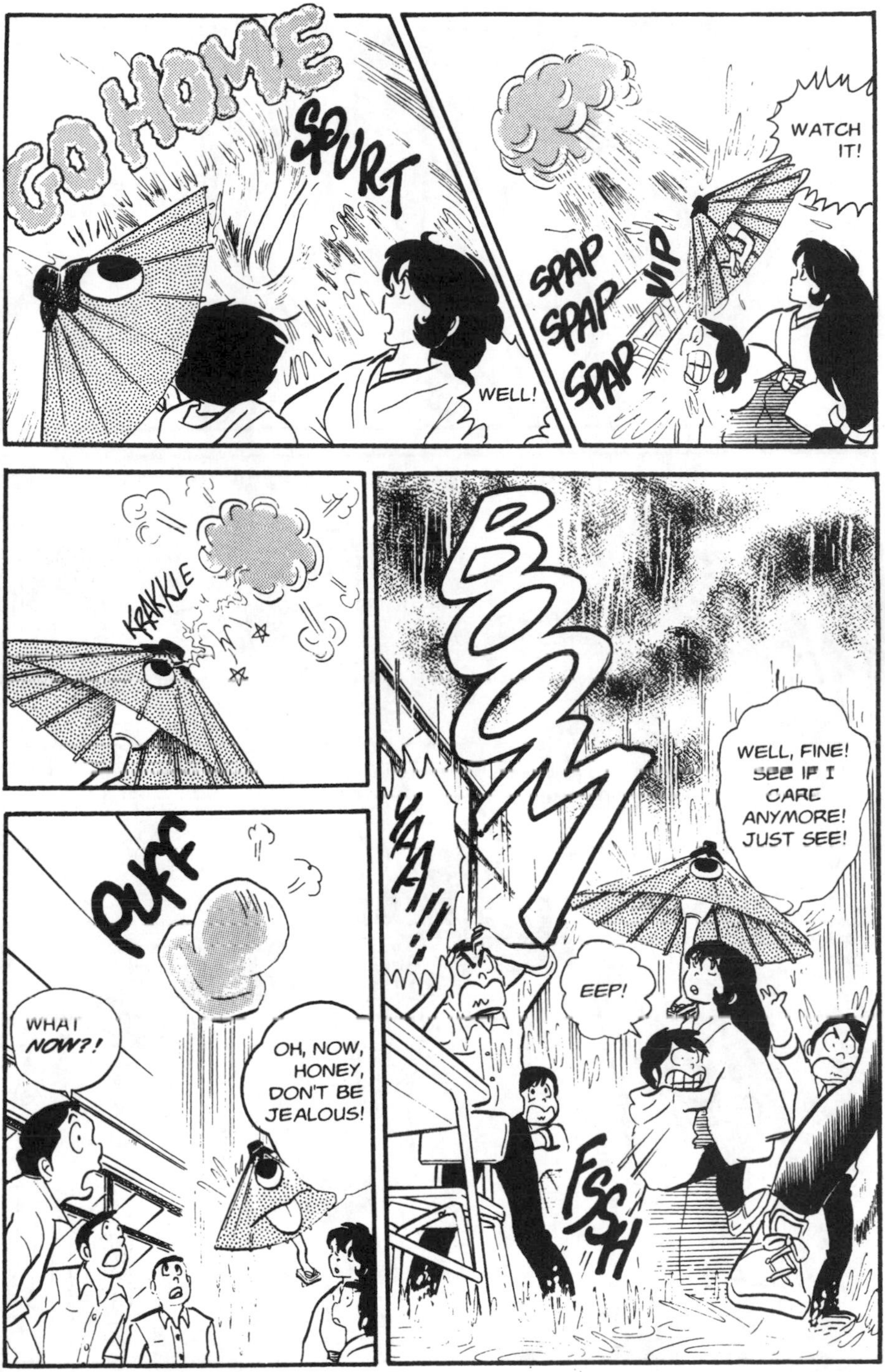
GO HOME
SPURT
WELL!
SPAP
SPAP
SPAP
VIP
WATCH IT!
KRAKKLE
PUFF
WHAT NOW?!
OH, NOW, HONEY, DON'T BE JEALOUS!
BOOM
YAAA!!!
WELL, FINE! SEE IF I CARE ANYMORE! JUST SEE!
EEP!
FSSH

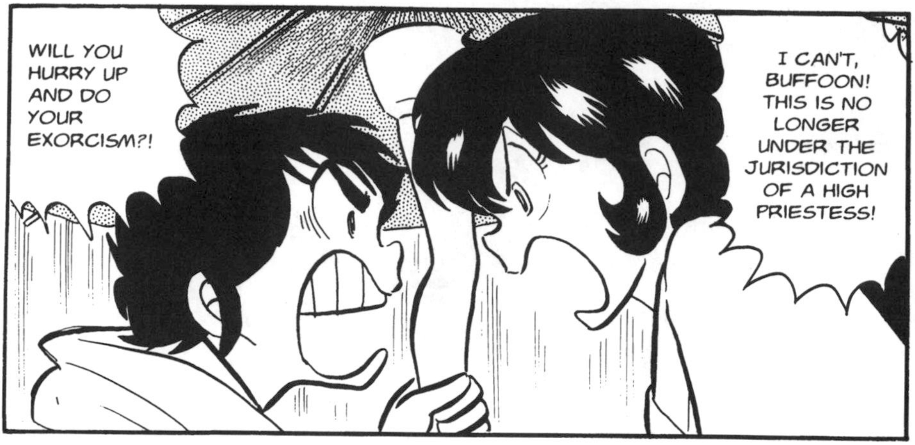
WILL YOU HURRY UP AND DO YOUR EXORCISM?!
I CAN'T, BUFFOON! THIS IS NO LONGER UNDER THE JURISDICTION OF A HIGH PRIESTESS!

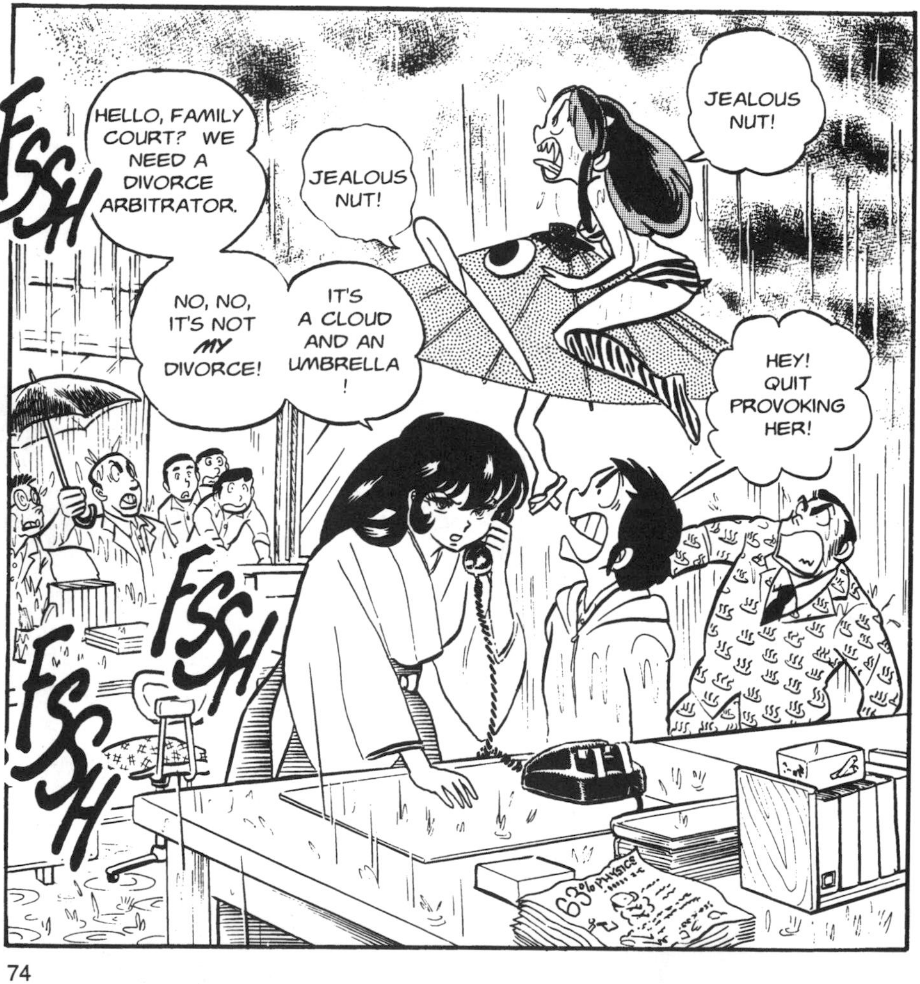
FSSH
HELLO, FAMILY COURT? WE NEED A DIVORCE ARBITRATOR.
JEALOUS NUT!
JEALOUS NUT!
NO, NO, IT'S NOT MY DIVORCE!
IT'S A CLOUD AND AN UMBRELLA!
HEY! QUIT PROVOKING HER!
FSSH
FSSH
63% PHYSICS

PART FIVE
THE CURSE OF THE COPY MAN

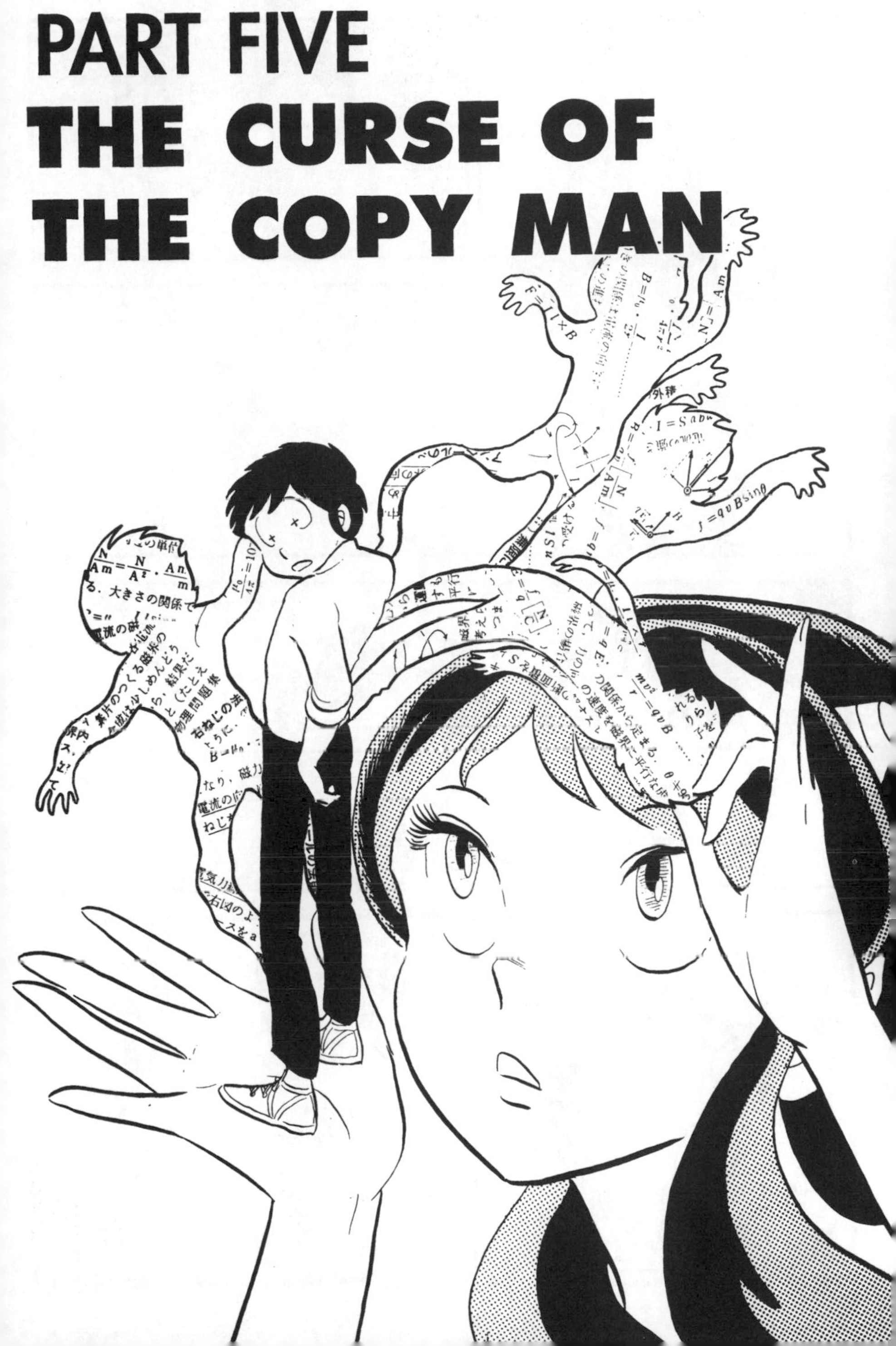

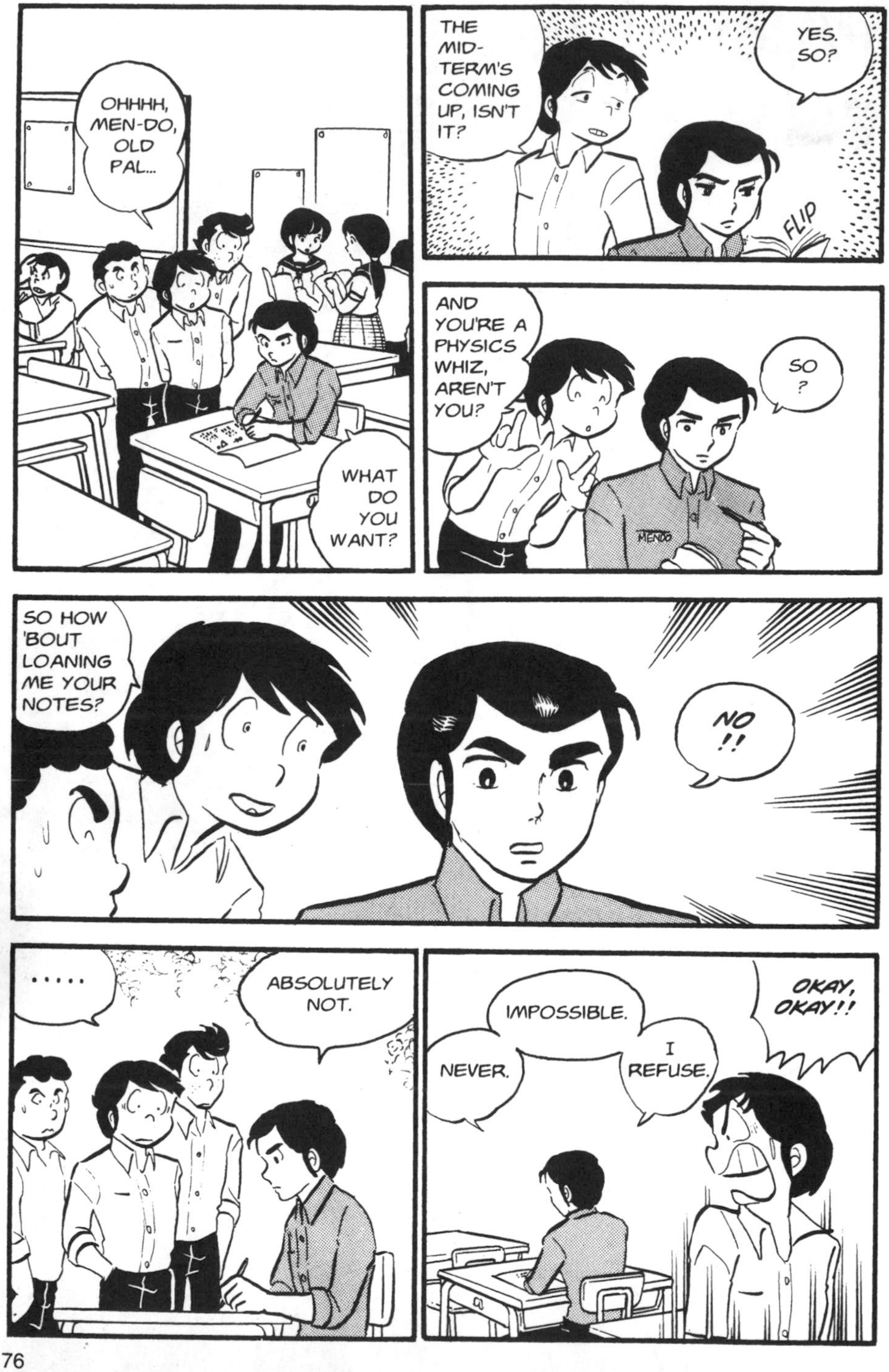
OHHHH, MEN-DO, OLD PAL...
WHAT DO YOU WANT?
THE MID-TERM'S COMING UP, ISN'T IT?
YES. SO?
FLIP
AND YOU'RE A PHYSICS WHIZ, AREN'T YOU?
SO ?
MENDO
SO HOW 'BOUT LOANING ME YOUR NOTES?
NO !!
.....
ABSOLUTELY NOT.
IMPOSSIBLE.
NEVER.
I REFUSE.
OKAY, OKAY!!

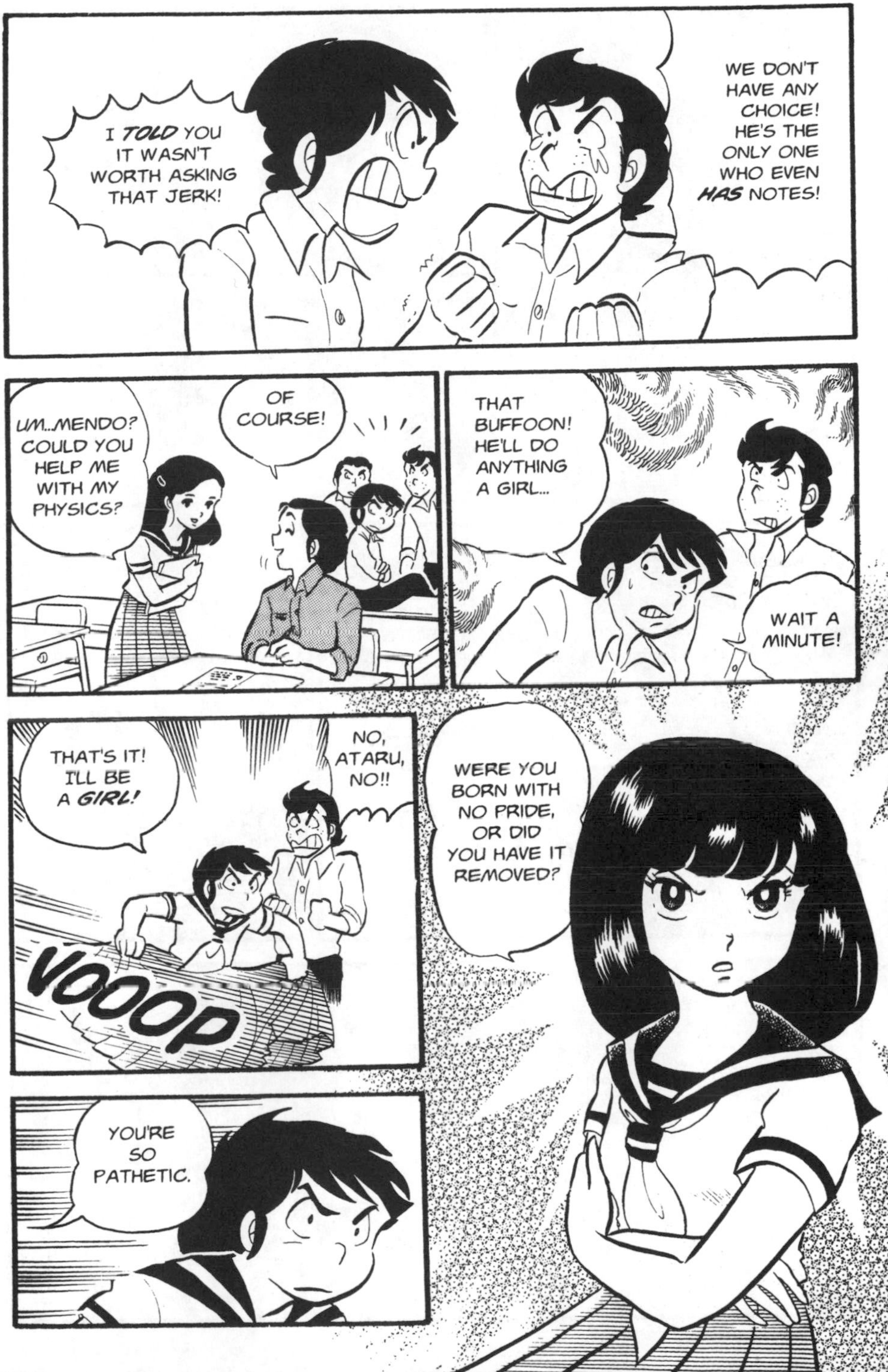
I TOLD YOU IT WASN'T WORTH ASKING THAT JERK!
WE DON'T HAVE ANY CHOICE! HE'S THE ONLY ONE WHO EVEN HAS NOTES!
UM...MENDO? COULD YOU HELP ME WITH MY PHYSICS?
OF COURSE!
THAT BUFFOON! HE'LL DO ANYTHING A GIRL...
WAIT A MINUTE!
THAT'S IT! I'LL BE A GIRL!
NO, ATARU, NO!!
VOOOP
WERE YOU BORN WITH NO PRIDE, OR DID YOU HAVE IT REMOVED?
YOU'RE SO PATHETIC.

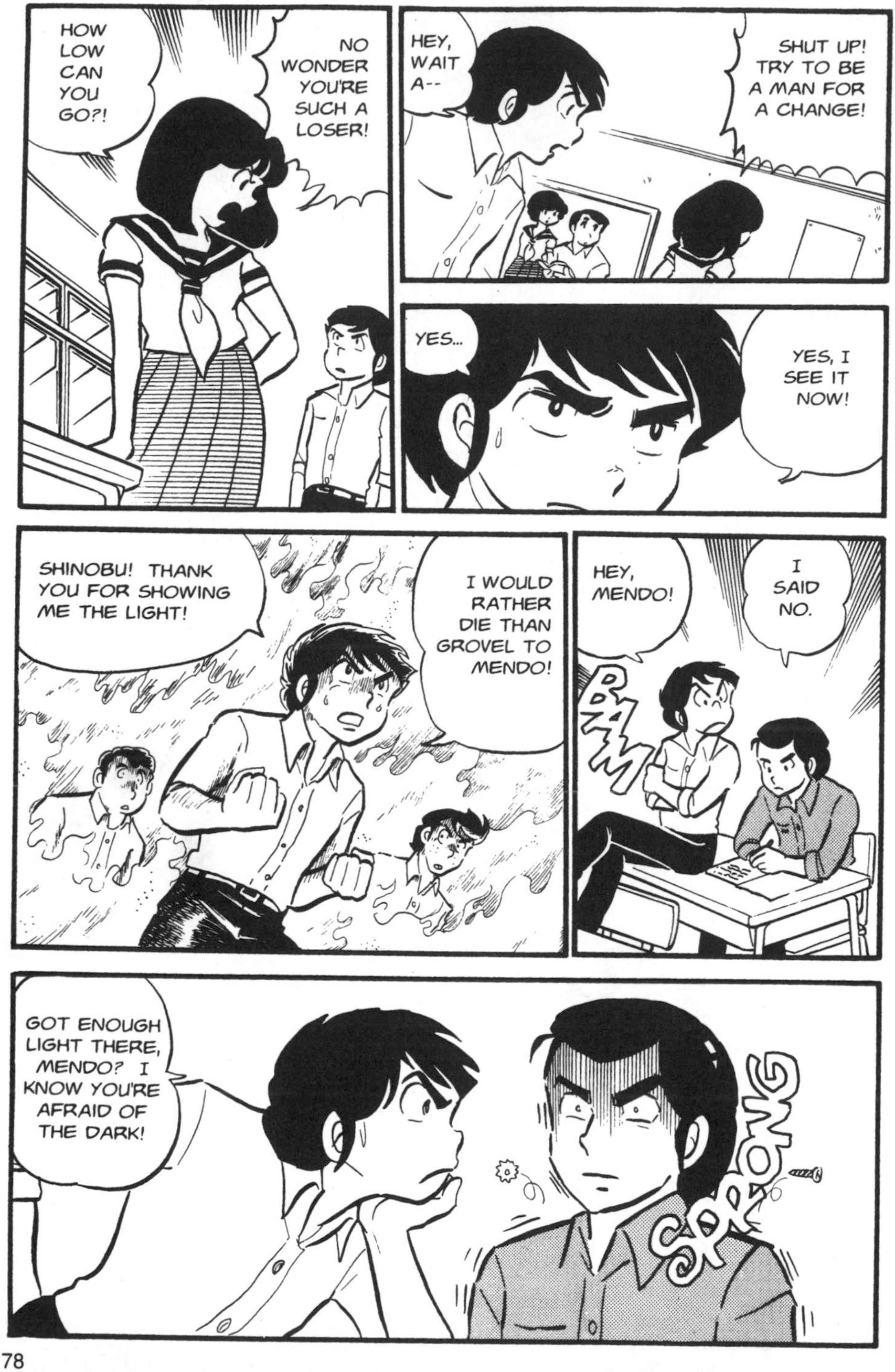
HOW LOW CAN YOU GO?!
NO WONDER YOU'RE SUCH A LOSER!
HEY, WAIT A--
SHUT UP! TRY TO BE A MAN FOR A CHANGE!
YES...
YES, I SEE IT NOW!
SHINOBU! THANK YOU FOR SHOWING ME THE LIGHT!
I WOULD RATHER DIE THAN GROVEL TO MENDO!
HEY, MENDO!
I SAID NO.
BAM
GOT ENOUGH LIGHT THERE, MENDO? I KNOW YOU'RE AFRAID OF THE DARK!
SPRONG

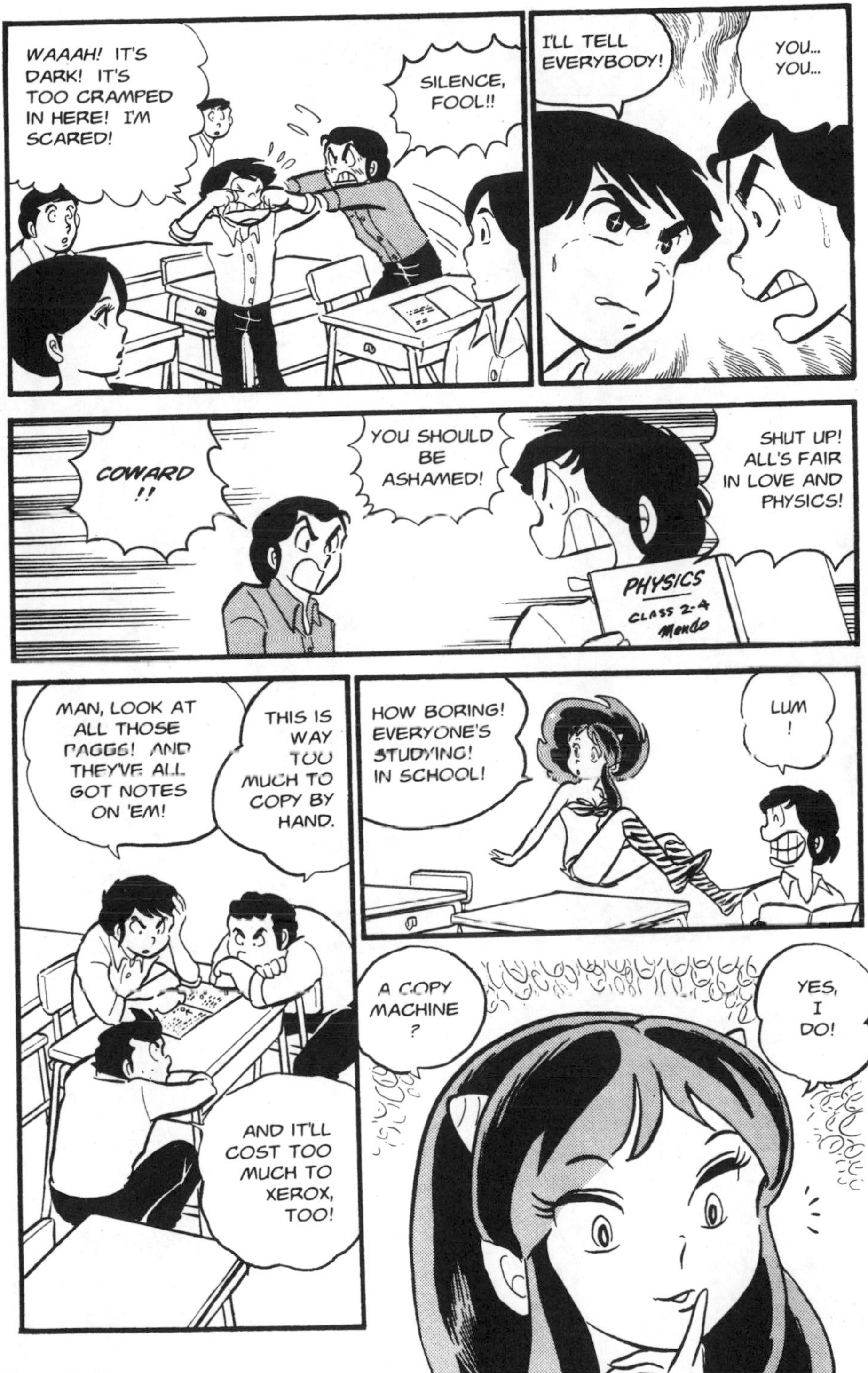
WAAAH! IT'S DARK! IT'S TOO CRAMPED IN HERE! I'M SCARED!
SILENCE, FOOL!!
I'LL TELL EVERYBODY!
YOU... YOU...
COWARD !!
YOU SHOULD BE ASHAMED!
SHUT UP! ALL'S FAIR IN LOVE AND PHYSICS!
PHYSICS
CLASS 2-4
Mendo
MAN, LOOK AT ALL THOSE PAGES! AND THEY'VE ALL GOT NOTES ON 'EM!
THIS IS WAY TOO MUCH TO COPY BY HAND.
AND IT'LL COST TOO MUCH TO XEROX, TOO!
HOW BORING! EVERYONE'S STUDYING! IN SCHOOL!
LUM !
A COPY MACHINE ?
YES, I DO!

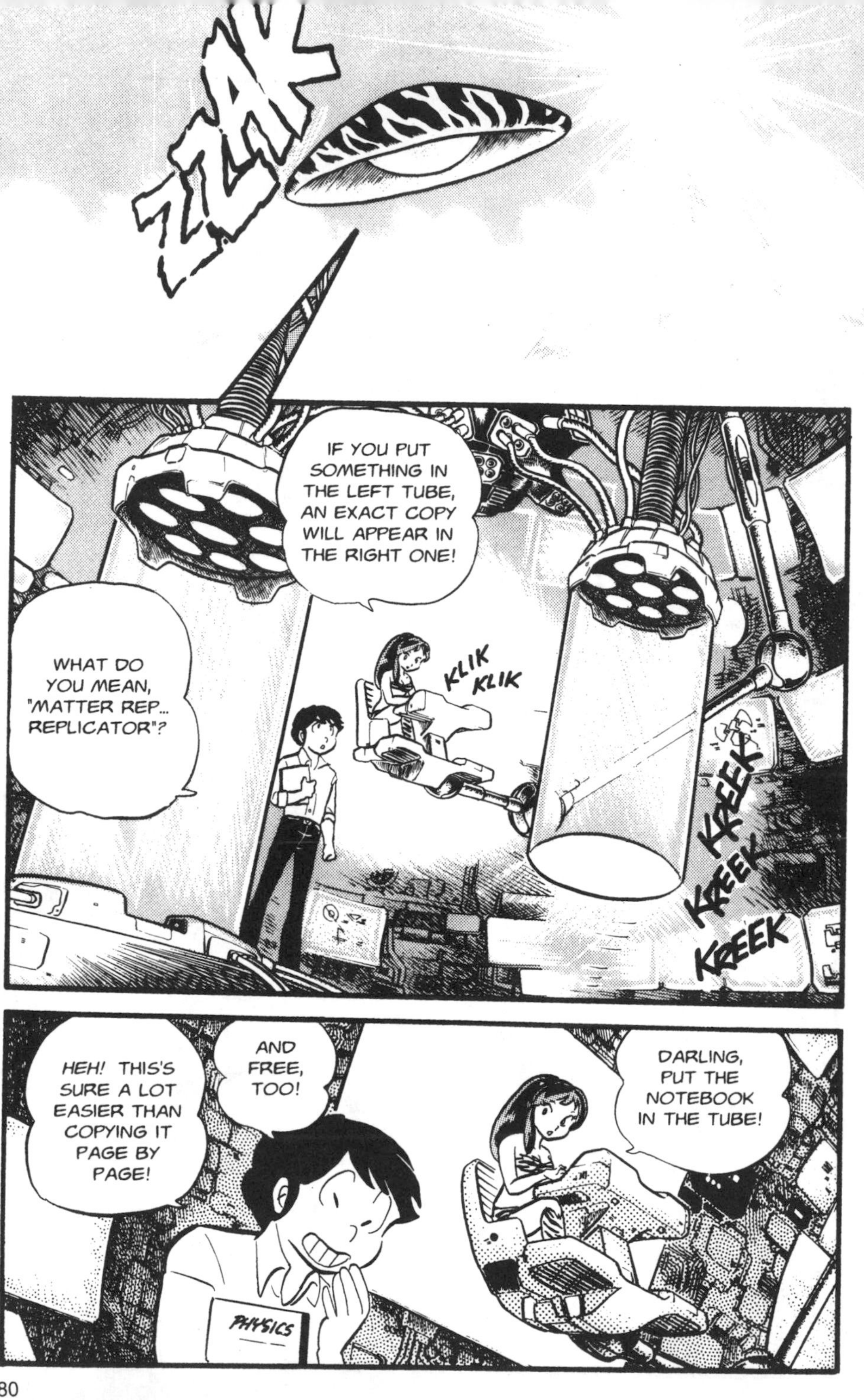
ZZZAK
WHAT DO YOU MEAN, "MATTER REP... REPLICATOR"?
IF YOU PUT SOMETHING IN THE LEFT TUBE, AN EXACT COPY WILL APPEAR IN THE RIGHT ONE!
KLIK KLIK
KREEK KREEK KREEK KREEK
HEH! THIS'S SURE A LOT EASIER THAN COPYING IT PAGE BY PAGE!
AND FREE, TOO!
DARLING, PUT THE NOTEBOOK IN THE TUBE!
PHYSICS

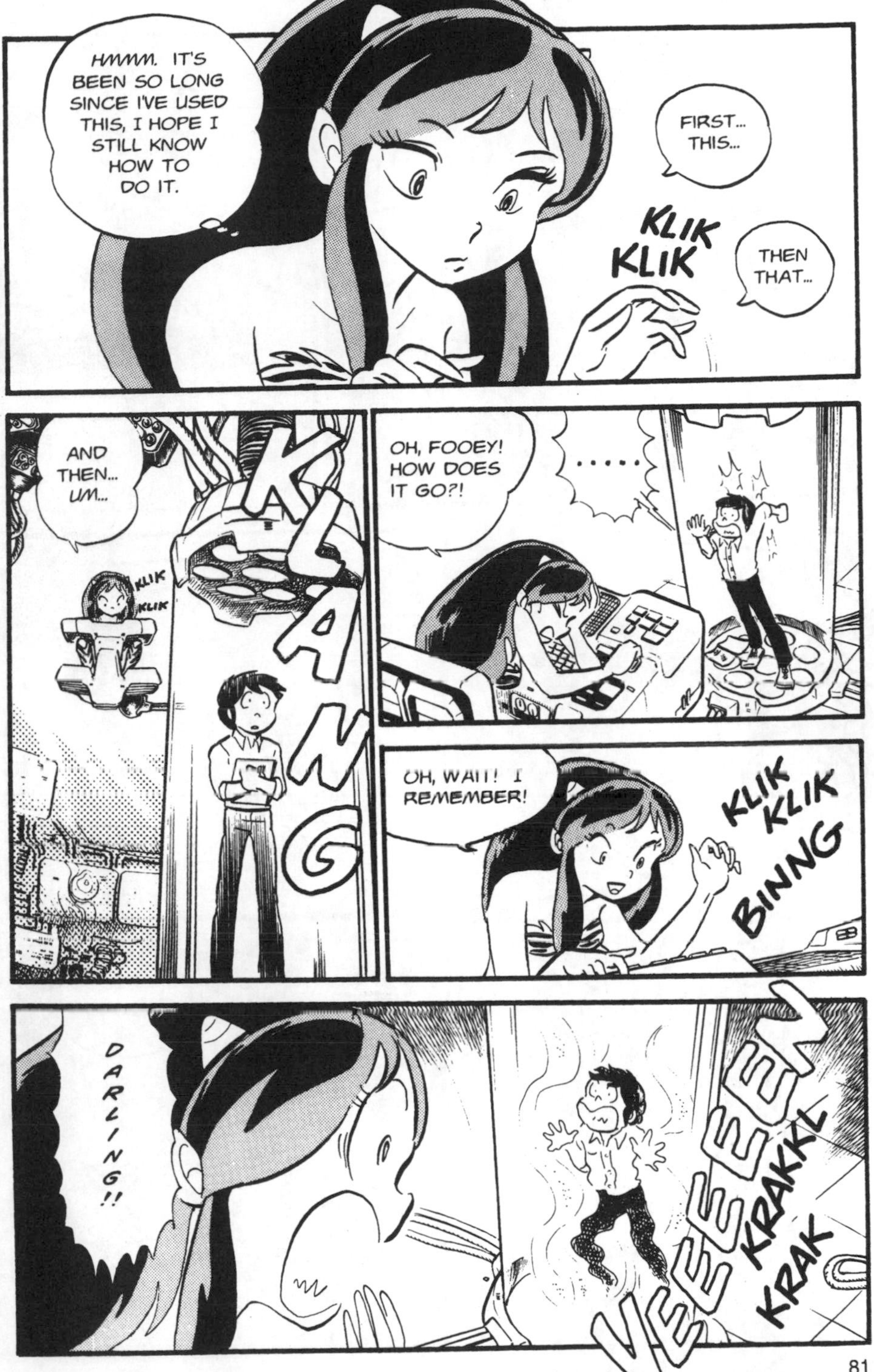
HMMM. IT'S BEEN SO LONG SINCE I'VE USED THIS, I HOPE I STILL KNOW HOW TO DO IT.
FIRST... THIS...
KLIK KLIK
THEN THAT...
AND THEN... UM...
KLIK KLIK
KLANG
OH, FOOEY! HOW DOES IT GO?!
.....
OH, WAIT! I REMEMBER!
KLIK KLIK
BINNG
DARLING!!
VEEEEEEN
KRAKKL KRAK

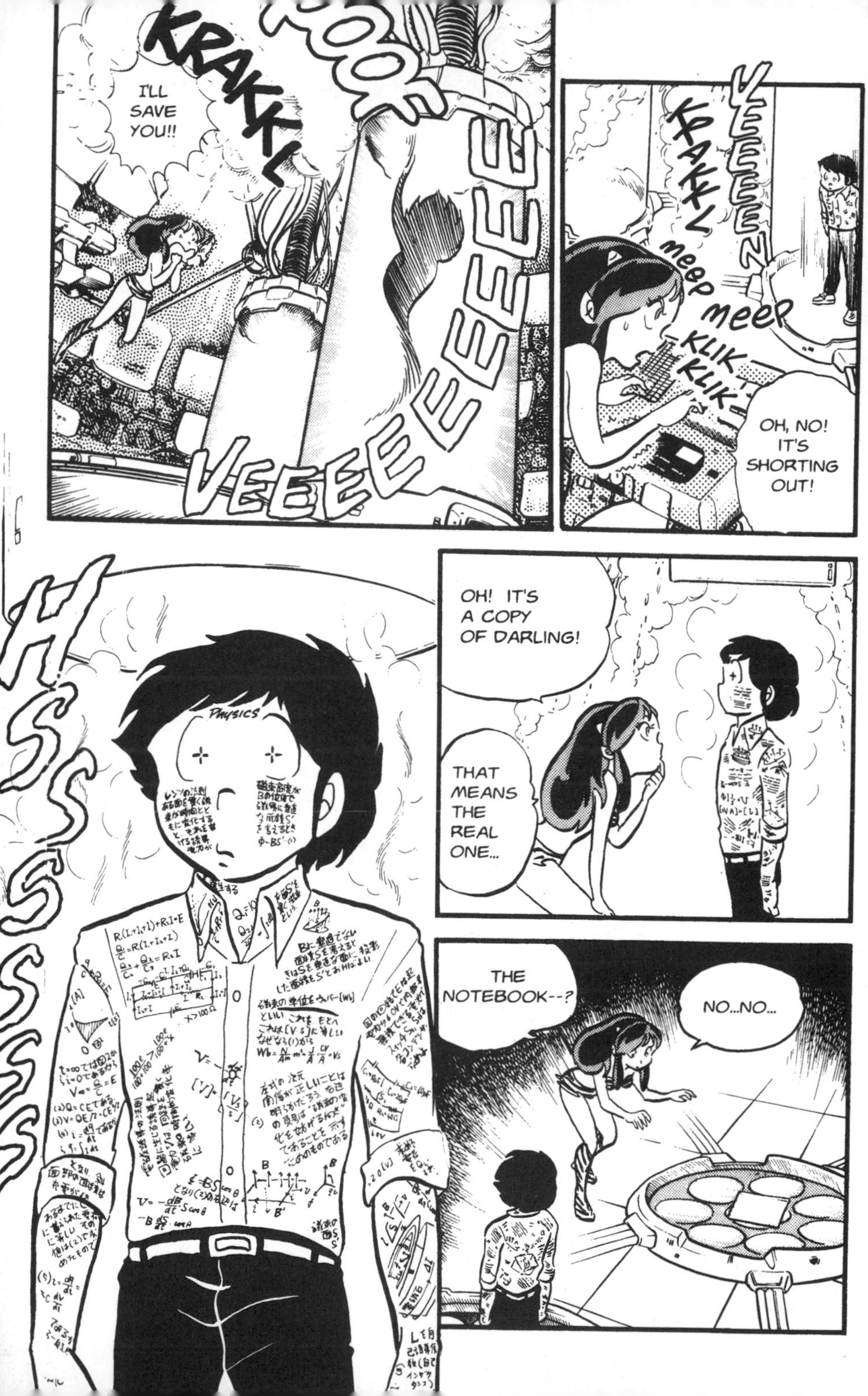
KRAKKL
I'LL SAVE YOU!!
VEEEEEEEEEEE
VEEEEN
KRAKKL
meep meep
KLIK KLIK
OH, NO! IT'S SHORTING OUT!
HISSSSSSS
PHYSICS
OH! IT'S A COPY OF DARLING!
THAT MEANS THE REAL ONE...
THE NOTEBOOK--?
NO...NO...

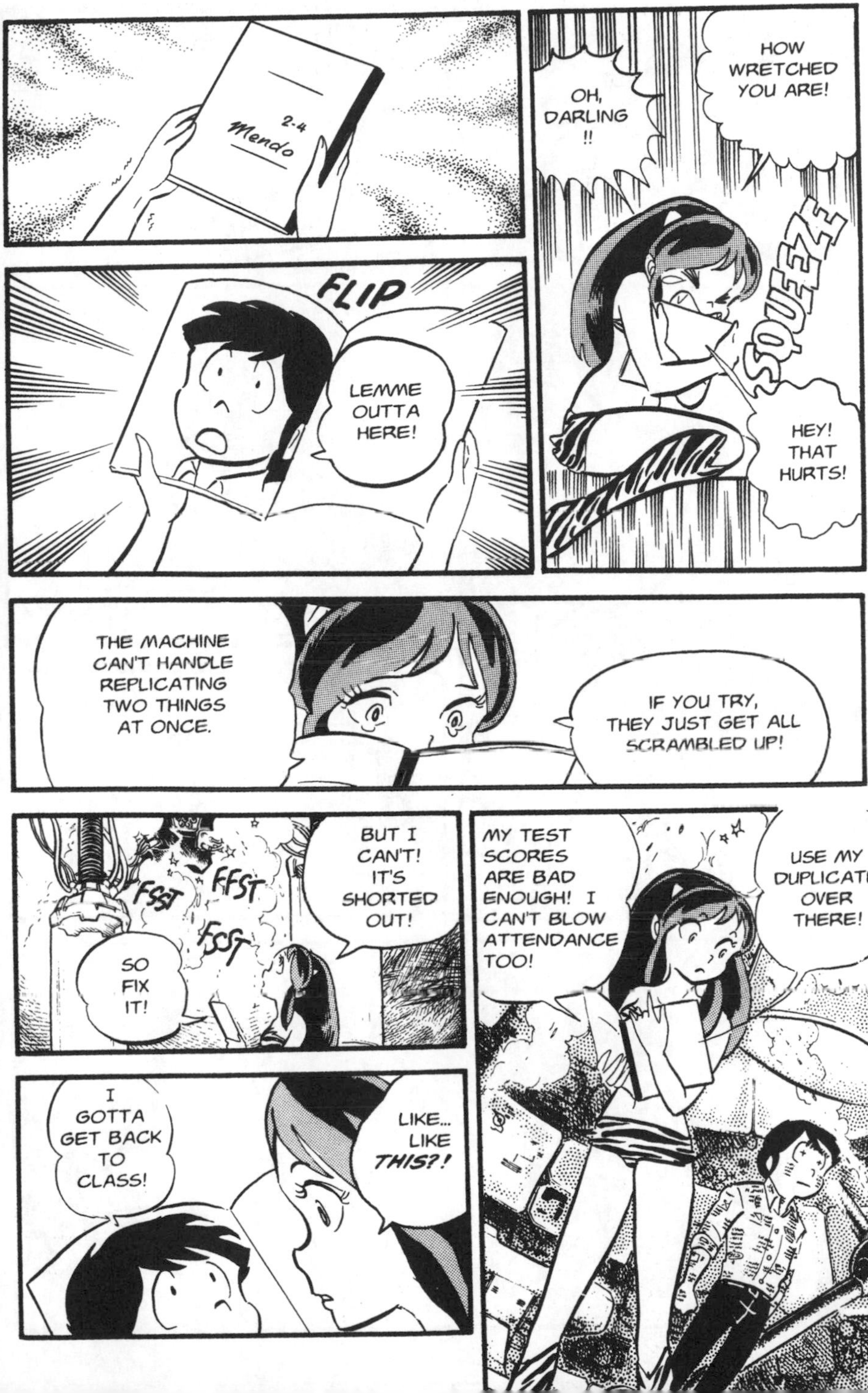
2-4
Mendo
FLIP
LEMME OUTTA HERE!
OH, DARLING !!
HOW WRETCHED YOU ARE!
SQUEEZE
HEY! THAT HURTS!
THE MACHINE CAN'T HANDLE REPLICATING TWO THINGS AT ONCE.
IF YOU TRY, THEY JUST GET ALL SCRAMBLED UP!
FSST
FFST
FSST
SO FIX IT!
BUT I CAN'T! IT'S SHORTED OUT!
I GOTTA GET BACK TO CLASS!
LIKE... LIKE *THIS?!*
MY TEST SCORES ARE BAD ENOUGH! I CAN'T BLOW ATTENDANCE TOO!
USE MY DUPLICATE OVER THERE!

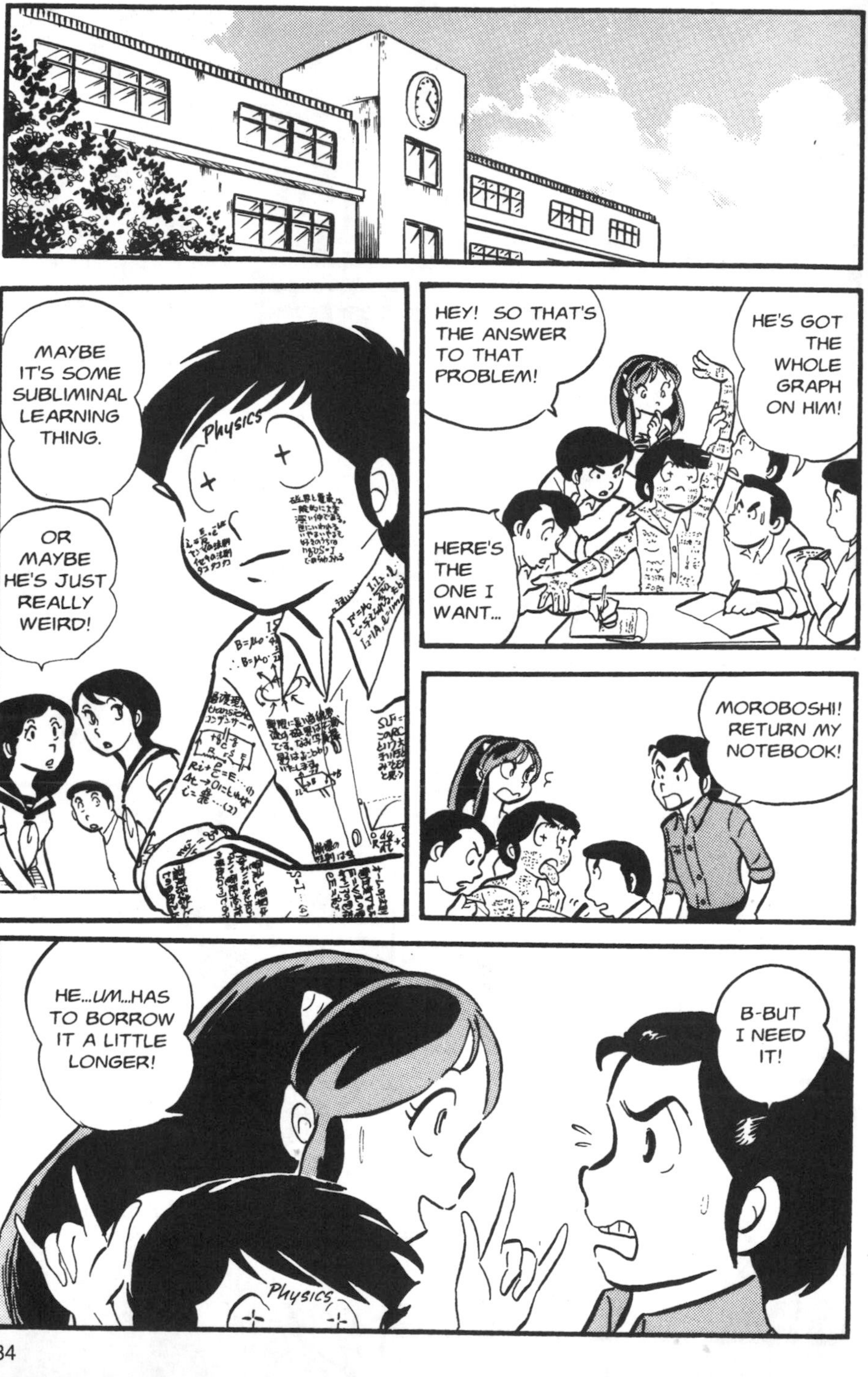

MAYBE IT'S SOME SUBLIMINAL LEARNING THING.
Physics
OR MAYBE HE'S JUST REALLY WEIRD!
HEY! SO THAT'S THE ANSWER TO THAT PROBLEM!
HE'S GOT THE WHOLE GRAPH ON HIM!
HERE'S THE ONE I WANT...
MOROBOSHI! RETURN MY NOTEBOOK!
HE...UM...HAS TO BORROW IT A LITTLE LONGER!
B-BUT I NEED IT!
Physics

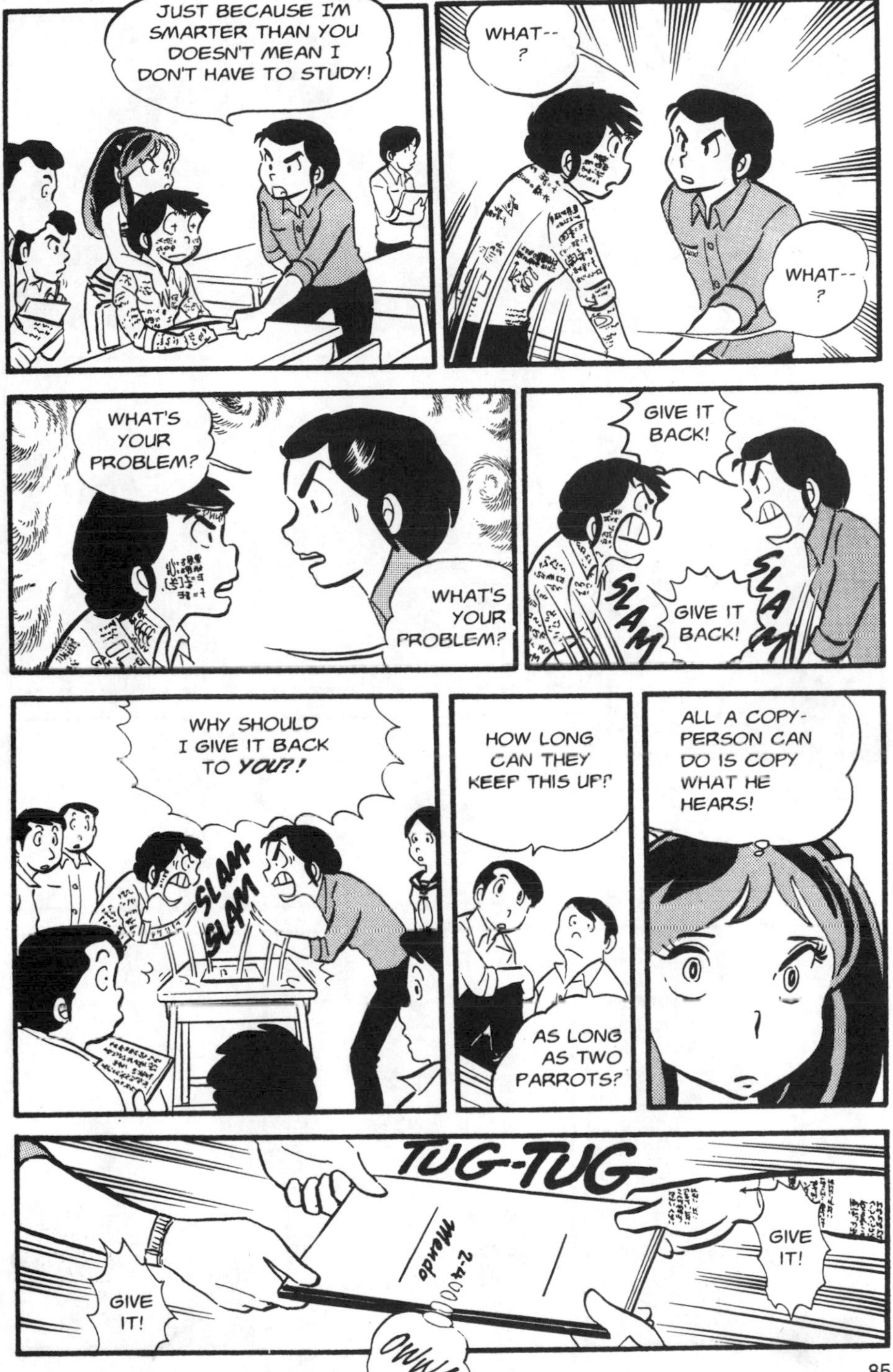
JUST BECAUSE I'M SMARTER THAN YOU DOESN'T MEAN I DON'T HAVE TO STUDY!
WHAT-- ?
WHAT-- ?
WHAT'S YOUR PROBLEM?
WHAT'S YOUR PROBLEM?
GIVE IT BACK!
SLAM
GIVE IT BACK!
SLAM
WHY SHOULD I GIVE IT BACK TO YOU?!
SLAM SLAM
HOW LONG CAN THEY KEEP THIS UP?
AS LONG AS TWO PARROTS?
ALL A COPY-PERSON CAN DO IS COPY WHAT HE HEARS!
TUG-TUG
Mendo
GIVE IT!
GIVE IT!
OWW!!

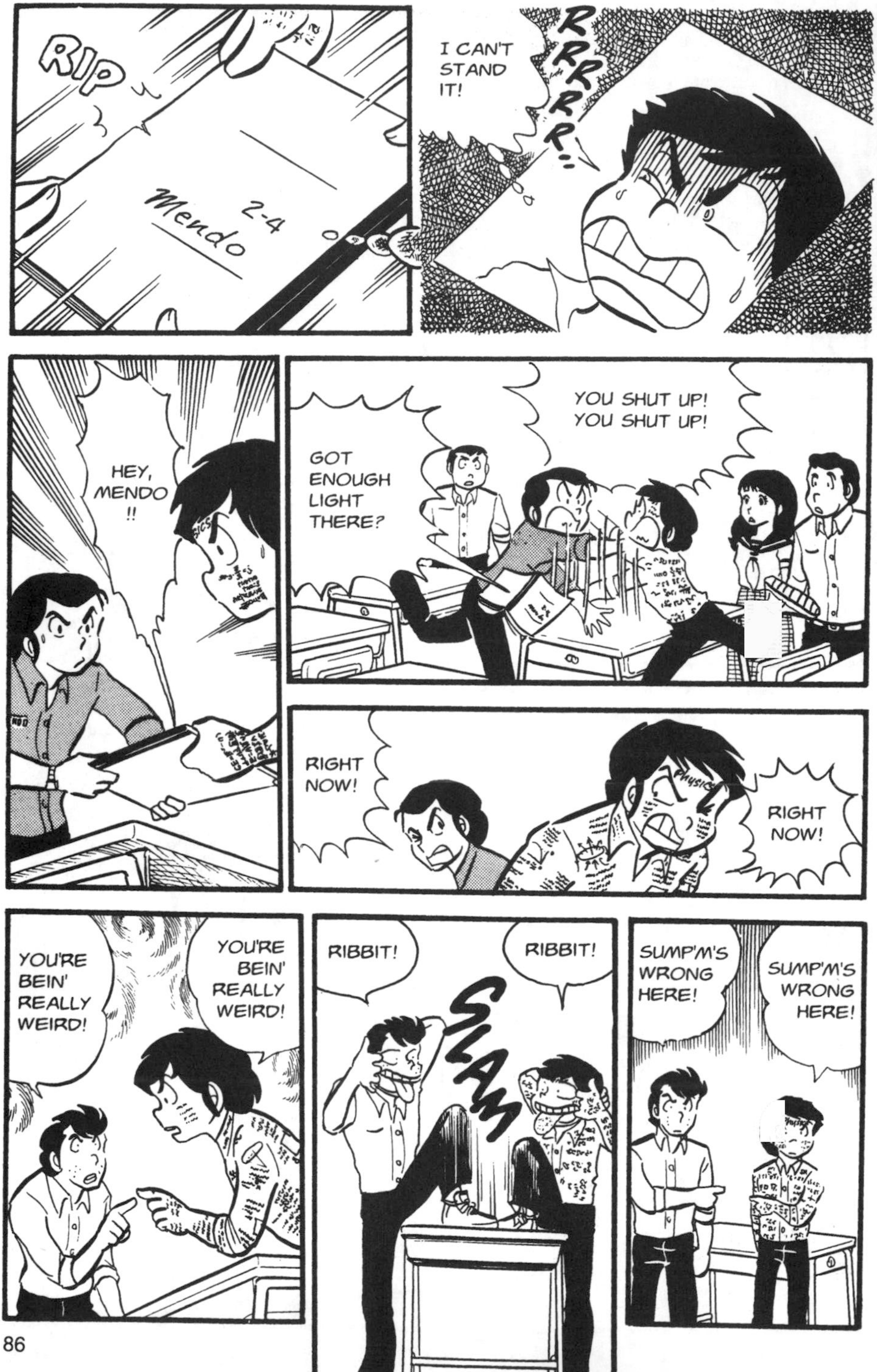
RIP
2-4
Mendo
I CAN'T STAND IT!
RRRRR..
HEY, MENDO !!
GOT ENOUGH LIGHT THERE?
YOU SHUT UP! YOU SHUT UP!
RIGHT NOW!
RIGHT NOW!
YOU'RE BEIN' REALLY WEIRD!
YOU'RE BEIN' REALLY WEIRD!
RIBBIT!
RIBBIT!
SLAM
SUMP'M'S WRONG HERE!
SUMP'M'S WRONG HERE!

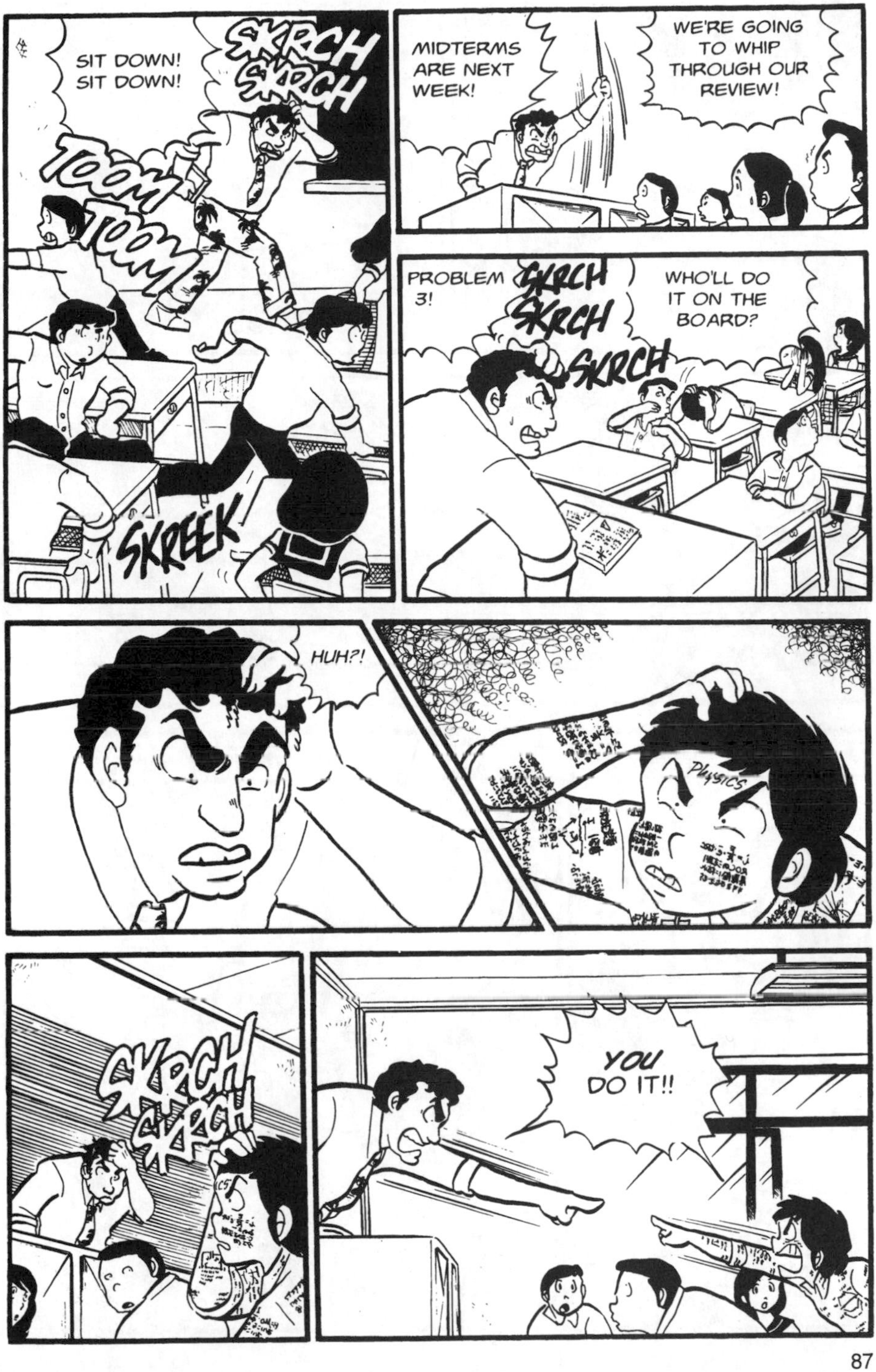
SIT DOWN! SIT DOWN!
SKRCH SKRCH
TOOM TOOM
SKREEK
MIDTERMS ARE NEXT WEEK!
WE'RE GOING TO WHIP THROUGH OUR REVIEW!
PROBLEM 3!
SKRCH SKRCH
SKRCH
WHO'LL DO IT ON THE BOARD?
HUH?!
PHYSICS
SKRCH SKRCH
YOU DO IT!!

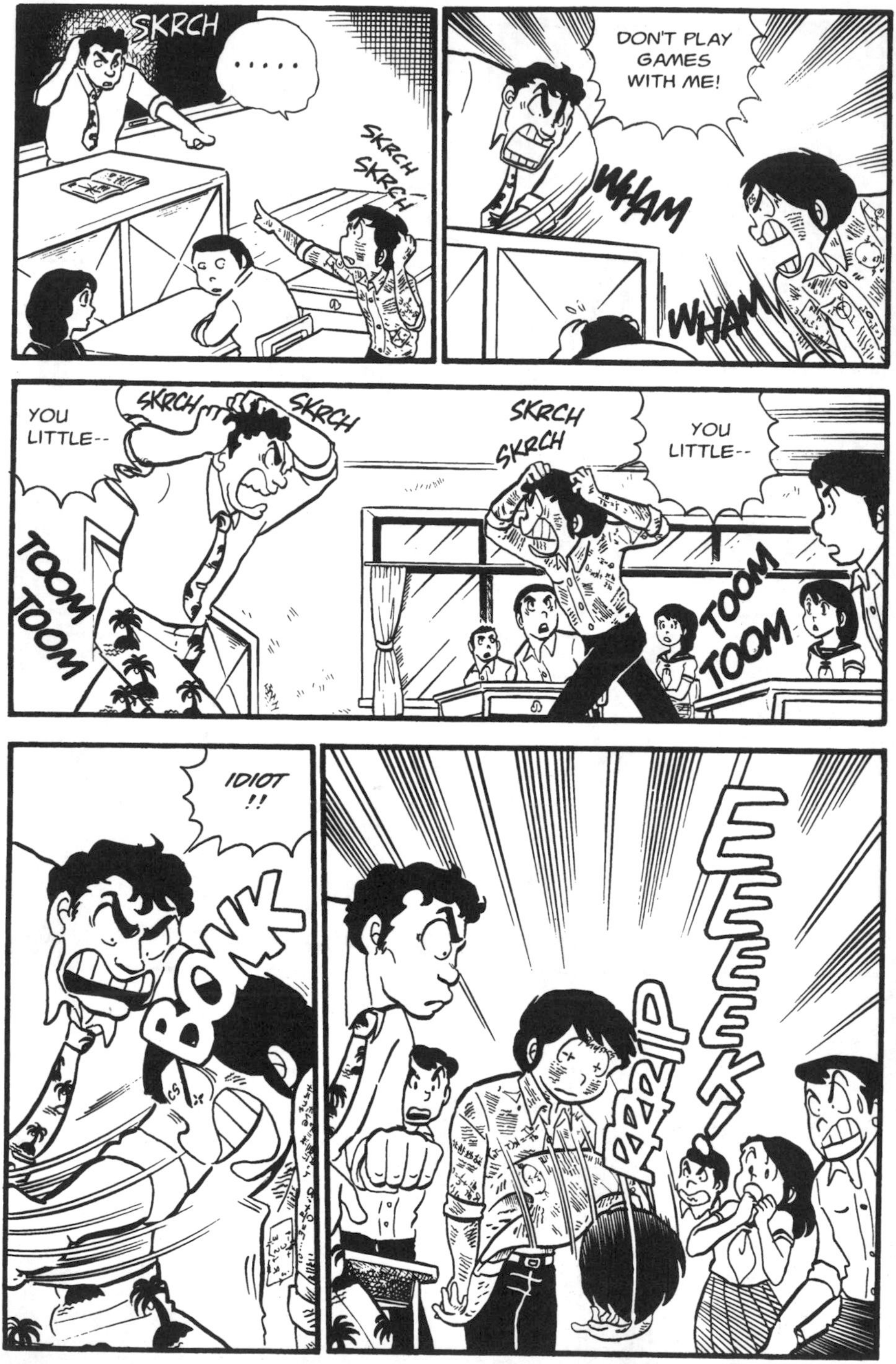
SKRCH
.....
SKRCH
SKRCH
DON'T PLAY GAMES WITH ME!
WHAM
WHAM
YOU LITTLE--
SKRCH
SKRCH
TOOM
TOOM
SKRCH
SKRCH
YOU LITTLE--
TOOM
TOOM
IDIOT !!
BONK
EEEEEK--
RRRRIP

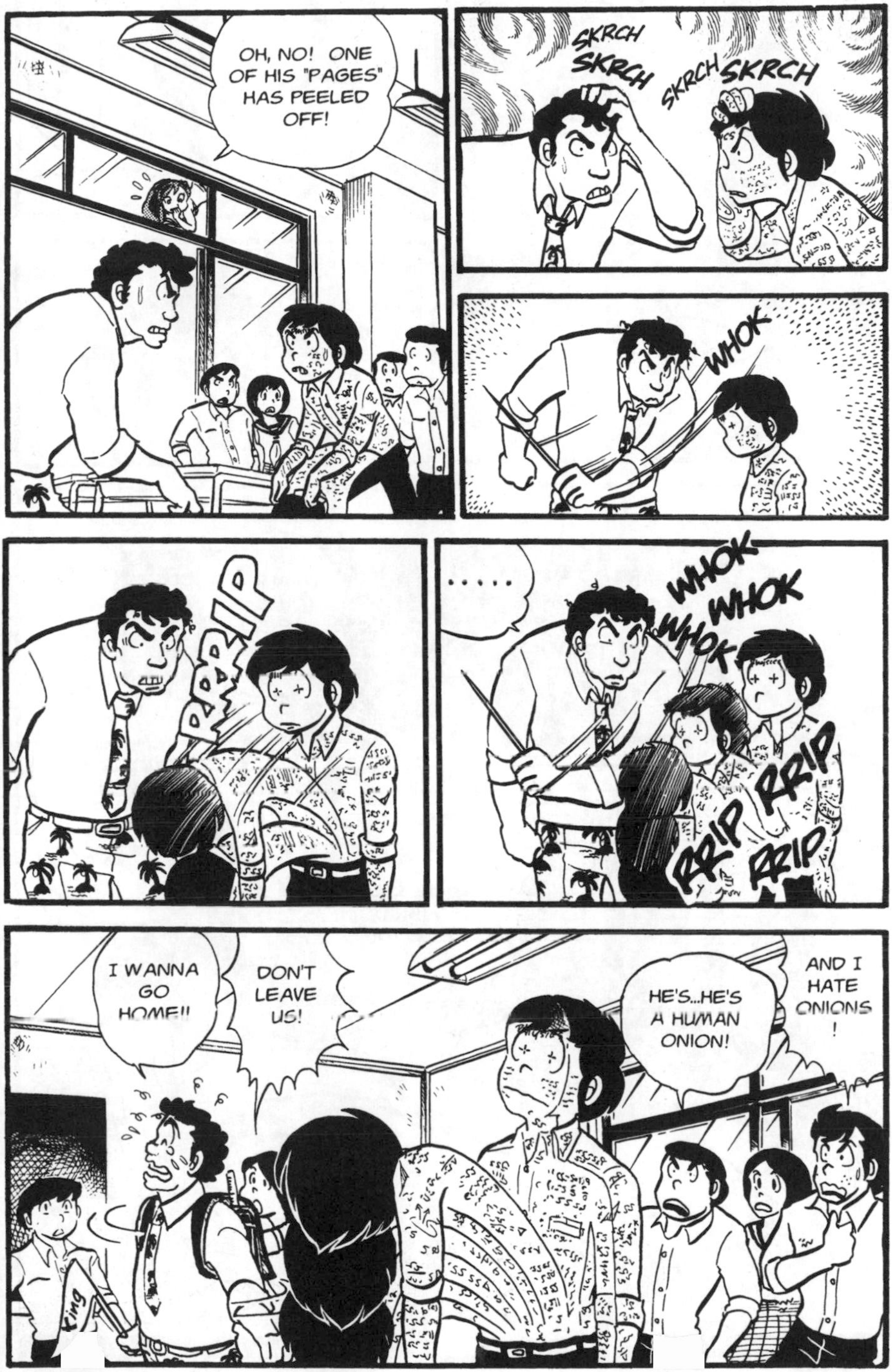
OH, NO! ONE OF HIS "PAGES" HAS PEELED OFF!
SKRCH SKRCH
SKRCH SKRCH
WHOK
RPPRIP
.....
WHOK WHOK WHOK
RRIP RRIP RRIP RRIP
I WANNA GO HOME!!
DON'T LEAVE US!
HE'S...HE'S A HUMAN ONION!
AND I HATE ONIONS!

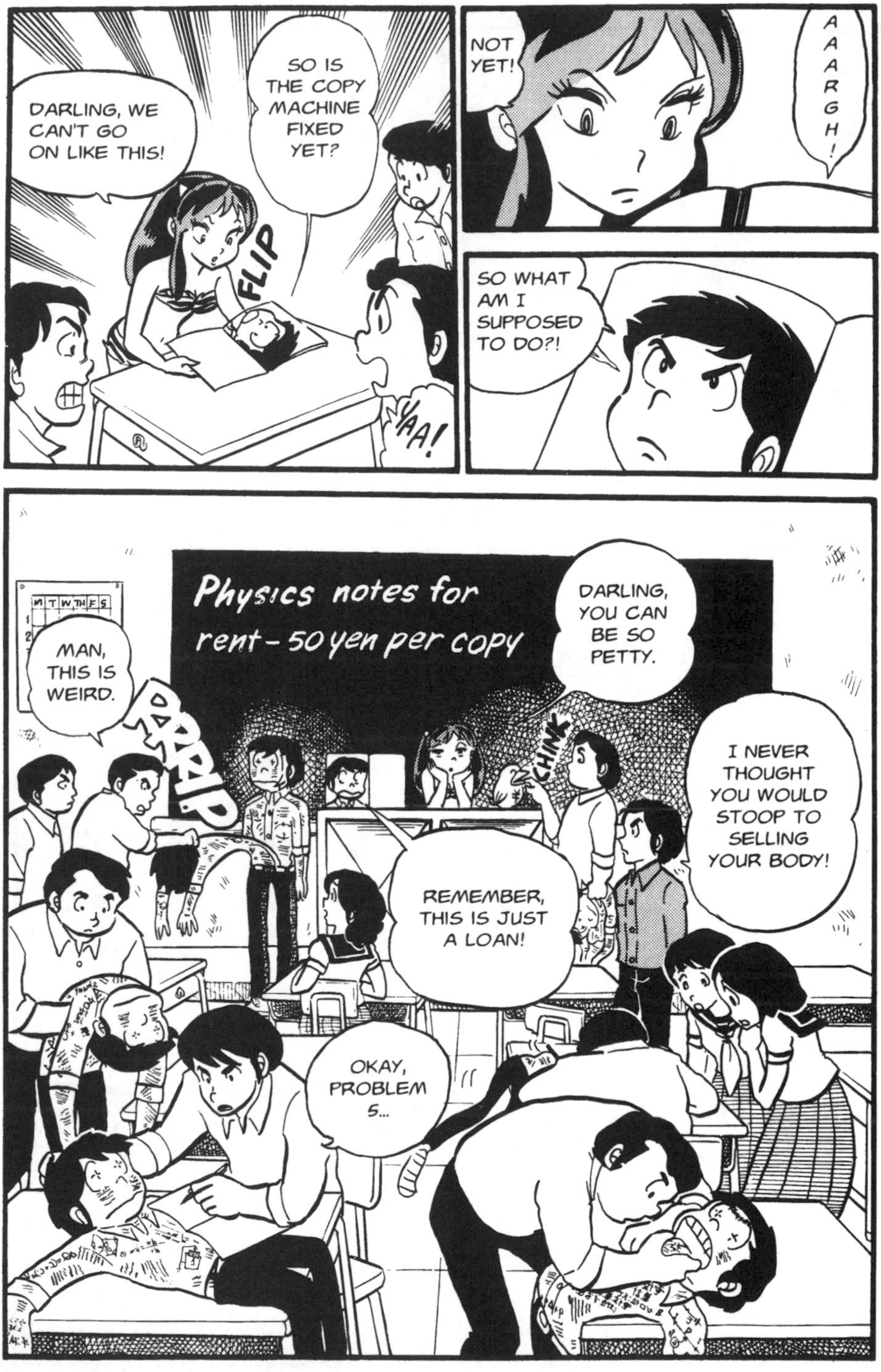
DARLING, WE CAN'T GO ON LIKE THIS!
SO IS THE COPY MACHINE FIXED YET?
FLIP
YAA!
NOT YET!
AAAARGH!
SO WHAT AM I SUPPOSED TO DO?!
Physics notes for rent - 50 yen per copy
MAN, THIS IS WEIRD.
DARLING, YOU CAN BE SO PETTY.
I NEVER THOUGHT YOU WOULD STOOP TO SELLING YOUR BODY!
REMEMBER, THIS IS JUST A LOAN!
OKAY, PROBLEM 5...

PART SIX
LIFE IS A BALL

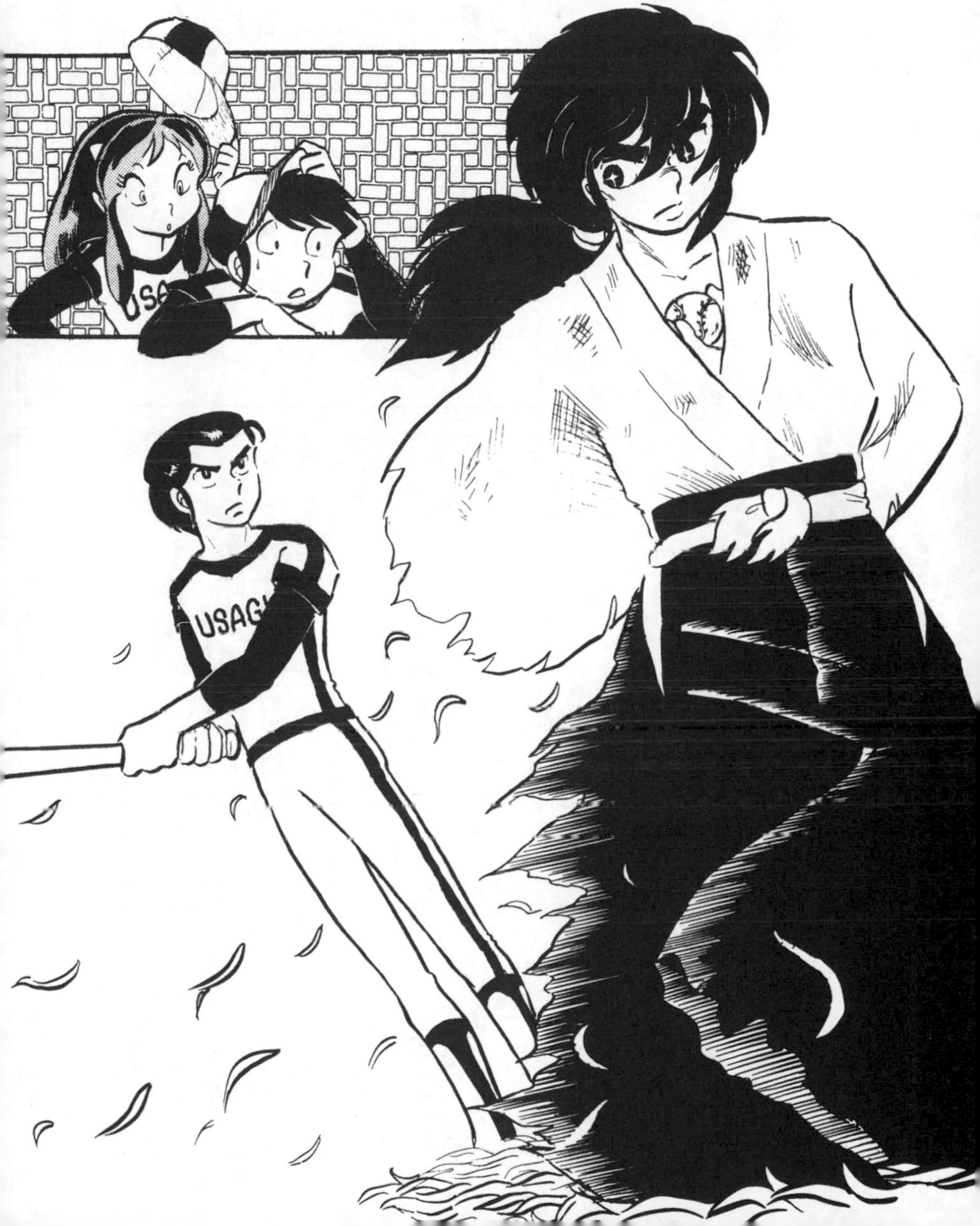

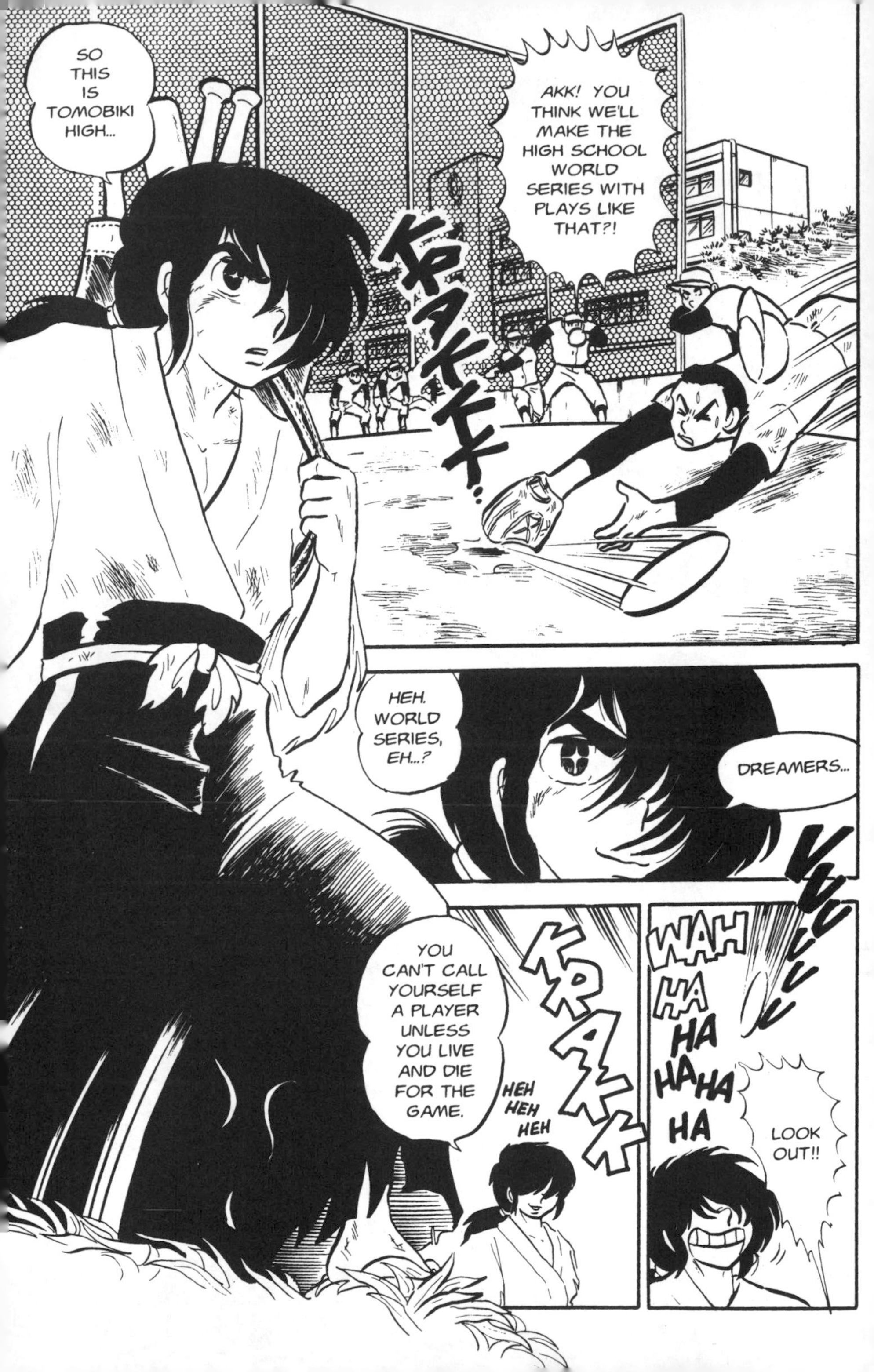
SO THIS IS TOMOBIKI HIGH...
AKK! YOU THINK WE'LL MAKE THE HIGH SCHOOL WORLD SERIES WITH PLAYS LIKE THAT?!
HEH. WORLD SERIES, EH...?
DREAMERS...
YOU CAN'T CALL YOURSELF A PLAYER UNLESS YOU LIVE AND DIE FOR THE GAME.
HEH HEH HEH
KRAKK
WAH HA HA HA HA HA HA
LOOK OUT!!

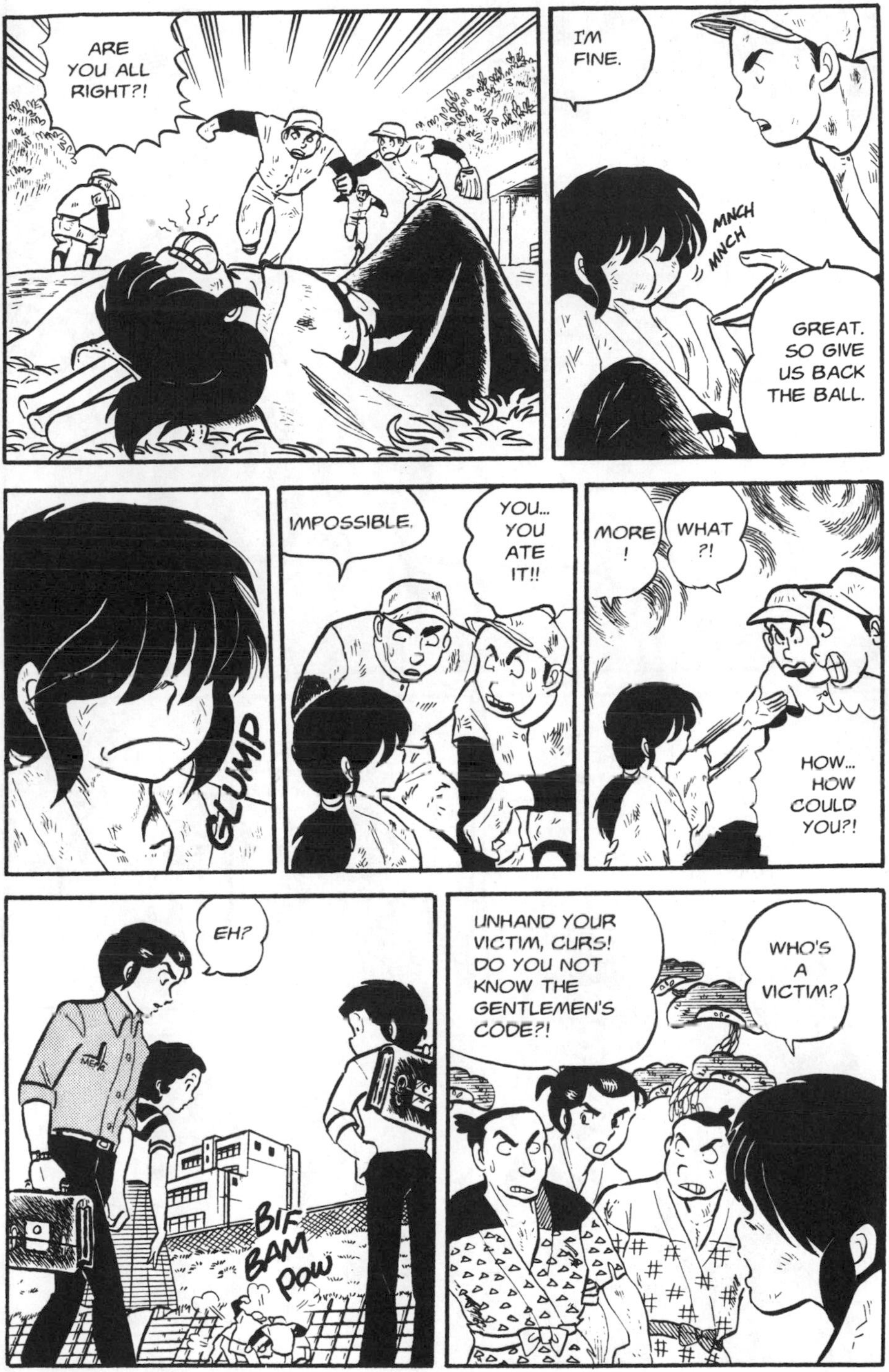
ARE YOU ALL RIGHT?!
I'M FINE.
MNCH MNCH
GREAT. SO GIVE US BACK THE BALL.
GLUMP
IMPOSSIBLE.
YOU... YOU ATE IT!!
MORE!
WHAT?!
HOW... HOW COULD YOU?!
EH?
BIF BAM POW
UNHAND YOUR VICTIM, CURS! DO YOU NOT KNOW THE GENTLEMEN'S CODE?!
WHO'S A VICTIM?

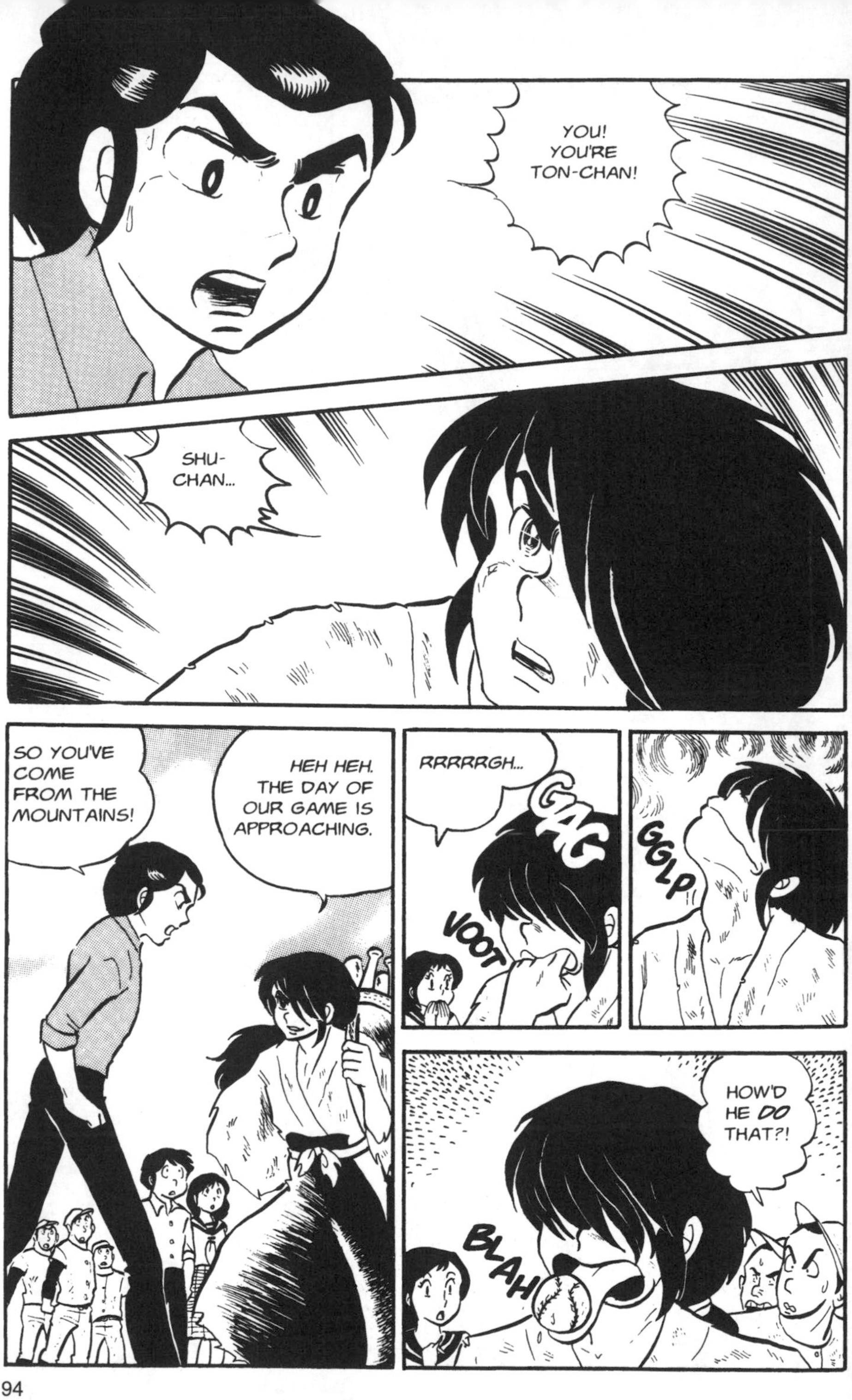
YOU! YOU'RE TON-CHAN!
SHU-CHAN...
SO YOU'VE COME FROM THE MOUNTAINS!
HEH HEH. THE DAY OF OUR GAME IS APPROACHING.
RRRRRGH...
GAG
VOOT
GGLP
HOW'D HE *DO* THAT?!
BLAH

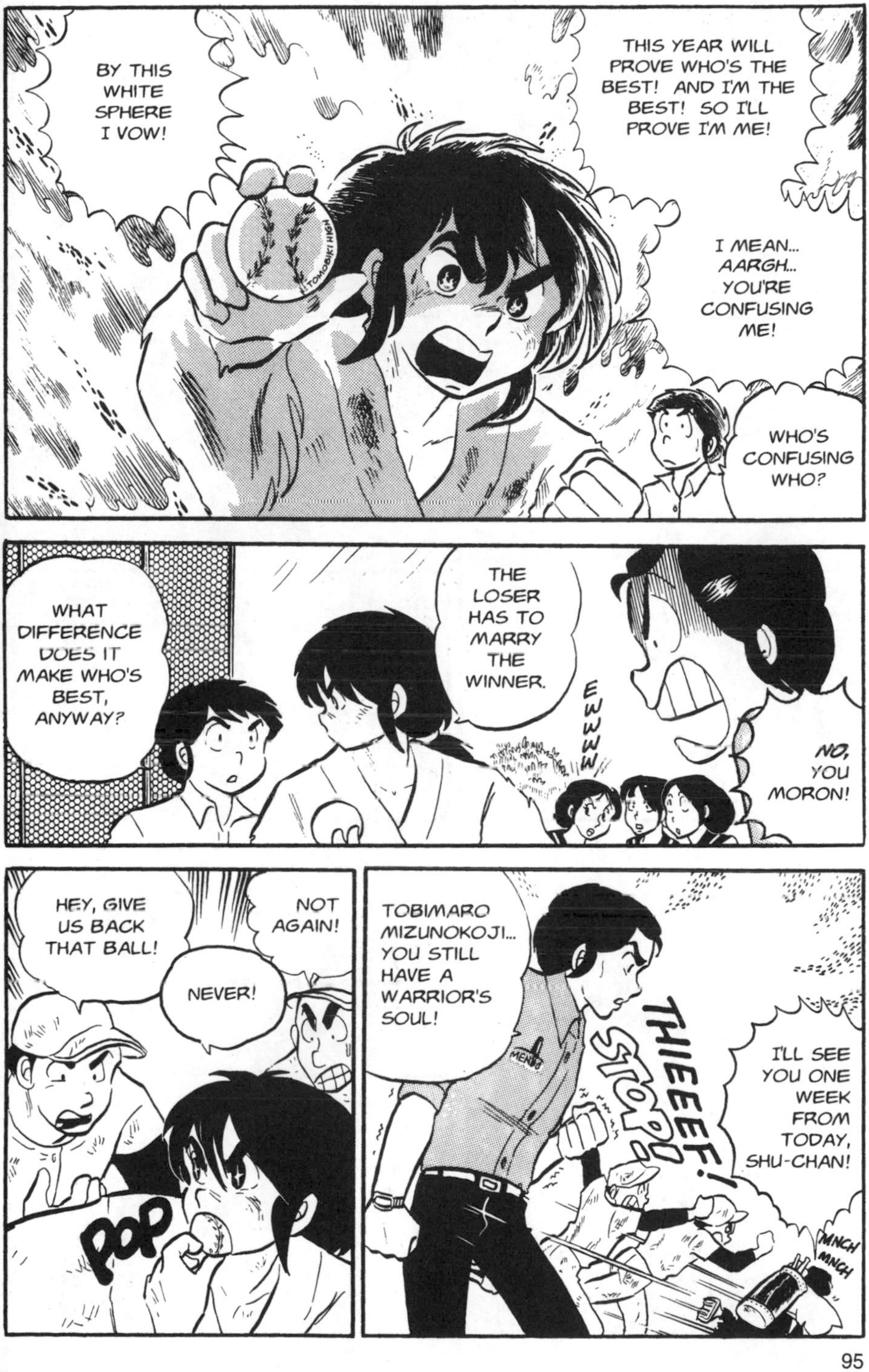
BY THIS WHITE SPHERE I VOW!
THIS YEAR WILL PROVE WHO'S THE BEST! AND I'M THE BEST! SO I'LL PROVE I'M ME!
TOMOBIKI HIGH
I MEAN... AARGH... YOU'RE CONFUSING ME!
WHO'S CONFUSING WHO?
WHAT DIFFERENCE DOES IT MAKE WHO'S BEST, ANYWAY?
THE LOSER HAS TO MARRY THE WINNER.
EWWWW
NO, YOU MORON!
HEY, GIVE US BACK THAT BALL!
NOT AGAIN!
NEVER!
POP
TOBIMARO MIZUNOKOJI... YOU STILL HAVE A WARRIOR'S SOUL!
THIEEEF!
STOP!
I'LL SEE YOU ONE WEEK FROM TODAY, SHU-CHAN!
MNCH MNCH

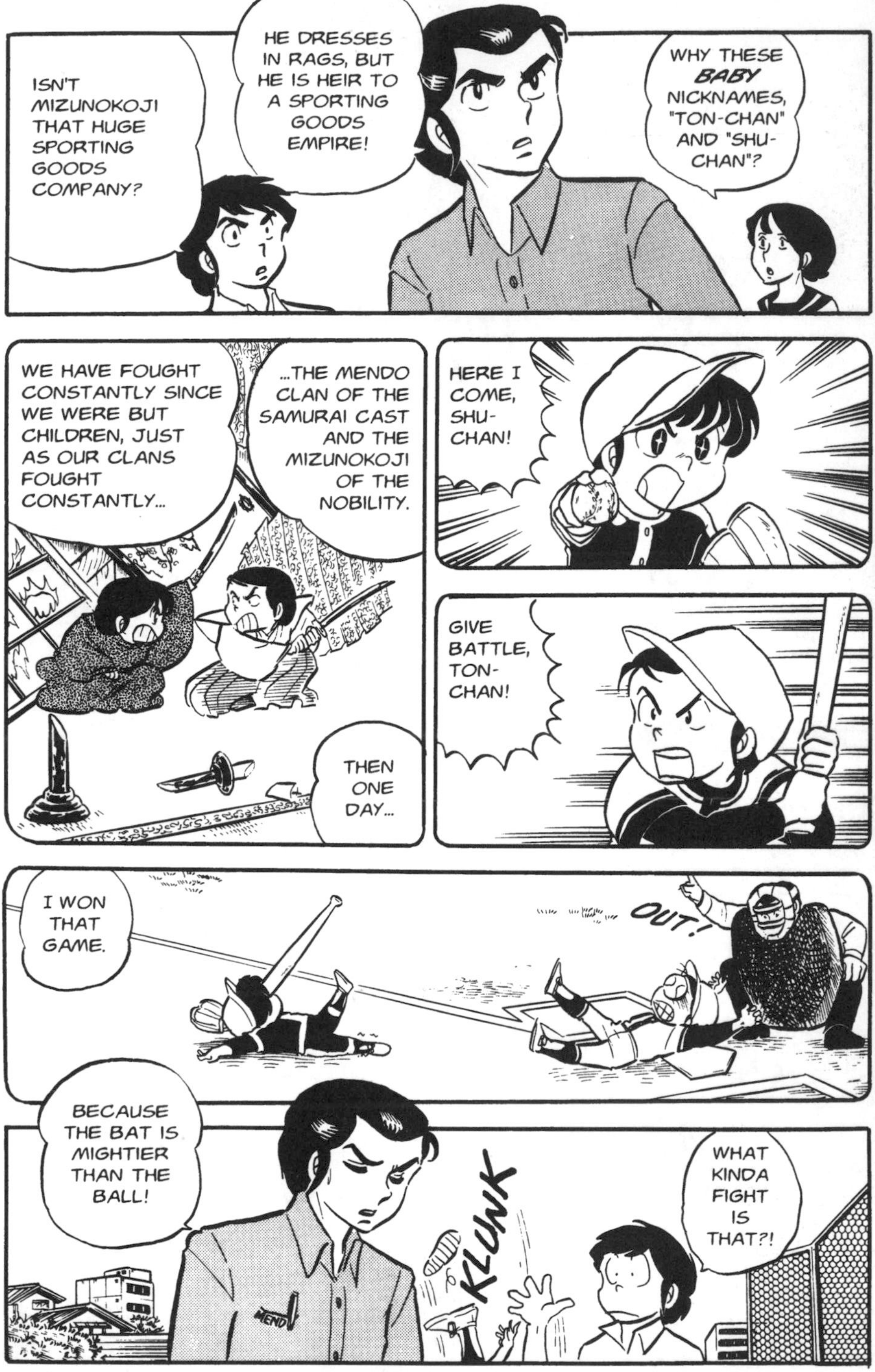
ISN'T MIZUNOKOJI THAT HUGE SPORTING GOODS COMPANY?
HE DRESSES IN RAGS, BUT HE IS HEIR TO A SPORTING GOODS EMPIRE!
WHY THESE *BABY* NICKNAMES, "TON-CHAN" AND "SHU-CHAN"?
WE HAVE FOUGHT CONSTANTLY SINCE WE WERE BUT CHILDREN, JUST AS OUR CLANS FOUGHT CONSTANTLY...
...THE MENDO CLAN OF THE SAMURAI CAST AND THE MIZUNOKOJI OF THE NOBILITY.
THEN ONE DAY...
HERE I COME, SHU-CHAN!
GIVE BATTLE, TON-CHAN!
I WON THAT GAME.
OUT!
BECAUSE THE BAT IS MIGHTIER THAN THE BALL!
KLUNK
MEND
WHAT KINDA FIGHT IS THAT?!

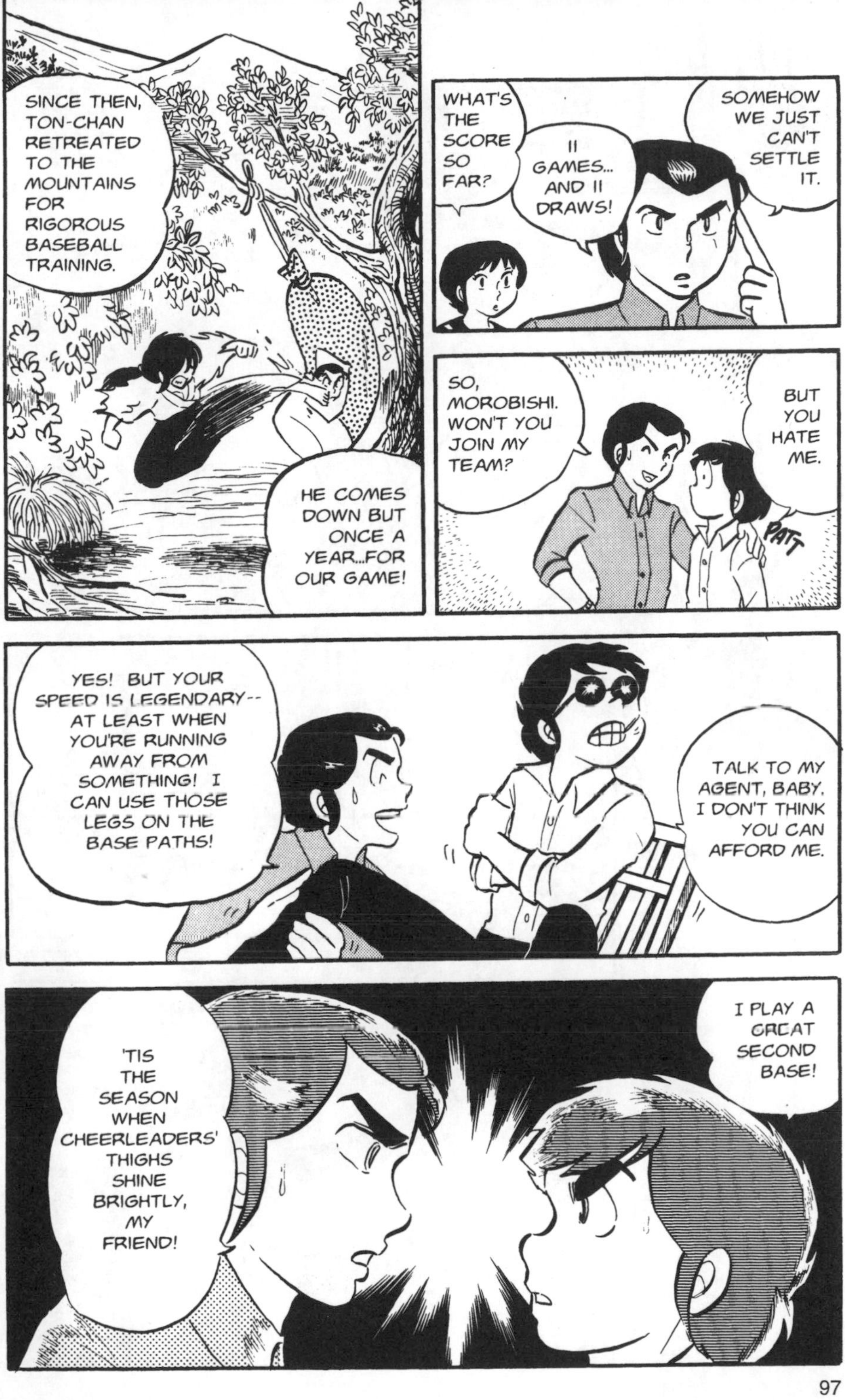
SINCE THEN, TON-CHAN RETREATED TO THE MOUNTAINS FOR RIGOROUS BASEBALL TRAINING.
HE COMES DOWN BUT ONCE A YEAR...FOR OUR GAME!
WHAT'S THE SCORE SO FAR?
11 GAMES... AND 11 DRAWS!
SOMEHOW WE JUST CAN'T SETTLE IT.
SO, MOROBISHI. WON'T YOU JOIN MY TEAM?
BUT YOU HATE ME.
PATT
YES! BUT YOUR SPEED IS LEGENDARY-- AT LEAST WHEN YOU'RE RUNNING AWAY FROM SOMETHING! I CAN USE THOSE LEGS ON THE BASE PATHS!
TALK TO MY AGENT, BABY. I DON'T THINK YOU CAN AFFORD ME.
'TIS THE SEASON WHEN CHEERLEADERS' THIGHS SHINE BRIGHTLY, MY FRIEND!
I PLAY A GREAT SECOND BASE!

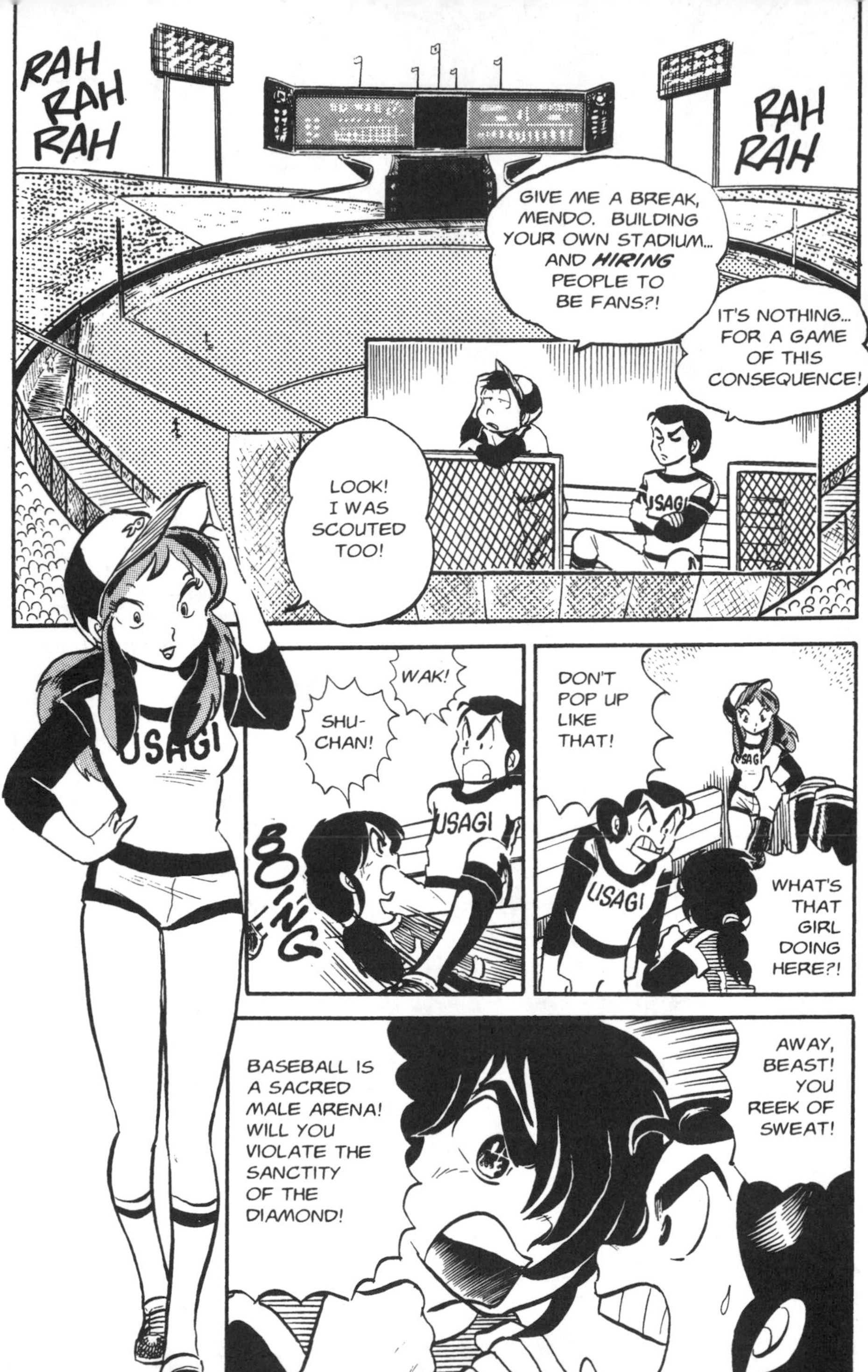
RAH RAH RAH
RAH RAH
GIVE ME A BREAK, MENDO. BUILDING YOUR OWN STADIUM... AND HIRING PEOPLE TO BE FANS?!
IT'S NOTHING... FOR A GAME OF THIS CONSEQUENCE!
LOOK! I WAS SCOUTED TOO!
USAGI
SHU-CHAN!
WAK!
BOING
USAGI
DON'T POP UP LIKE THAT!
WHAT'S THAT GIRL DOING HERE?!
USAGI
BASEBALL IS A SACRED MALE ARENA! WILL YOU VIOLATE THE SANCTITY OF THE DIAMOND!
AWAY, BEAST! YOU REEK OF SWEAT!

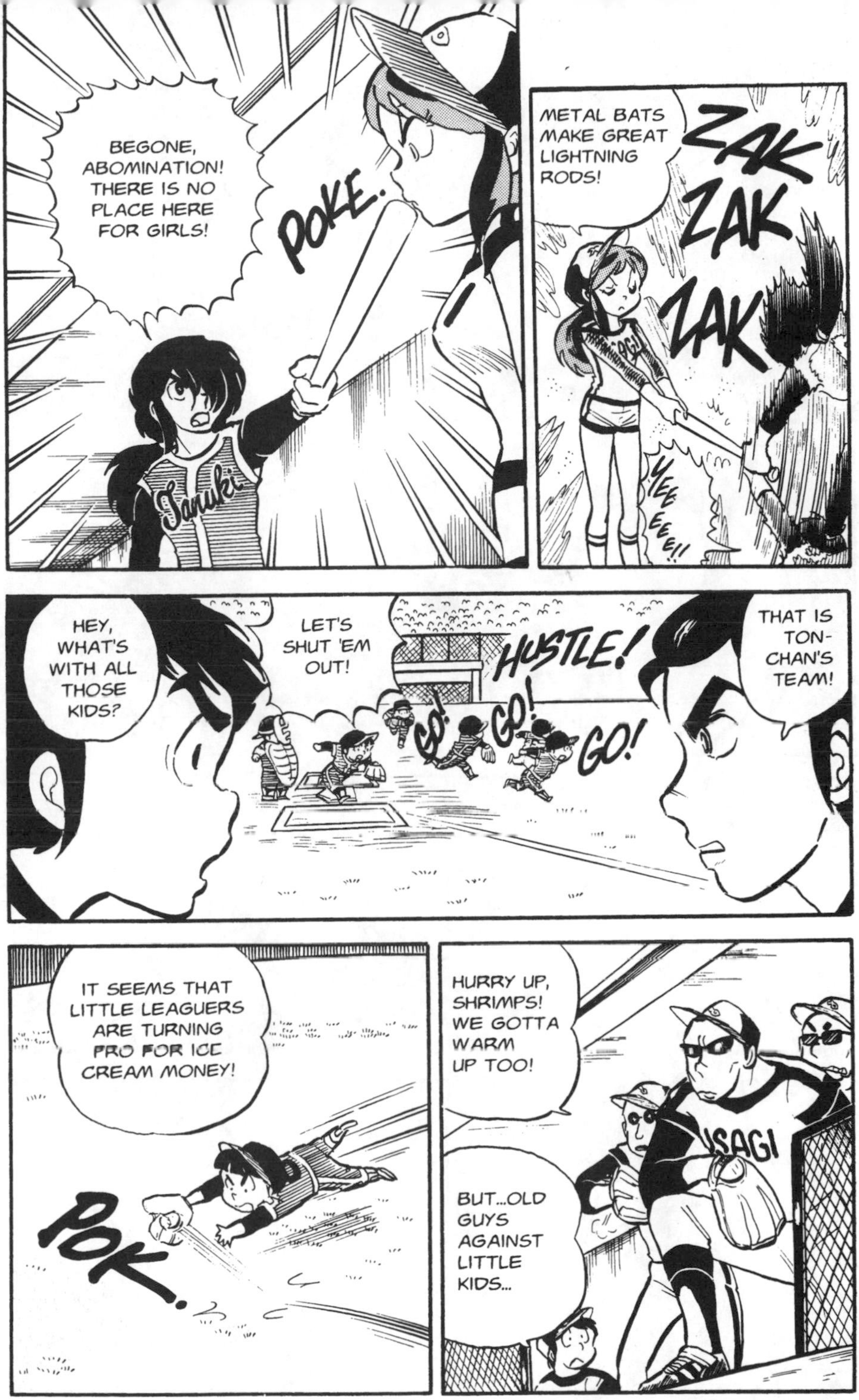
BEGONE, ABOMINATION! THERE IS NO PLACE HERE FOR GIRLS!
POKE.
Sanuki
METAL BATS MAKE GREAT LIGHTNING RODS!
ZAK ZAK ZAK
YEEEEE!!
HEY, WHAT'S WITH ALL THOSE KIDS?
LET'S SHUT 'EM OUT!
HUSTLE!
GO! GO! GO!
THAT IS TON-CHAN'S TEAM!
IT SEEMS THAT LITTLE LEAGUERS ARE TURNING PRO FOR ICE CREAM MONEY!
POK.
HURRY UP, SHRIMPS! WE GOTTA WARM UP TOO!
USAGI
BUT...OLD GUYS AGAINST LITTLE KIDS...

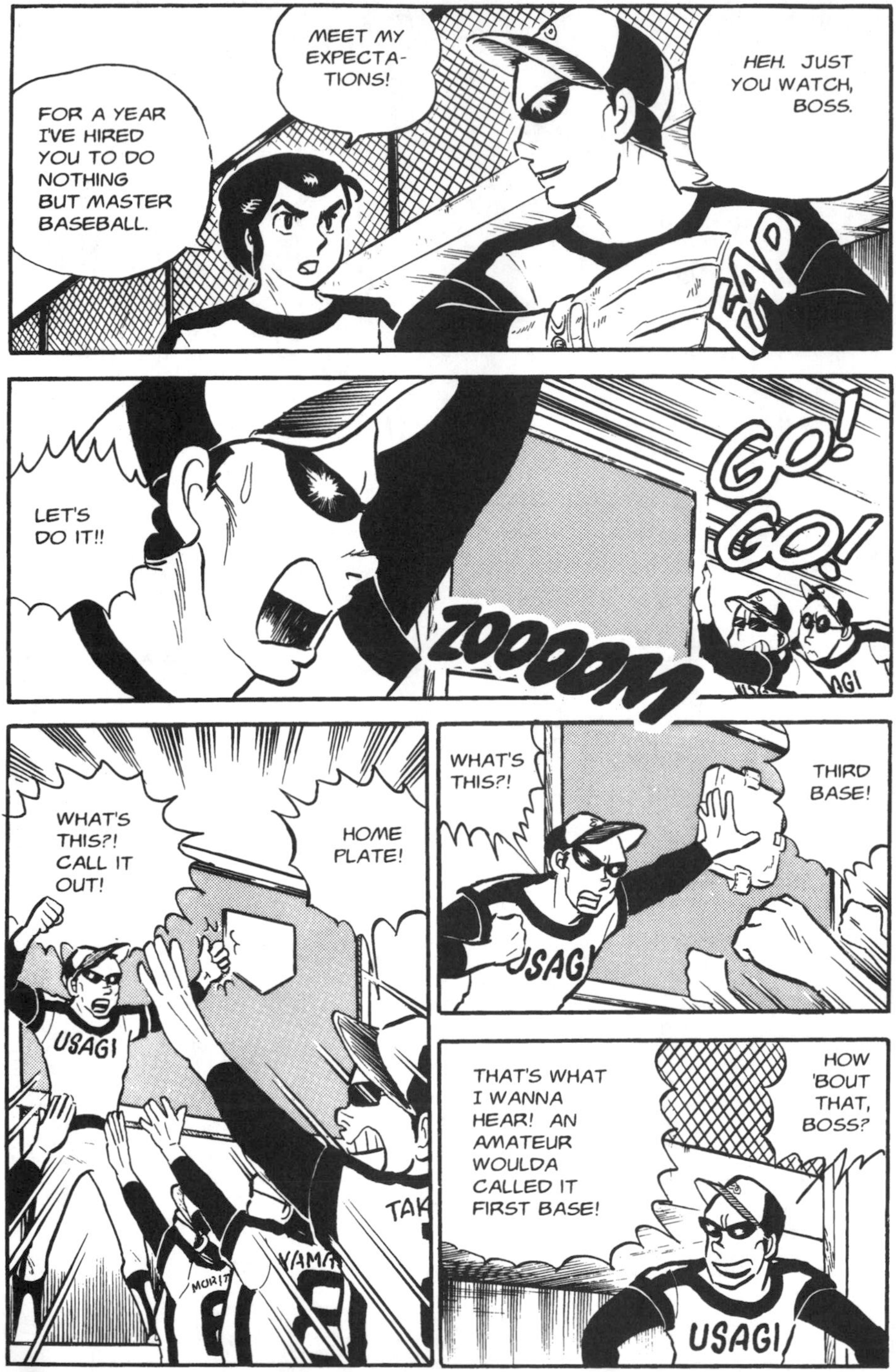
FOR A YEAR I'VE HIRED YOU TO DO NOTHING BUT MASTER BASEBALL.
MEET MY EXPECTATIONS!
HEH. JUST YOU WATCH, BOSS.
LET'S DO IT!!
GO! GO!
ZOOOOM
WHAT'S THIS?! CALL IT OUT!
HOME PLATE!
WHAT'S THIS?!
THIRD BASE!
HOW 'BOUT THAT, BOSS?
THAT'S WHAT I WANNA HEAR! AN AMATEUR WOULDA CALLED IT FIRST BASE!

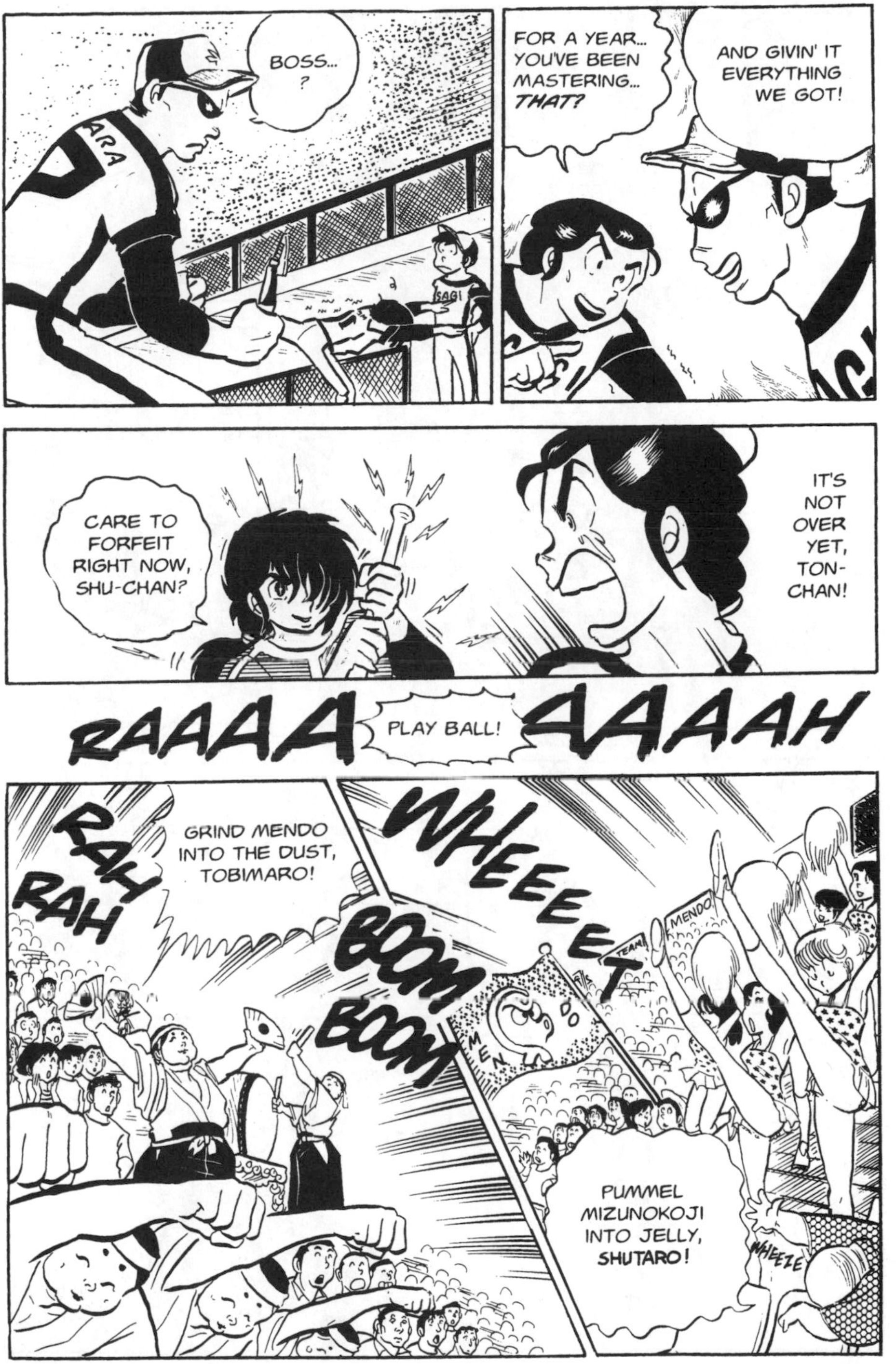
BOSS... ?
FOR A YEAR... YOU'VE BEEN MASTERING... *THAT?*
AND GIVIN' IT EVERYTHING WE GOT!
CARE TO FORFEIT RIGHT NOW, SHU-CHAN?
IT'S NOT OVER YET, TON-CHAN!
RAAAA
PLAY BALL!
AAAAH
RAH RAH
GRIND MENDO INTO THE DUST, TOBIMARO!
WHEEEEET
BOOM BOOM BOOM
MENDO
PUMMEL MIZUNOKOJI INTO JELLY, **SHUTARO**!
WHEEZE

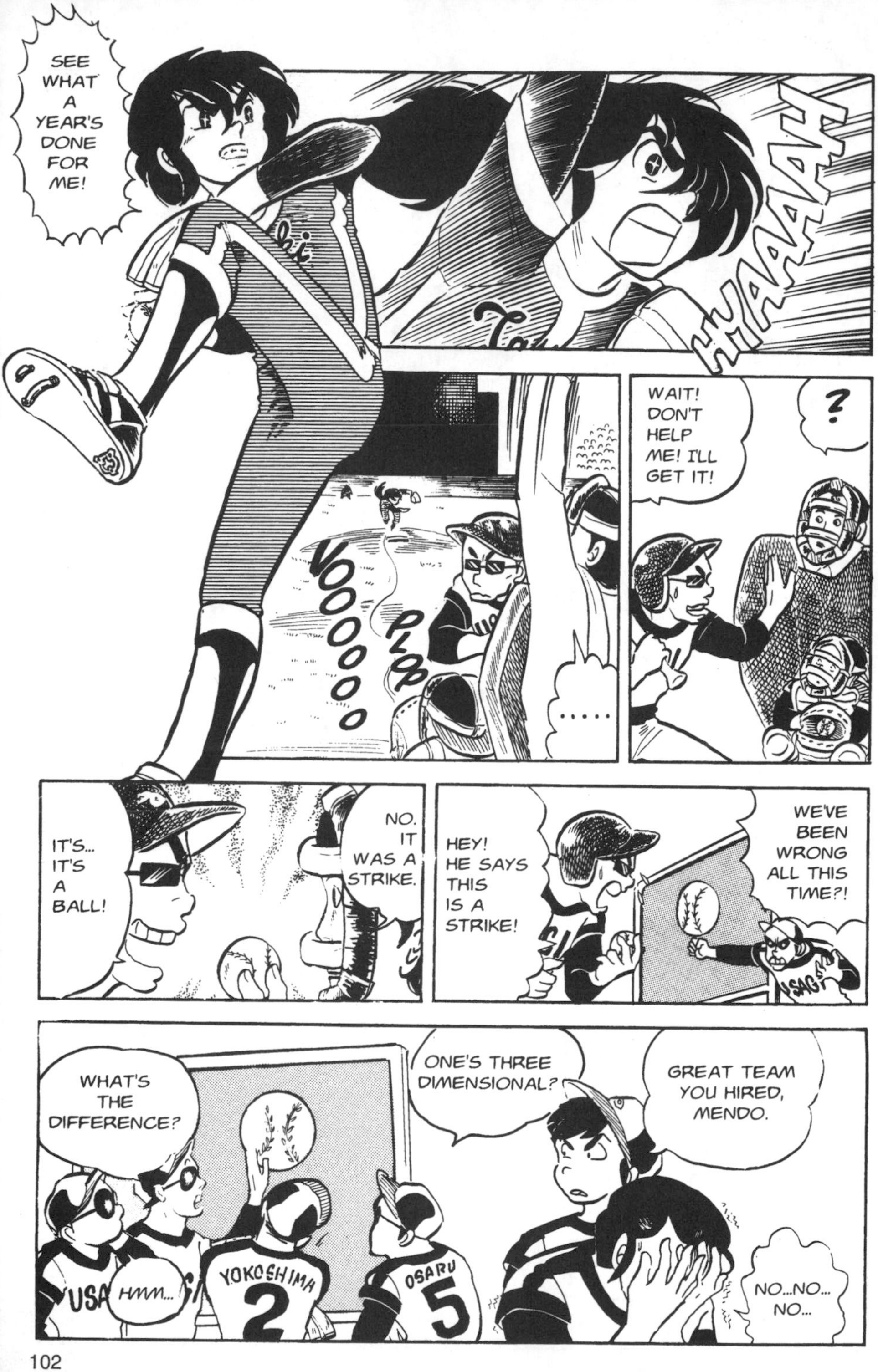

SEE WHAT A YEAR'S DONE FOR ME!
HYAAAAH
VOOOOOOO
PLOP
.....
WAIT! DON'T HELP ME! I'LL GET IT!
?
IT'S... IT'S A BALL!
NO. IT WAS A STRIKE.
HEY! HE SAYS THIS IS A STRIKE!
WE'VE BEEN WRONG ALL THIS TIME?!
WHAT'S THE DIFFERENCE?
HMM...
YOKOSHIMA 2
OSARU 5
ONE'S THREE DIMENSIONAL?
GREAT TEAM YOU HIRED, MENDO.
NO...NO... NO...

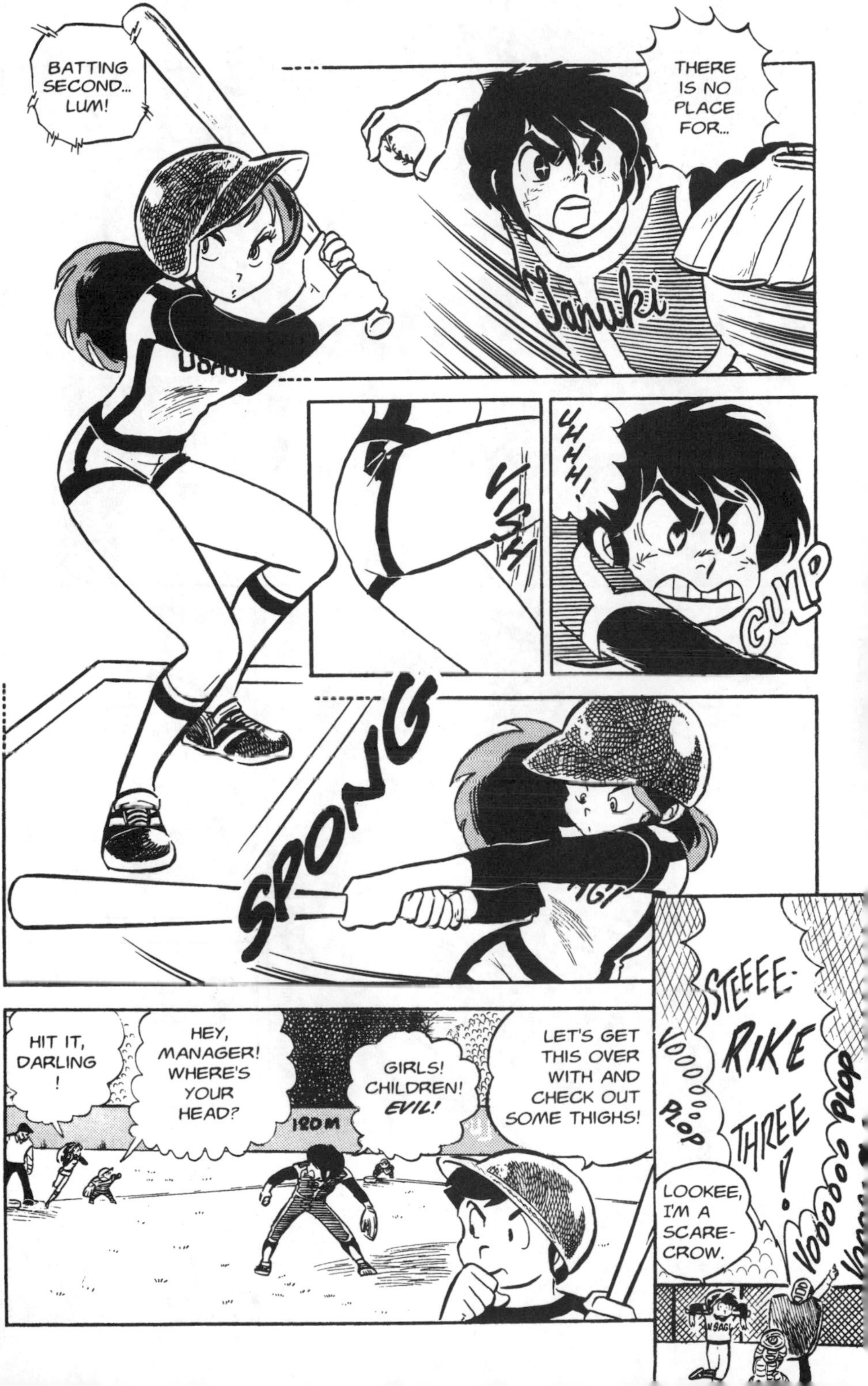
BATTING SECOND... LUM!
THERE IS NO PLACE FOR...
VISH
UHHH!
GULP
SPONG
HIT IT, DARLING!
HEY, MANAGER! WHERE'S YOUR HEAD?
GIRLS! CHILDREN! *EVIL!*
120M
LET'S GET THIS OVER WITH AND CHECK OUT SOME THIGHS!
STEEEE-RIKE THREE!
VOOOOOO PLOP
VOOOOOOO PLOP
LOOKEE, I'M A SCARE-CROW.

BATTING FOURTH-- MENDO!

CRACKLE!

ROOOOOOOAR

CLINCHH

HE'S CALLING HIS SHOT!

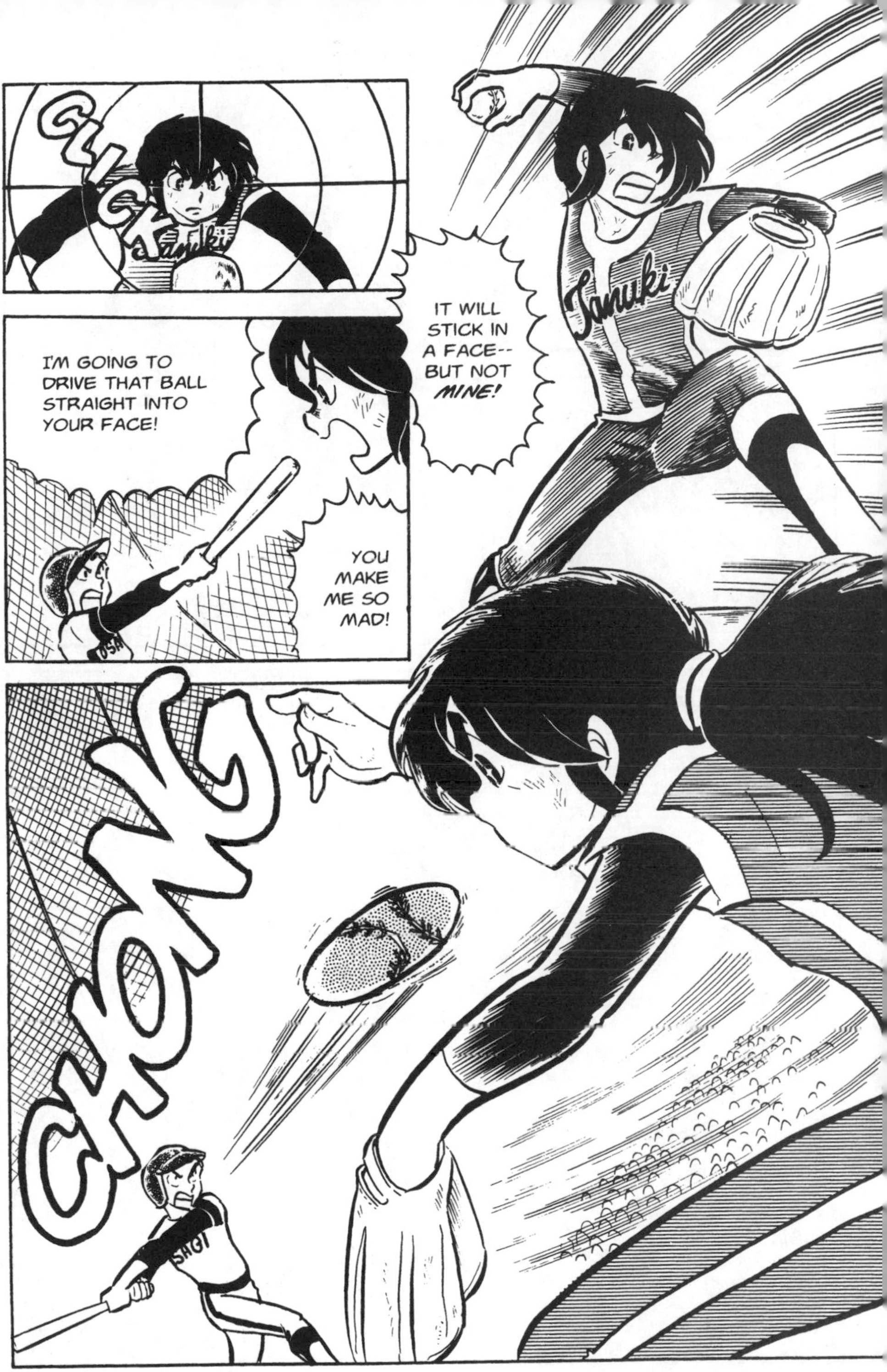
CLICK
I'M GOING TO DRIVE THAT BALL STRAIGHT INTO YOUR FACE!
YOU MAKE ME SO MAD!
IT WILL STICK IN A FACE-- BUT NOT *MINE!*
CHONG

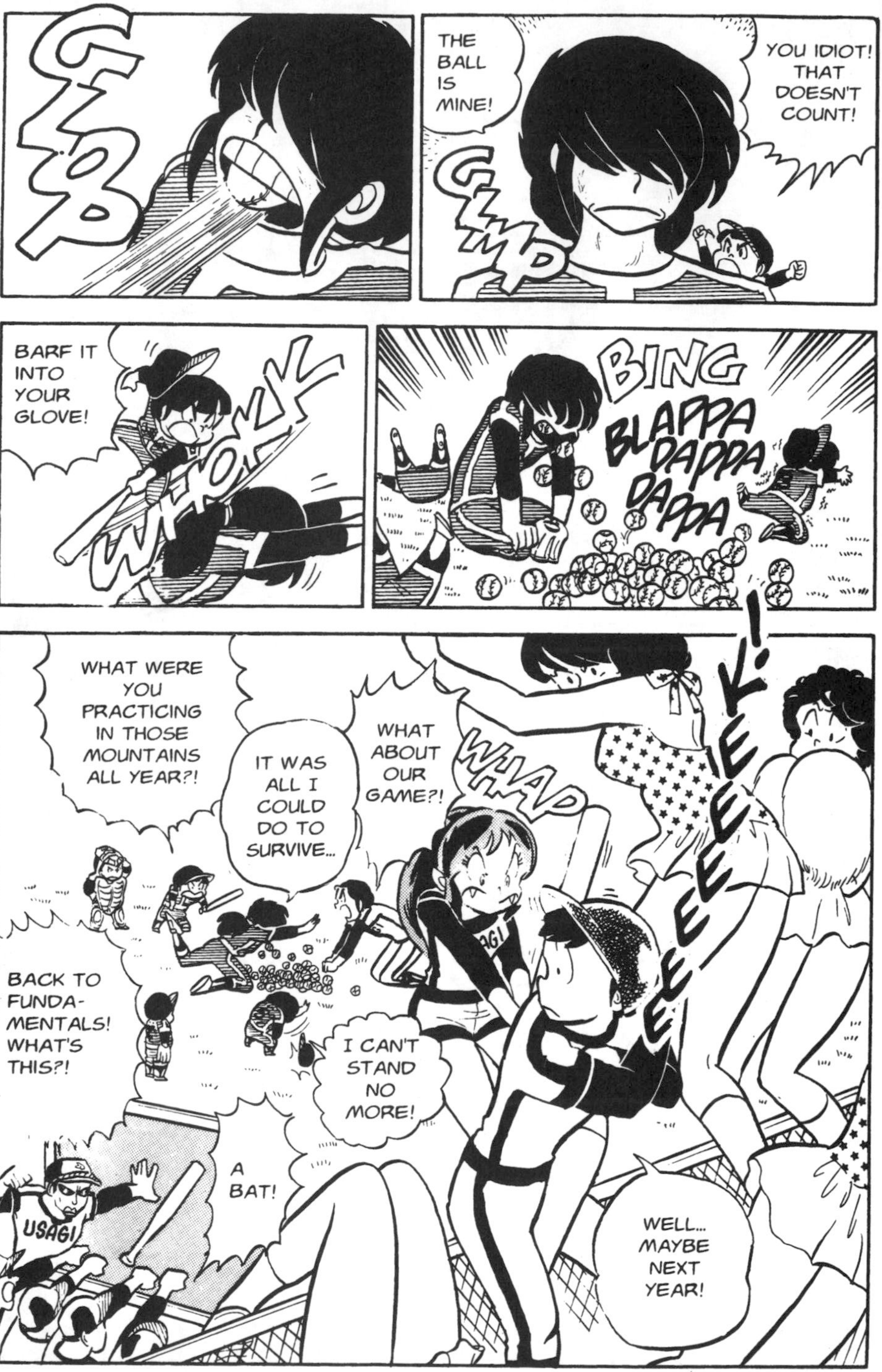
GLOMP
THE BALL IS MINE!
GLMP
YOU IDIOT! THAT DOESN'T COUNT!
BARF IT INTO YOUR GLOVE!
WHOK
BING
BLAPPA DAPPA DAPPA
WHAT WERE YOU PRACTICING IN THOSE MOUNTAINS ALL YEAR?!
IT WAS ALL I COULD DO TO SURVIVE...
WHAT ABOUT OUR GAME?!
WHAP
EEEEEEEK!
BACK TO FUNDA-MENTALS! WHAT'S THIS?!
I CAN'T STAND NO MORE!
A BAT!
WELL... MAYBE NEXT YEAR!
USAGI

PART SEVEN
THE RED CLOAK

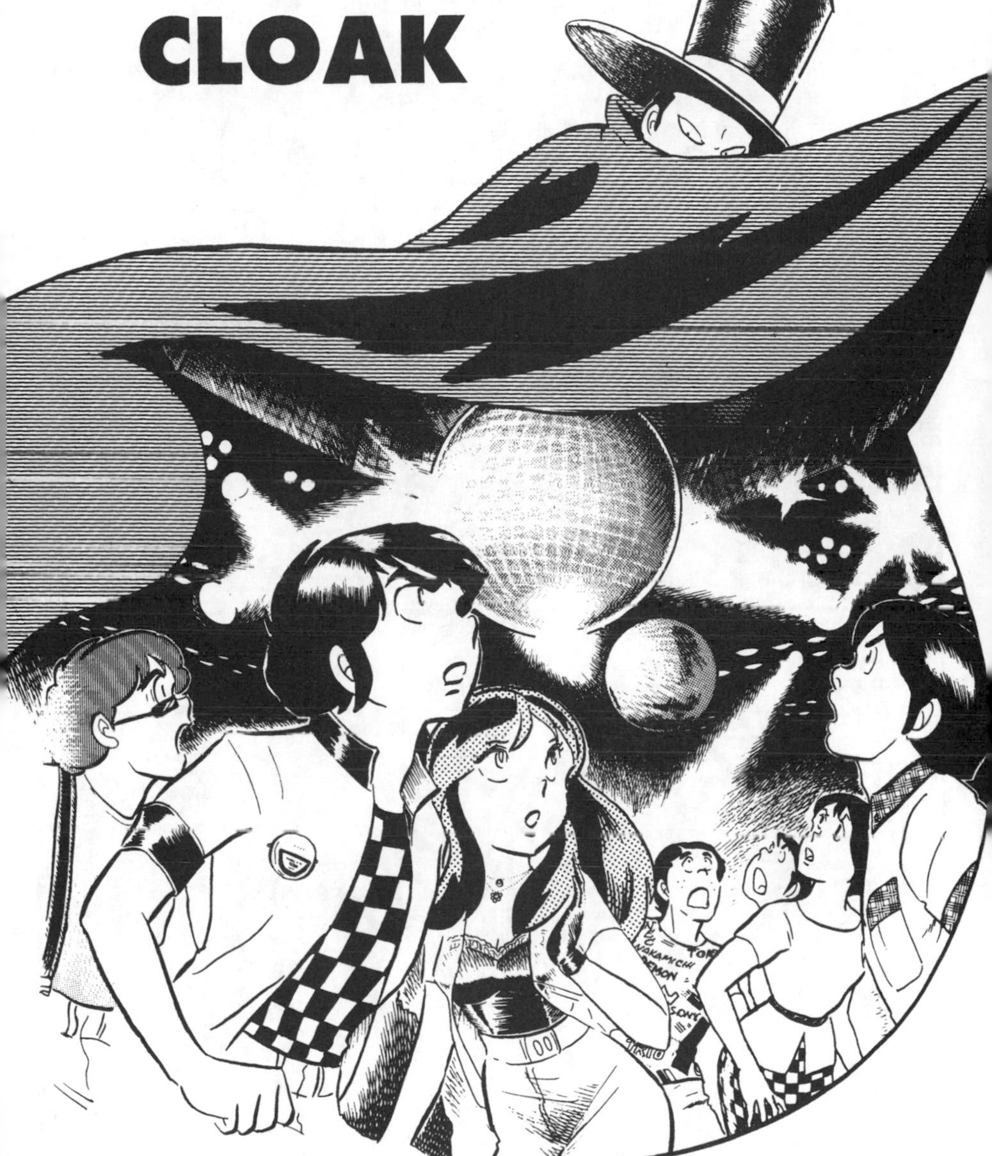

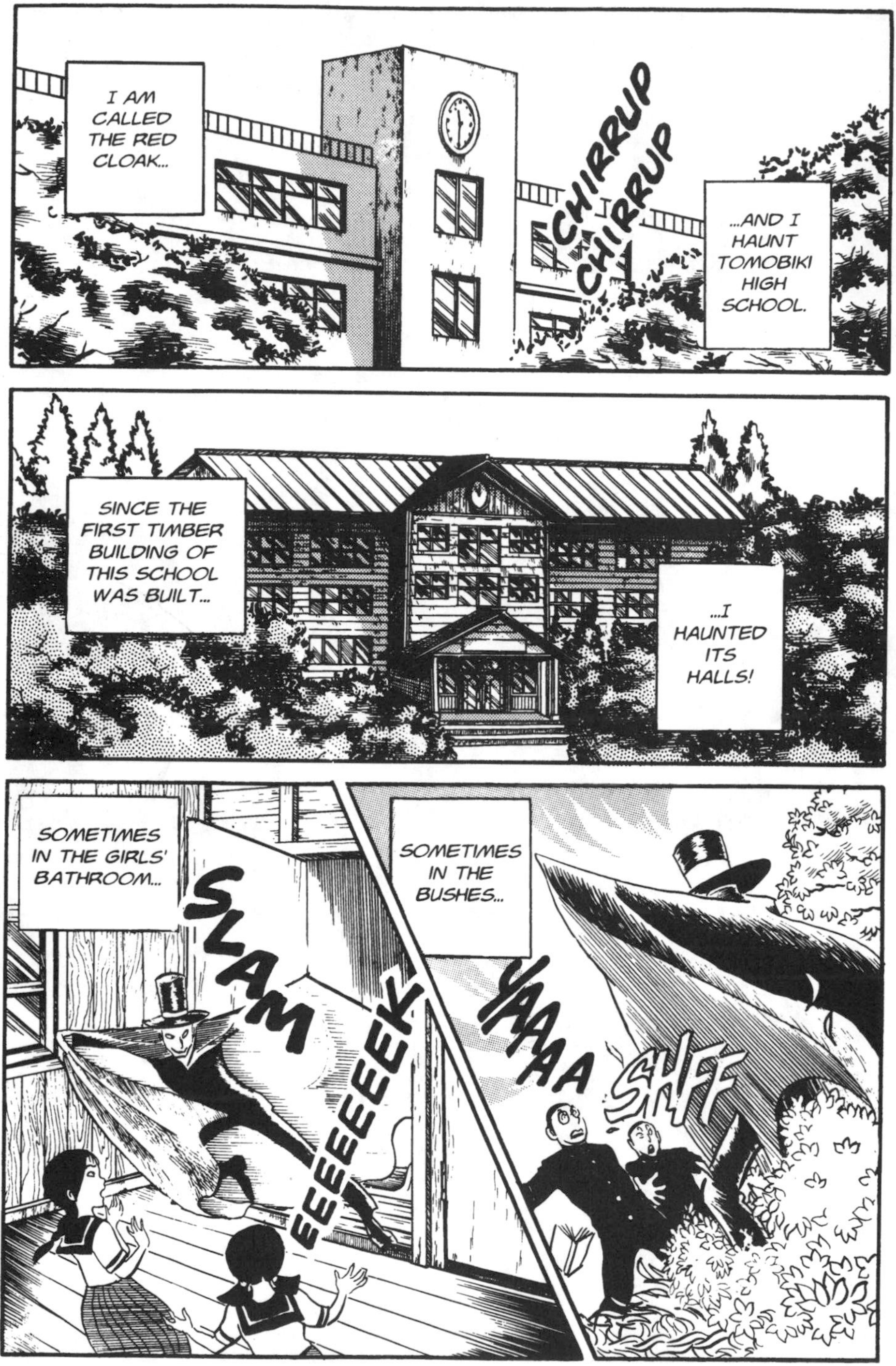
I AM CALLED THE RED CLOAK...
CHIRRUP CHIRRUP
...AND I HAUNT TOMOBIKI HIGH SCHOOL.
SINCE THE FIRST TIMBER BUILDING OF THIS SCHOOL WAS BUILT...
...I HAUNTED ITS HALLS!
SOMETIMES IN THE GIRLS' BATHROOM...
SLAM
EEEEEEEK
SOMETIMES IN THE BUSHES...
YAAAAA
SHFF

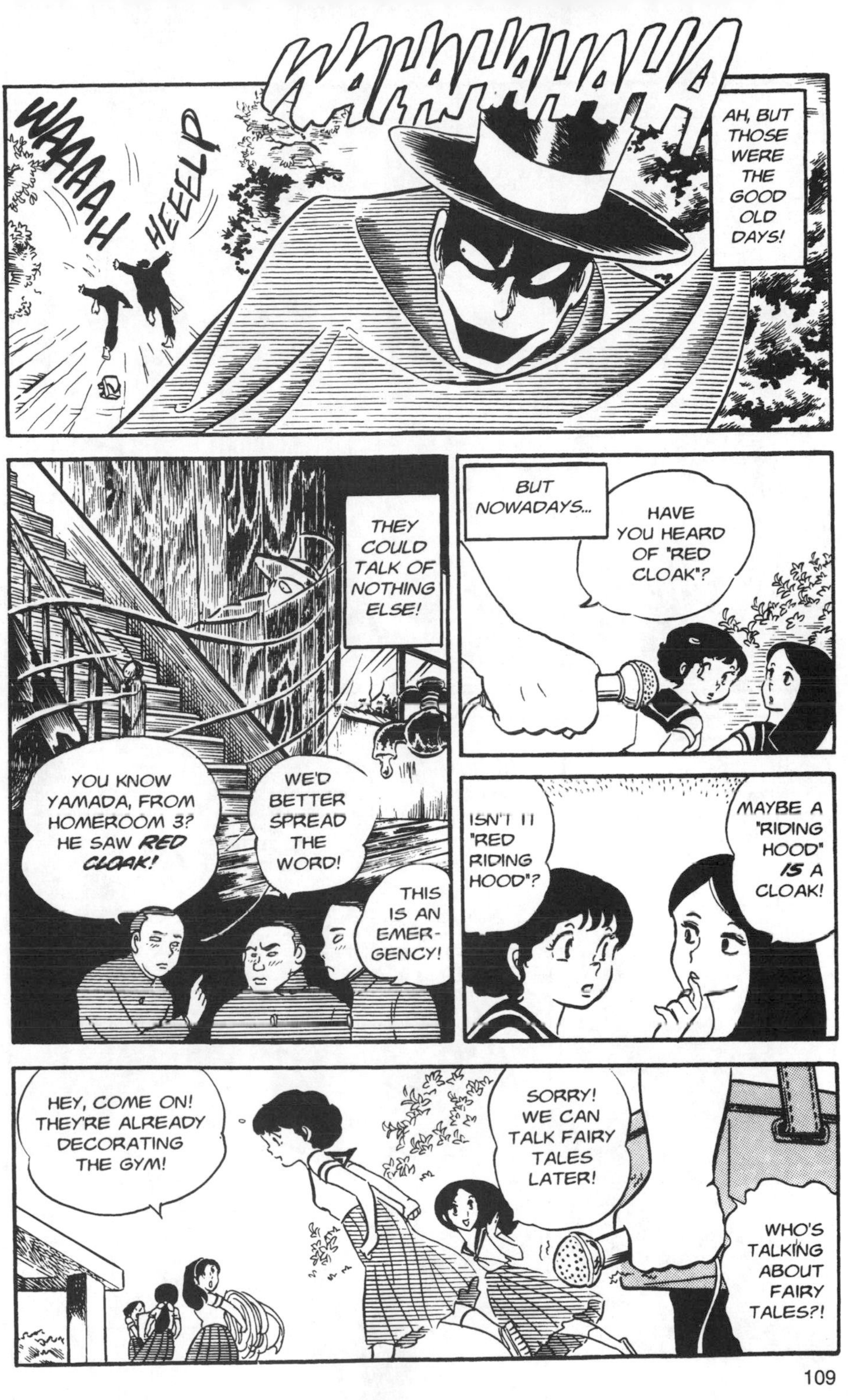
WAHAHAHAHAHA
WAAAAAH
HEEELP
AH, BUT THOSE WERE THE GOOD OLD DAYS!
THEY COULD TALK OF NOTHING ELSE!
YOU KNOW YAMADA, FROM HOMEROOM 3? HE SAW **RED CLOAK!**
WE'D BETTER SPREAD THE WORD!
THIS IS AN EMERGENCY!
BUT NOWADAYS...
HAVE YOU HEARD OF "RED CLOAK"?
ISN'T IT "RED RIDING HOOD"?
MAYBE A "RIDING HOOD" ***IS*** A CLOAK!
HEY, COME ON! THEY'RE ALREADY DECORATING THE GYM!
SORRY! WE CAN TALK FAIRY TALES LATER!
WHO'S TALKING ABOUT FAIRY TALES?!

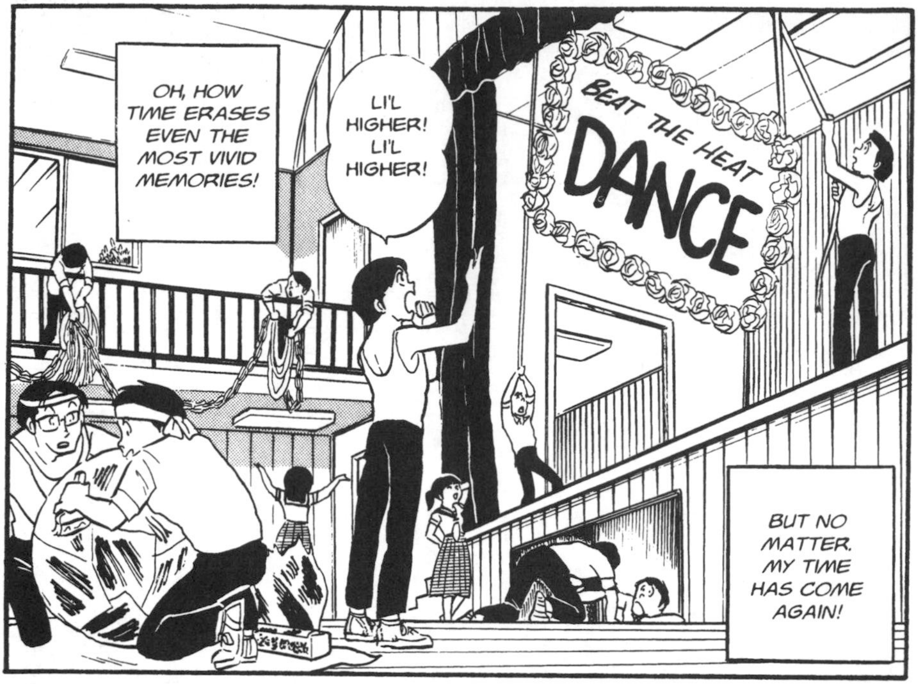
OH, HOW TIME ERASES EVEN THE MOST VIVID MEMORIES!
LI'L HIGHER! LI'L HIGHER!
BEAT THE HEAT DANCE
BUT NO MATTER. MY TIME HAS COME AGAIN!

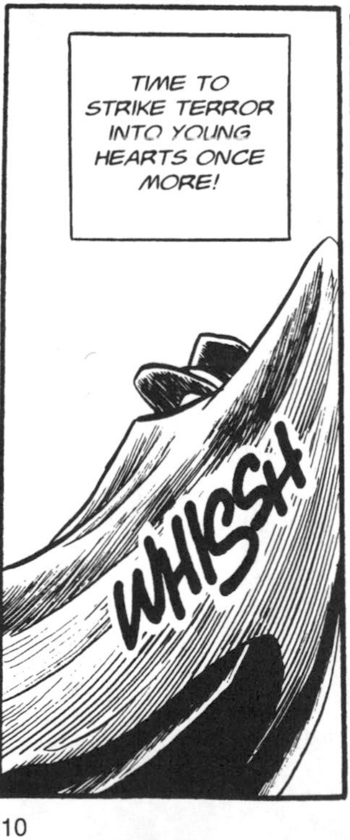
TIME TO STRIKE TERROR INTO YOUNG HEARTS ONCE MORE!
WHISSH

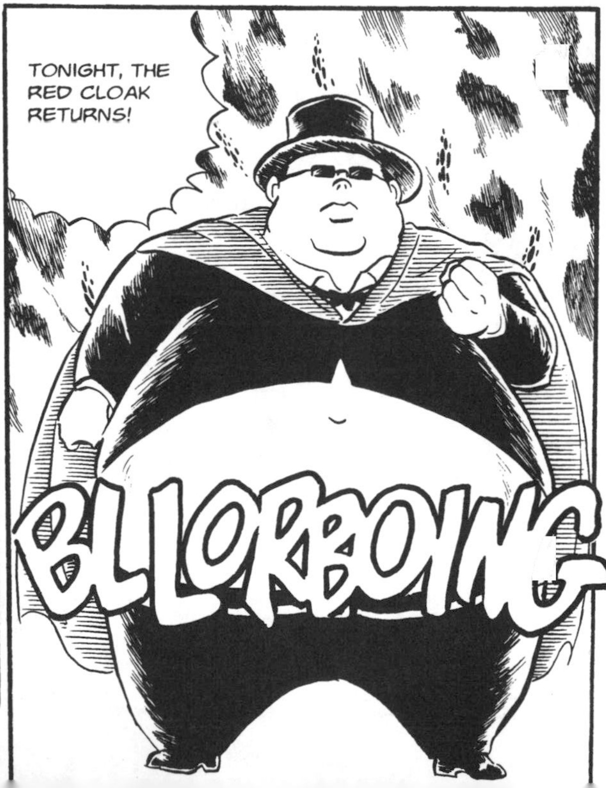
TONIGHT, THE RED CLOAK RETURNS!
BLLORBOING

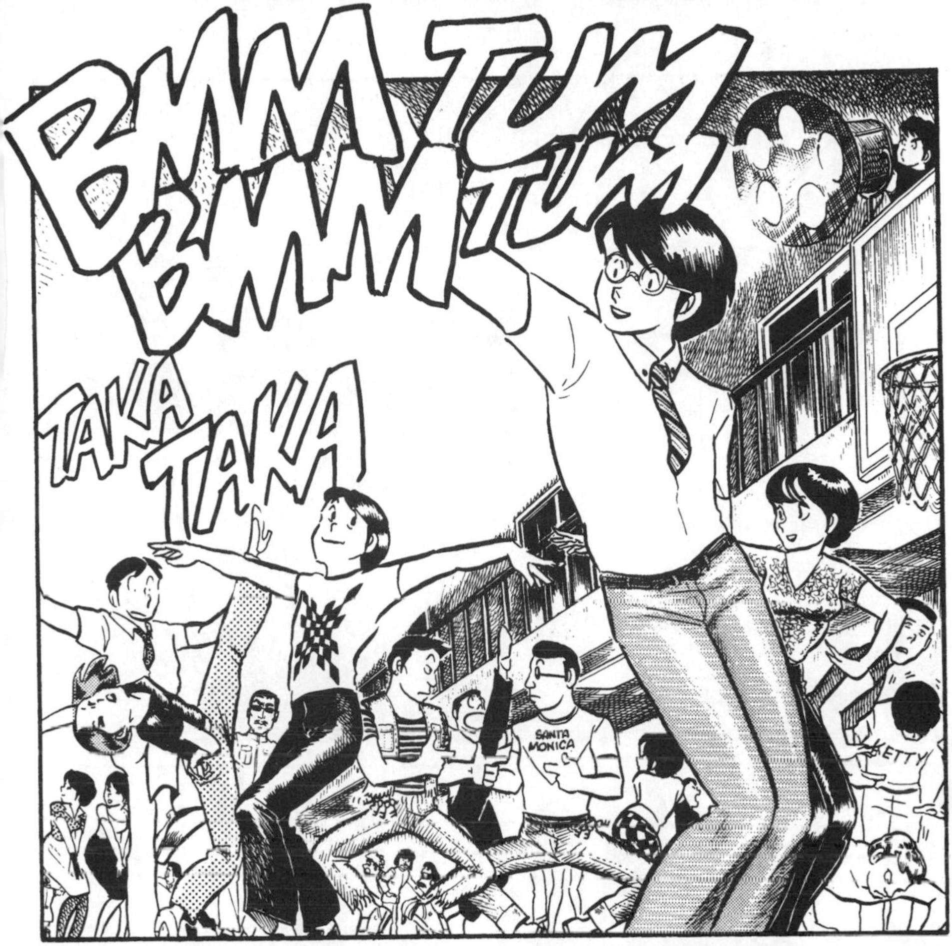
BMM TUM
BMM TUM
TAKA
TAKA
SANTA MONICA
KETTY

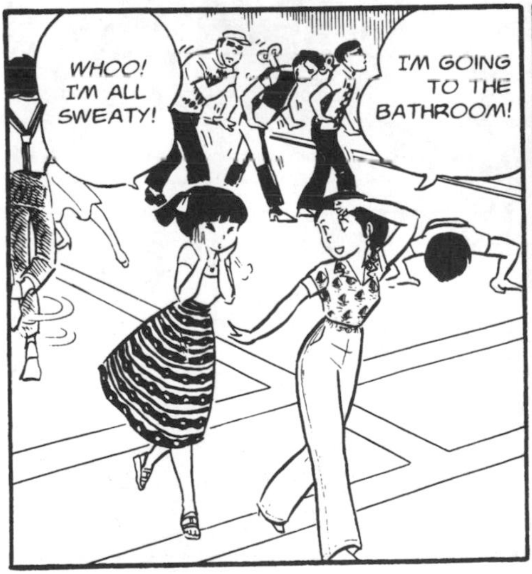
WHOO! I'M ALL SWEATY!
I'M GOING TO THE BATHROOM!

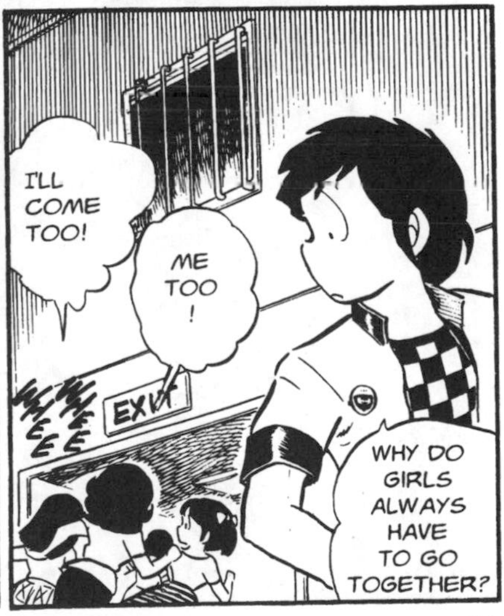
I'LL COME TOO!
ME TOO !
EXIT
WHY DO GIRLS ALWAYS HAVE TO GO TOGETHER?

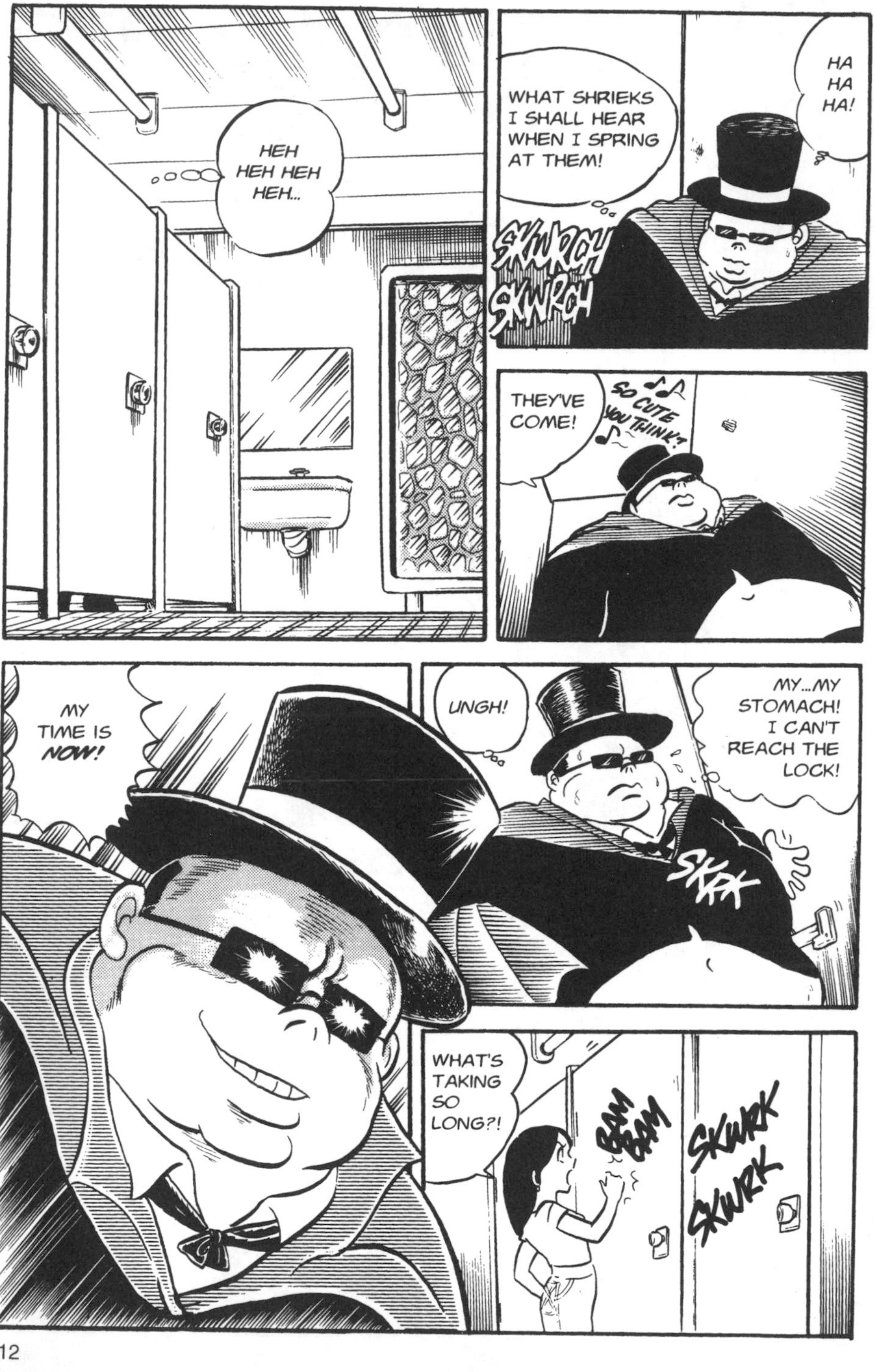
HEH HEH HEH HEH...
WHAT SHRIEKS I SHALL HEAR WHEN I SPRING AT THEM!
HA HA HA!
SKWRCH SKWRCH
THEY'VE COME!
SO CUTE YOU THINK?
MY TIME IS NOW!
UNGH!
MY...MY STOMACH! I CAN'T REACH THE LOCK!
SKRK
WHAT'S TAKING SO LONG?!
BAM BAM
SKWRK SKWRK

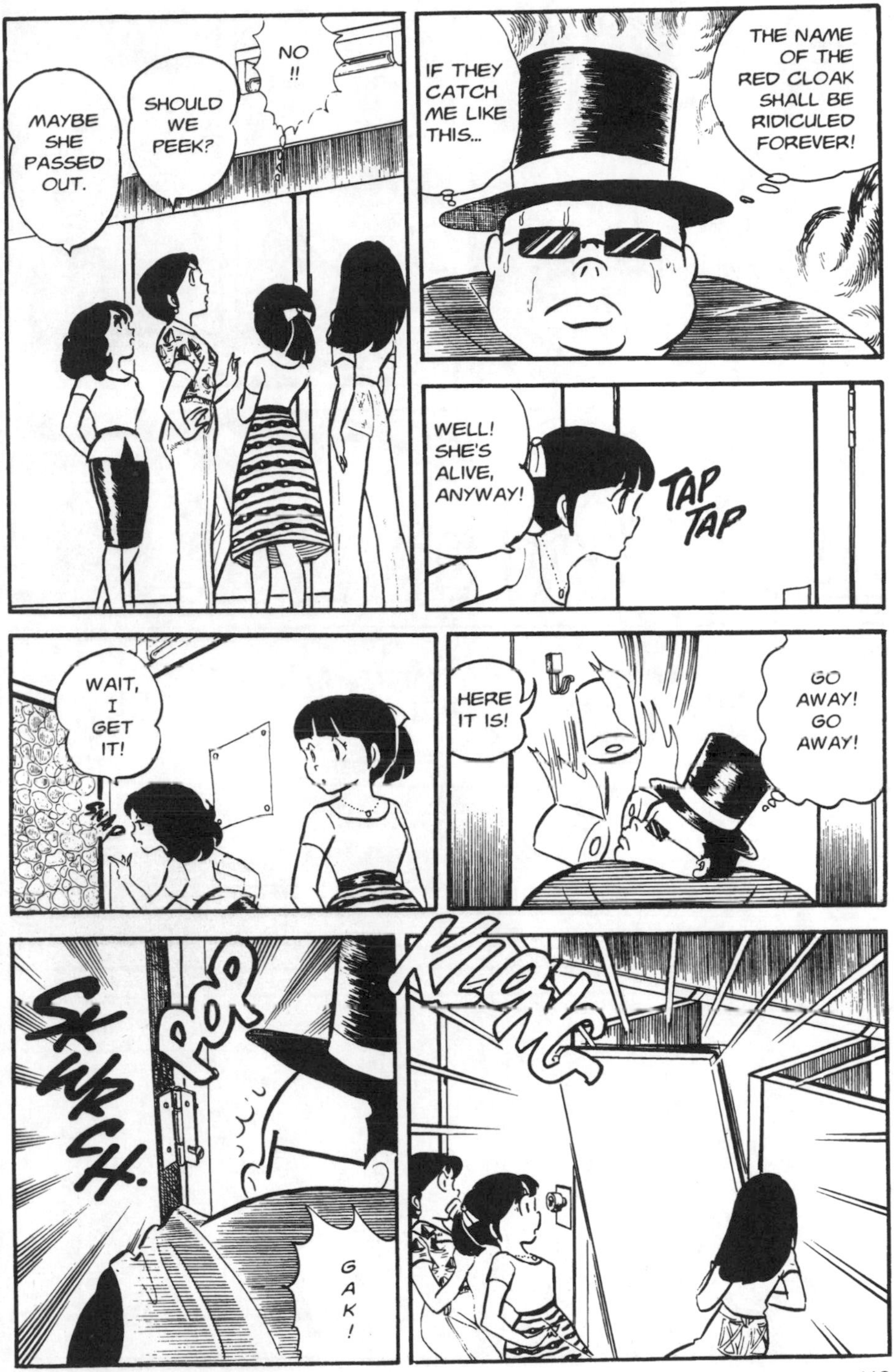
MAYBE SHE PASSED OUT.
SHOULD WE PEEK?
NO !!
IF THEY CATCH ME LIKE THIS...
THE NAME OF THE RED CLOAK SHALL BE RIDICULED FOREVER!
WELL! SHE'S ALIVE, ANYWAY!
TAP TAP
WAIT, I GET IT!
HERE IT IS!
GO AWAY! GO AWAY!
SKWRCH.
POP
GAK!
KLONK

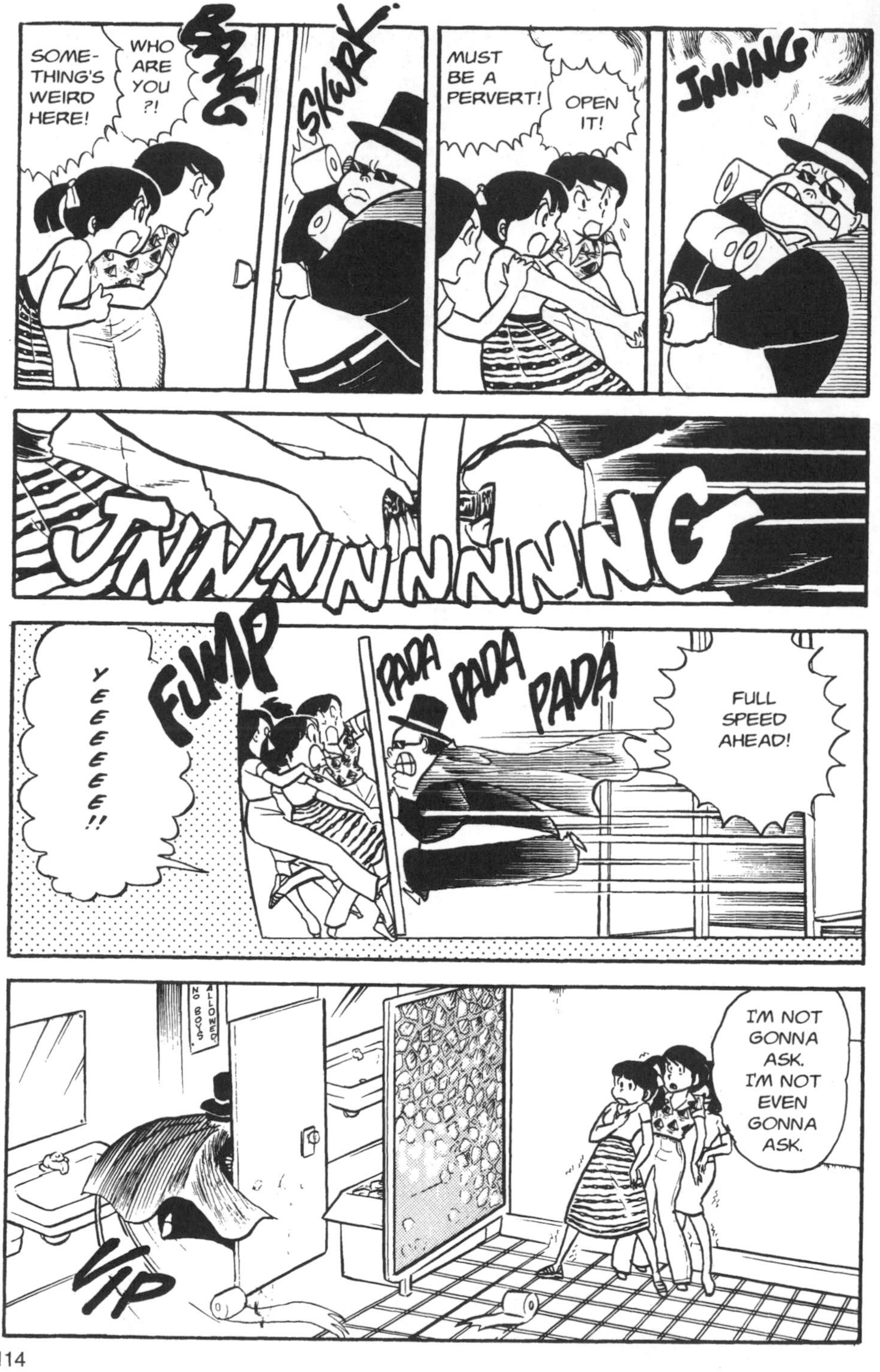
SOME-THING'S WEIRD HERE!
WHO ARE YOU ?!
BANG
SKWRK
MUST BE A PERVERT!
OPEN IT!
JNNNG
JNNNNNNNNG
YEEEEEEE!!
FUMP
PADA BADA PADA
FULL SPEED AHEAD!
NO BOYS ALLOWED
VIP
I'M NOT GONNA ASK. I'M NOT EVEN GONNA ASK.

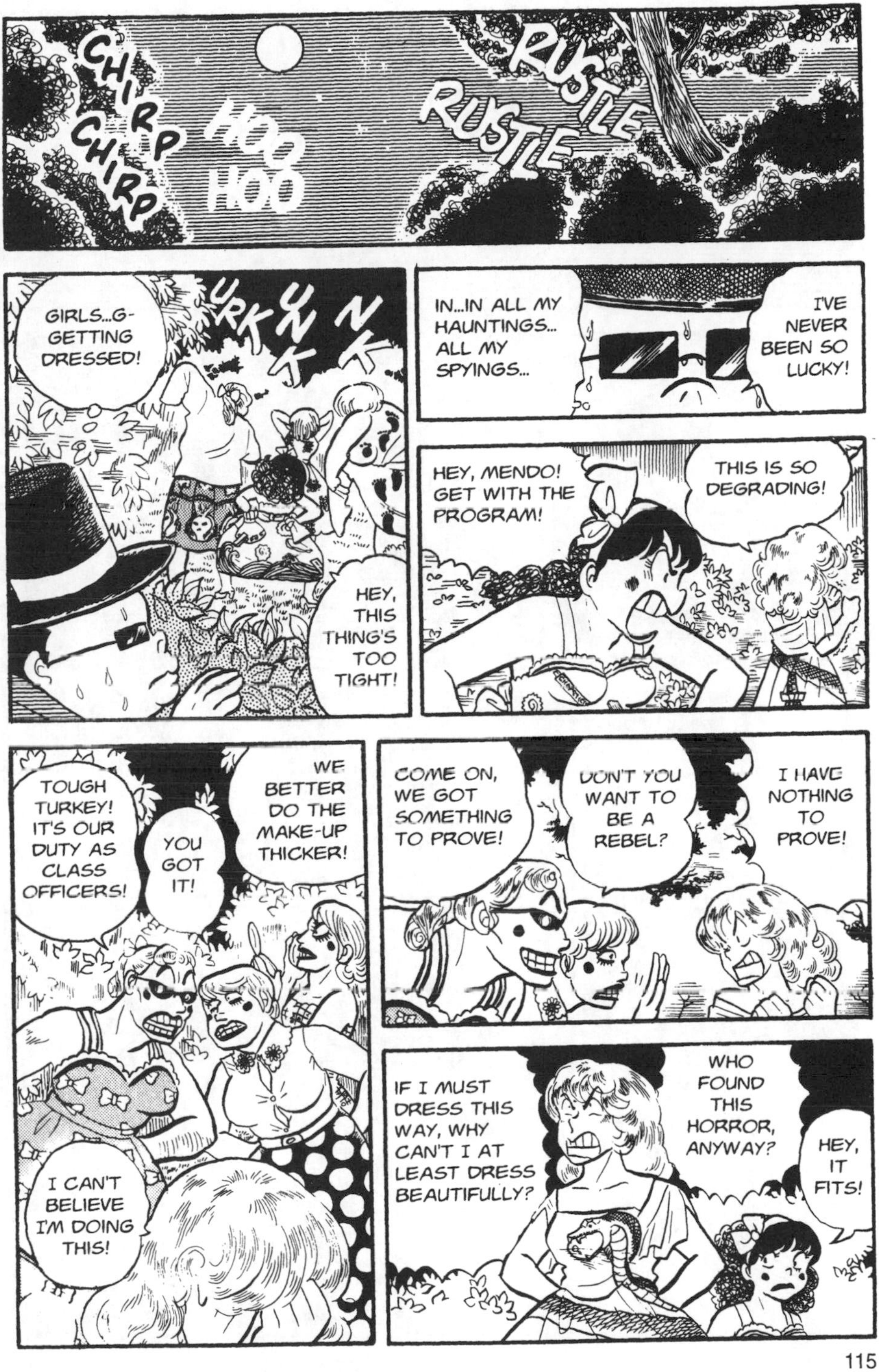
CHIRP CHIRP
CHIRP CHIRP
HOO HOO
RUSTLE
RUSTLE
GIRLS...G-GETTING DRESSED!
URK
JUNK JUNK
HEY, THIS THING'S TOO TIGHT!
IN...IN ALL MY HAUNTINGS... ALL MY SPYINGS...
I'VE NEVER BEEN SO LUCKY!
HEY, MENDO! GET WITH THE PROGRAM!
THIS IS SO DEGRADING!
TOUGH TURKEY! IT'S OUR DUTY AS CLASS OFFICERS!
YOU GOT IT!
WE BETTER DO THE MAKE-UP THICKER!
I CAN'T BELIEVE I'M DOING THIS!
COME ON, WE GOT SOMETHING TO PROVE!
DON'T YOU WANT TO BE A REBEL?
I HAVE NOTHING TO PROVE!
IF I MUST DRESS THIS WAY, WHY CAN'T I AT LEAST DRESS BEAUTIFULLY?
WHO FOUND THIS HORROR, ANYWAY?
HEY, IT FITS!

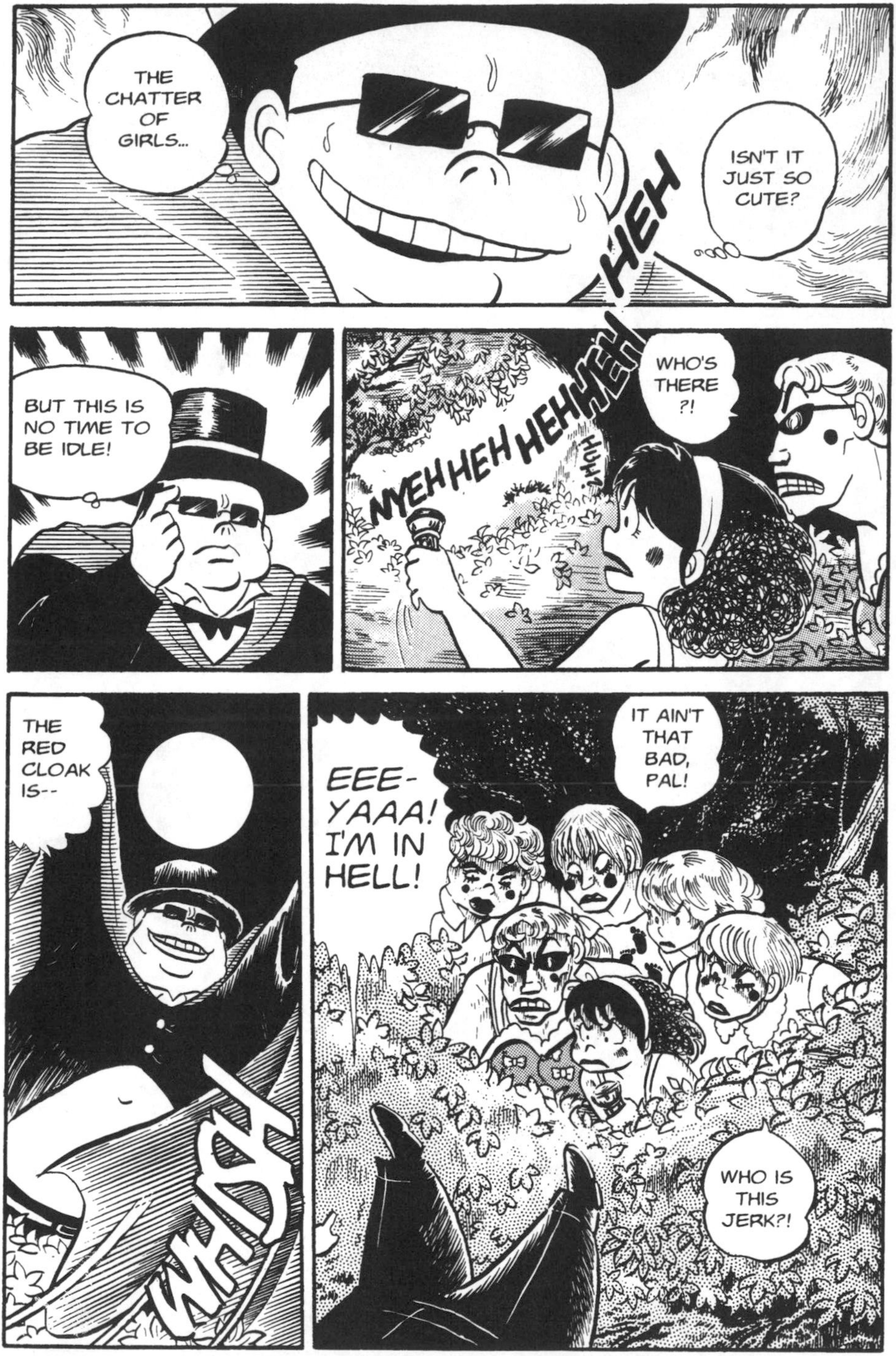
THE CHATTER OF GIRLS...
ISN'T IT JUST SO CUTE?
BUT THIS IS NO TIME TO BE IDLE!
NYEH HEH HEH HEH HEH HEH
HUH?!
WHO'S THERE ?!
THE RED CLOAK IS--
WHISH
EEE-YAAA! I'M IN HELL!
IT AIN'T THAT BAD, PAL!
WHO IS THIS JERK?!

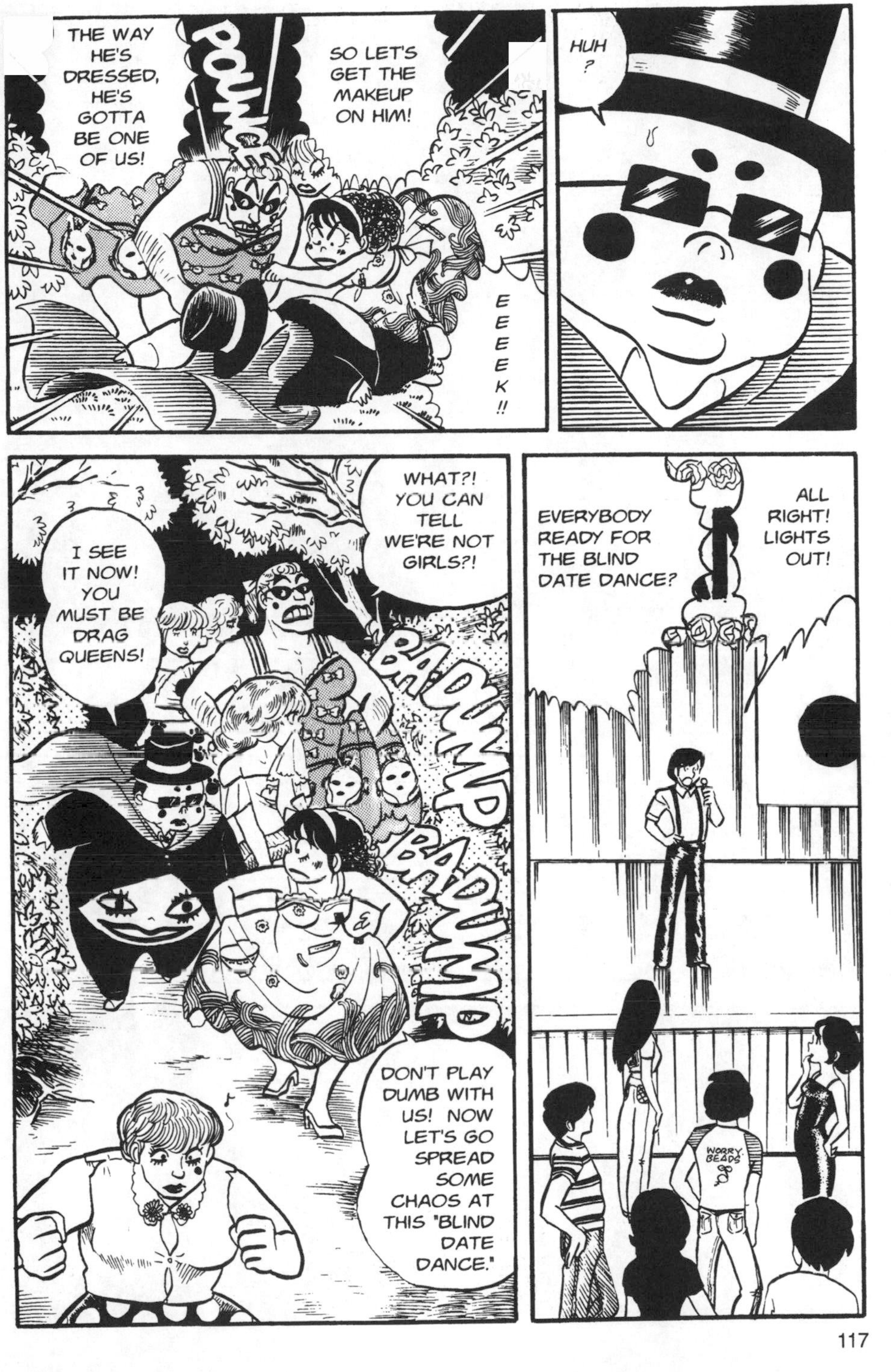
THE WAY HE'S DRESSED, HE'S GOTTA BE ONE OF US!
POUNCE
SO LET'S GET THE MAKEUP ON HIM!
EEEEEK!!
HUH?
I SEE IT NOW! YOU MUST BE DRAG QUEENS!
WHAT?! YOU CAN TELL WE'RE NOT GIRLS?!
BADUMP
BADUMP
BADUMP
DON'T PLAY DUMB WITH US! NOW LET'S GO SPREAD SOME CHAOS AT THIS "BLIND DATE DANCE."
EVERYBODY READY FOR THE BLIND DATE DANCE?
ALL RIGHT! LIGHTS OUT!
WORRY BEADS

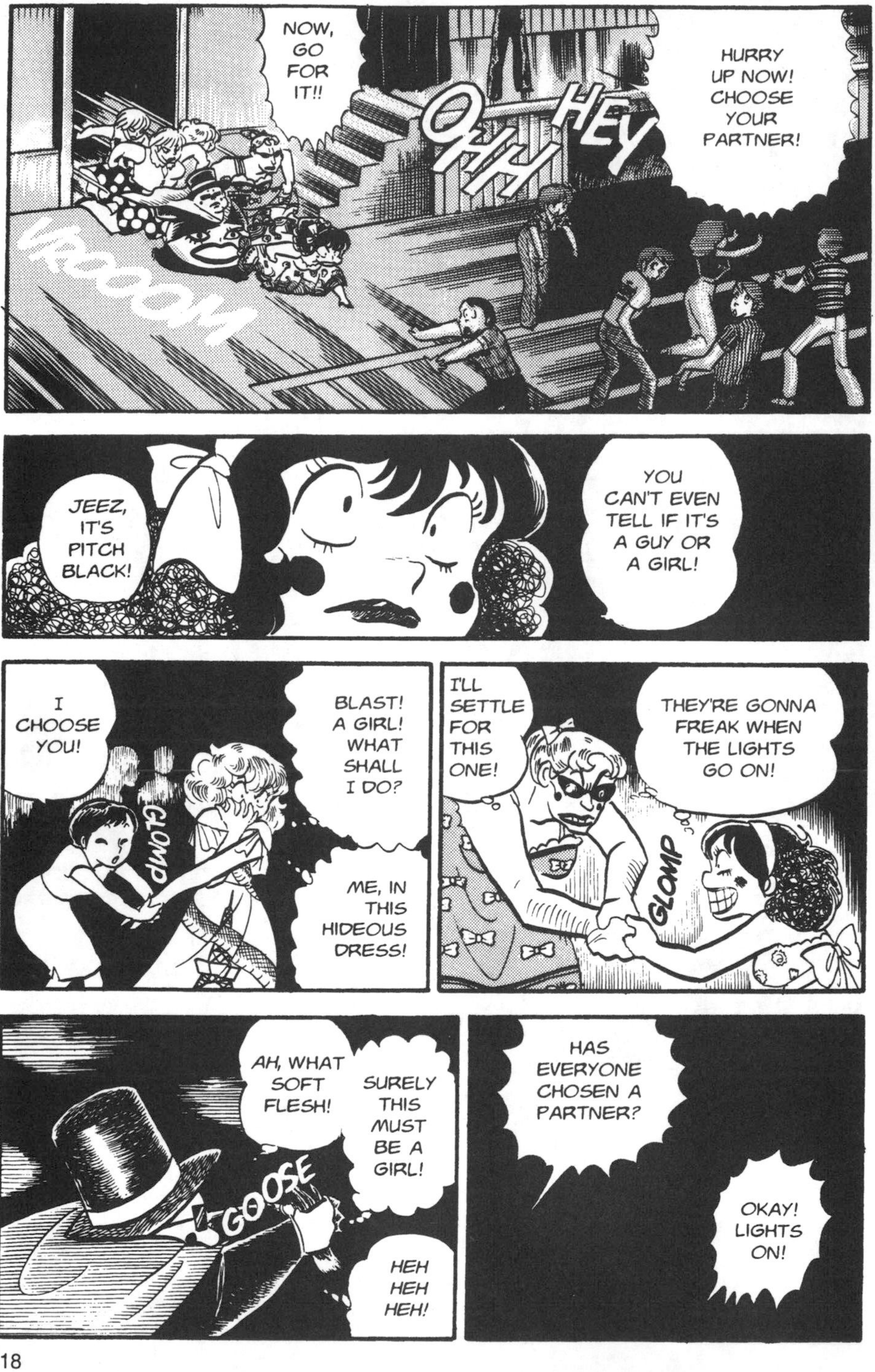
NOW, GO FOR IT!!
VROOOM
OHH
HEY
HURRY UP NOW! CHOOSE YOUR PARTNER!
JEEZ, IT'S PITCH BLACK!
YOU CAN'T EVEN TELL IF IT'S A GUY OR A GIRL!
I CHOOSE YOU!
GLOMP
BLAST! A GIRL! WHAT SHALL I DO?
ME, IN THIS HIDEOUS DRESS!
I'LL SETTLE FOR THIS ONE!
THEY'RE GONNA FREAK WHEN THE LIGHTS GO ON!
GLOMP
AH, WHAT SOFT FLESH!
SURELY THIS MUST BE A GIRL!
GOOSE
HEH HEH HEH!
HAS EVERYONE CHOSEN A PARTNER?
OKAY! LIGHTS ON!

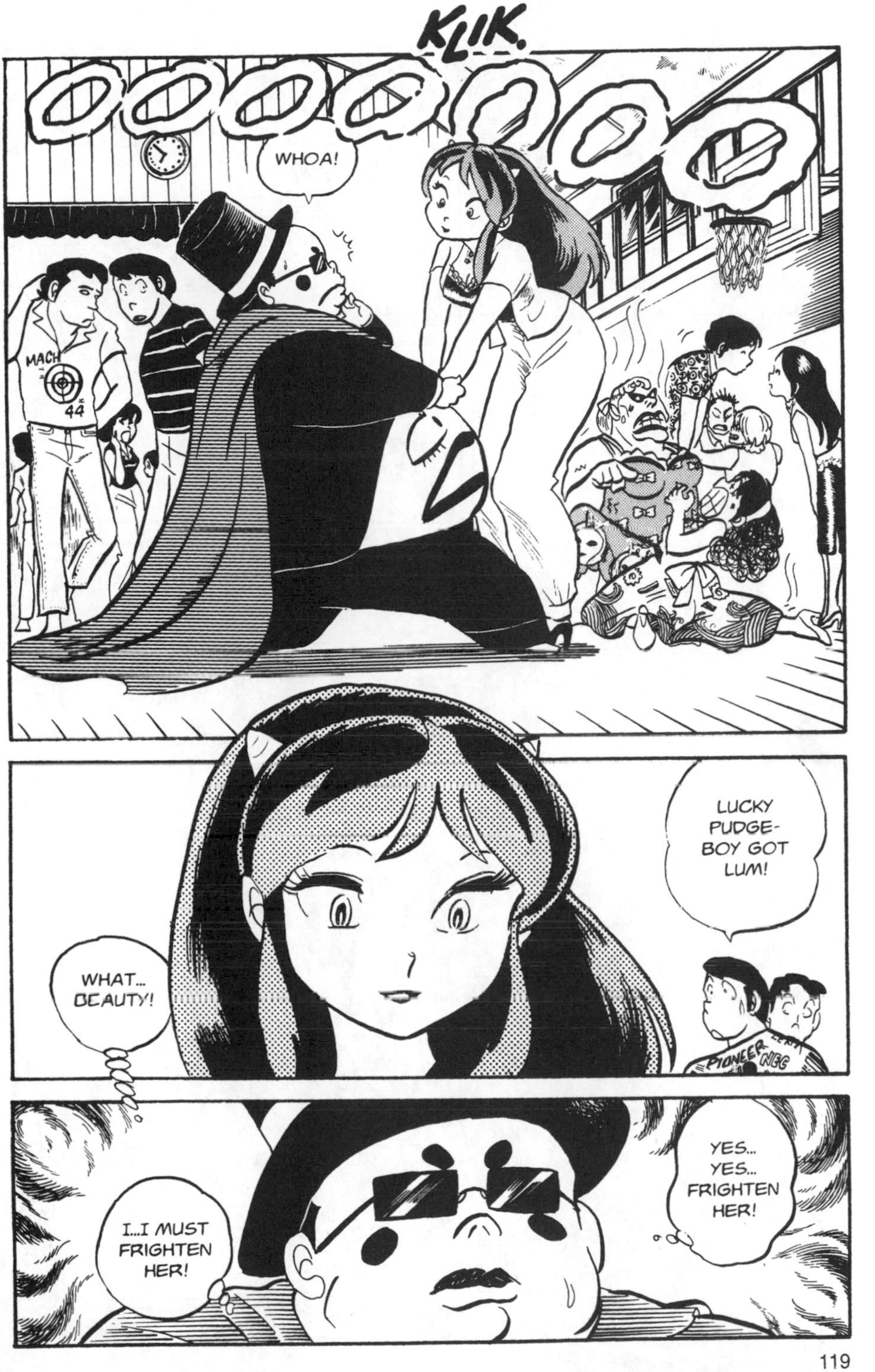
KLIK.
WHOA!
MACH
44
WHAT... BEAUTY!
LUCKY PUDGE-BOY GOT LUM!
PIONEER
I...I MUST FRIGHTEN HER!
YES... YES... FRIGHTEN HER!

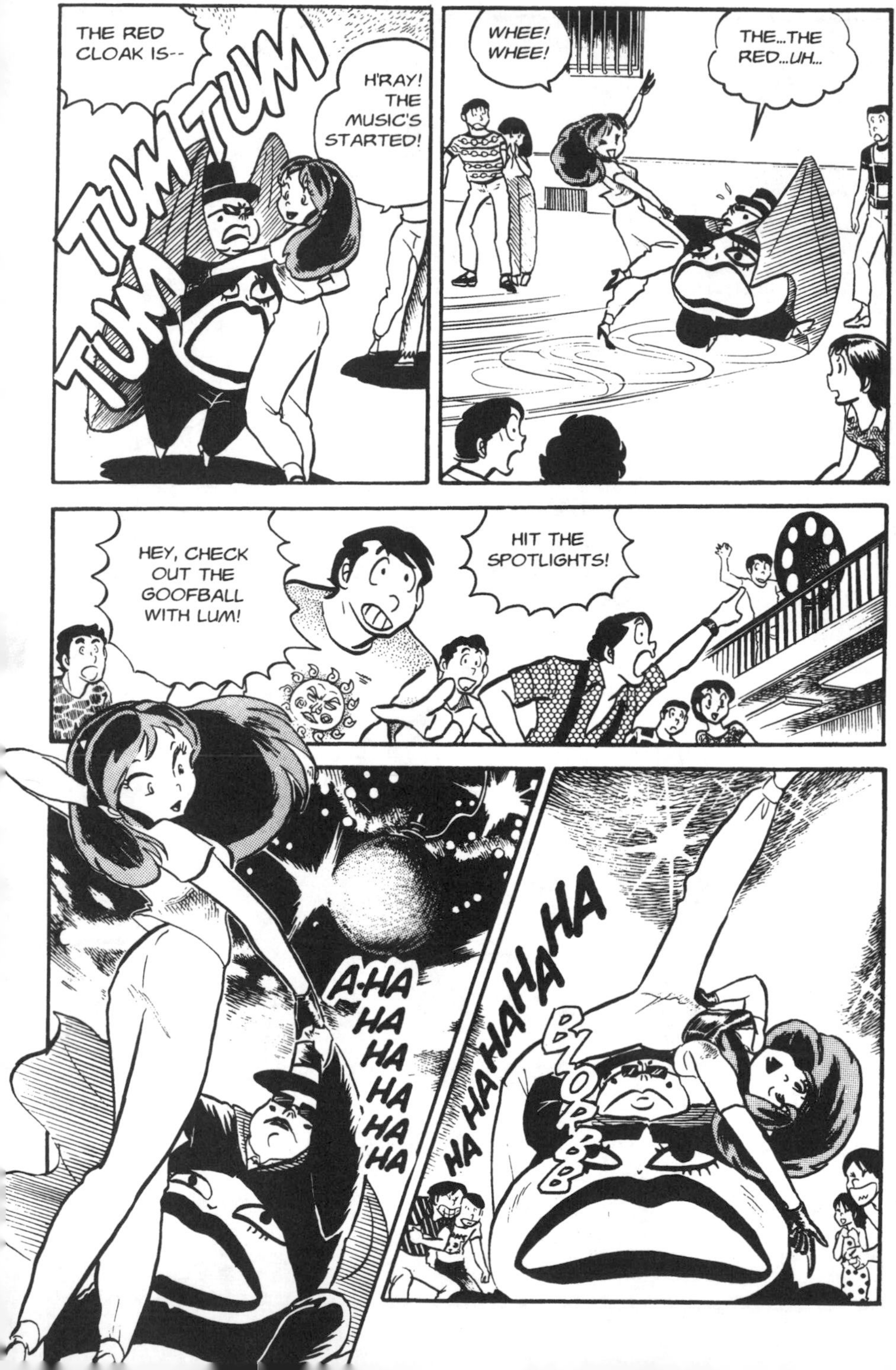
THE RED CLOAK IS--
TUM TUM TUM TUM
H'RAY! THE MUSIC'S STARTED!
WHEE! WHEE!
THE...THE RED...UH...
HEY, CHECK OUT THE GOOFBALL WITH LUM!
HIT THE SPOTLIGHTS!
A-HA HA HA HA HA HA HA
HA HA HA HA HA HA HA
BLOOPBOOB

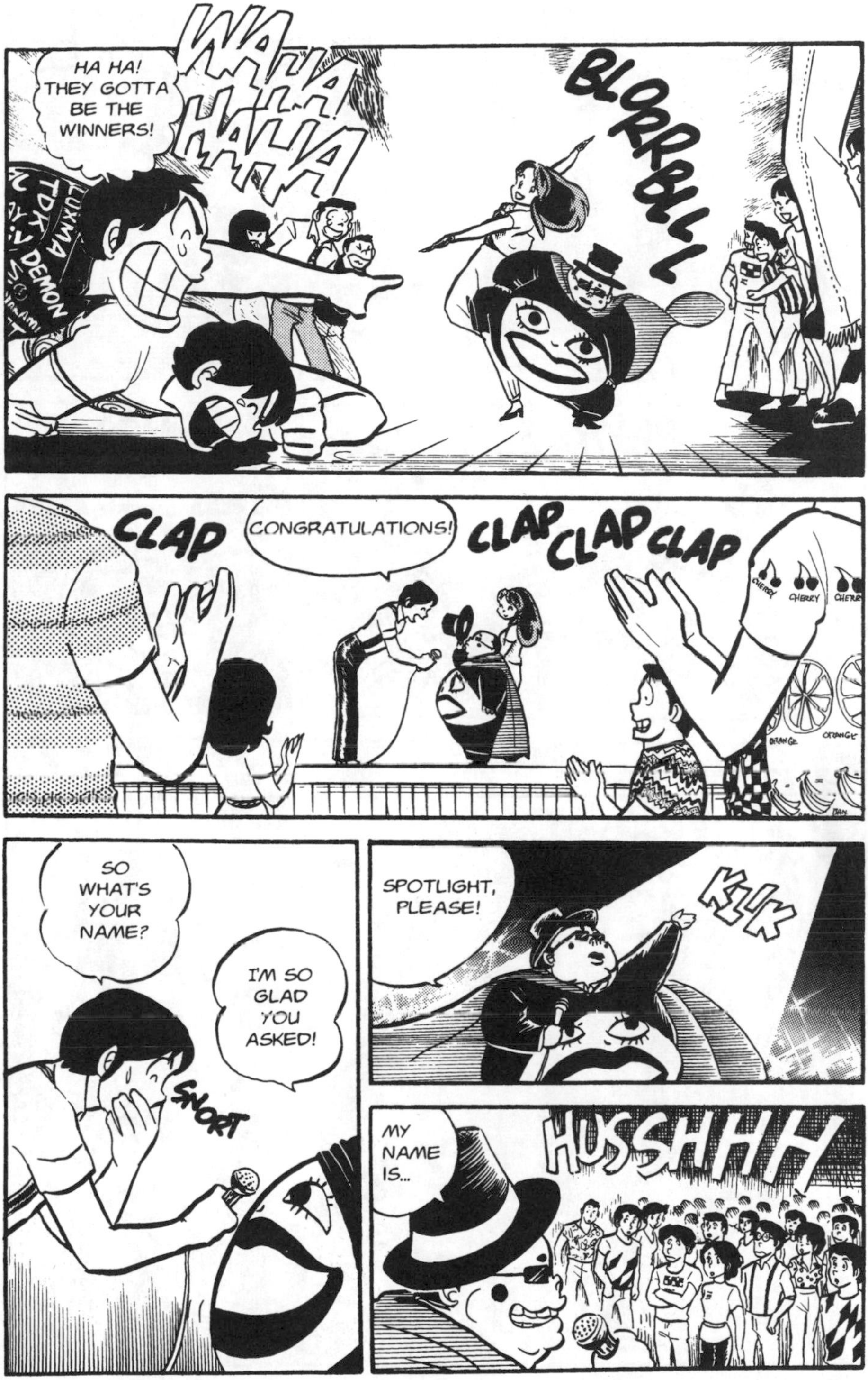
HA HA! THEY GOTTA BE THE WINNERS!
WAHAHA HA-HA! HAHA
BLORRBLLL
LUXMA
TDK
DEMON
CLAP
CONGRATULATIONS!
CLAP CLAP CLAP
CHERRY
CHERRY
CHERRY
ORANGE
ORANGE
SO WHAT'S YOUR NAME?
I'M SO GLAD YOU ASKED!
SNORT
SPOTLIGHT, PLEASE!
KLIK
MY NAME IS...
HUSSHHH

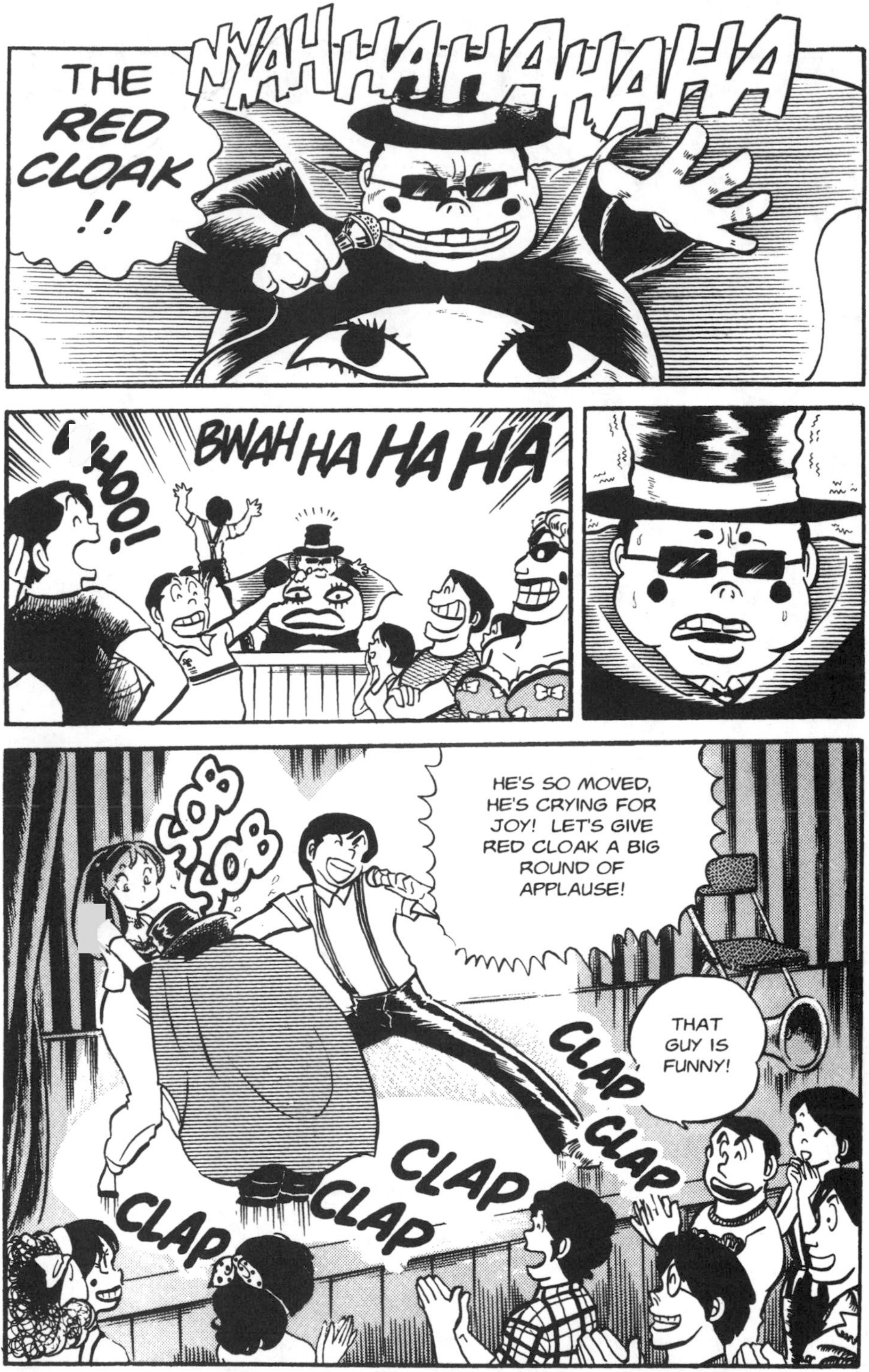
THE RED CLOAK !!
NYAHHAHAHAHAHA
HOO!
BWAH HA HA HA HA
SOB SOB
HE'S SO MOVED, HE'S CRYING FOR JOY! LET'S GIVE RED CLOAK A BIG ROUND OF APPLAUSE!
THAT GUY IS FUNNY!
CLAP CLAP
CLAP CLAP
CLAP CLAP

PART EIGHT
SURF'S UP!

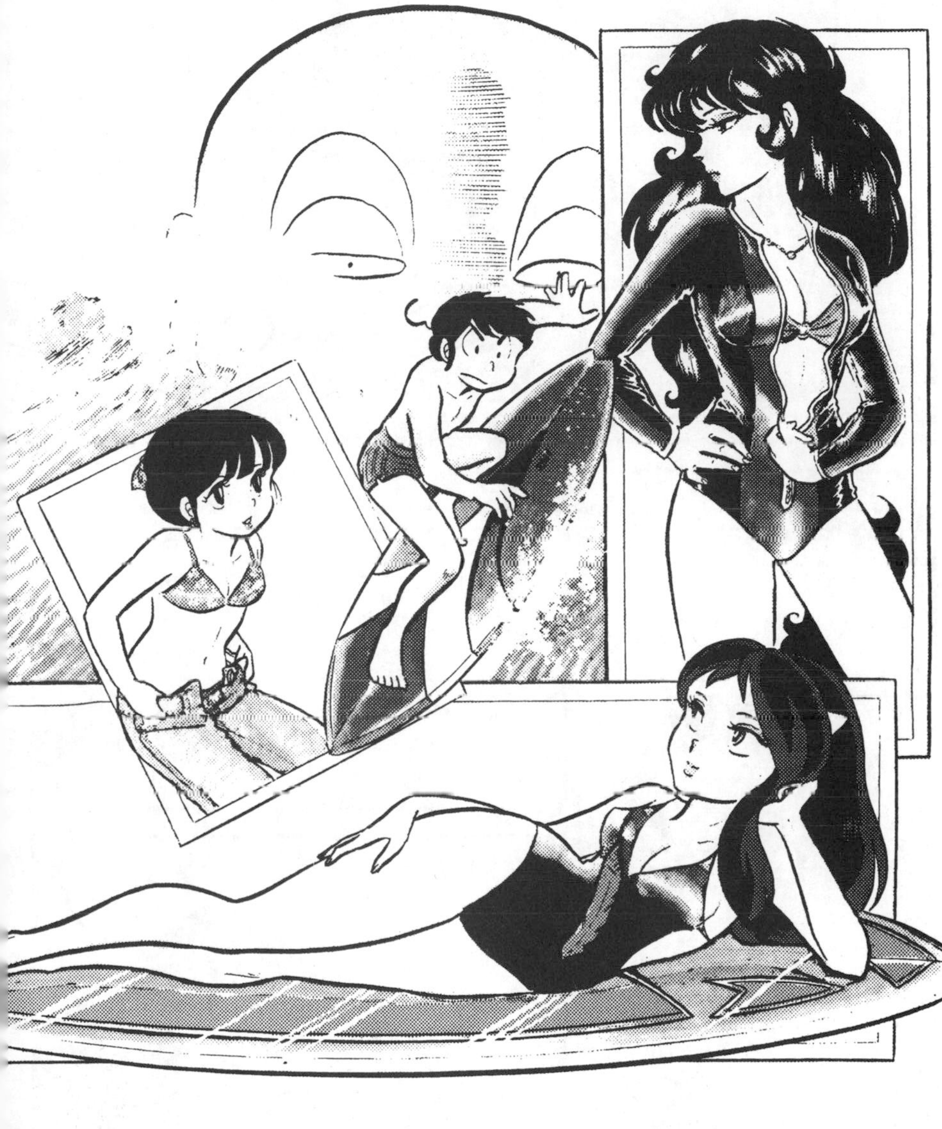

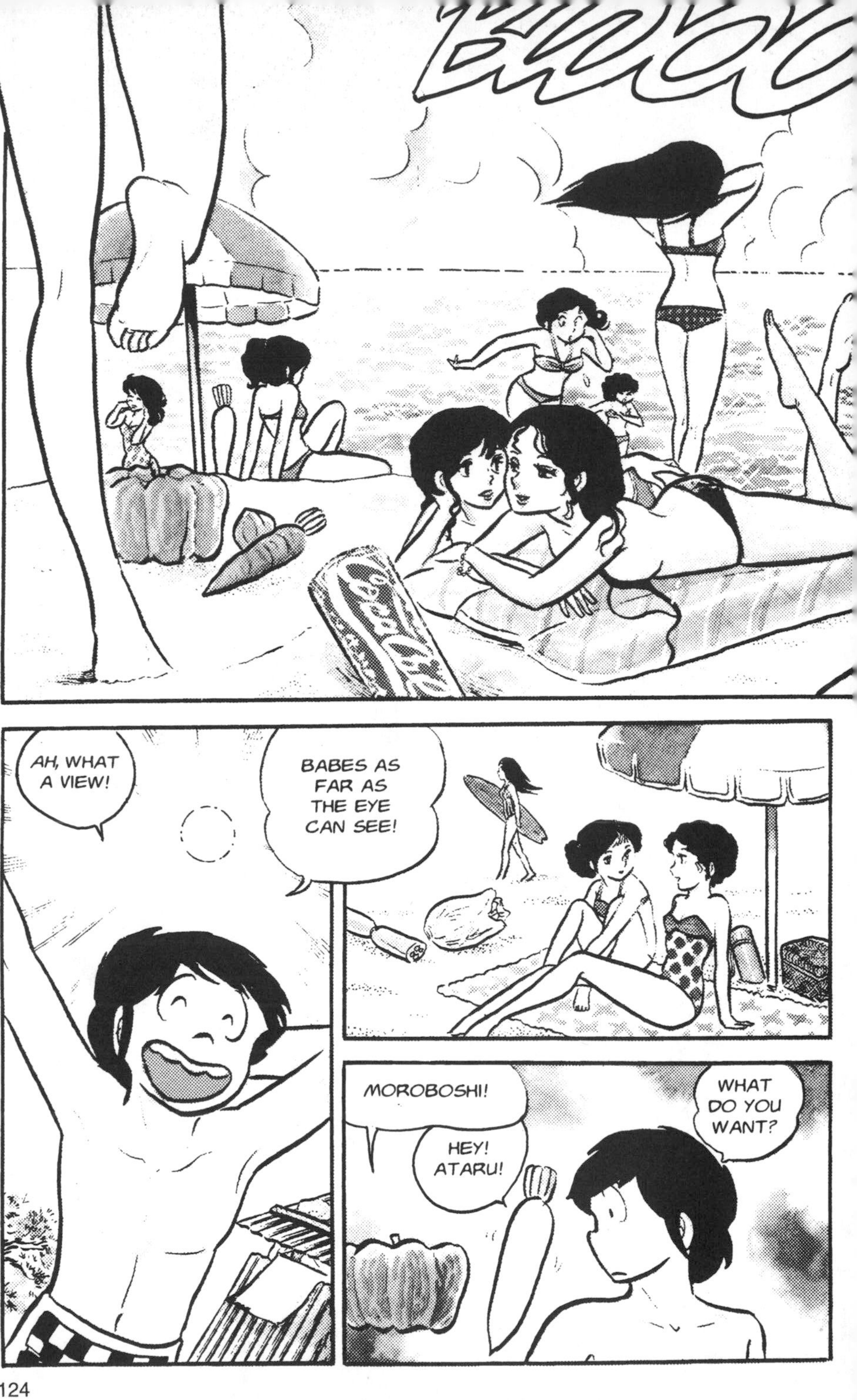
AH, WHAT A VIEW!
BABES AS FAR AS THE EYE CAN SEE!
MOROBOSHI!
HEY! ATARU!
WHAT DO YOU WANT?

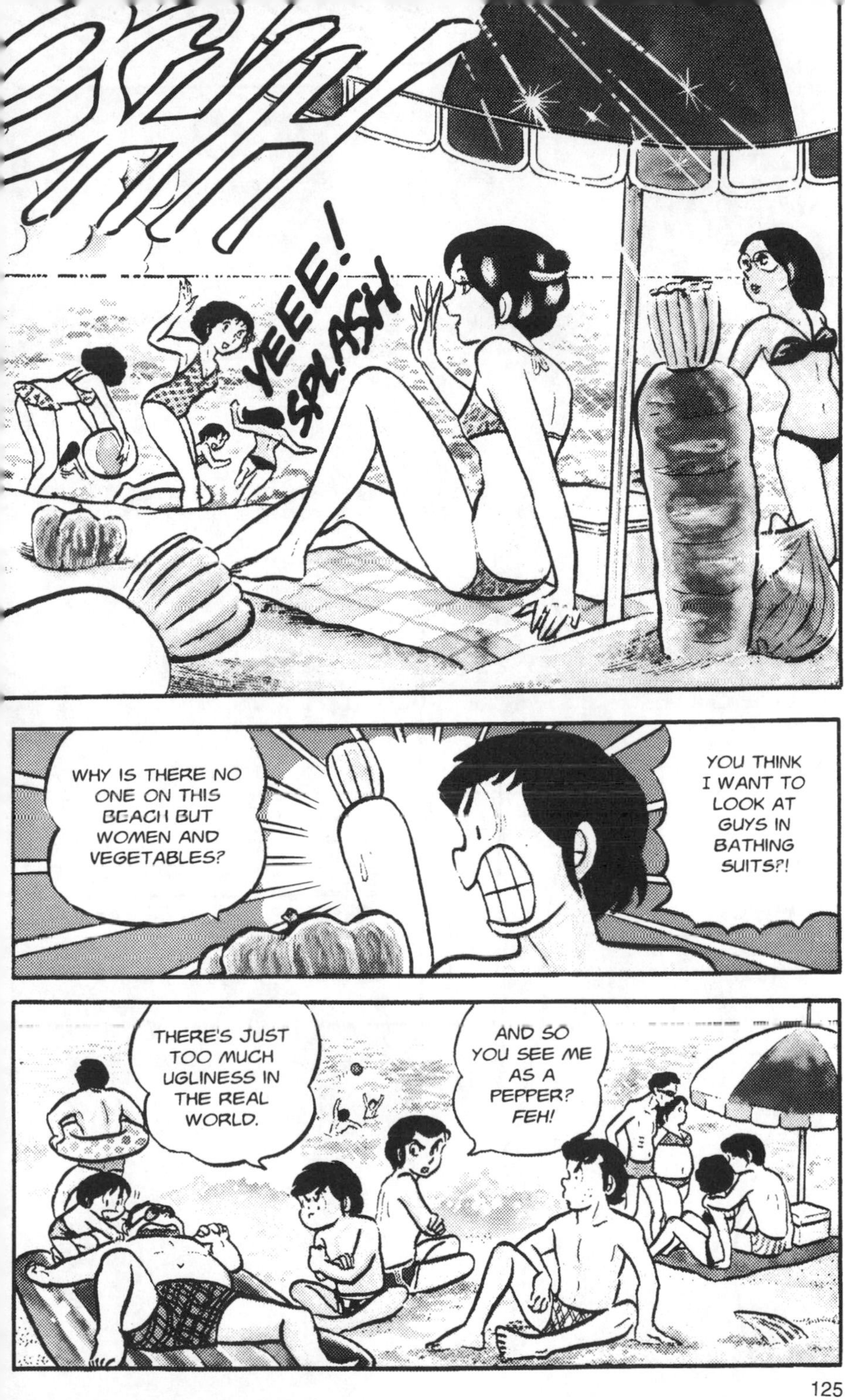
YEEE! SPLASH
WHY IS THERE NO ONE ON THIS BEACH BUT WOMEN AND VEGETABLES?
YOU THINK I WANT TO LOOK AT GUYS IN BATHING SUITS?!
THERE'S JUST TOO MUCH UGLINESS IN THE REAL WORLD.
AND SO YOU SEE ME AS A PEPPER? FEH!

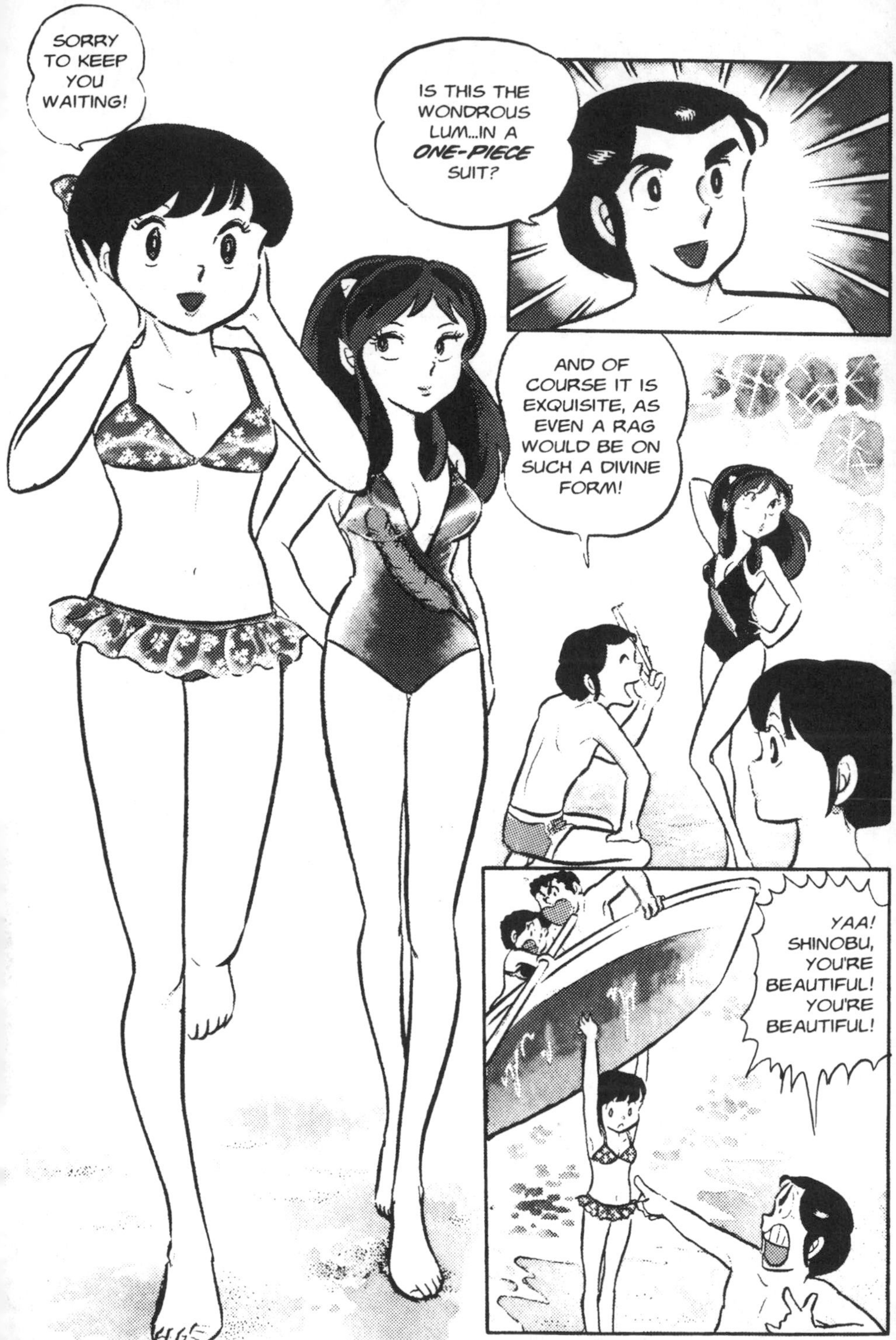
SORRY TO KEEP YOU WAITING!
IS THIS THE WONDROUS LUM...IN A *ONE-PIECE* SUIT?
AND OF COURSE IT IS EXQUISITE, AS EVEN A RAG WOULD BE ON SUCH A DIVINE FORM!
YAA! SHINOBU, YOU'RE BEAUTIFUL! YOU'RE BEAUTIFUL!

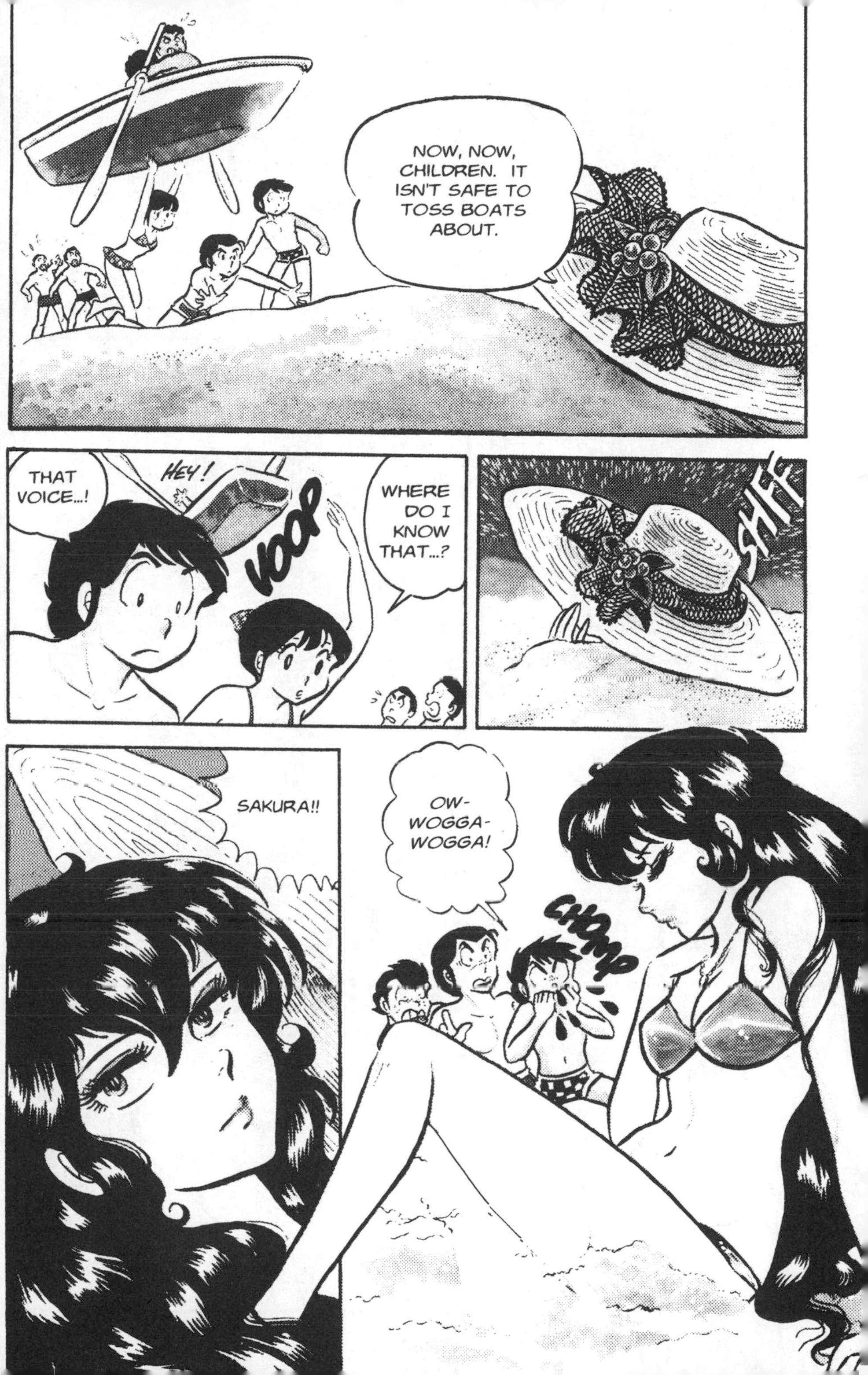
NOW, NOW, CHILDREN. IT ISN'T SAFE TO TOSS BOATS ABOUT.
THAT VOICE...!
HEY!
VOOP
WHERE DO I KNOW THAT...?
SHFF
SAKURA!!
OW-WOGGA-WOGGA!
CHOMP

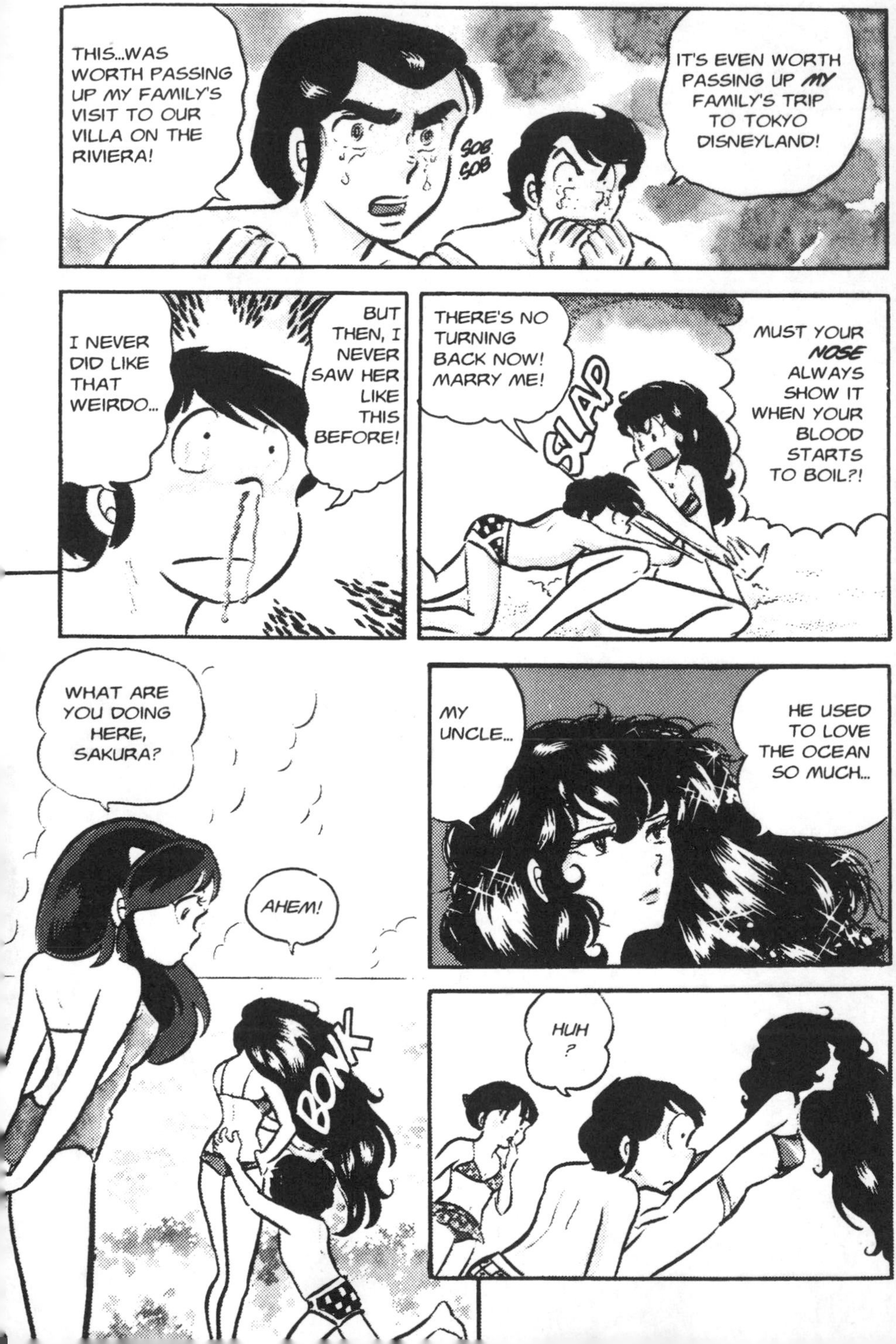
THIS...WAS WORTH PASSING UP MY FAMILY'S VISIT TO OUR VILLA ON THE RIVIERA!
SOB SOB
IT'S EVEN WORTH PASSING UP MY FAMILY'S TRIP TO TOKYO DISNEYLAND!
I NEVER DID LIKE THAT WEIRDO...
BUT THEN, I NEVER SAW HER LIKE THIS BEFORE!
THERE'S NO TURNING BACK NOW! MARRY ME!
SLAP
MUST YOUR NOSE ALWAYS SHOW IT WHEN YOUR BLOOD STARTS TO BOIL?!
WHAT ARE YOU DOING HERE, SAKURA?
AHEM!
BONK
MY UNCLE...
HE USED TO LOVE THE OCEAN SO MUCH...
HUH?

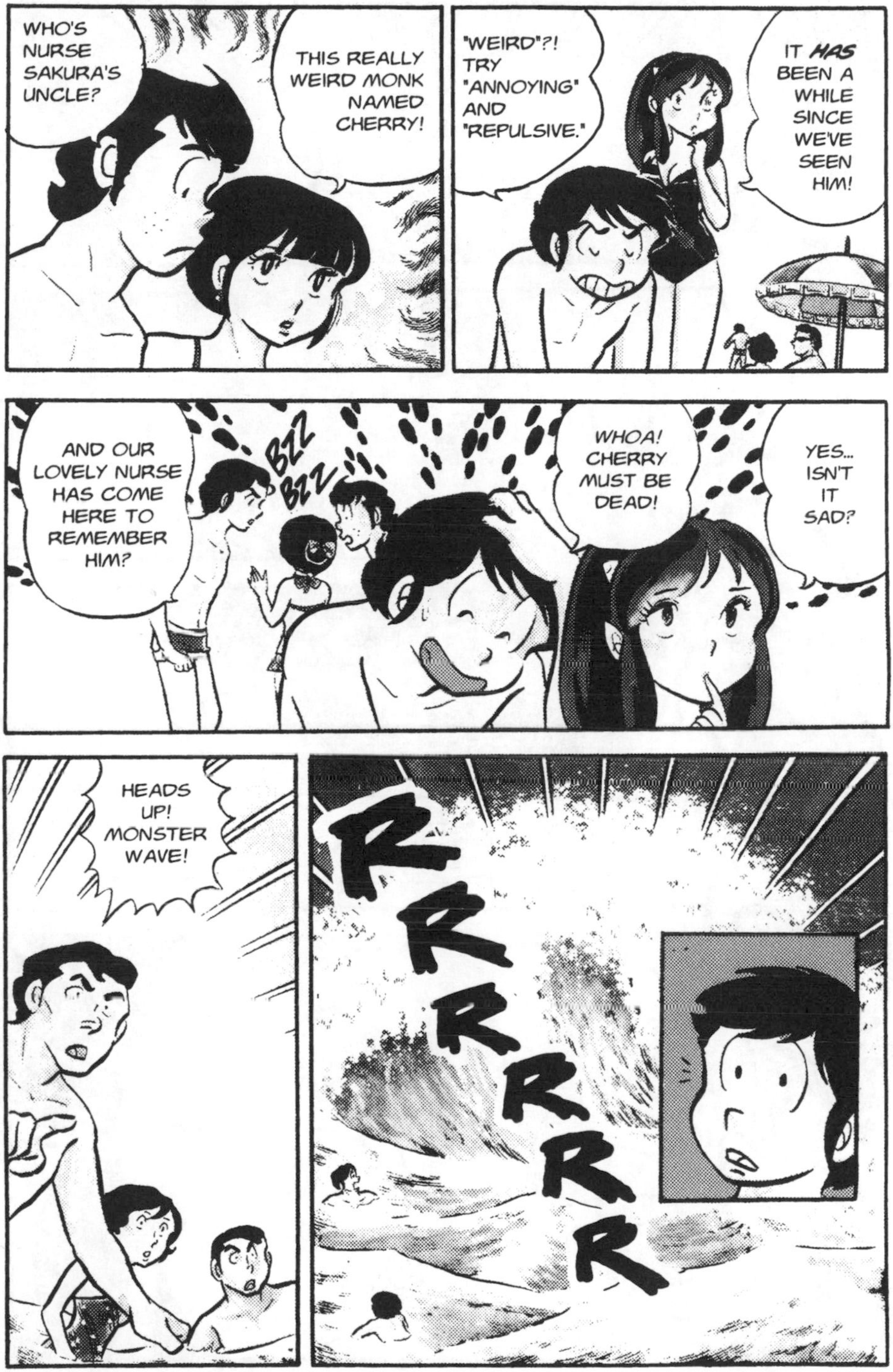
WHO'S NURSE SAKURA'S UNCLE?
THIS REALLY WEIRD MONK NAMED CHERRY!
"WEIRD"?! TRY "ANNOYING" AND "REPULSIVE."
IT HAS BEEN A WHILE SINCE WE'VE SEEN HIM!
AND OUR LOVELY NURSE HAS COME HERE TO REMEMBER HIM?
BZZ BZZ
WHOA! CHERRY MUST BE DEAD!
YES... ISN'T IT SAD?
HEADS UP! MONSTER WAVE!
RRRRRRRR

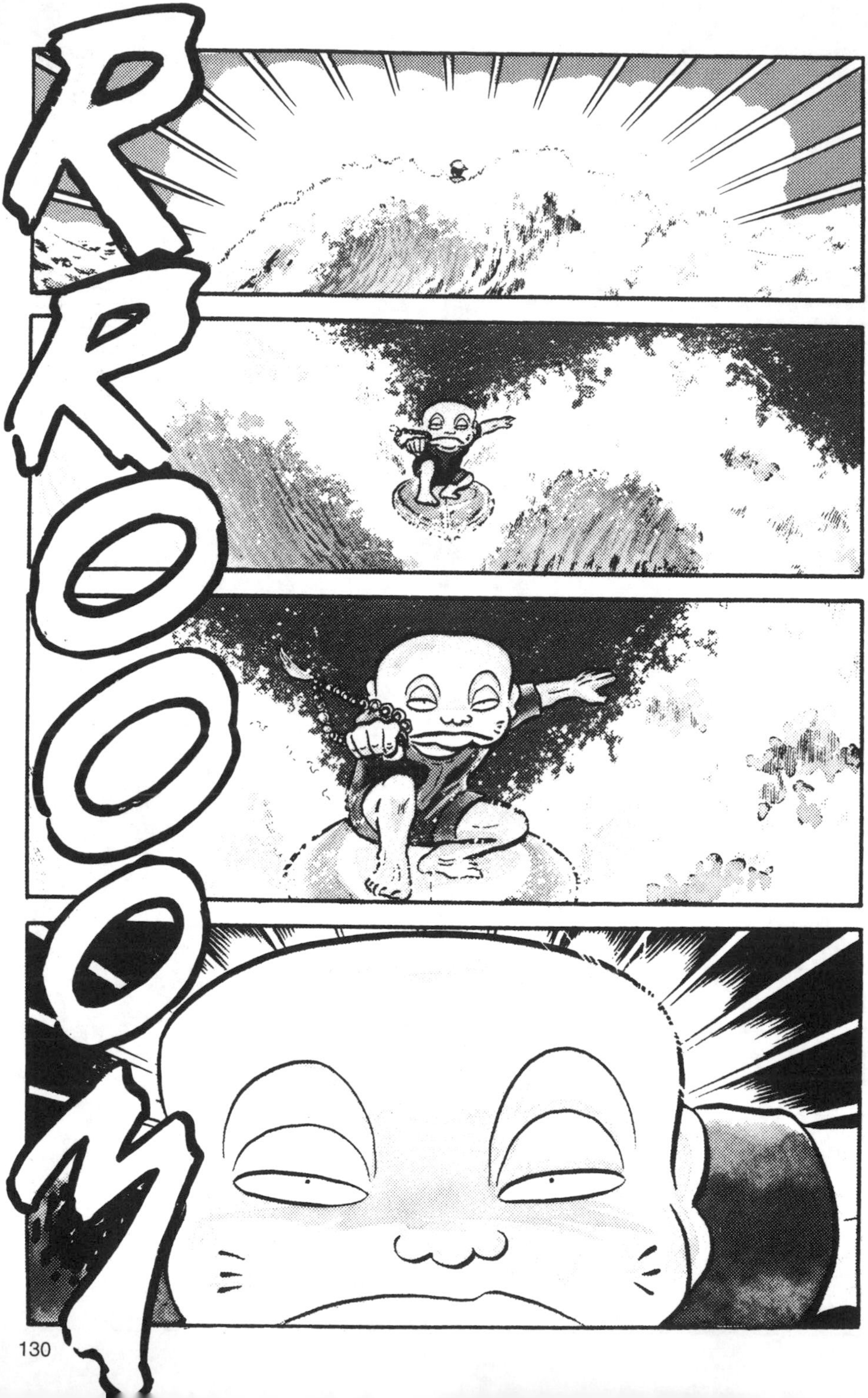
RROOOOM

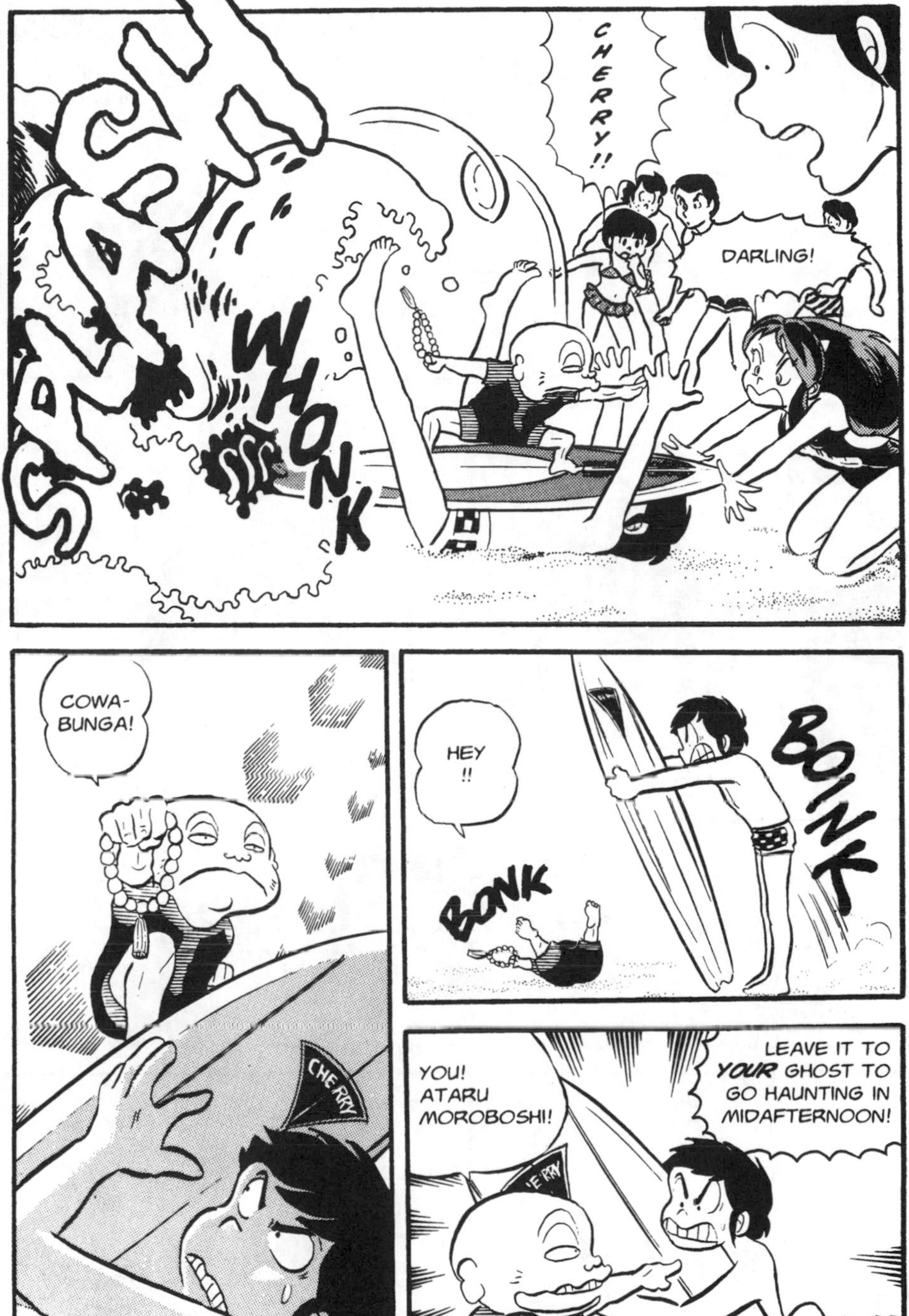
SPLASH
WHONK
CHERRY!!
DARLING!
COWA-BUNGA!
CHERRY
HEY !!
BOINK
BONK
YOU! ATARU MOROBOSHI!
LEAVE IT TO YOUR GHOST TO GO HAUNTING IN MIDAFTERNOON!

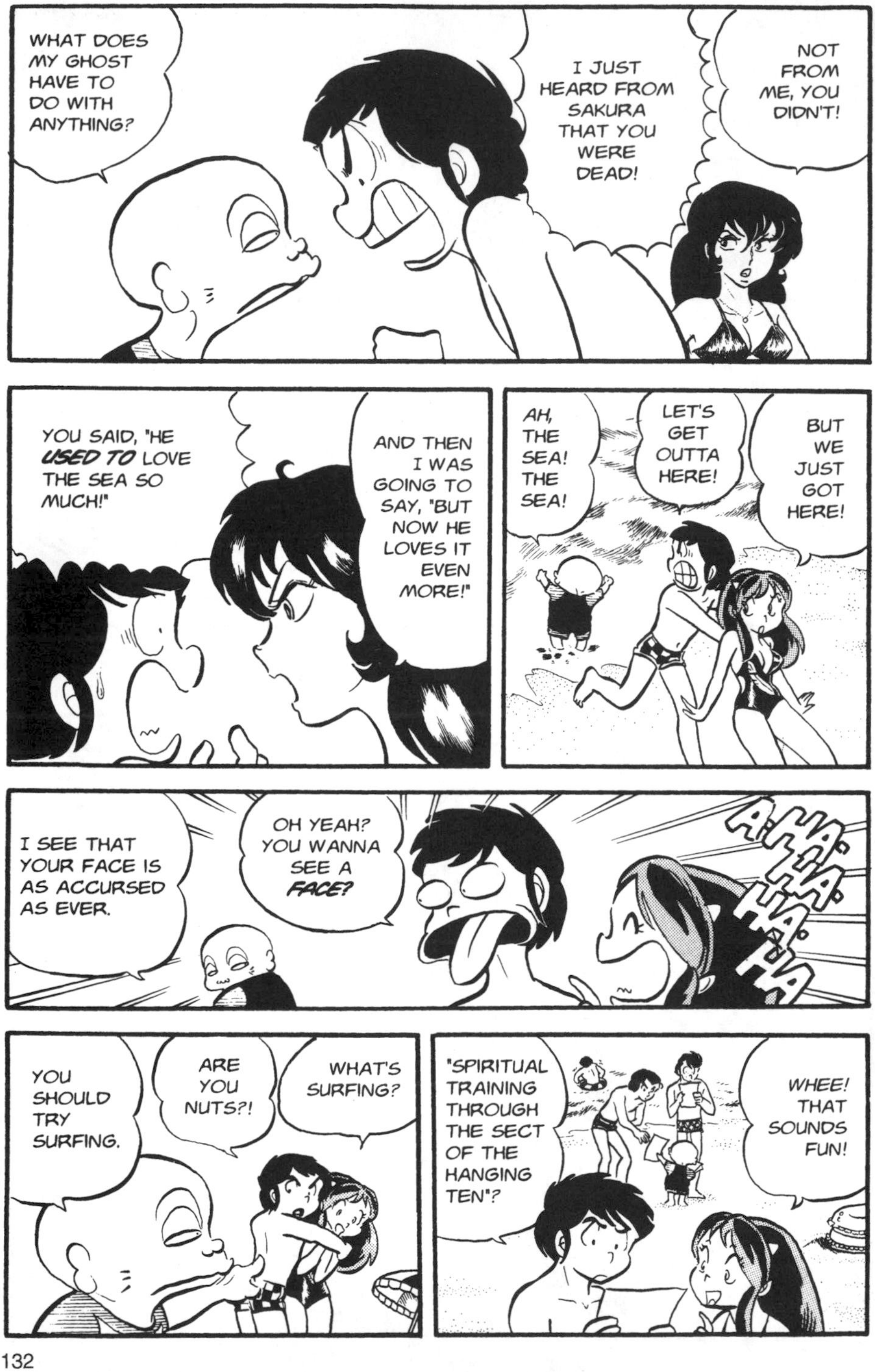
WHAT DOES MY GHOST HAVE TO DO WITH ANYTHING?
I JUST HEARD FROM SAKURA THAT YOU WERE DEAD!
NOT FROM ME, YOU DIDN'T!
YOU SAID, "HE USED TO LOVE THE SEA SO MUCH!"
AND THEN I WAS GOING TO SAY, "BUT NOW HE LOVES IT EVEN MORE!"
AH, THE SEA! THE SEA!
LET'S GET OUTTA HERE!
BUT WE JUST GOT HERE!
I SEE THAT YOUR FACE IS AS ACCURSED AS EVER.
OH YEAH? YOU WANNA SEE A FACE?
A-HA-HA-HA-HA
YOU SHOULD TRY SURFING.
ARE YOU NUTS?!
WHAT'S SURFING?
"SPIRITUAL TRAINING THROUGH THE SECT OF THE HANGING TEN"?
WHEE! THAT SOUNDS FUN!

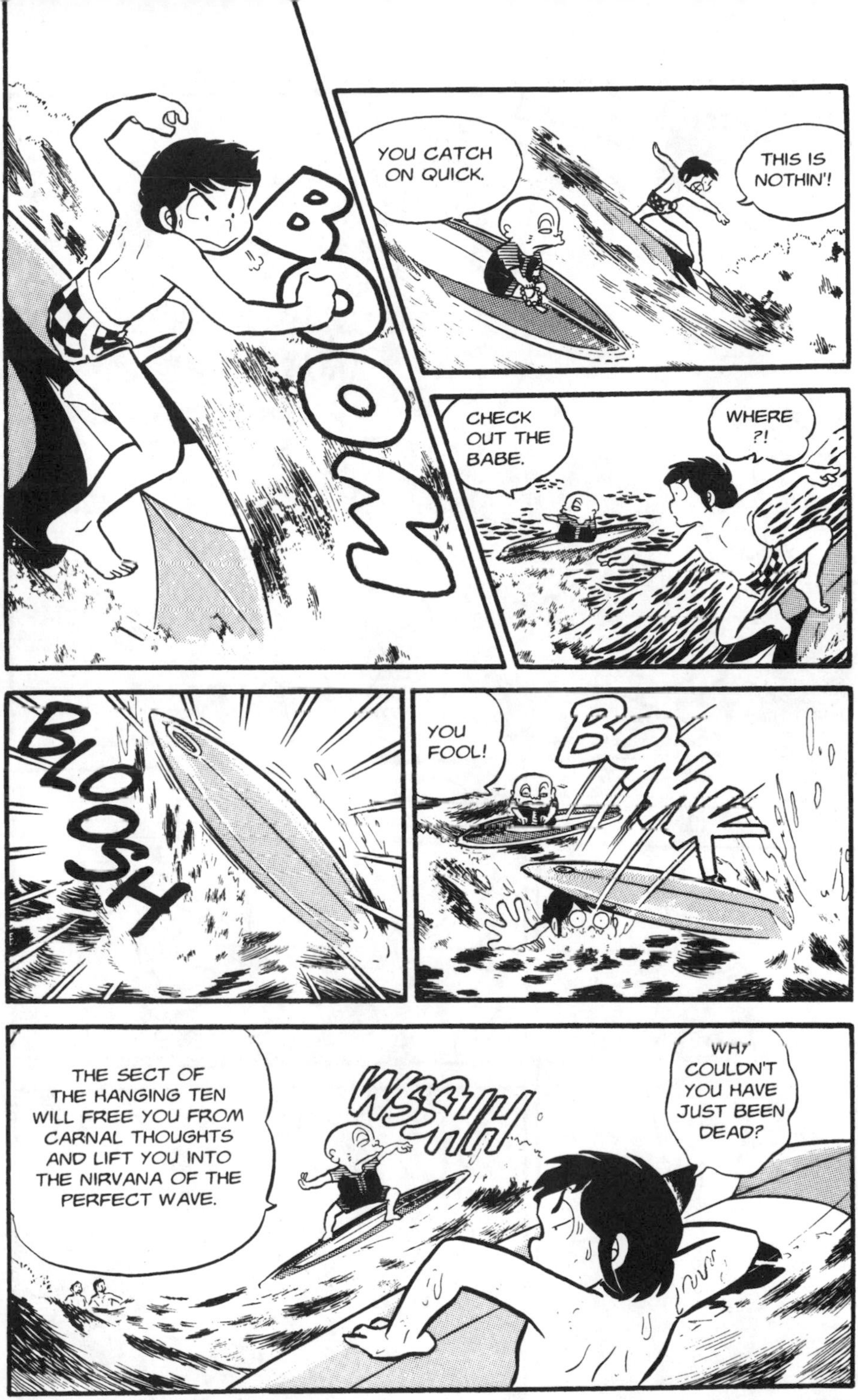
BOOM
YOU CATCH ON QUICK.
THIS IS NOTHIN'!
CHECK OUT THE BABE.
WHERE ?!
BLOSH
YOU FOOL!
BONK
THE SECT OF THE HANGING TEN WILL FREE YOU FROM CARNAL THOUGHTS AND LIFT YOU INTO THE NIRVANA OF THE PERFECT WAVE.
WSSSHH
WHY COULDN'T YOU HAVE JUST BEEN DEAD?

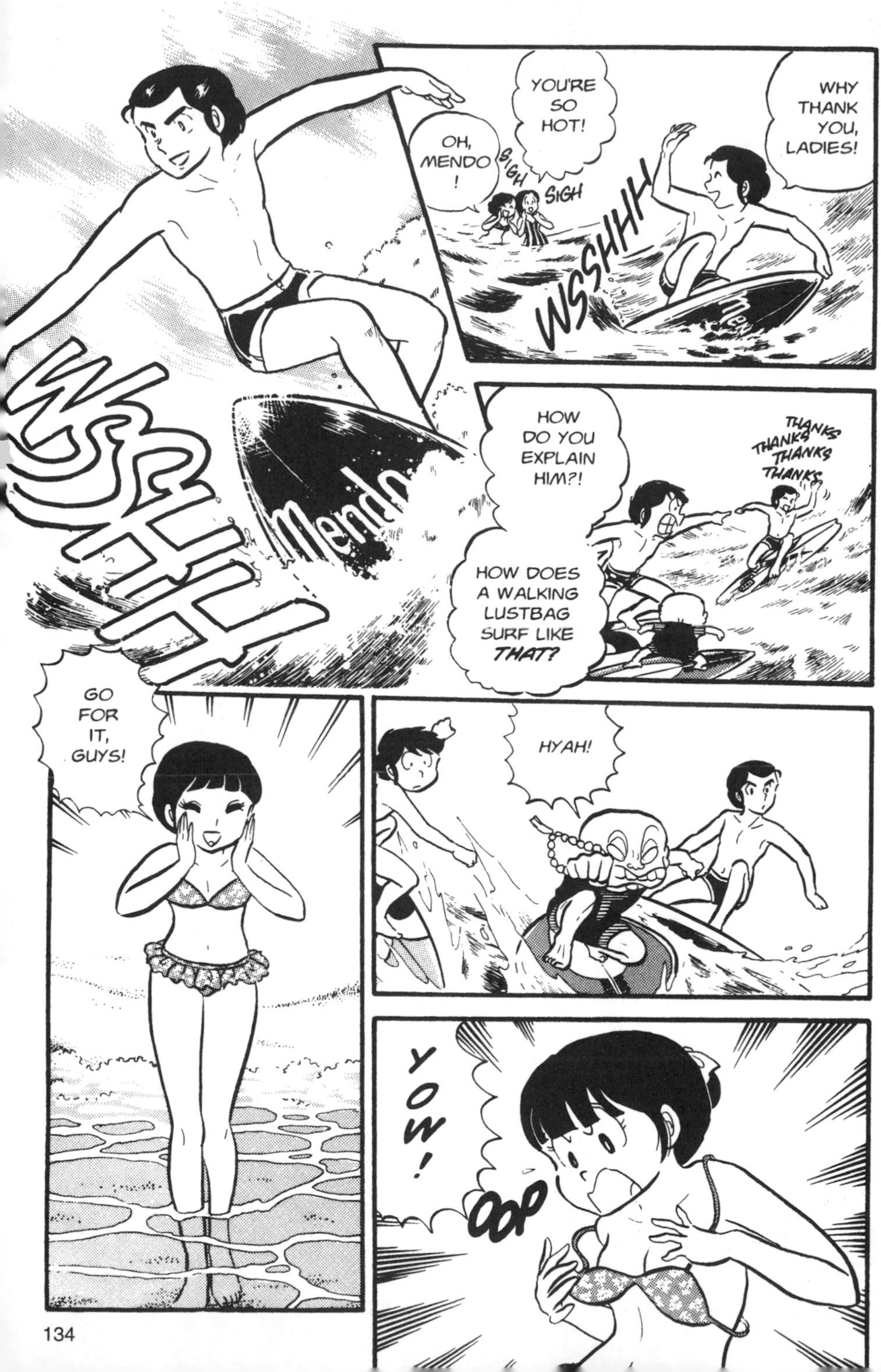

WSSHHH
Mendo
OH, MENDO!
SIGH
SIGH
YOU'RE SO HOT!
WSSHHH
WHY THANK YOU, LADIES!
HOW DO YOU EXPLAIN HIM?!
HOW DOES A WALKING LUSTBAG SURF LIKE *THAT?*
THANKS THANKS THANKS THANKS
GO FOR IT, GUYS!
HYAH!
YOW!
OOP

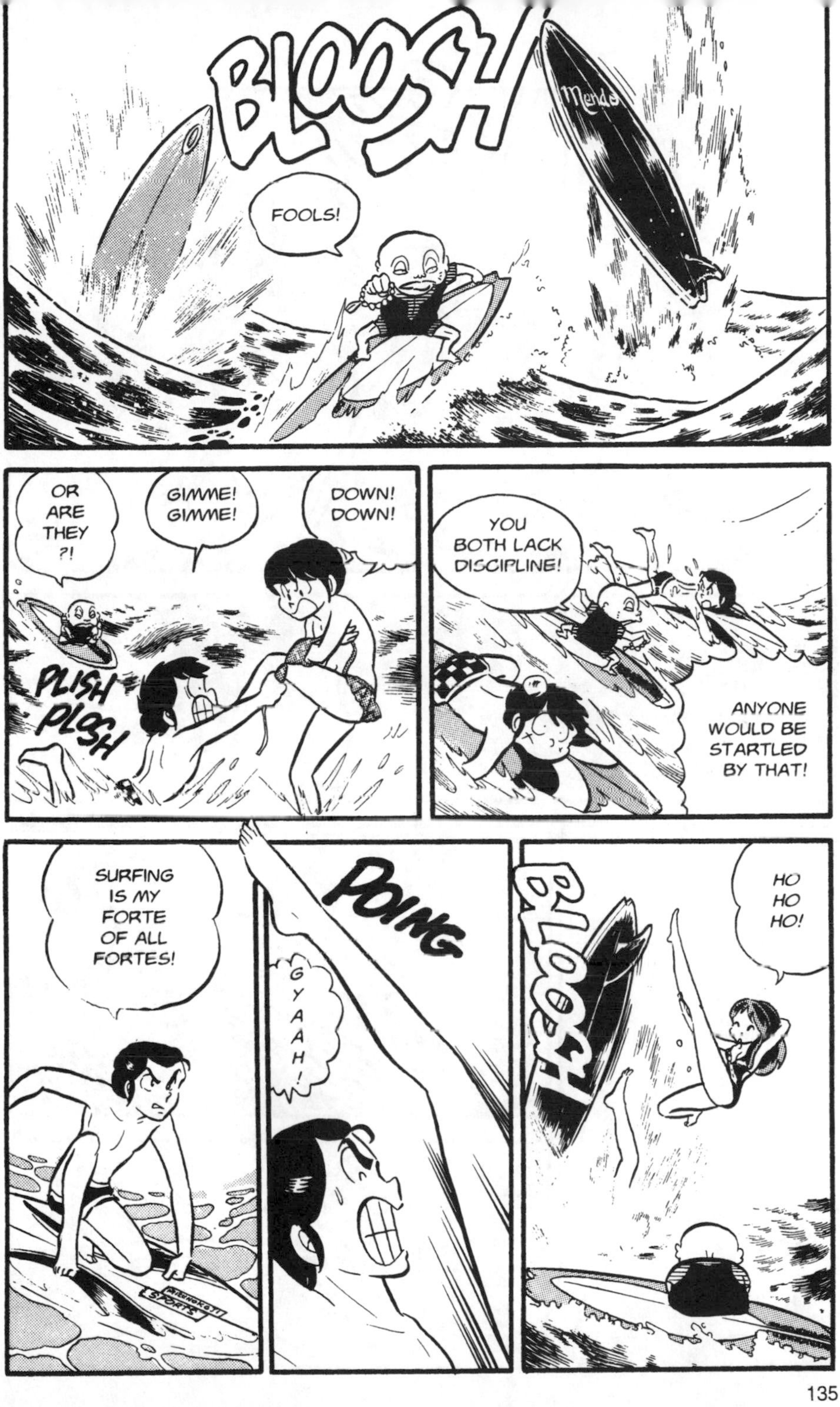
BLOOSH
Mendo
FOOLS!
OR ARE THEY ?!
GIMME! GIMME!
DOWN! DOWN!
PLISH PLOSH
YOU BOTH LACK DISCIPLINE!
ANYONE WOULD BE STARTLED BY THAT!
SURFING IS MY FORTE OF ALL FORTES!
SPORTS
POING
GYAAAH!
BLOOSH
HO HO HO!

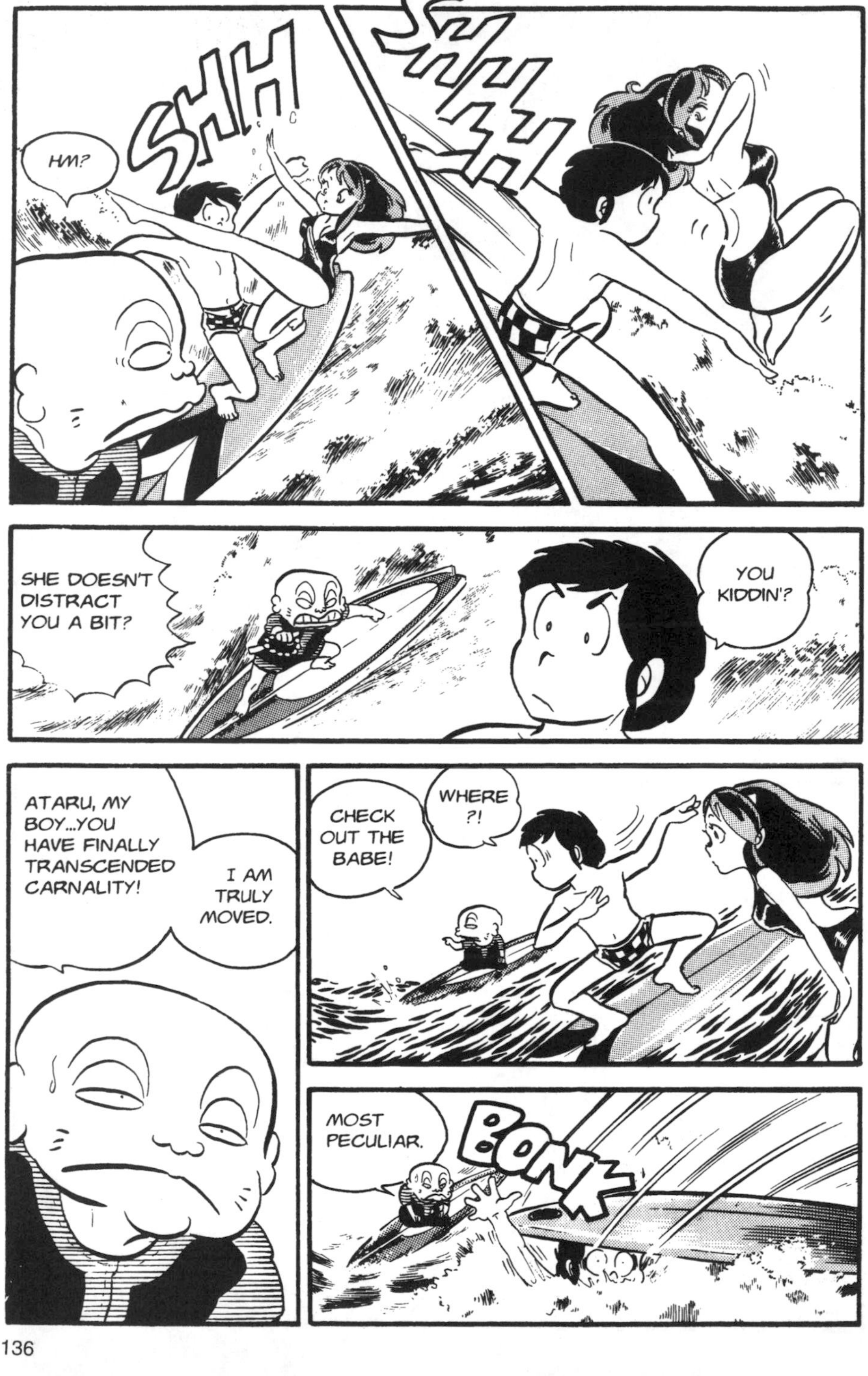
SHH
HM?
SHHHH
SHE DOESN'T DISTRACT YOU A BIT?
YOU KIDDIN'?
ATARU, MY BOY...YOU HAVE FINALLY TRANSCENDED CARNALITY!
I AM TRULY MOVED.
CHECK OUT THE BABE!
WHERE ?!
MOST PECULIAR.
BONK

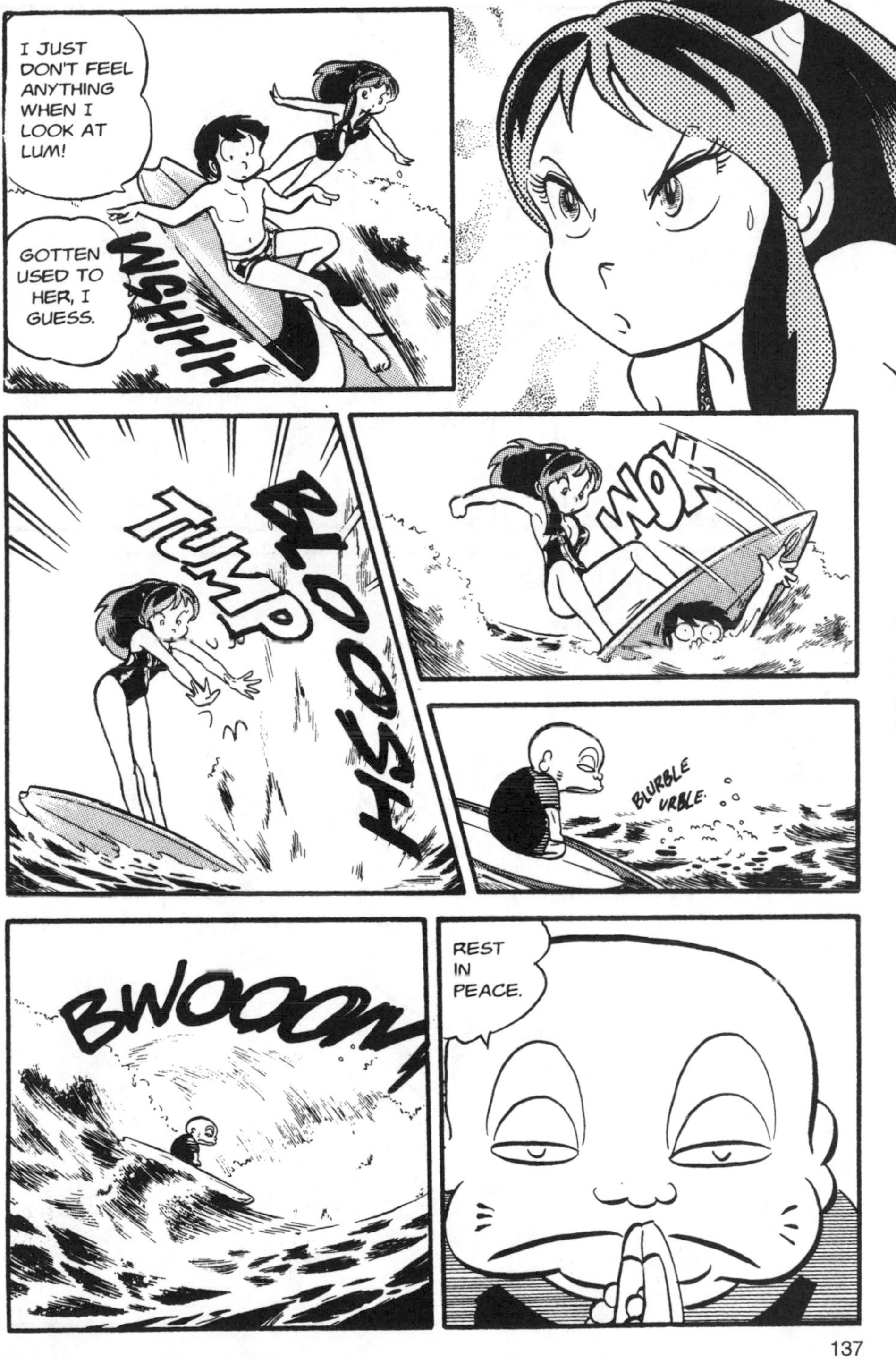
I JUST DON'T FEEL ANYTHING WHEN I LOOK AT LUM!
GOTTEN USED TO HER, I GUESS.
WSHHHH
BLOOOSH
TUMP
WOK!
BLURBLE URBLE
BWOOOOM
REST IN PEACE.

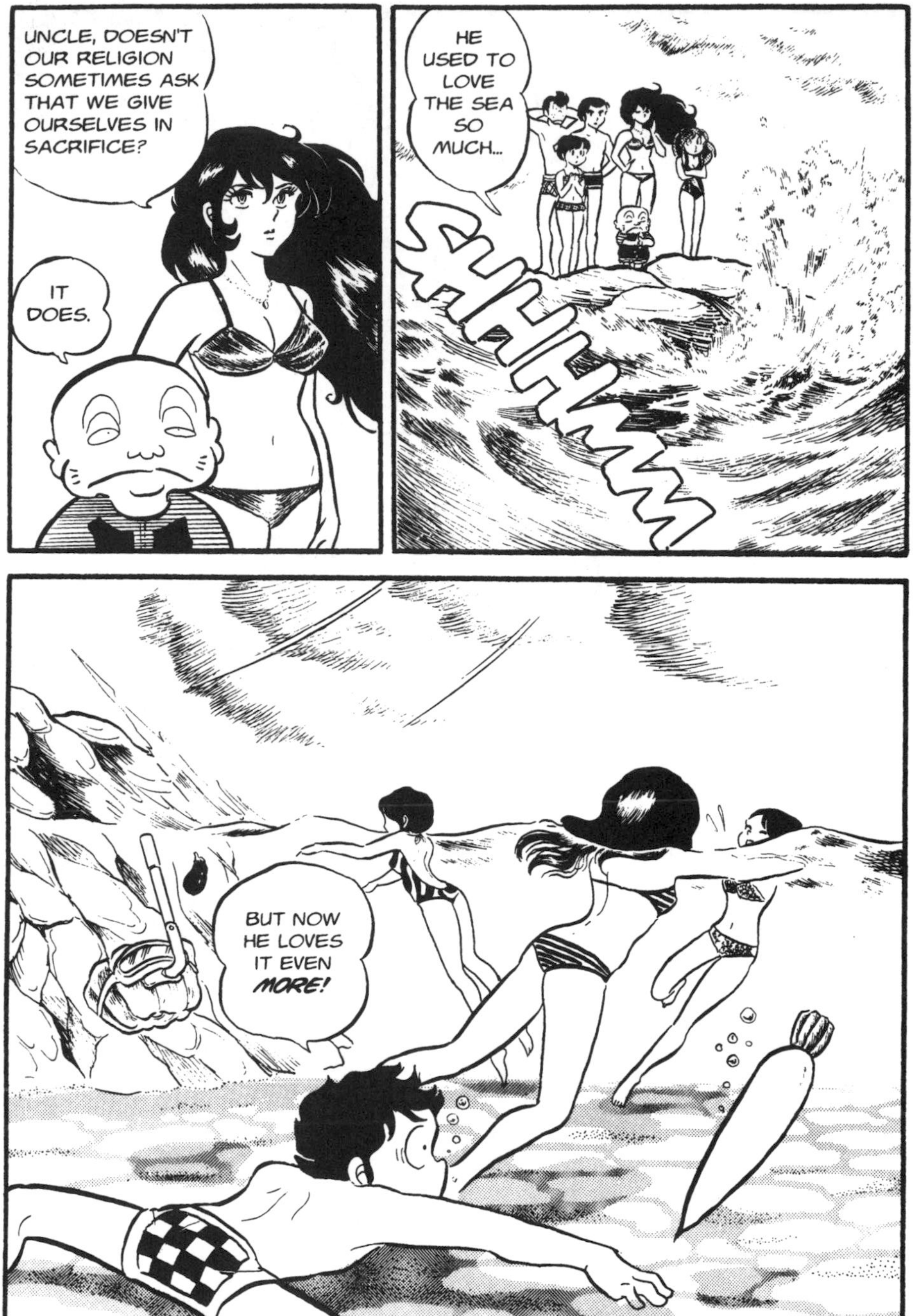
UNCLE, DOESN'T OUR RELIGION SOMETIMES ASK THAT WE GIVE OURSELVES IN SACRIFICE?
IT DOES.
HE USED TO LOVE THE SEA SO MUCH...
SHHHMMM
BUT NOW HE LOVES IT EVEN *MORE!*

PART NINE
SWIMSUIT THIEF

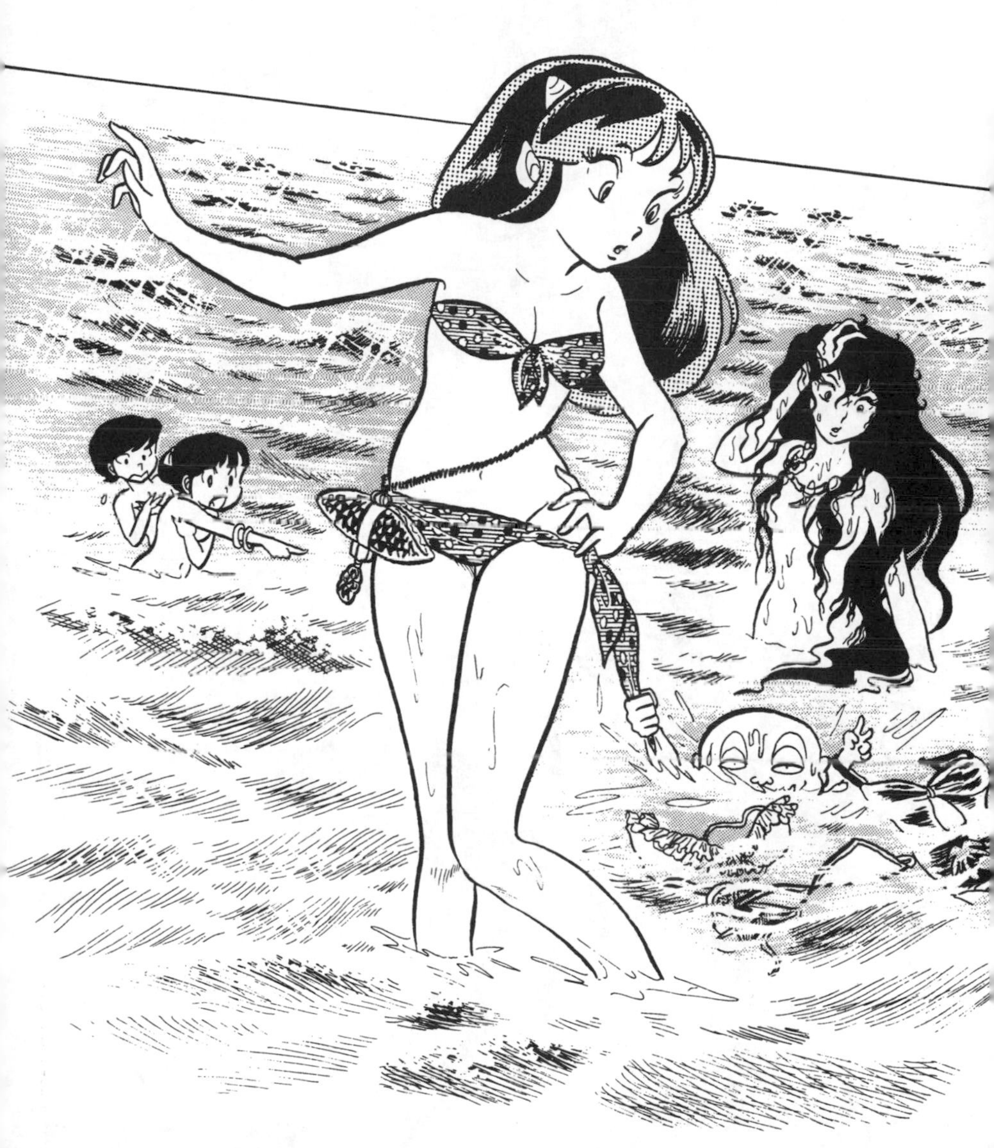

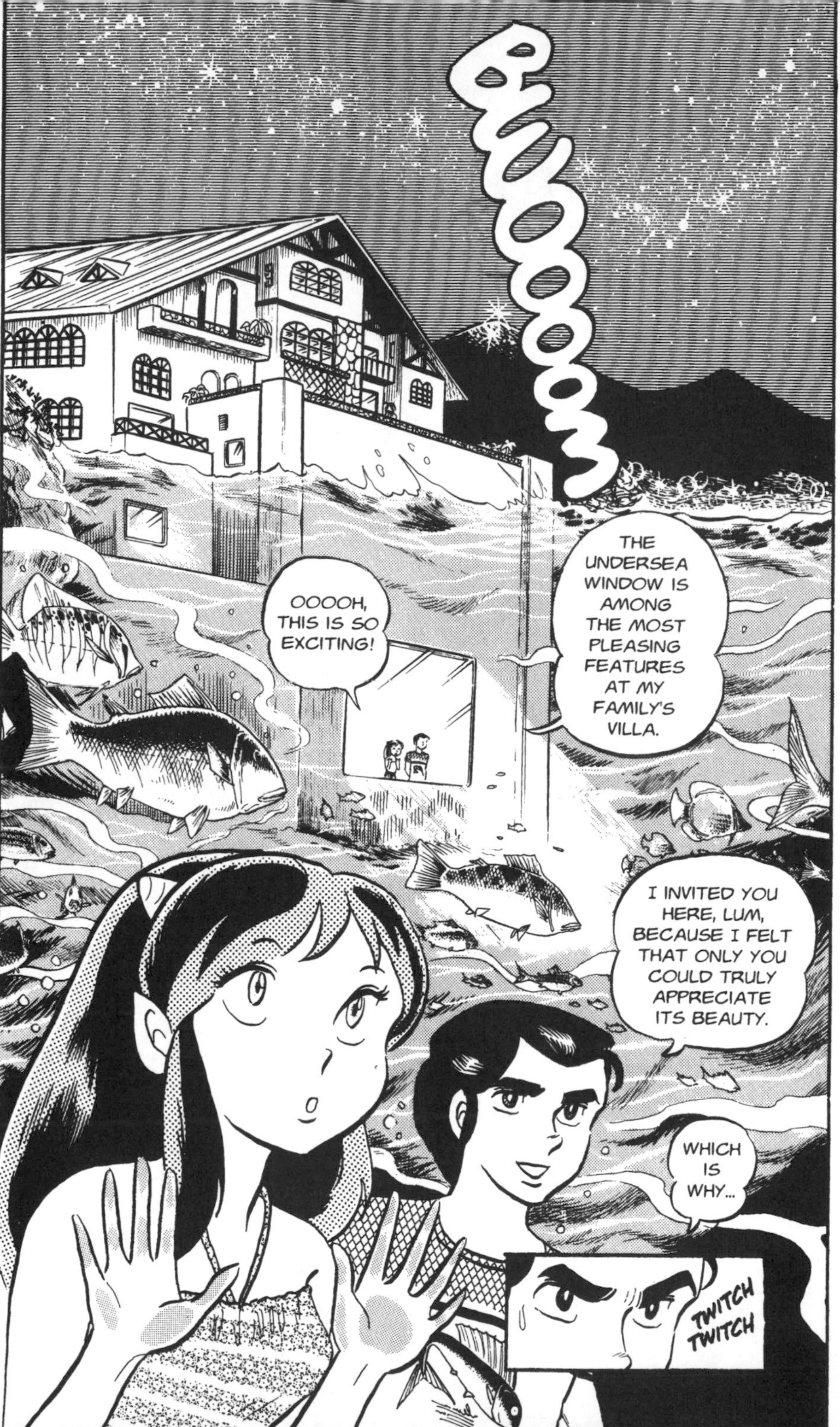

BLOOOOOM
OOOOH, THIS IS SO EXCITING!
THE UNDERSEA WINDOW IS AMONG THE MOST PLEASING FEATURES AT MY FAMILY'S VILLA.
I INVITED YOU HERE, LUM, BECAUSE I FELT THAT ONLY YOU COULD TRULY APPRECIATE ITS BEAUTY.
WHICH IS WHY...
TWITCH TWITCH

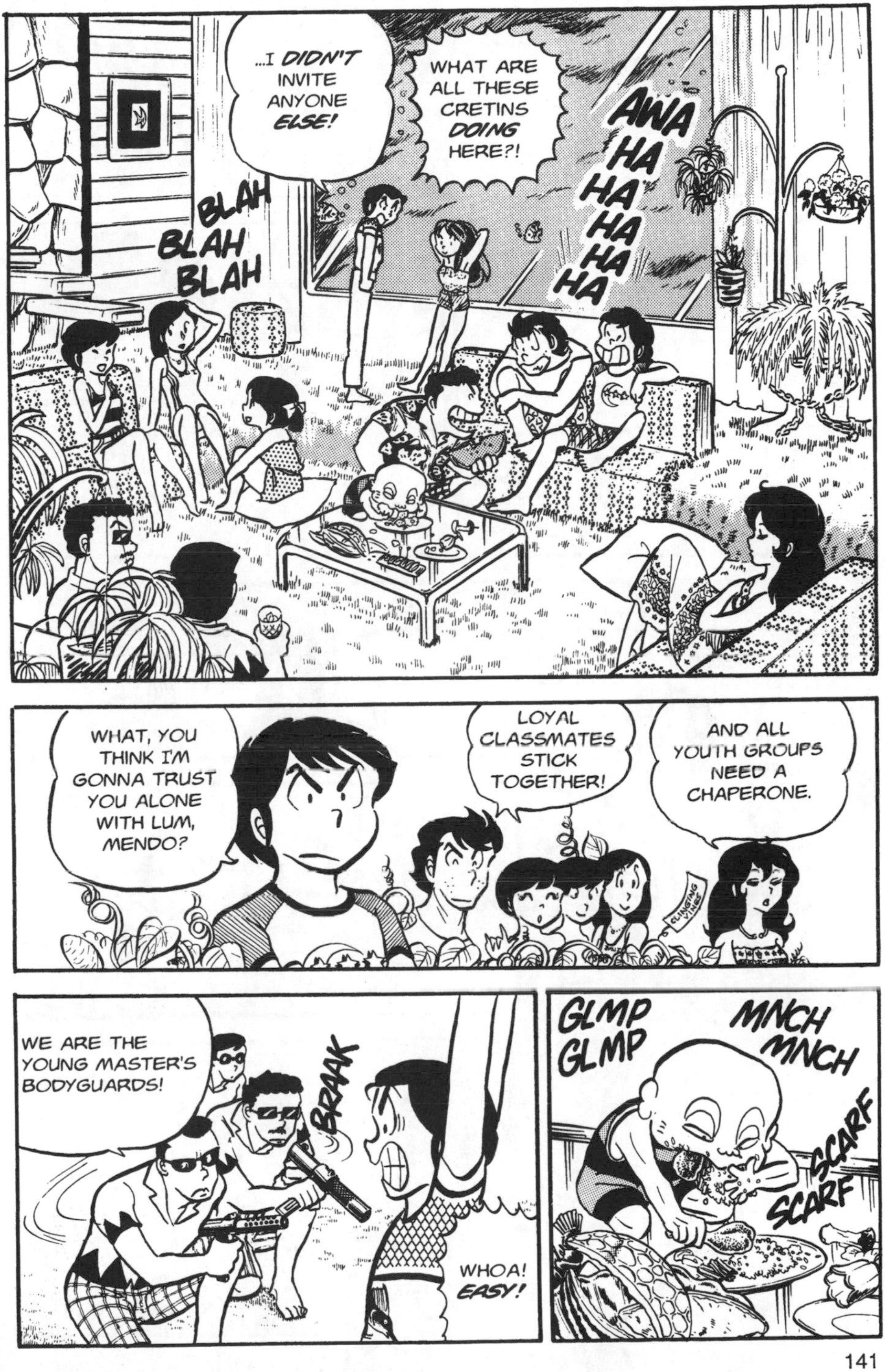
...I DIDN'T INVITE ANYONE ELSE!
WHAT ARE ALL THESE CRETINS DOING HERE?!
AWA HA HA HA HA HA HA
BLAH BLAH BLAH
WHAT, YOU THINK I'M GONNA TRUST YOU ALONE WITH LUM, MENDO?
LOYAL CLASSMATES STICK TOGETHER!
CLINGING VINES
AND ALL YOUTH GROUPS NEED A CHAPERONE.
WE ARE THE YOUNG MASTER'S BODYGUARDS!
BRAAK
WHOA! EASY!
GLMP GLMP
MNCH MNCH
SCARF SCARF

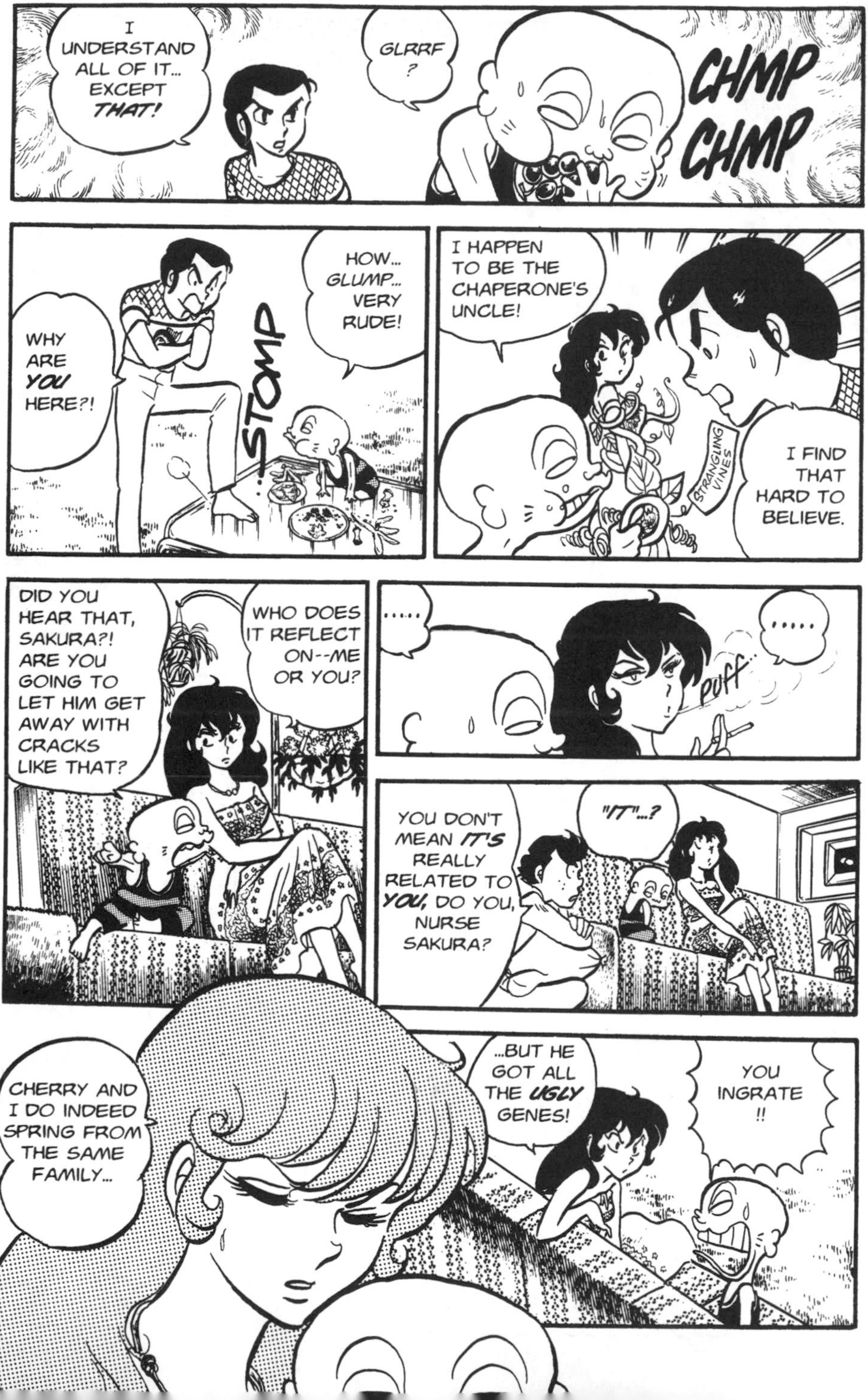
I UNDERSTAND ALL OF IT... EXCEPT THAT!
GLRRF ?
CHMP CHMP
WHY ARE YOU HERE?!
STOMP
HOW... GLUMP... VERY RUDE!
I HAPPEN TO BE THE CHAPERONE'S UNCLE!
STRANGLING VINES
I FIND THAT HARD TO BELIEVE.
DID YOU HEAR THAT, SAKURA?! ARE YOU GOING TO LET HIM GET AWAY WITH CRACKS LIKE THAT?
WHO DOES IT REFLECT ON--ME OR YOU?
.....
PUFF
.....
YOU DON'T MEAN IT'S REALLY RELATED TO YOU, DO YOU, NURSE SAKURA?
"IT"...?
CHERRY AND I DO INDEED SPRING FROM THE SAME FAMILY...
...BUT HE GOT ALL THE UGLY GENES!
YOU INGRATE !!

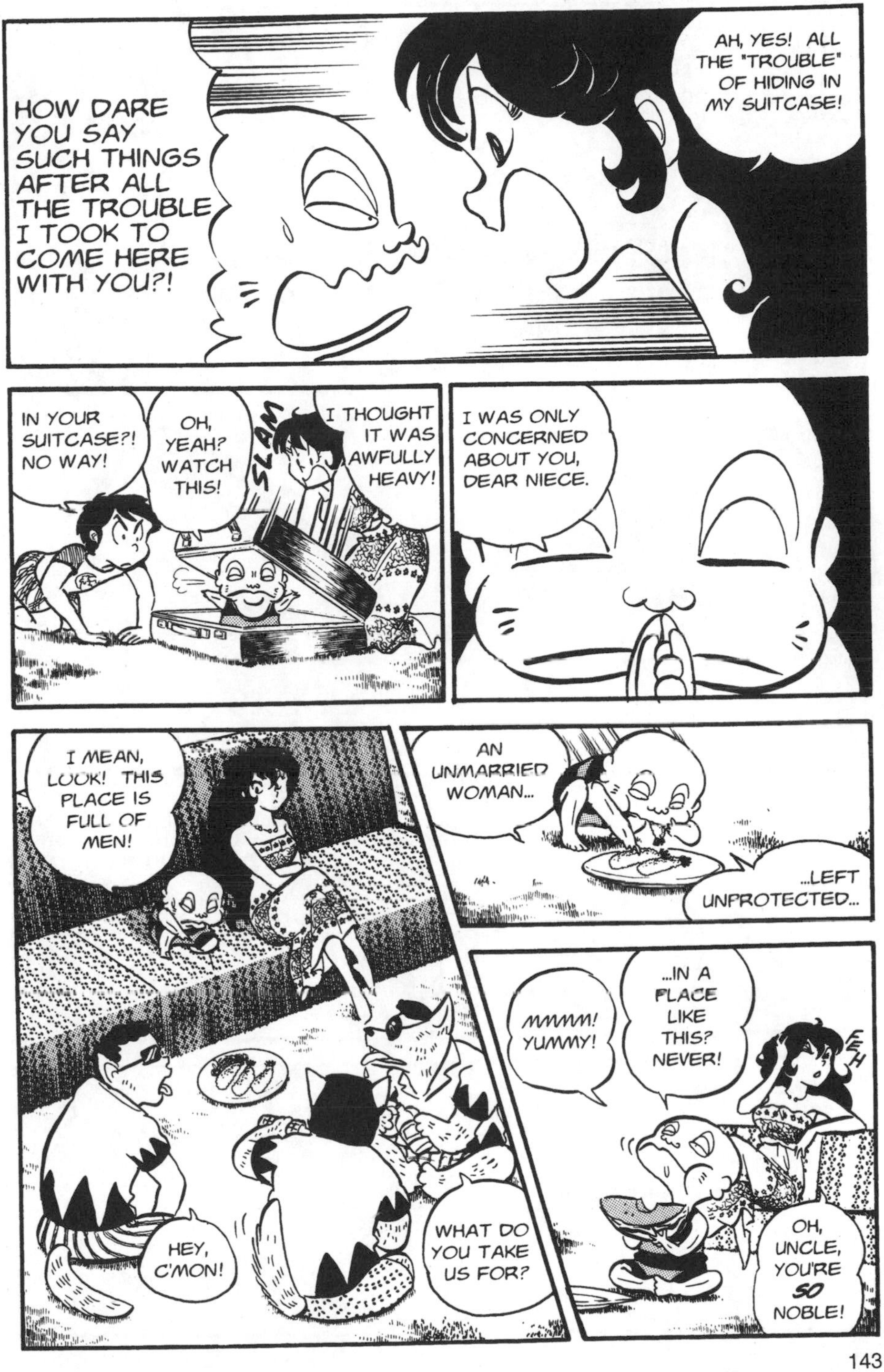
HOW DARE YOU SAY SUCH THINGS AFTER ALL THE TROUBLE I TOOK TO COME HERE WITH YOU?!
AH, YES! ALL THE "TROUBLE" OF HIDING IN MY SUITCASE!
IN YOUR SUITCASE?! NO WAY!
OH, YEAH? WATCH THIS!
SLAM
I THOUGHT IT WAS AWFULLY HEAVY!
I WAS ONLY CONCERNED ABOUT YOU, DEAR NIECE.
I MEAN, LOOK! THIS PLACE IS FULL OF MEN!
HEY, C'MON!
WHAT DO YOU TAKE US FOR?
AN UNMARRIED WOMAN...
...LEFT UNPROTECTED...
MMMM! YUMMY!
...IN A PLACE LIKE THIS? NEVER!
FEH
OH, UNCLE, YOU'RE SO NOBLE!

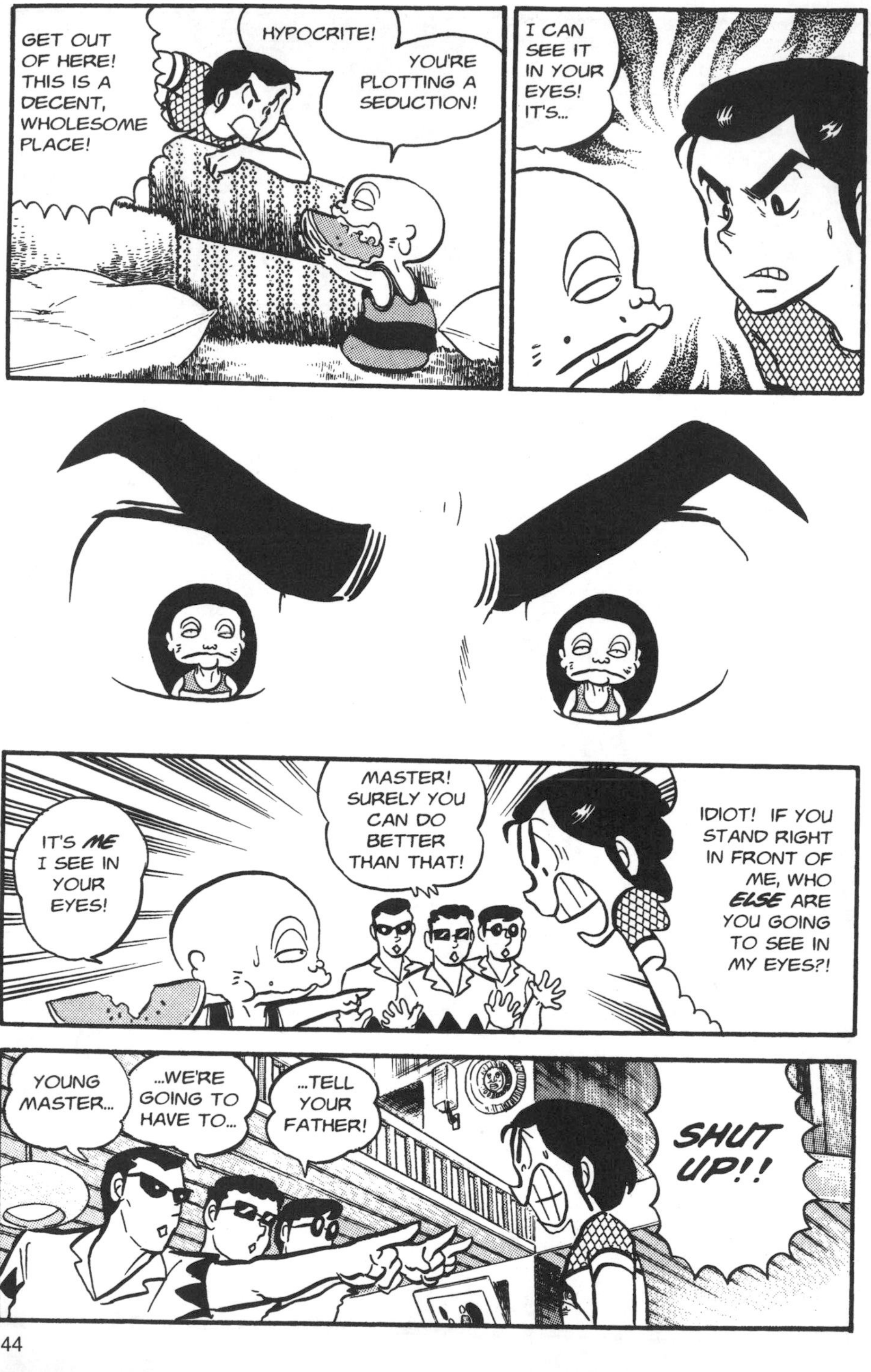
GET OUT OF HERE! THIS IS A DECENT, WHOLESOME PLACE!
HYPOCRITE!
YOU'RE PLOTTING A SEDUCTION!
I CAN SEE IT IN YOUR EYES! IT'S...
IT'S *ME* I SEE IN YOUR EYES!
MASTER! SURELY YOU CAN DO BETTER THAN THAT!
IDIOT! IF YOU STAND RIGHT IN FRONT OF ME, WHO *ELSE* ARE YOU GOING TO SEE IN MY EYES?!
YOUNG MASTER...
...WE'RE GOING TO HAVE TO...
...TELL YOUR FATHER!
SHUT UP!!

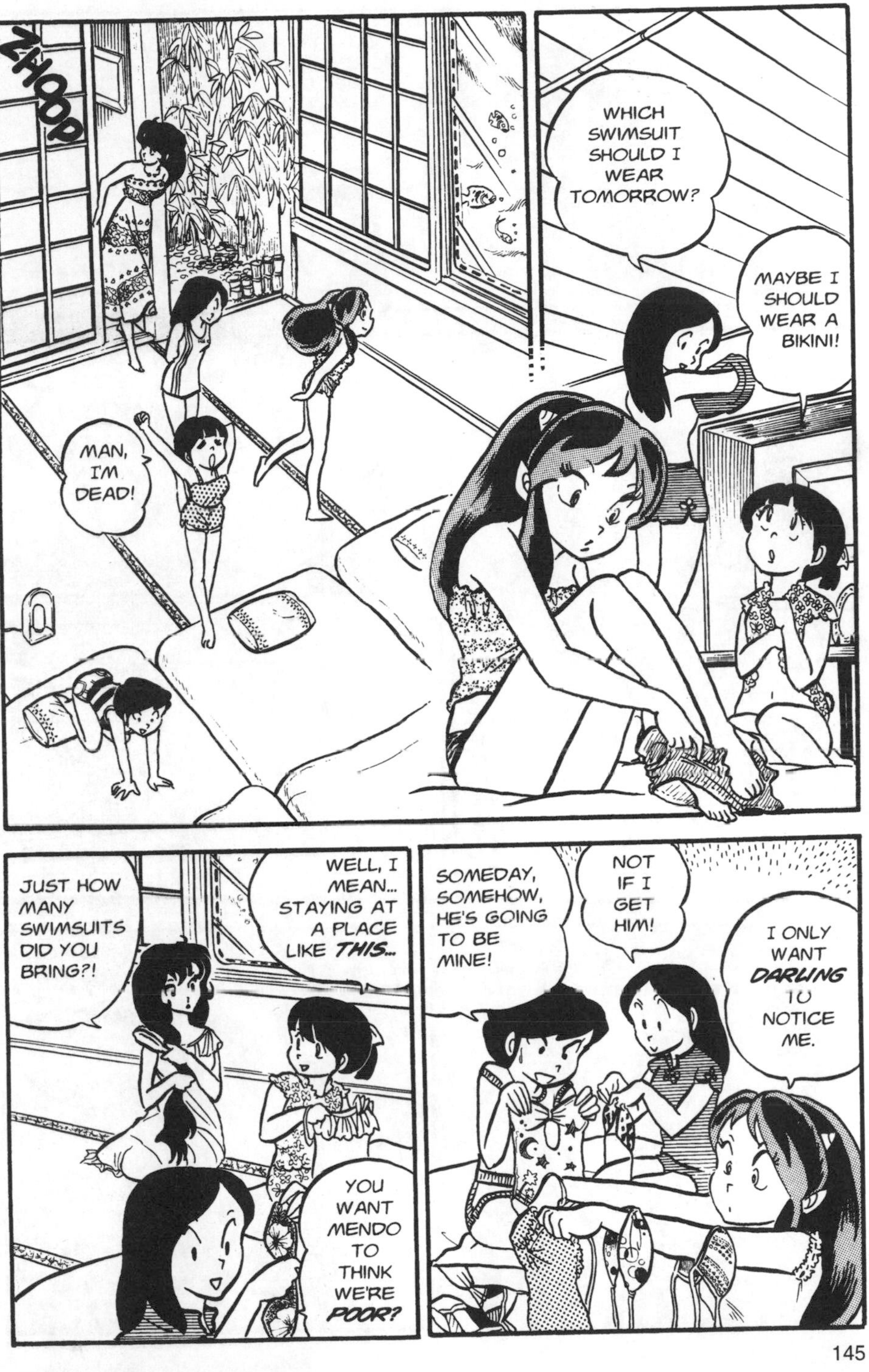
ZHOOP
MAN, I'M DEAD!
WHICH SWIMSUIT SHOULD I WEAR TOMORROW?
MAYBE I SHOULD WEAR A BIKINI!
JUST HOW MANY SWIMSUITS DID YOU BRING?!
WELL, I MEAN... STAYING AT A PLACE LIKE THIS...
YOU WANT MENDO TO THINK WE'RE POOR?
SOMEDAY, SOMEHOW, HE'S GOING TO BE MINE!
NOT IF I GET HIM!
I ONLY WANT DARLING TO NOTICE ME.

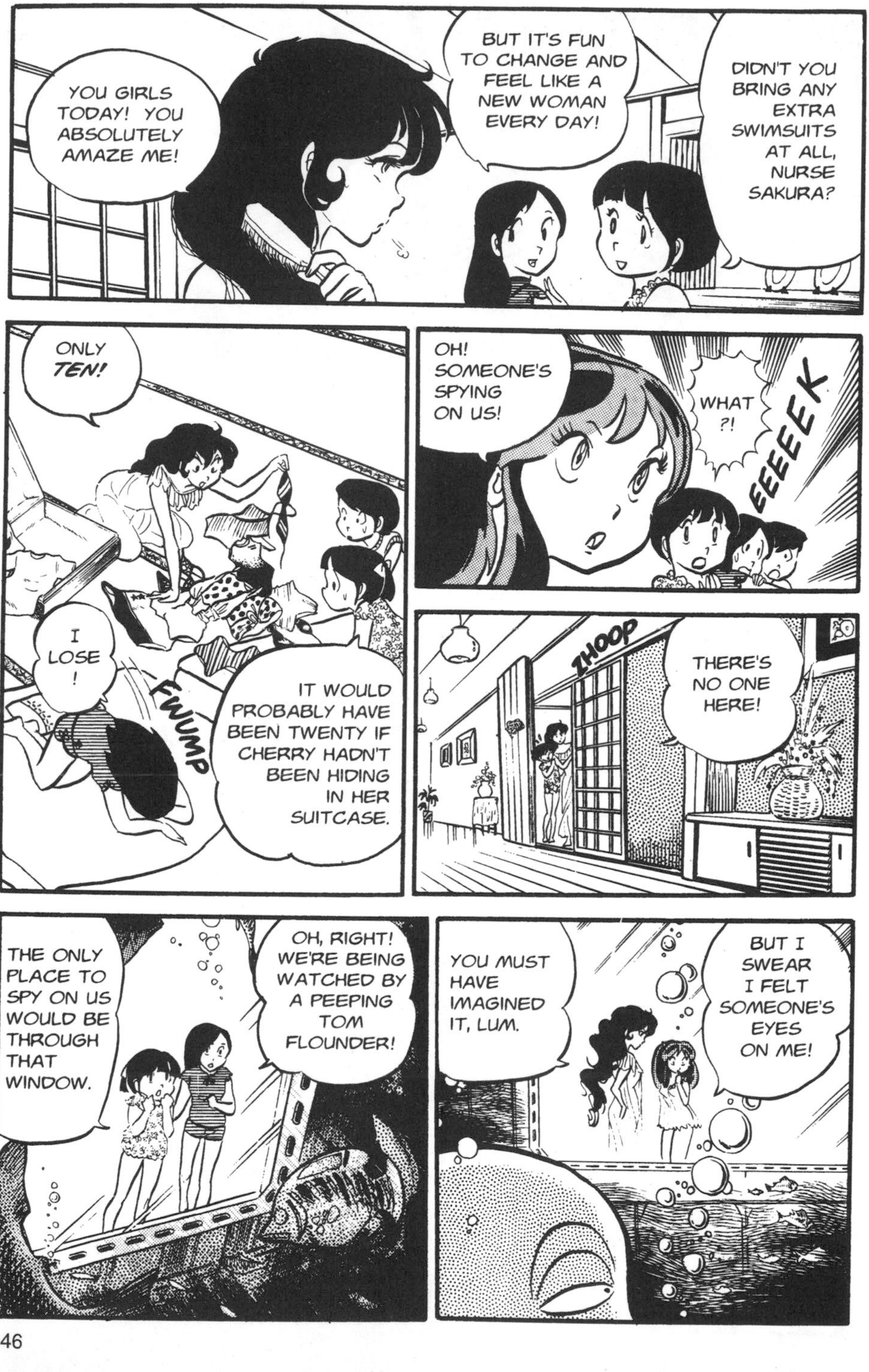
YOU GIRLS TODAY! YOU ABSOLUTELY AMAZE ME!
BUT IT'S FUN TO CHANGE AND FEEL LIKE A NEW WOMAN EVERY DAY!
DIDN'T YOU BRING ANY EXTRA SWIMSUITS AT ALL, NURSE SAKURA?
ONLY *TEN!*
I LOSE!
FWUMP
IT WOULD PROBABLY HAVE BEEN TWENTY IF CHERRY HADN'T BEEN HIDING IN HER SUITCASE.
OH! SOMEONE'S SPYING ON US!
WHAT ?!
EEEEEK
ZHOOP
THERE'S NO ONE HERE!
THE ONLY PLACE TO SPY ON US WOULD BE THROUGH THAT WINDOW.
OH, RIGHT! WE'RE BEING WATCHED BY A PEEPING TOM FLOUNDER!
YOU MUST HAVE IMAGINED IT, LUM.
BUT I SWEAR I FELT SOMEONE'S EYES ON ME!

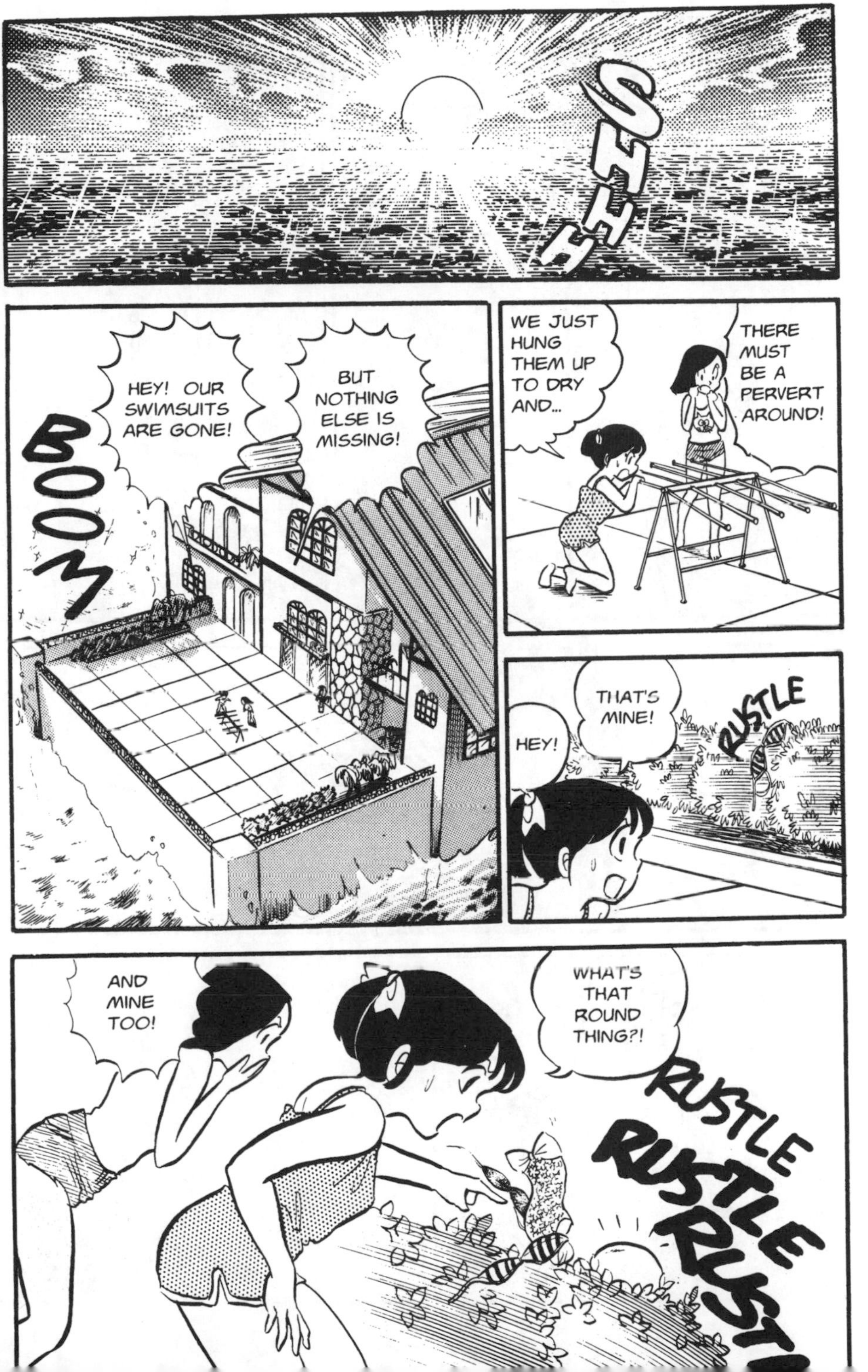
SHHHH
BOOM
HEY! OUR SWIMSUITS ARE GONE!
BUT NOTHING ELSE IS MISSING!
WE JUST HUNG THEM UP TO DRY AND...
THERE MUST BE A PERVERT AROUND!
HEY!
THAT'S MINE!
RUSTLE
AND MINE TOO!
WHAT'S THAT ROUND THING?!
RUSTLE
RUSTLE
RUST

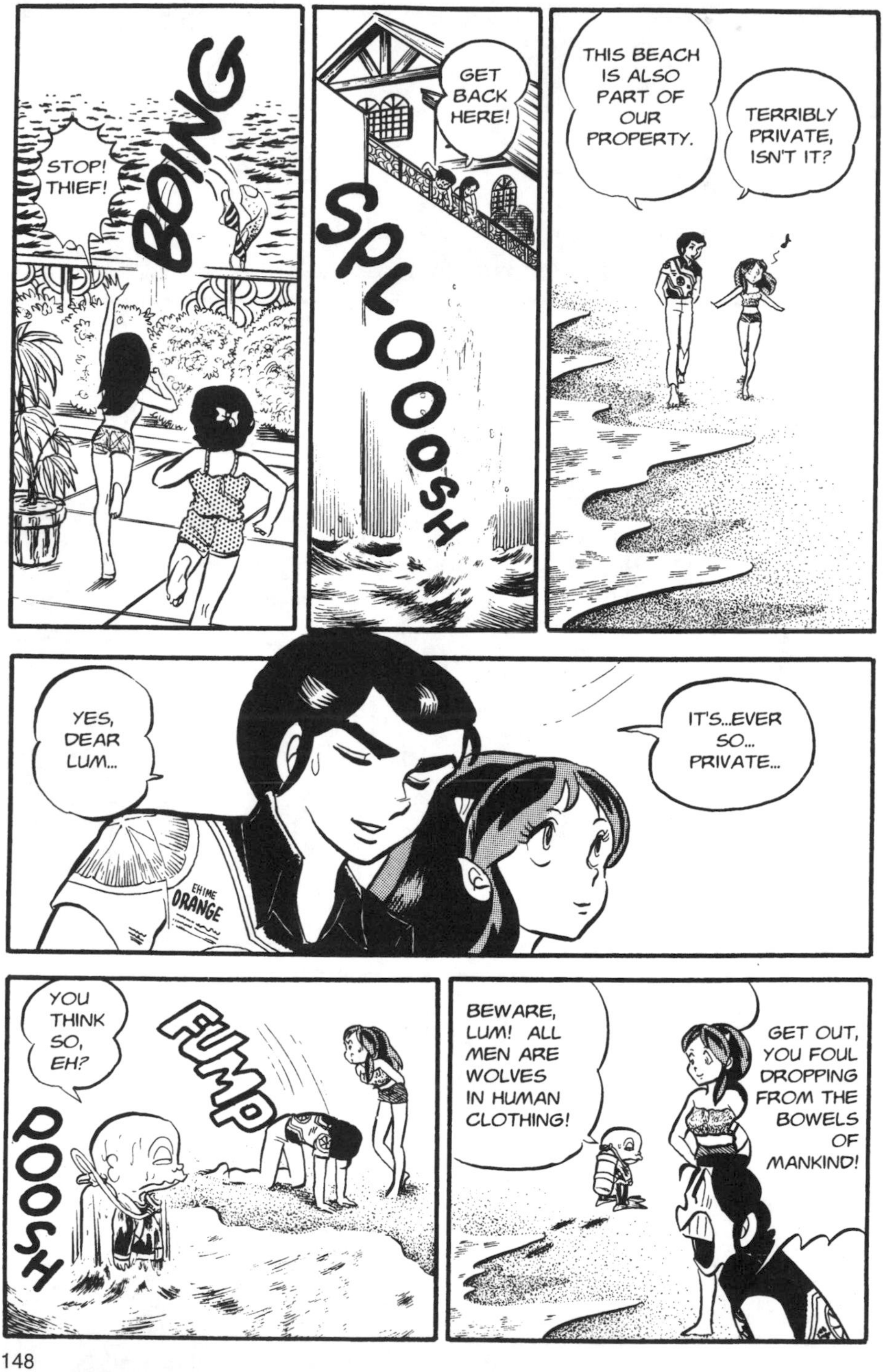
STOP! THIEF!
BOING
GET BACK HERE!
SPLOOOSH
THIS BEACH IS ALSO PART OF OUR PROPERTY.
TERRIBLY PRIVATE, ISN'T IT?
YES, DEAR LUM...
IT'S...EVER SO... PRIVATE...
EHIME ORANGE
YOU THINK SO, EH?
FUMP
POOOSH
BEWARE, LUM! ALL MEN ARE WOLVES IN HUMAN CLOTHING!
GET OUT, YOU FOUL DROPPING FROM THE BOWELS OF MANKIND!

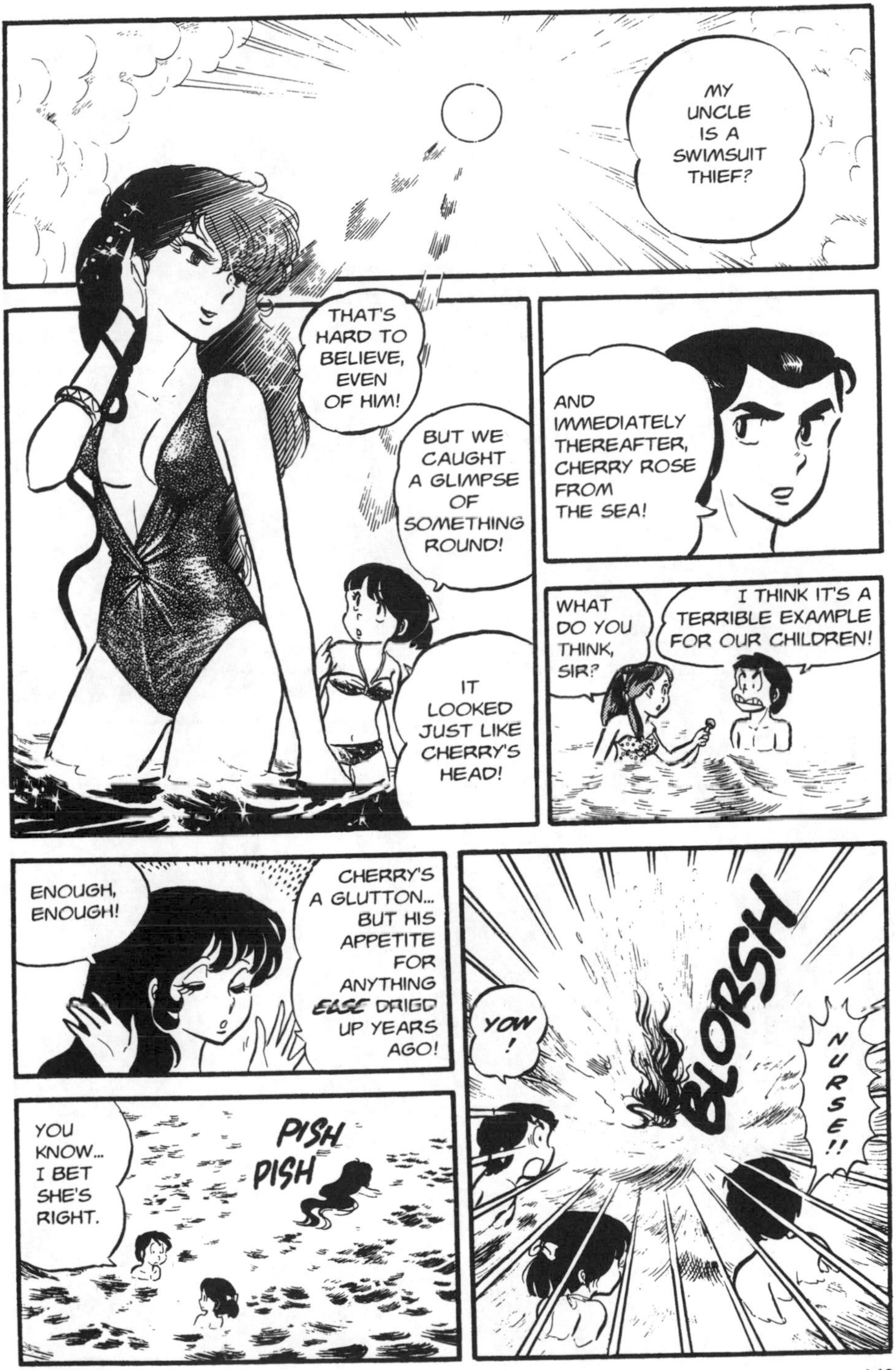
MY UNCLE IS A SWIMSUIT THIEF?
THAT'S HARD TO BELIEVE, EVEN OF HIM!
BUT WE CAUGHT A GLIMPSE OF SOMETHING ROUND!
IT LOOKED JUST LIKE CHERRY'S HEAD!
AND IMMEDIATELY THEREAFTER, CHERRY ROSE FROM THE SEA!
WHAT DO YOU THINK, SIR?
I THINK IT'S A TERRIBLE EXAMPLE FOR OUR CHILDREN!
ENOUGH, ENOUGH!
CHERRY'S A GLUTTON... BUT HIS APPETITE FOR ANYTHING ELSE DRIED UP YEARS AGO!
YOU KNOW... I BET SHE'S RIGHT.
PISH PISH
YOW!
BLORSH
NURSE!!

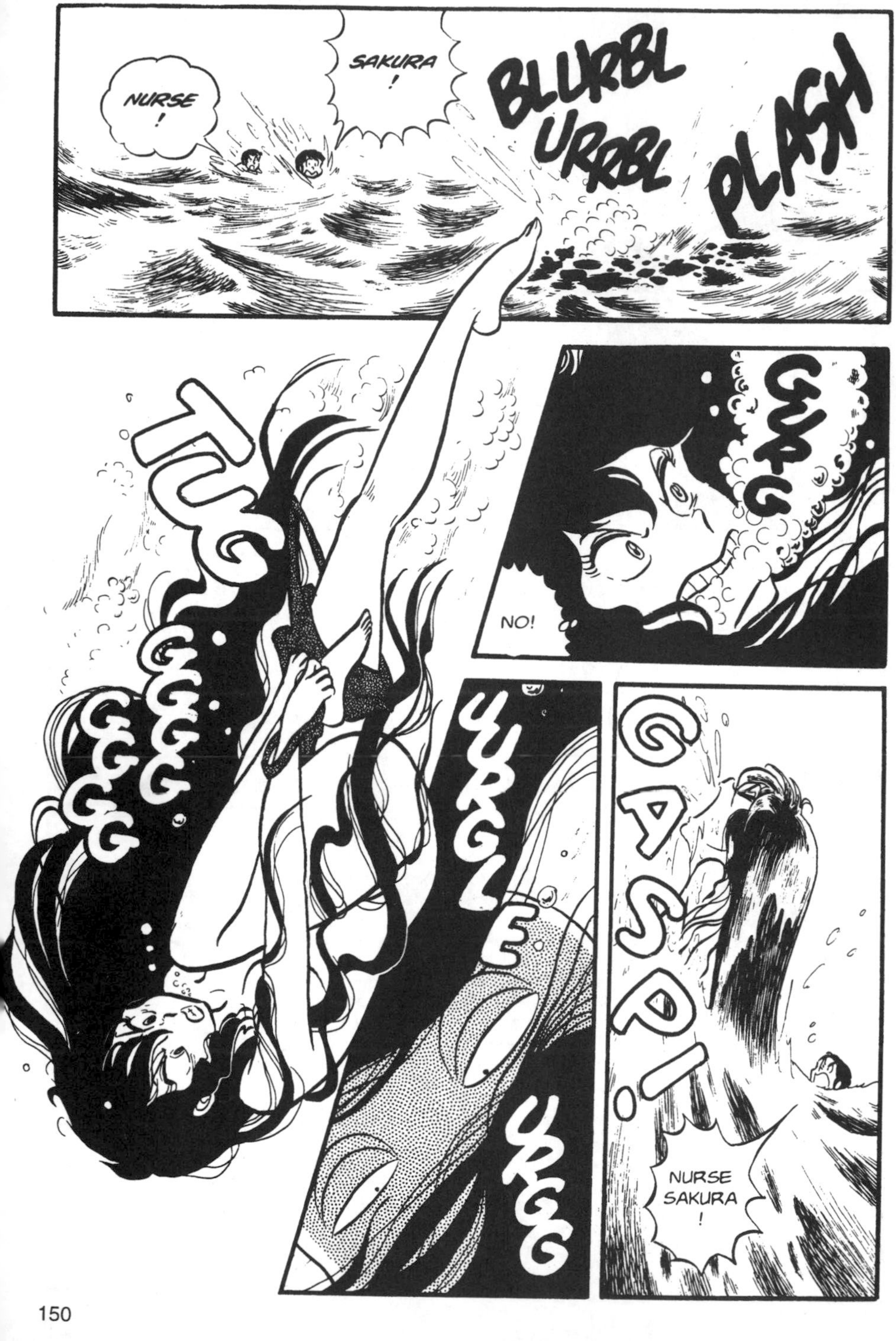
NURSE !
SAKURA !
BLURBL URRBL
PLASH
TUG GGGG GGGG
GURG
NO!
URGLE
URGG
GASP!
NURSE SAKURA !

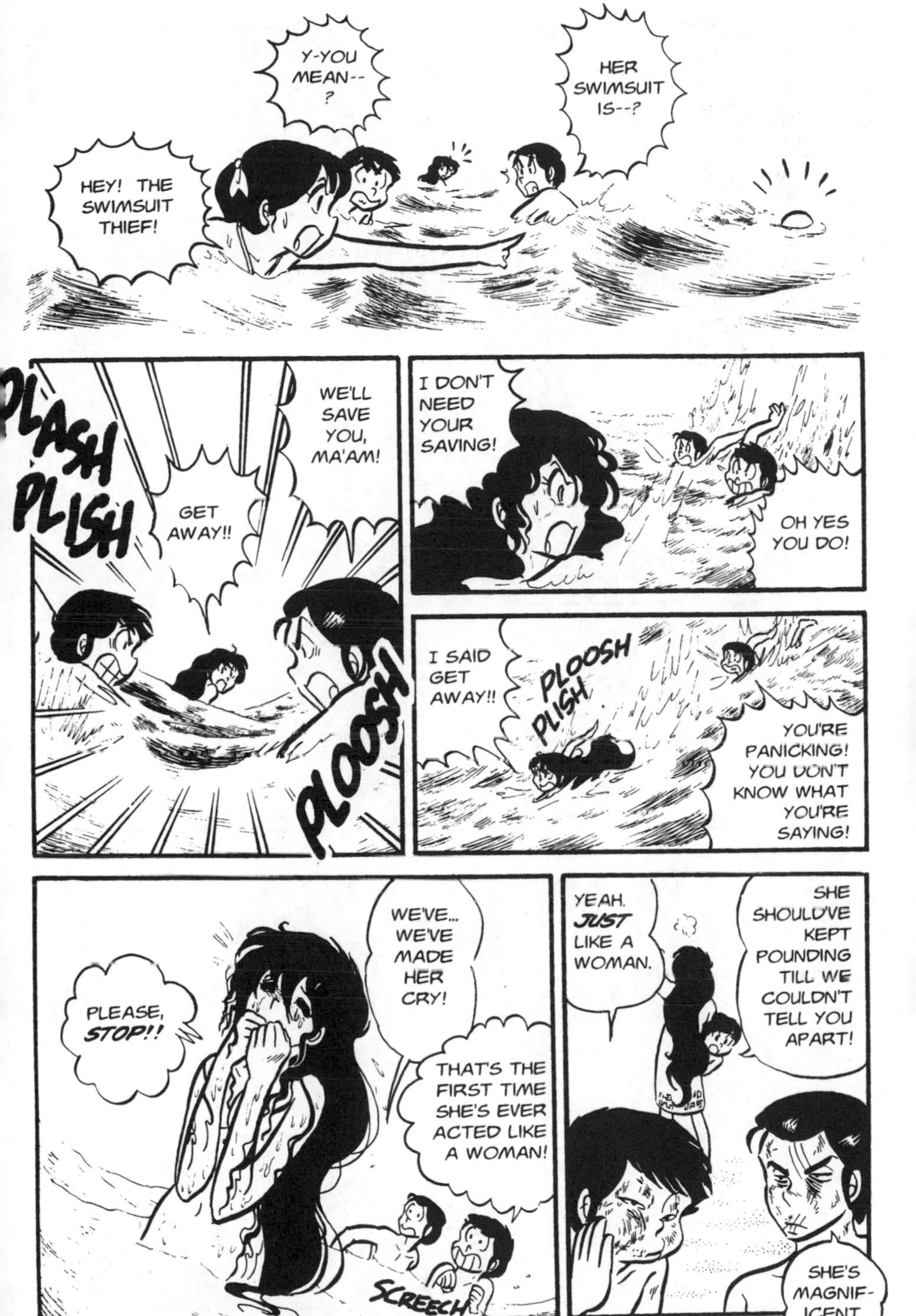
Y-YOU MEAN--?
HER SWIMSUIT IS--?
HEY! THE SWIMSUIT THIEF!
PLASH PLISH
WE'LL SAVE YOU, MA'AM!
GET AWAY!!
PLOOSH
I DON'T NEED YOUR SAVING!
OH YES YOU DO!
I SAID GET AWAY!!
PLOOSH PLISH
YOU'RE PANICKING! YOU DON'T KNOW WHAT YOU'RE SAYING!
WE'VE... WE'VE MADE HER CRY!
PLEASE, STOP!!
THAT'S THE FIRST TIME SHE'S EVER ACTED LIKE A WOMAN!
SCREECH
YEAH. JUST LIKE A WOMAN.
SHE SHOULD'VE KEPT POUNDING TILL WE COULDN'T TELL YOU APART!
SHE'S MAGNIF- ICENT.

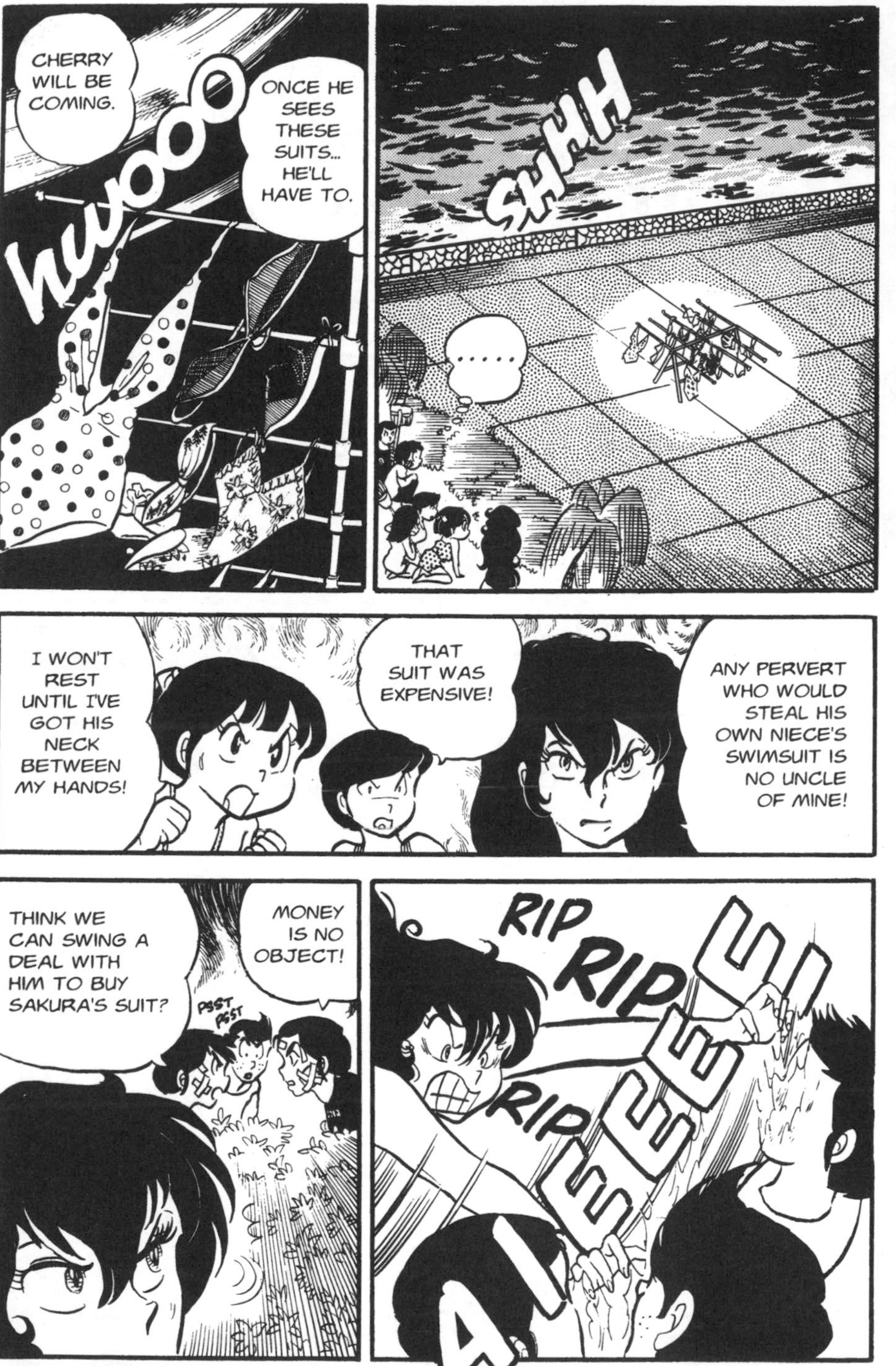
CHERRY WILL BE COMING.
HWOOOO
ONCE HE SEES THESE SUITS... HE'LL HAVE TO.
SHHH
......
I WON'T REST UNTIL I'VE GOT HIS NECK BETWEEN MY HANDS!
THAT SUIT WAS EXPENSIVE!
ANY PERVERT WHO WOULD STEAL HIS OWN NIECE'S SWIMSUIT IS NO UNCLE OF MINE!
THINK WE CAN SWING A DEAL WITH HIM TO BUY SAKURA'S SUIT?
MONEY IS NO OBJECT!
PSST PSST
RIP
RIP
RIP
AIEEEEE!!

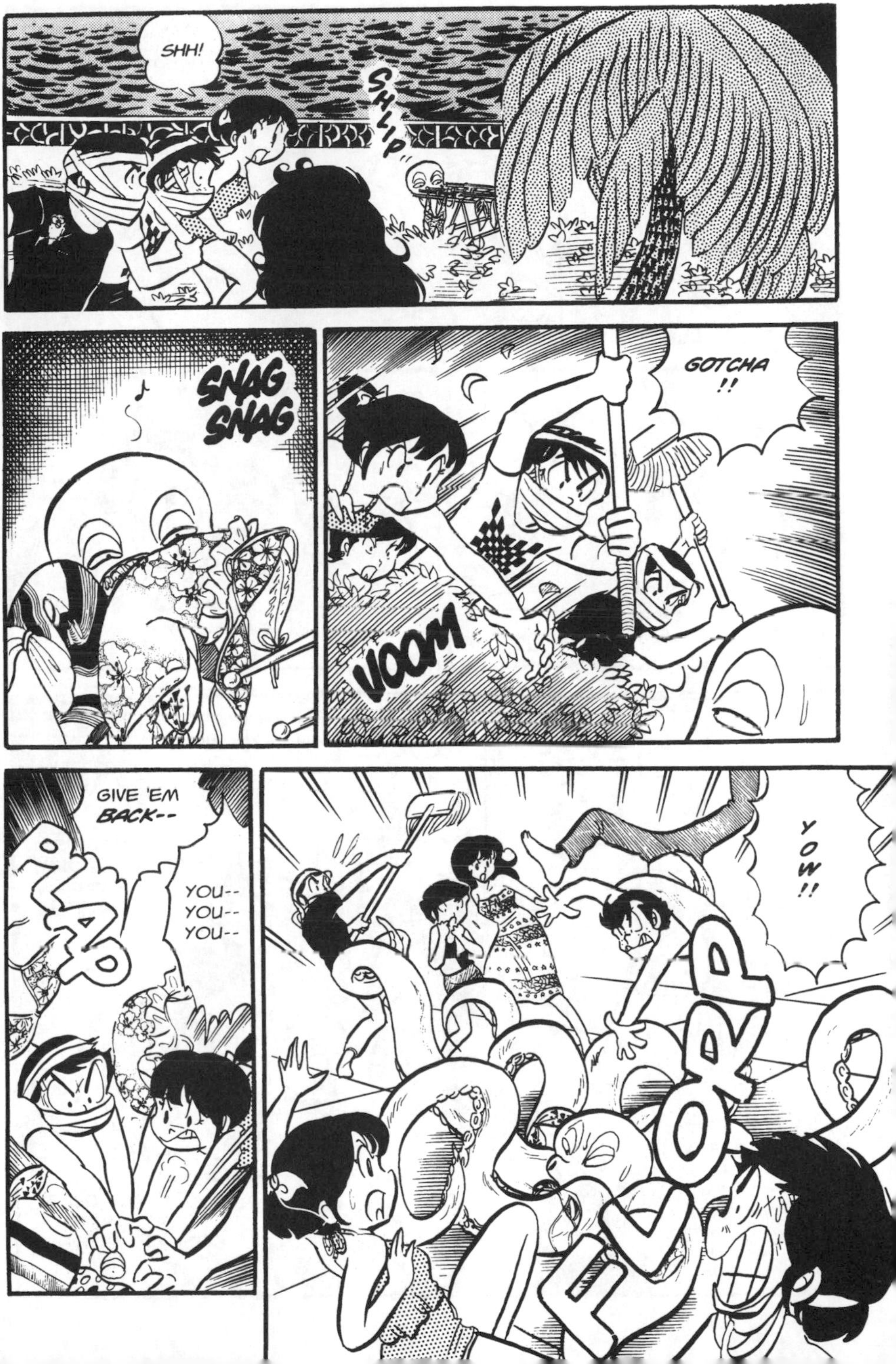
SHH!
SHLIP
SNAG SNAG
GOTCHA !!
VOOM
GIVE 'EM BACK--
PLAP
YOU-- YOU-- YOU--
YOW!!
FLORP

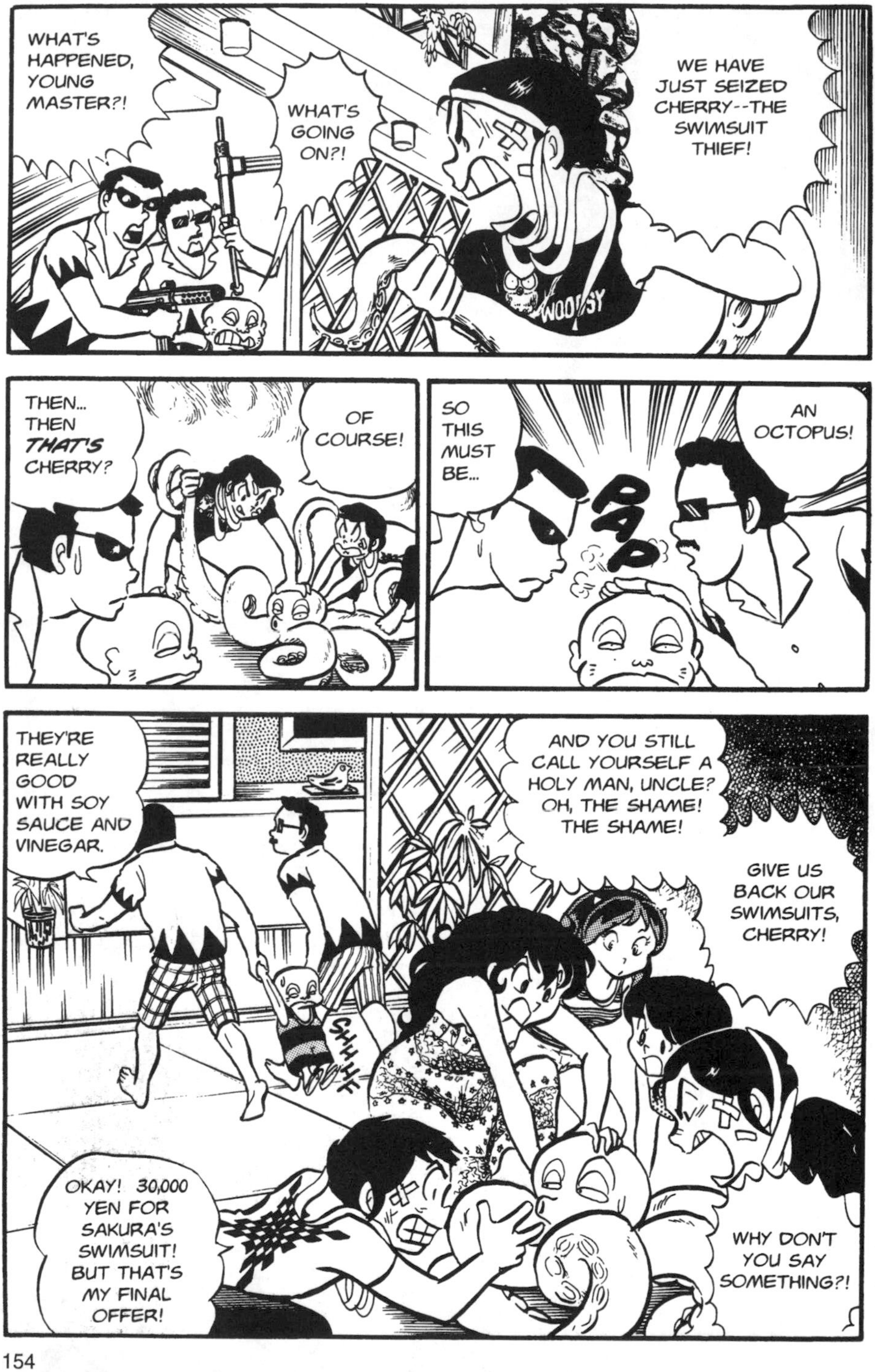
WHAT'S HAPPENED, YOUNG MASTER?!
WHAT'S GOING ON?!
WE HAVE JUST SEIZED CHERRY--THE SWIMSUIT THIEF!
WOODSY
THEN... THEN *THAT'S* CHERRY?
OF COURSE!
SO THIS MUST BE...
AN OCTOPUS!
PAP
THEY'RE REALLY GOOD WITH SOY SAUCE AND VINEGAR.
AND YOU STILL CALL YOURSELF A HOLY MAN, UNCLE? OH, THE SHAME! THE SHAME!
GIVE US BACK OUR SWIMSUITS, CHERRY!
SHHHF
OKAY! 30,000 YEN FOR SAKURA'S SWIMSUIT! BUT THAT'S MY FINAL OFFER!
WHY DON'T YOU SAY SOMETHING?!

PART TEN
LET'S HAVE THAT BIKINI!

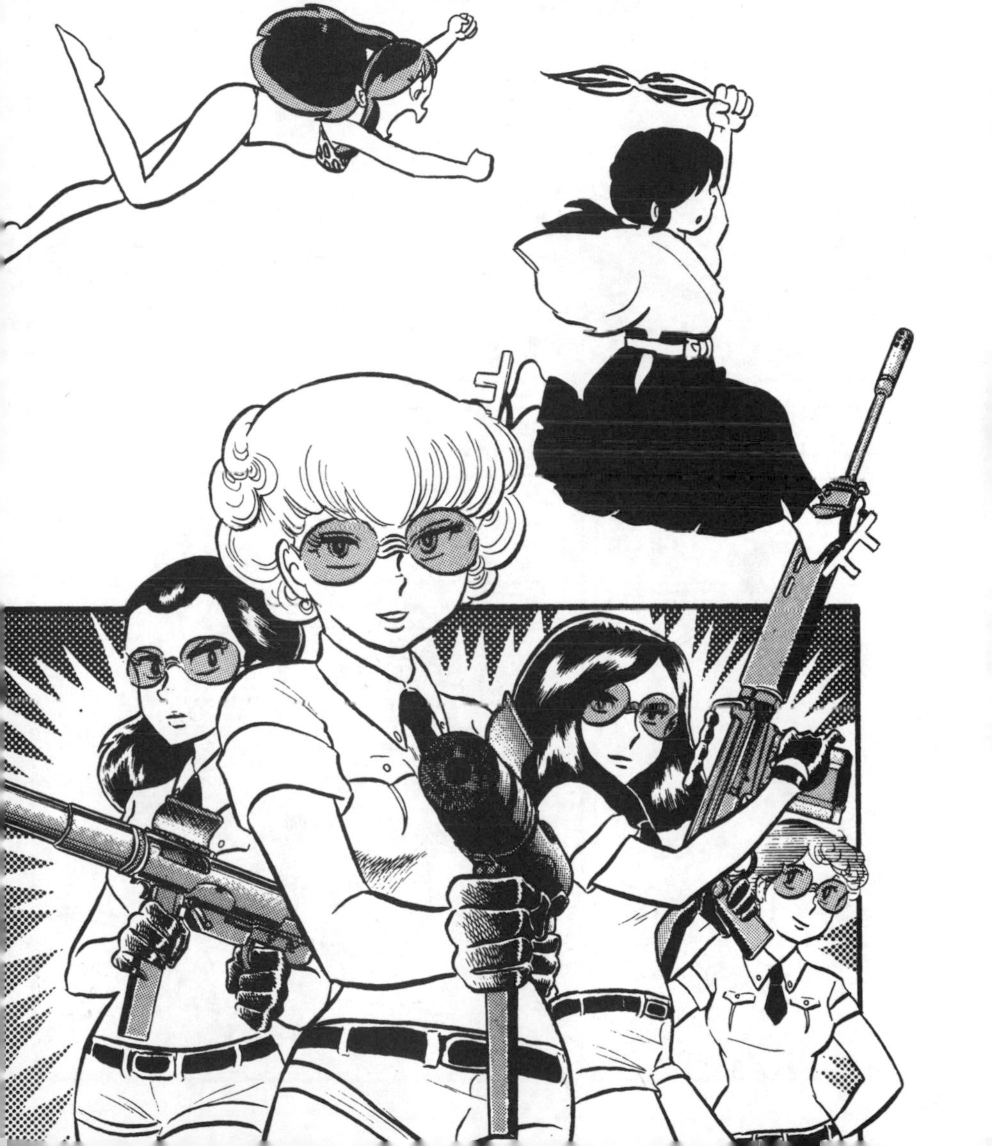

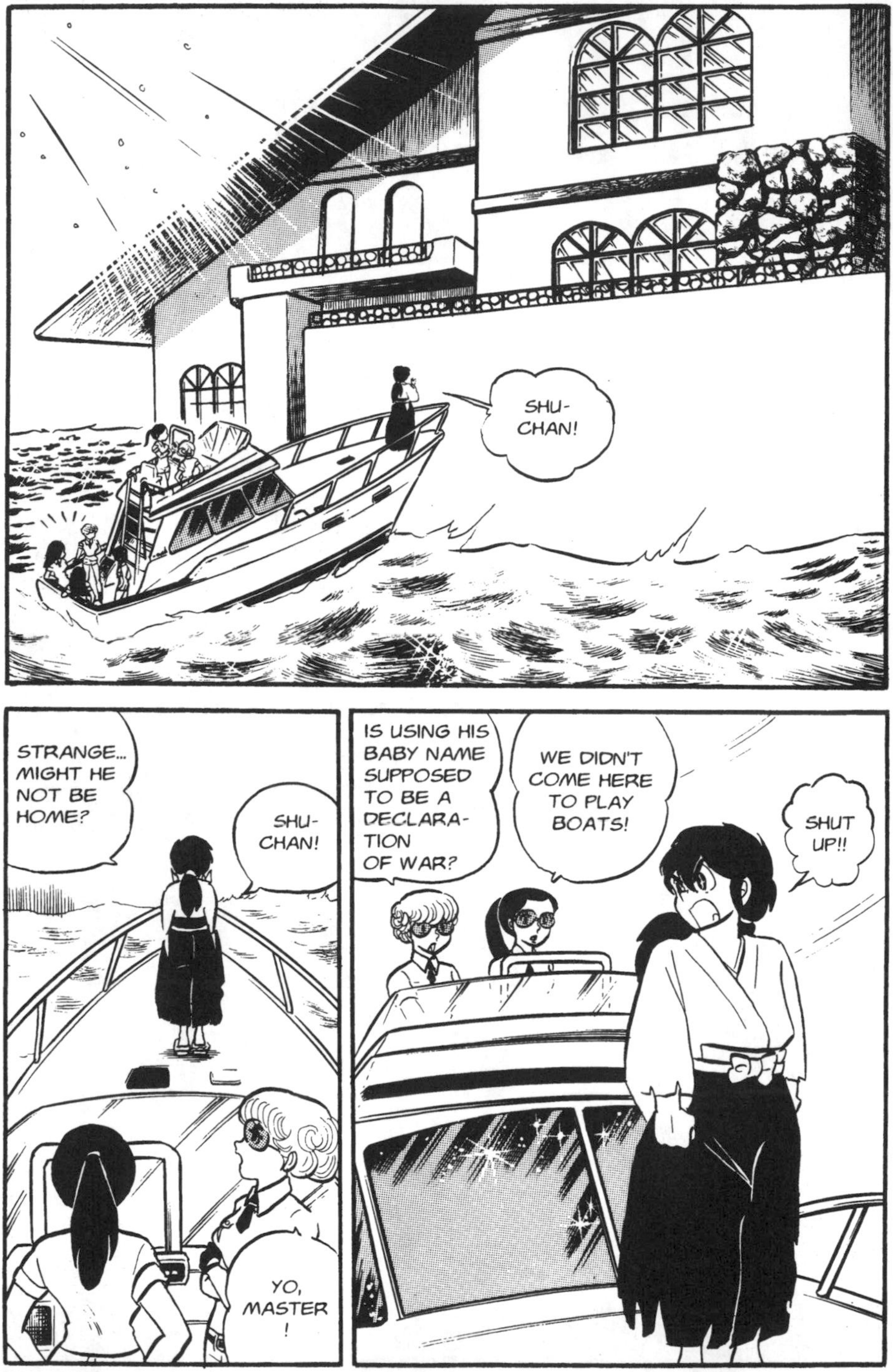
SHU-CHAN!
STRANGE... MIGHT HE NOT BE HOME?
SHU-CHAN!
YO, MASTER!
IS USING HIS BABY NAME SUPPOSED TO BE A DECLARATION OF WAR?
WE DIDN'T COME HERE TO PLAY BOATS!
SHUT UP!!

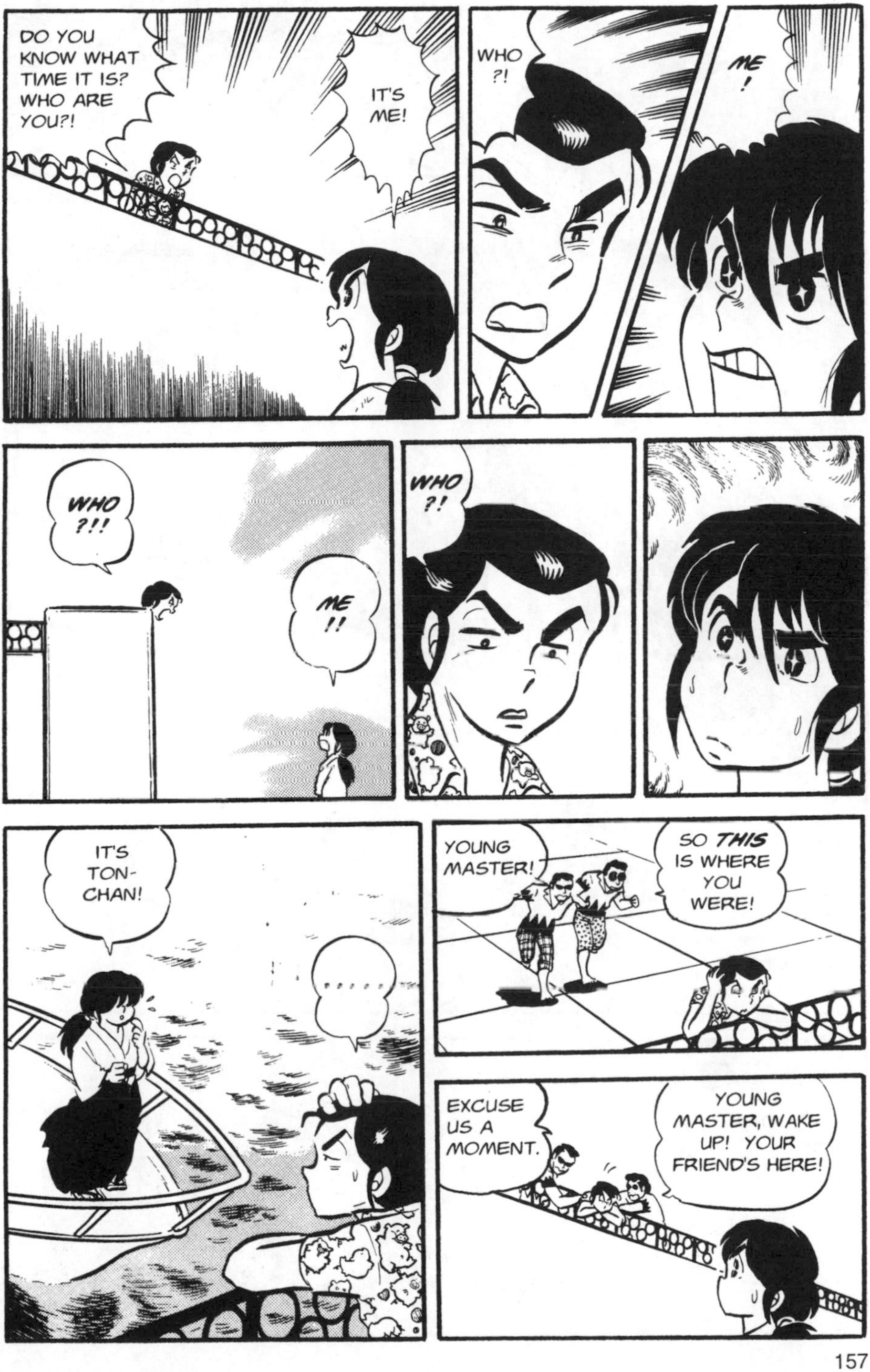
DO YOU KNOW WHAT TIME IT IS? WHO ARE YOU?!
IT'S ME!
WHO ?!
ME !
WHO ?!!
ME !!
WHO ?!
IT'S TON-CHAN!
......
YOUNG MASTER!
SO THIS IS WHERE YOU WERE!
EXCUSE US A MOMENT.
YOUNG MASTER, WAKE UP! YOUR FRIEND'S HERE!

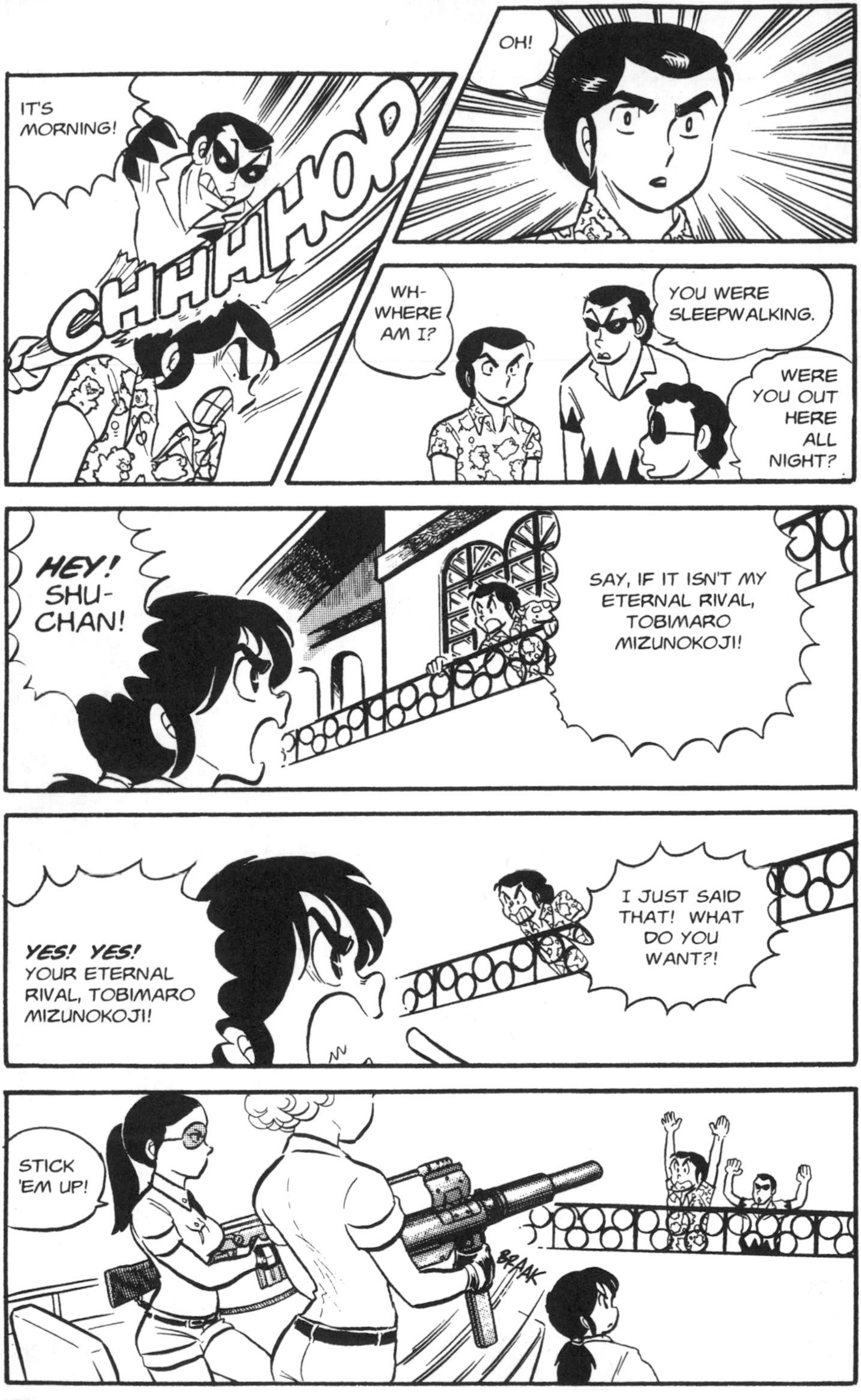
IT'S MORNING!
CHHHHOP
OH!
WH- WHERE AM I?
YOU WERE SLEEPWALKING.
WERE YOU OUT HERE ALL NIGHT?
HEY! SHU-CHAN!
SAY, IF IT ISN'T MY ETERNAL RIVAL, TOBIMARO MIZUNOKOJI!
YES! YES! YOUR ETERNAL RIVAL, TOBIMARO MIZUNOKOJI!
I JUST SAID THAT! WHAT DO YOU WANT?!
STICK 'EM UP!
BRAAK

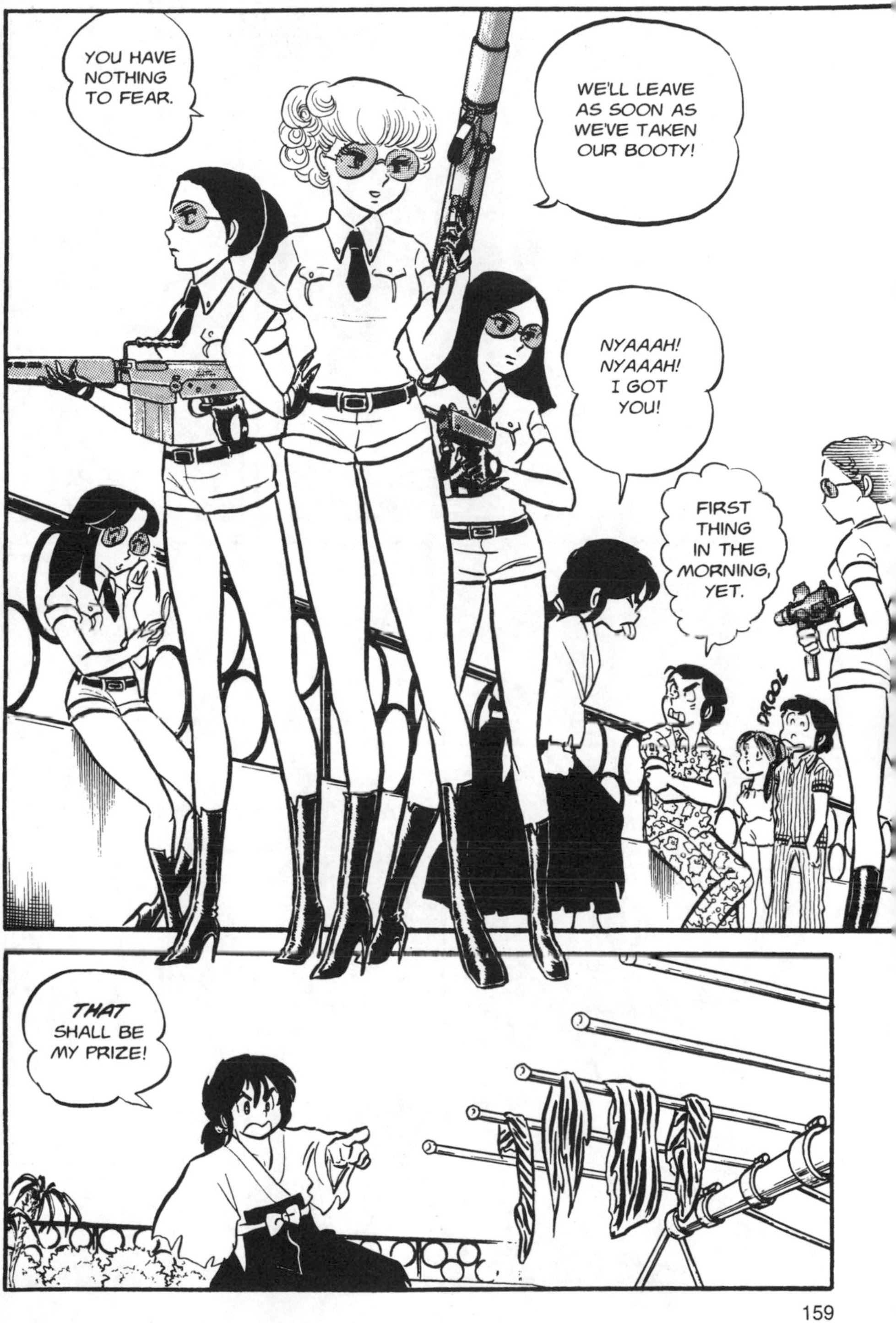
YOU HAVE NOTHING TO FEAR.
WE'LL LEAVE AS SOON AS WE'VE TAKEN OUR BOOTY!
NYAAAH! NYAAAH! I GOT YOU!
FIRST THING IN THE MORNING, YET.
DROOL
THAT SHALL BE MY PRIZE!

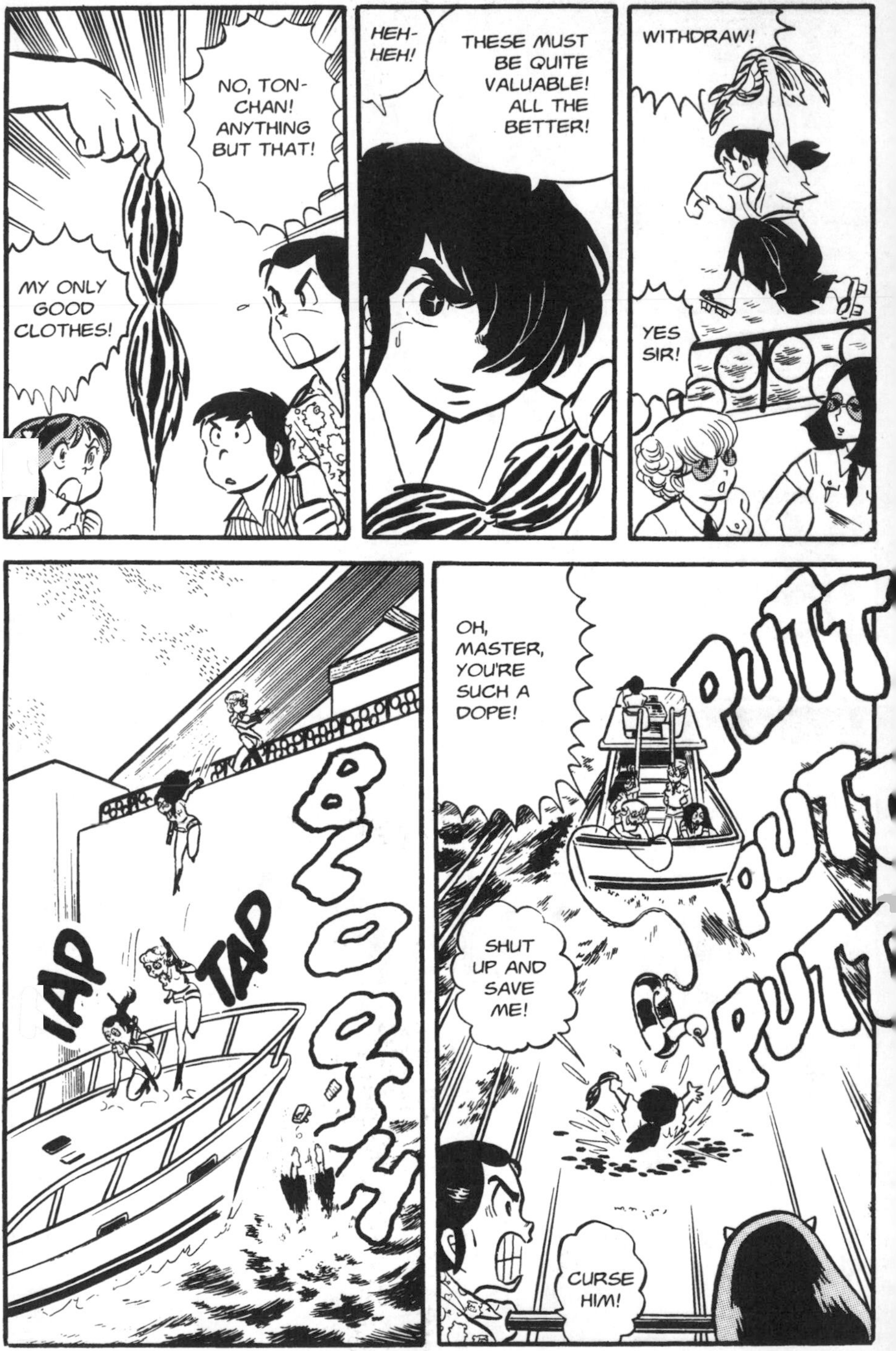
NO, TON-CHAN! ANYTHING BUT THAT!
MY ONLY GOOD CLOTHES!
HEH-HEH!
THESE MUST BE QUITE VALUABLE! ALL THE BETTER!
WITHDRAW!
YES SIR!
TAP
TAP
BLOOSH
OH, MASTER, YOU'RE SUCH A DOPE!
SHUT UP AND SAVE ME!
CURSE HIM!

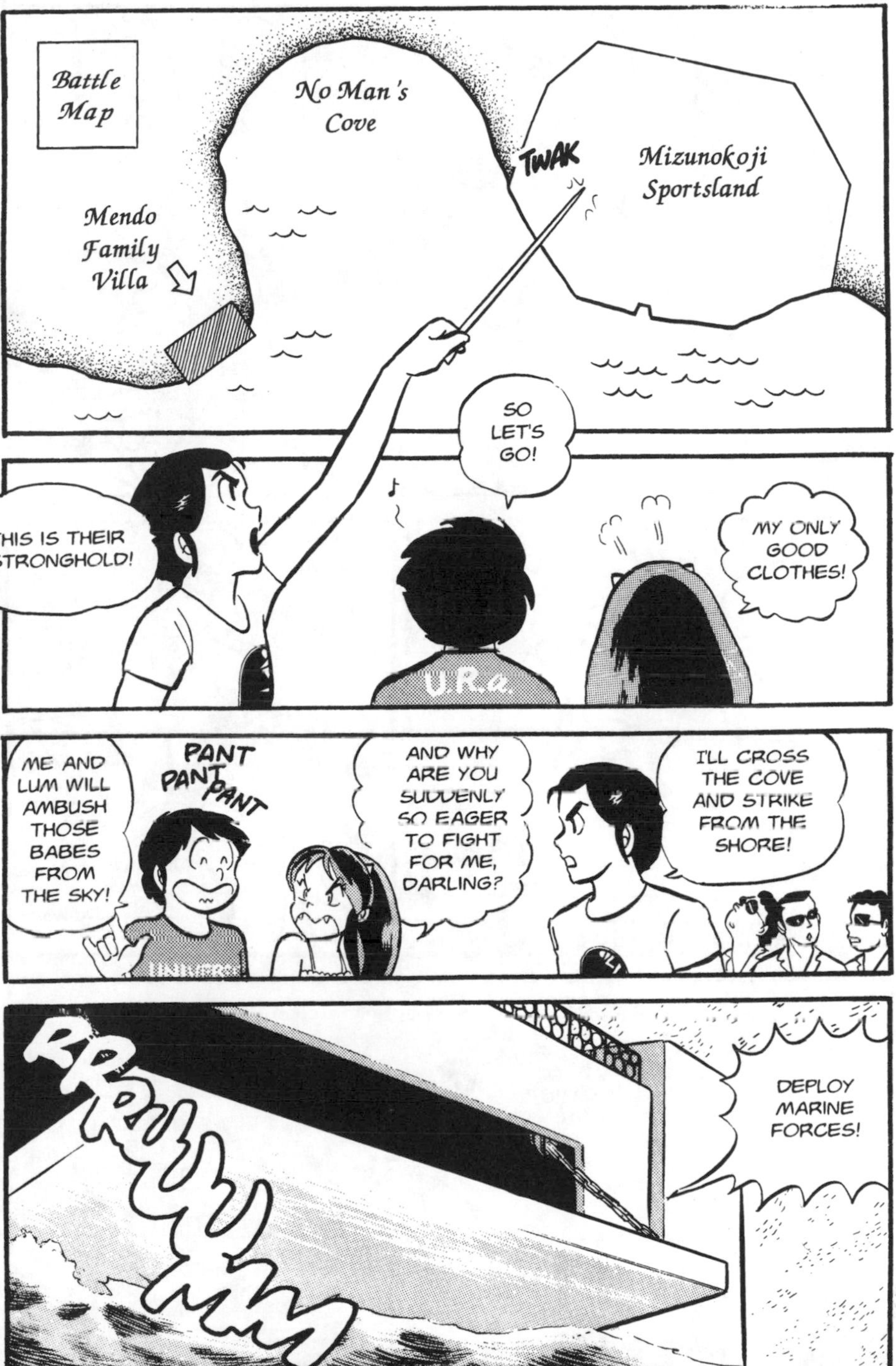
Battle Map
No Man's Cove
TWAK
Mizunokoji Sportsland
Mendo Family Villa
THIS IS THEIR STRONGHOLD!
SO LET'S GO!
MY ONLY GOOD CLOTHES!
ME AND LUM WILL AMBUSH THOSE BABES FROM THE SKY!
PANT PANT PANT
AND WHY ARE YOU SUDDENLY SO EAGER TO FIGHT FOR ME, DARLING?
I'LL CROSS THE COVE AND STRIKE FROM THE SHORE!
RRRUUMMM
DEPLOY MARINE FORCES!

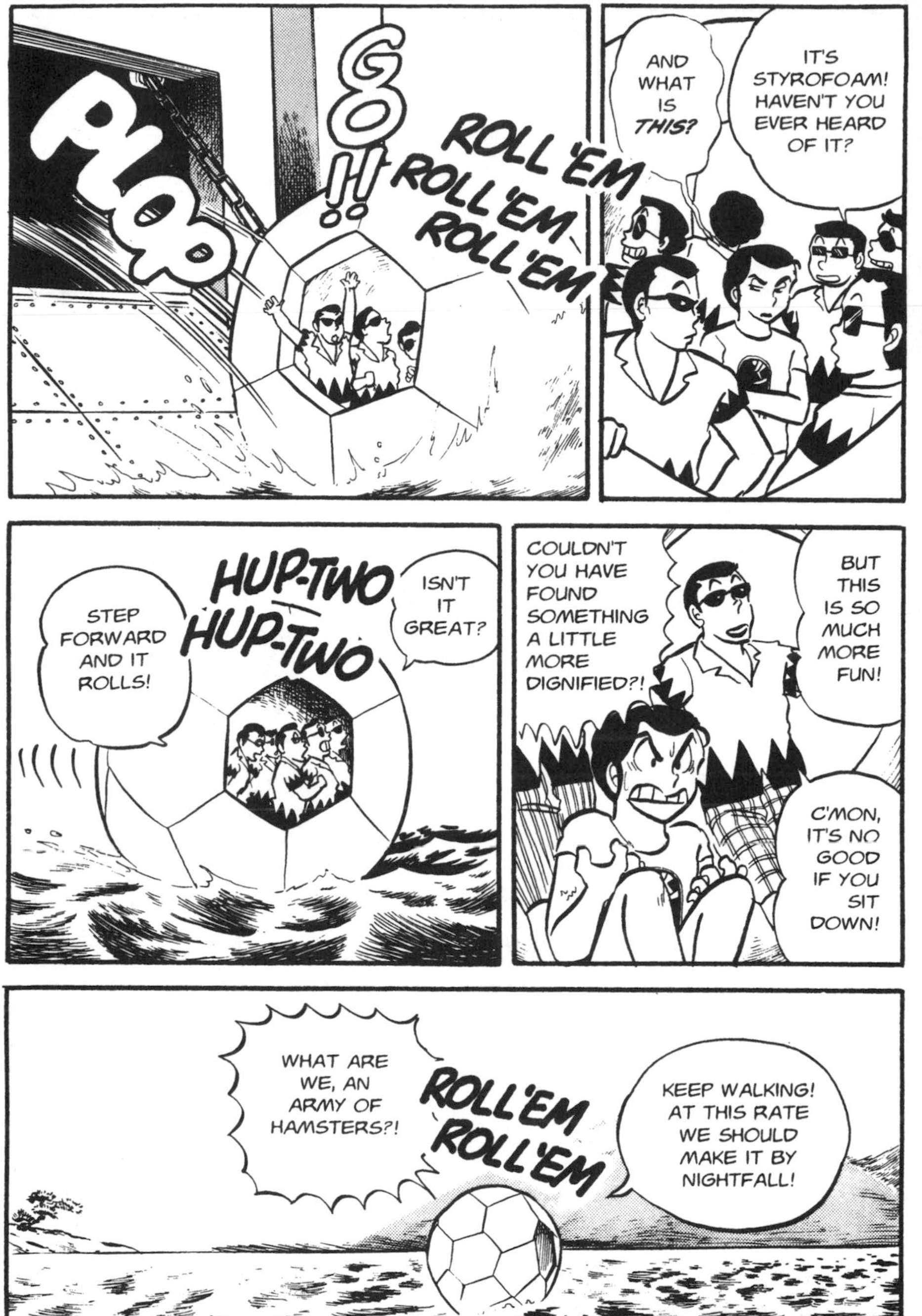
PLOP
GO!!
ROLL 'EM
ROLL 'EM
ROLL 'EM
AND WHAT IS *THIS?*
IT'S STYROFOAM! HAVEN'T YOU EVER HEARD OF IT?
STEP FORWARD AND IT ROLLS!
HUP-TWO
HUP-TWO
ISN'T IT GREAT?
COULDN'T YOU HAVE FOUND SOMETHING A LITTLE MORE DIGNIFIED?!
BUT THIS IS SO MUCH MORE FUN!
C'MON, IT'S NO GOOD IF YOU SIT DOWN!
WHAT ARE WE, AN ARMY OF HAMSTERS?!
ROLL'EM
ROLL'EM
KEEP WALKING! AT THIS RATE WE SHOULD MAKE IT BY NIGHTFALL!

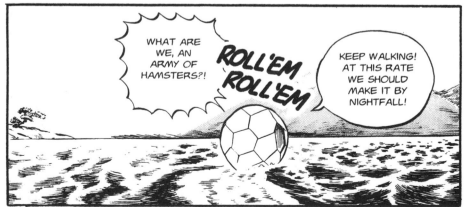

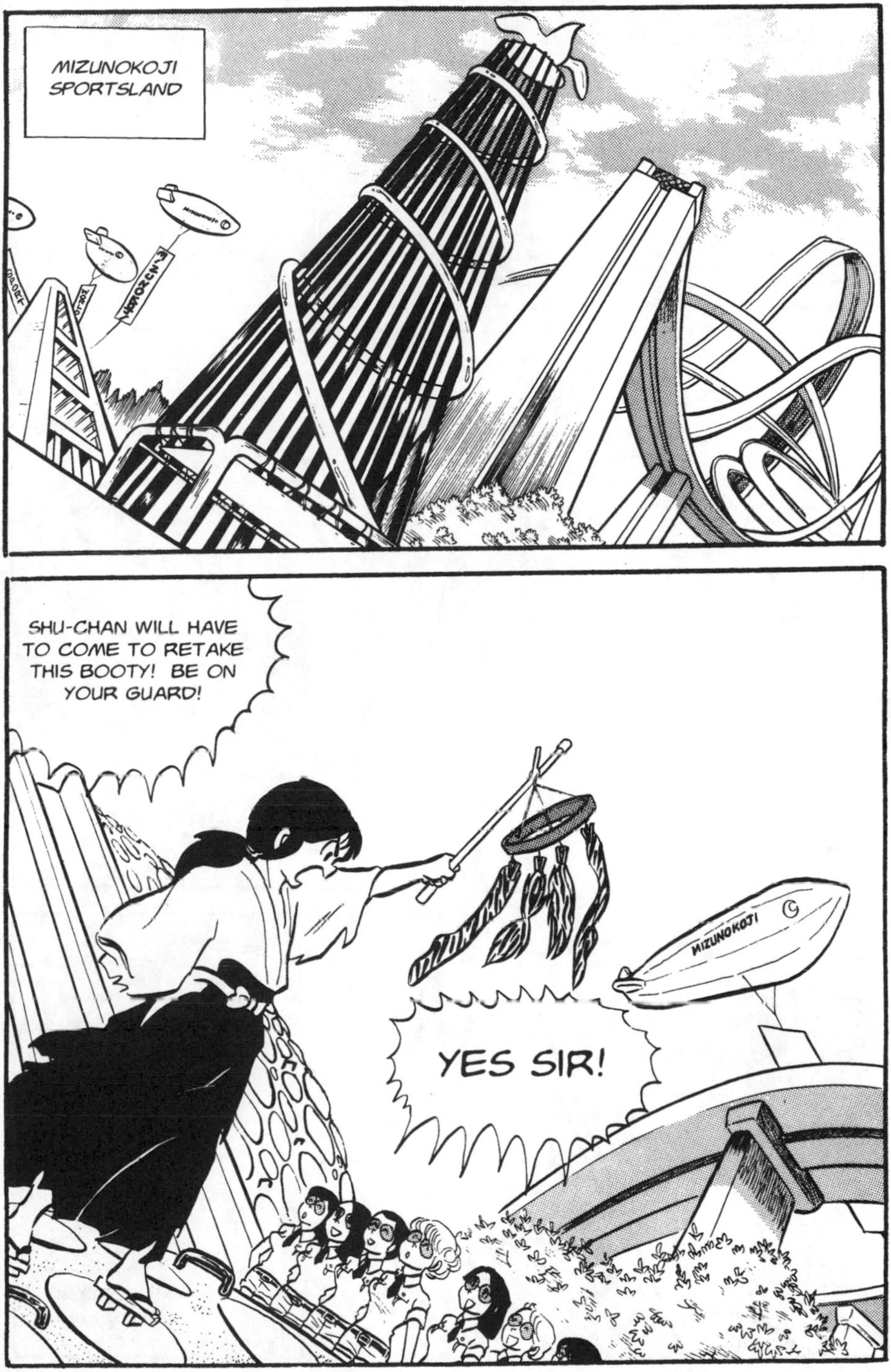
MIZUNOKOJI SPORTSLAND
SHU-CHAN WILL HAVE TO COME TO RETAKE THIS BOOTY! BE ON YOUR GUARD!
MIZUNOKOJI
YES SIR!

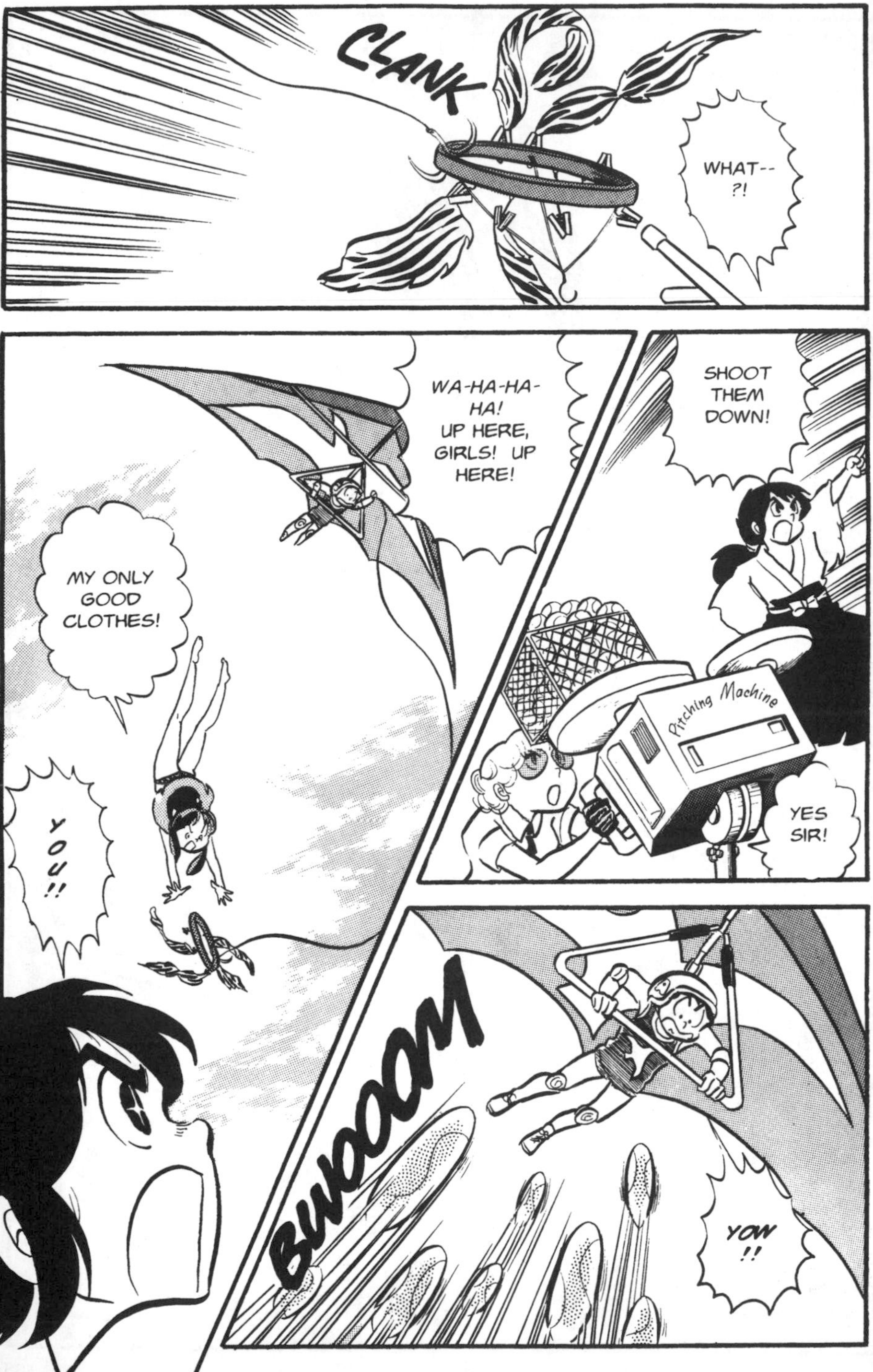
CLANK
WHAT-- ?!
MY ONLY GOOD CLOTHES!
YOU!!
WA-HA-HA-HA! UP HERE, GIRLS! UP HERE!
SHOOT THEM DOWN!
Pitching Machine
YES SIR!
BWOOOM
YOW !!

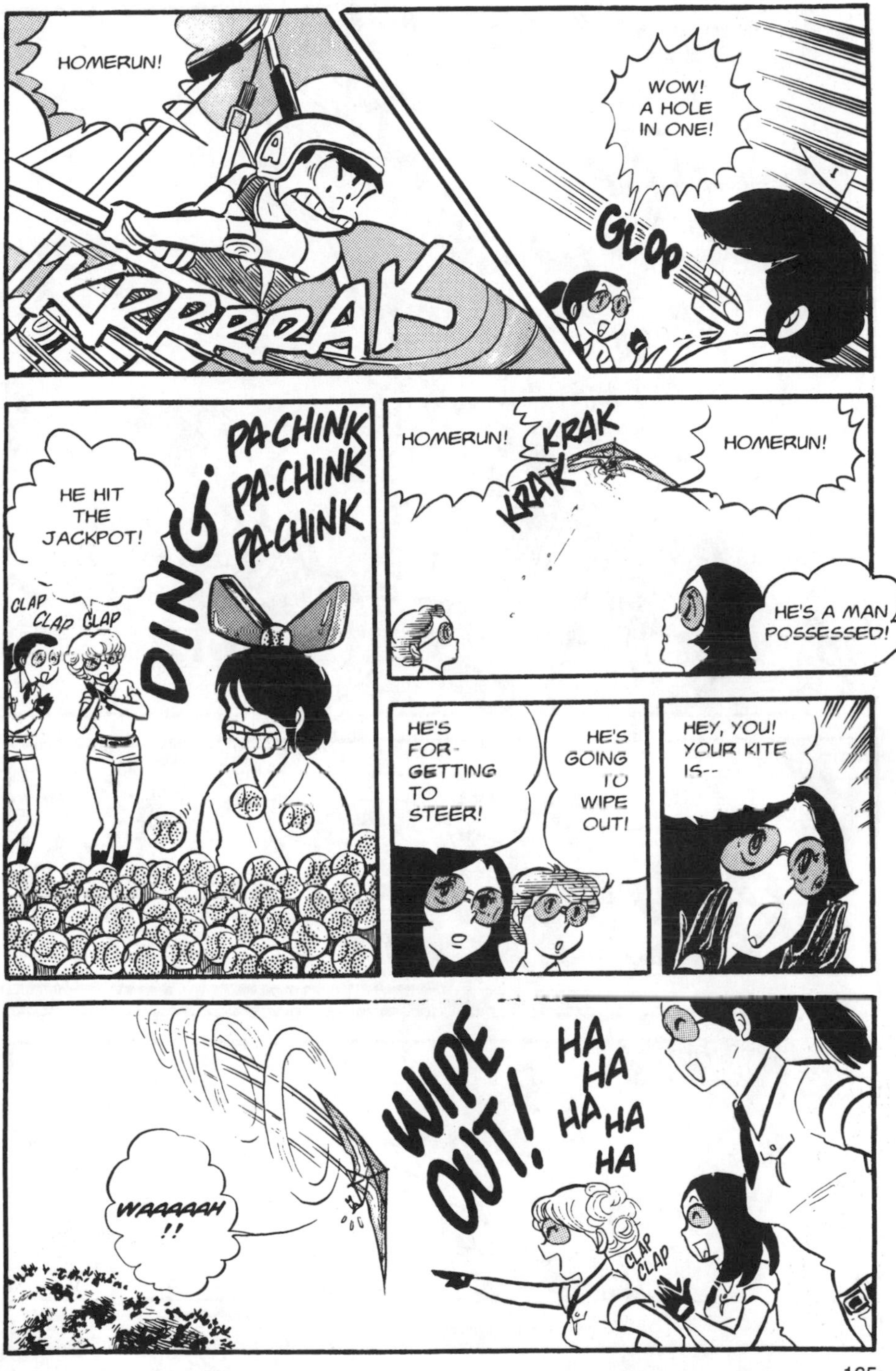
HOMERUN!
KRRRRAK
WOW! A HOLE IN ONE!
GLOP
HE HIT THE JACKPOT!
CLAP CLAP CLAP
DING!
PA-CHINK PA-CHINK PA-CHINK
HOMERUN!
KRAK KRAK
HOMERUN!
HE'S A MAN POSSESSED!
HE'S FOR-GETTING TO STEER!
HE'S GOING TO WIPE OUT!
HEY, YOU! YOUR KITE IS--
WAAAAAH !!
WIPE OUT!
HA HA HA HA HA
CLAP CLAP

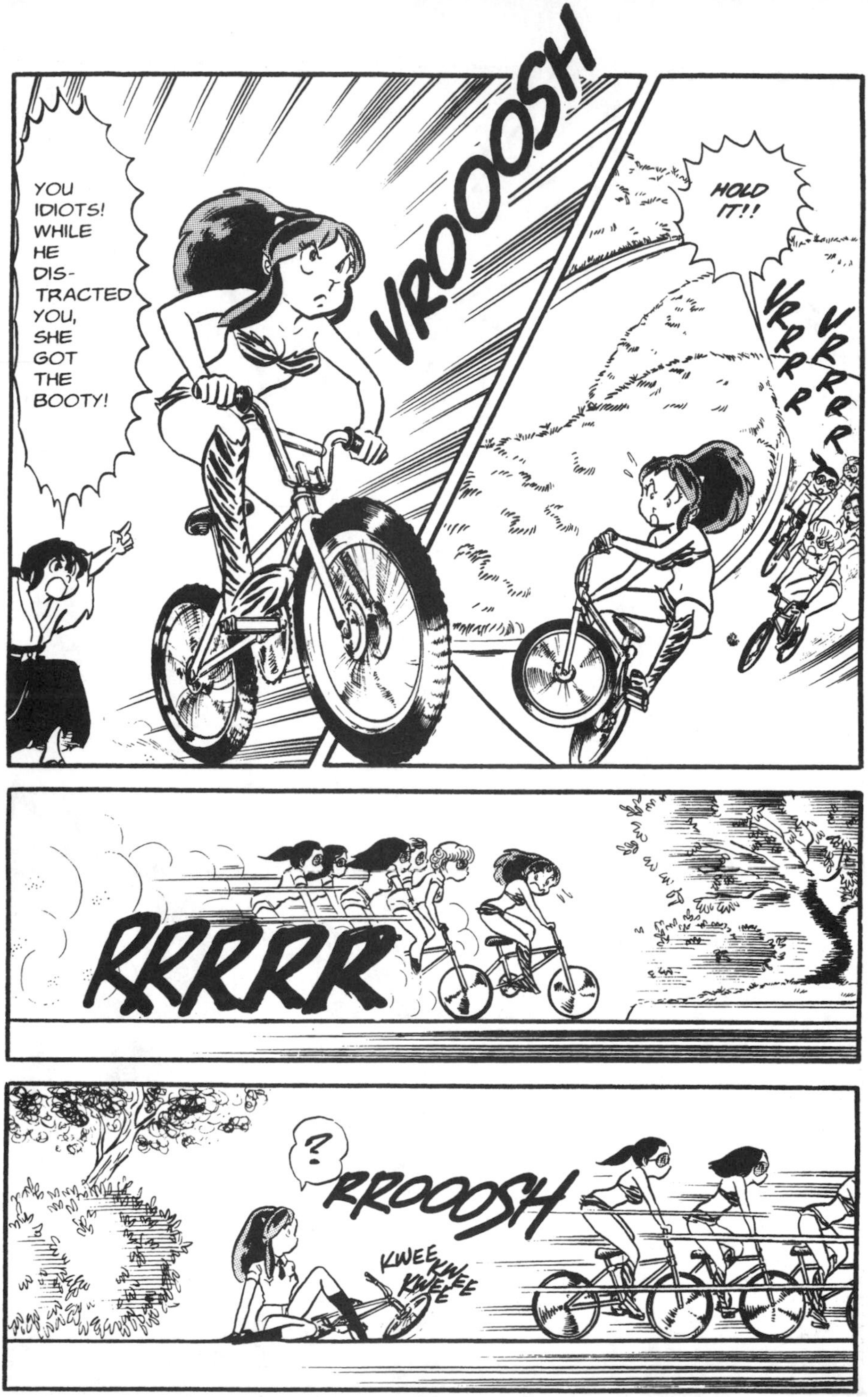
YOU IDIOTS! WHILE HE DISTRACTED YOU, SHE GOT THE BOOTY!
VROOOSH
HOLD IT!!
VRRRRR
VRRRRR
RRRRRR
?
RROOOSH
KWEE KWEE KWEEE

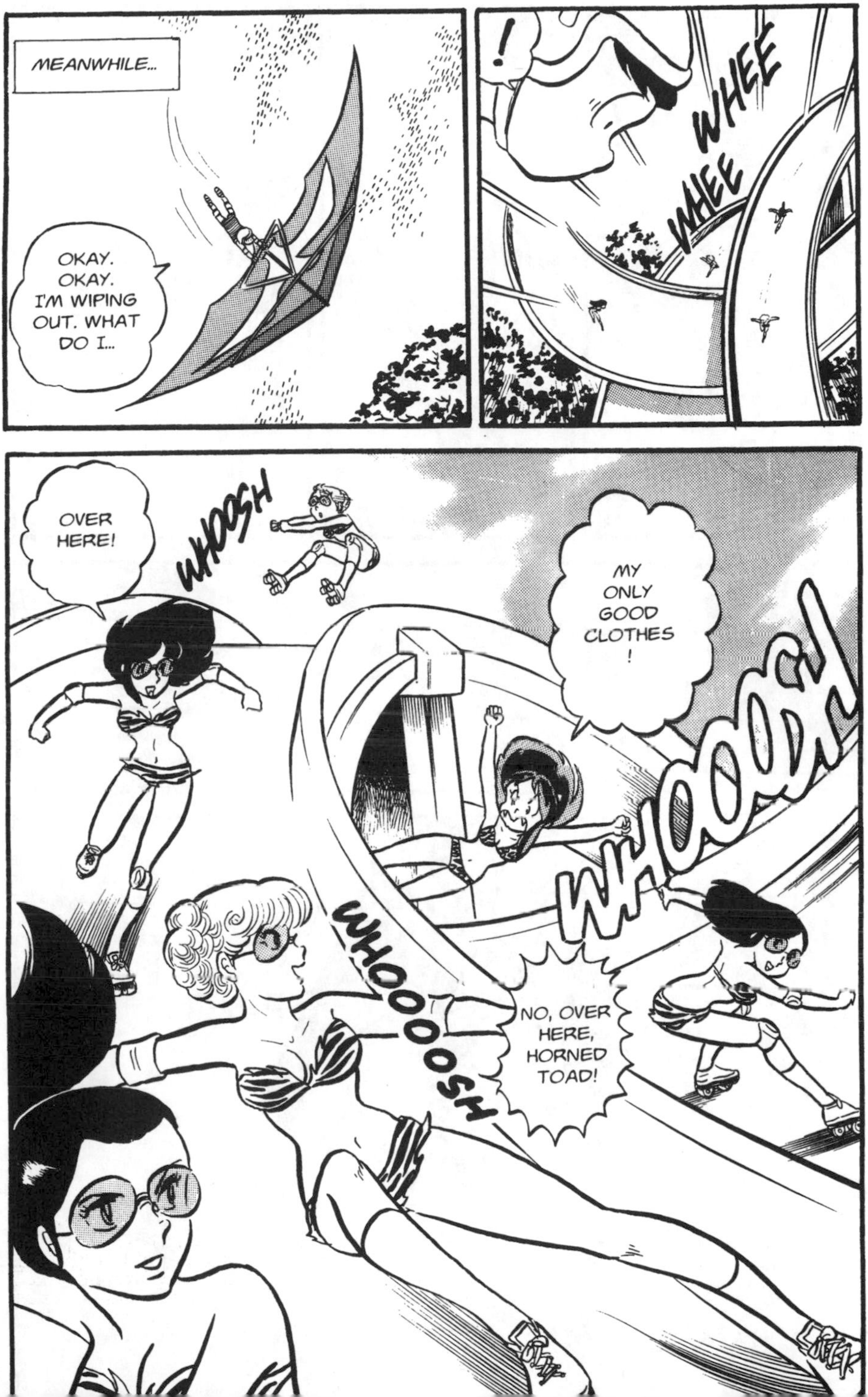
MEANWHILE...
OKAY. OKAY. I'M WIPING OUT. WHAT DO I...
!
WHEE
WHEE
OVER HERE!
WHOOSH
MY ONLY GOOD CLOTHES !
WHOOOSH
WHOOOOOOSH
NO, OVER HERE, HORNED TOAD!

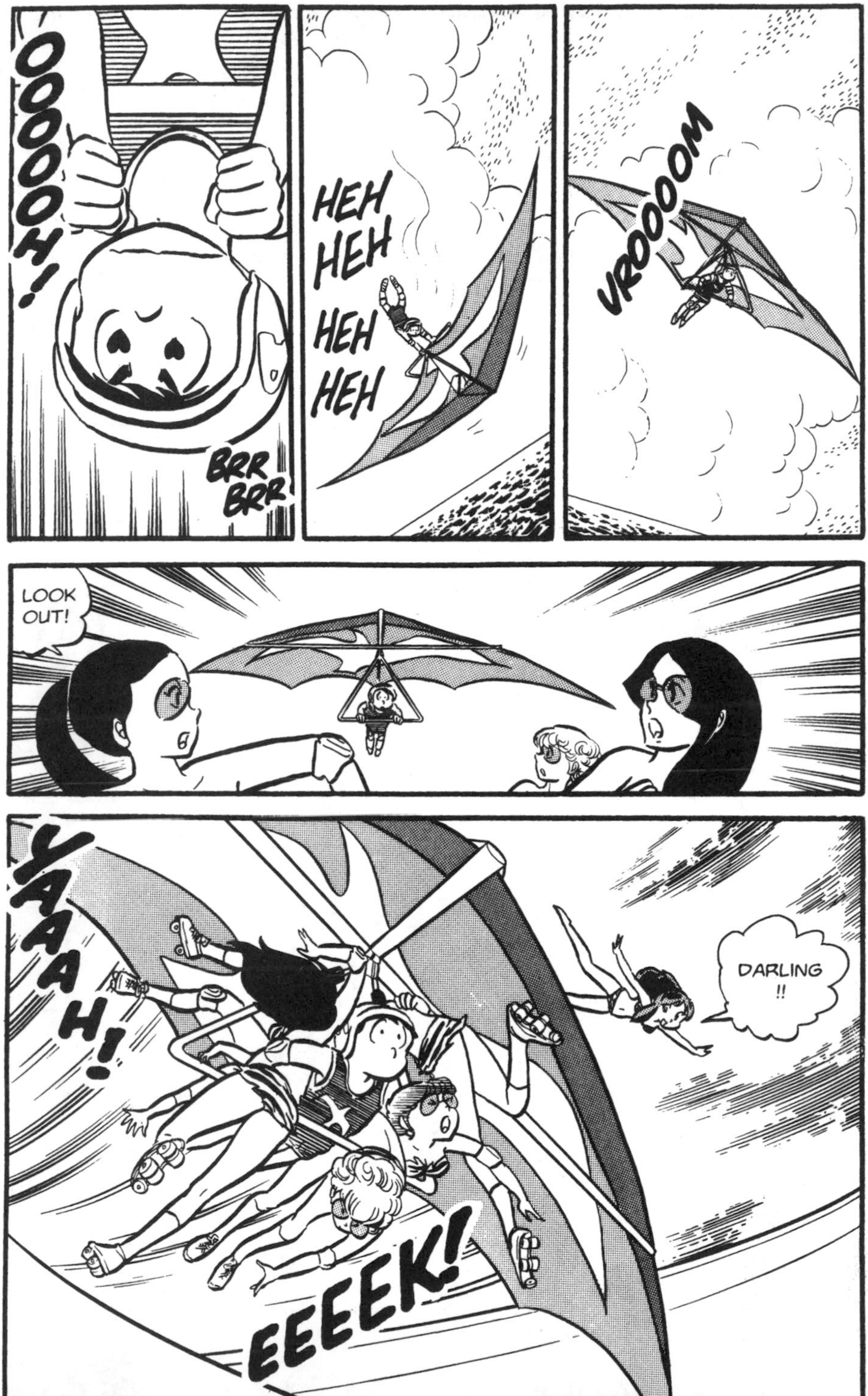
OOOOOOH!!
BRR BRR
HEH HEH HEH HEH
VROOOOM
LOOK OUT!
YAAAAH!!
DARLING !!
EEEEK!

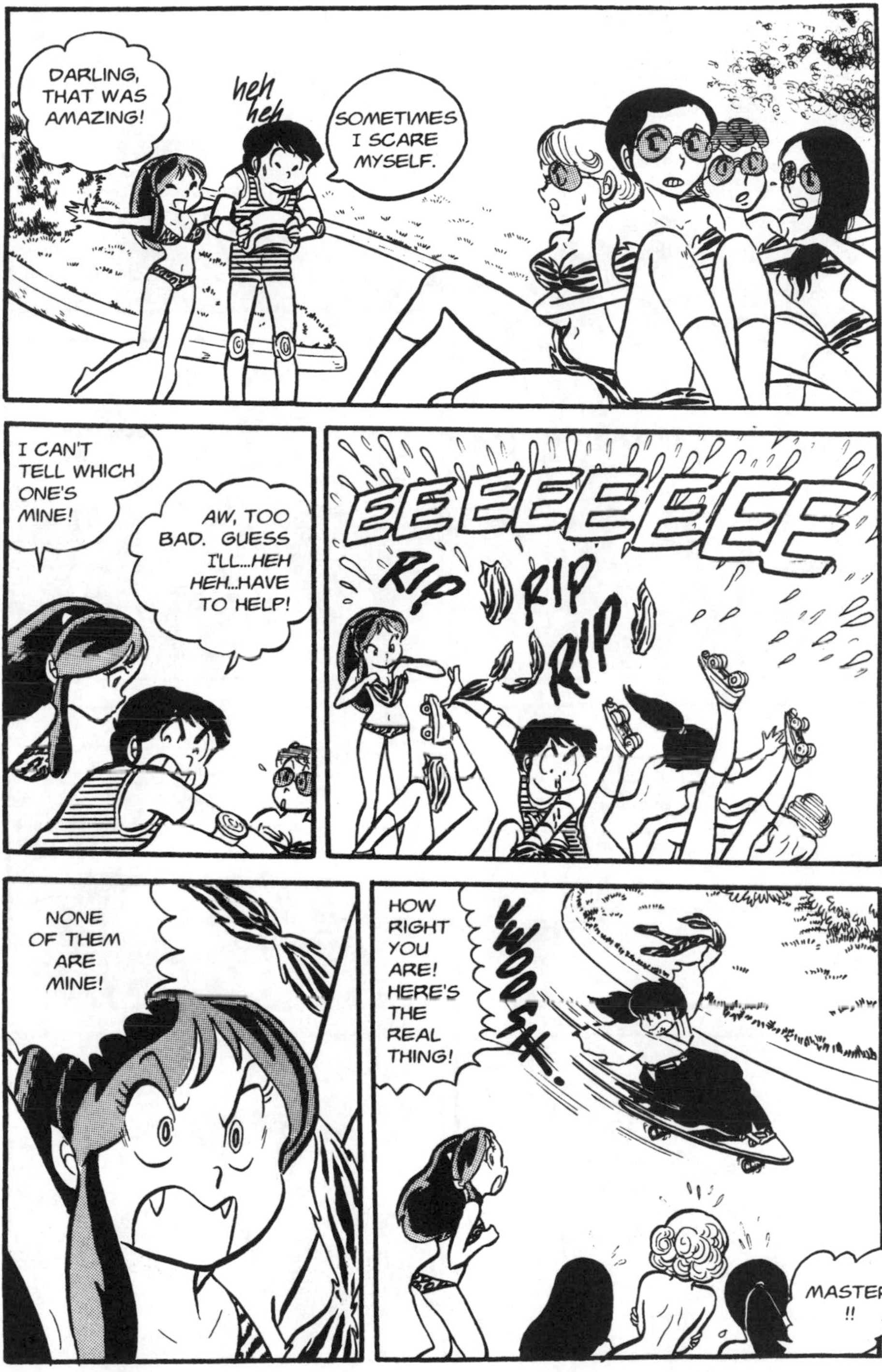
DARLING, THAT WAS AMAZING!
heh heh
SOMETIMES I SCARE MYSELF.
I CAN'T TELL WHICH ONE'S MINE!
AW, TOO BAD. GUESS I'LL...HEH HEH...HAVE TO HELP!
EEEEEEEE
RIP RIP RIP
NONE OF THEM ARE MINE!
HOW RIGHT YOU ARE! HERE'S THE REAL THING!
WOOSH!
MASTER !!

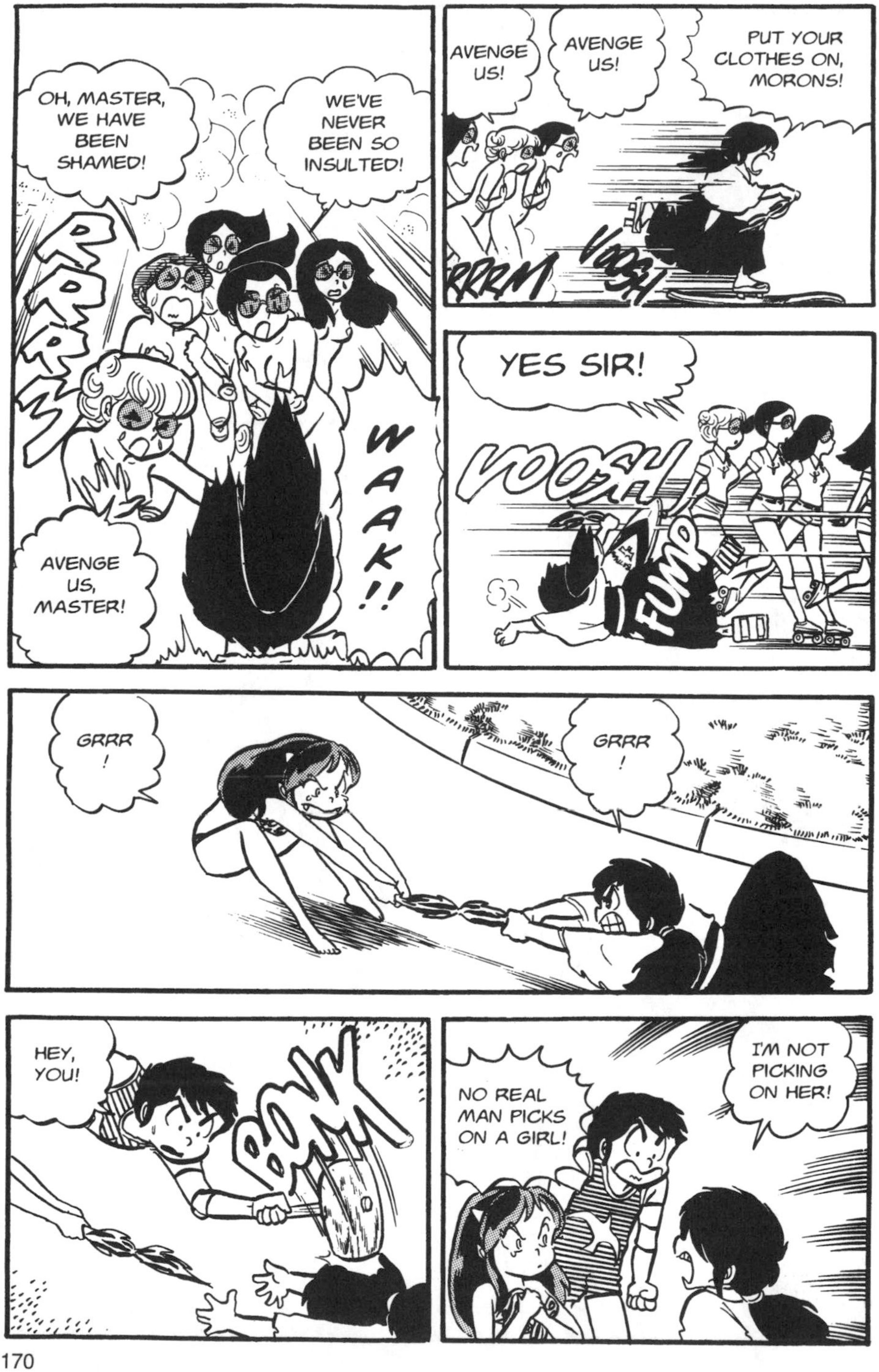
OH, MASTER, WE HAVE BEEN SHAMED!
WE'VE NEVER BEEN SO INSULTED!
PRRRM
AVENGE US, MASTER!
WAAAK!!
AVENGE US!
AVENGE US!
PUT YOUR CLOTHES ON, MORONS!
RRRM
VOOSH
YES SIR!
VOOSH
FUMP
GRRR !
GRRR !
HEY, YOU!
BONK
NO REAL MAN PICKS ON A GIRL!
I'M NOT PICKING ON HER!

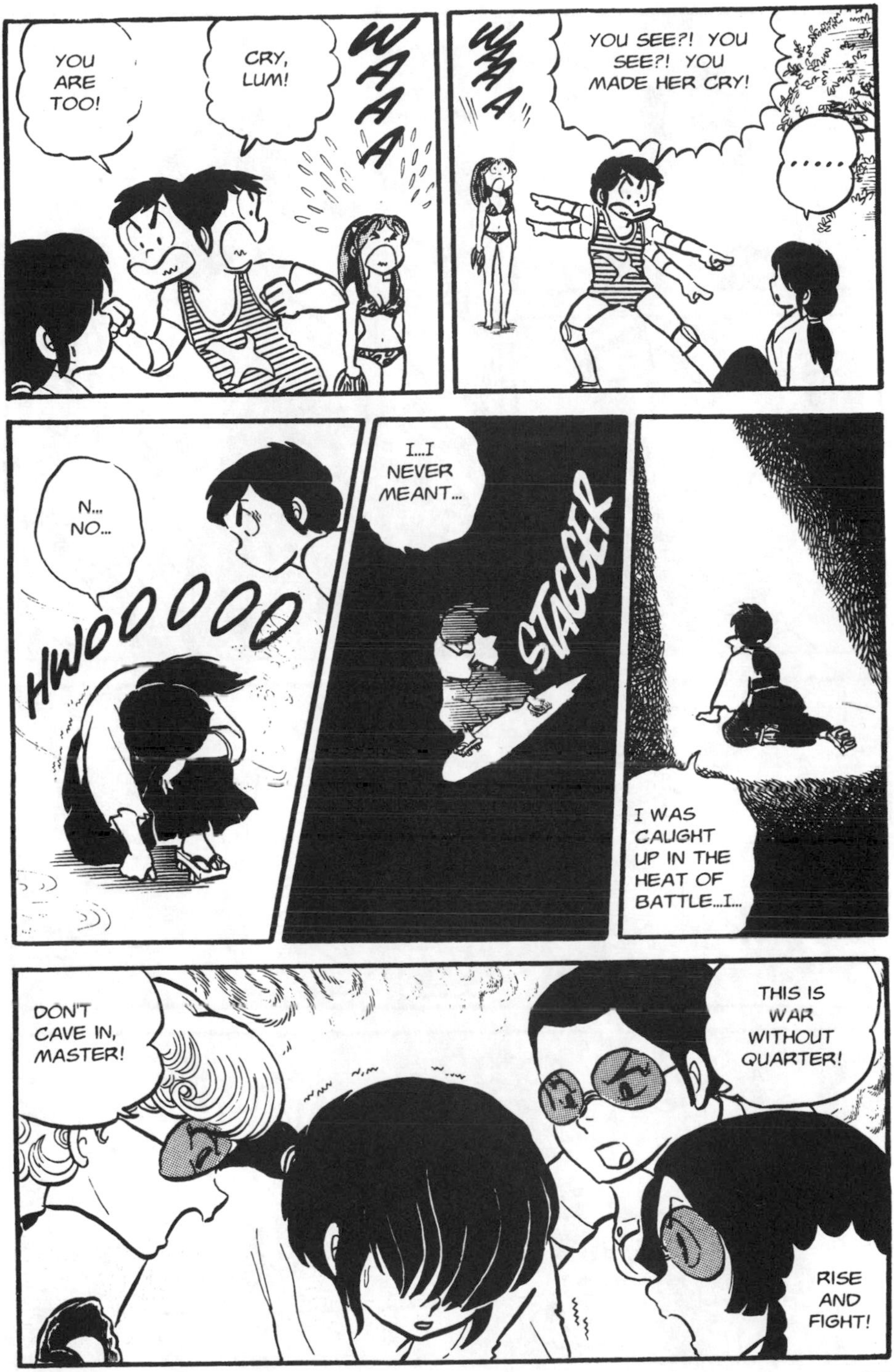
YOU ARE TOO!
CRY, LUM!
WAAAA
WAAA
YOU SEE?! YOU SEE?! YOU MADE HER CRY!
.....
N... NO...
HWOOOOOO
I...I NEVER MEANT...
STAGGER
I WAS CAUGHT UP IN THE HEAT OF BATTLE...I...
DON'T CAVE IN, MASTER!
THIS IS WAR WITHOUT QUARTER!
RISE AND FIGHT!

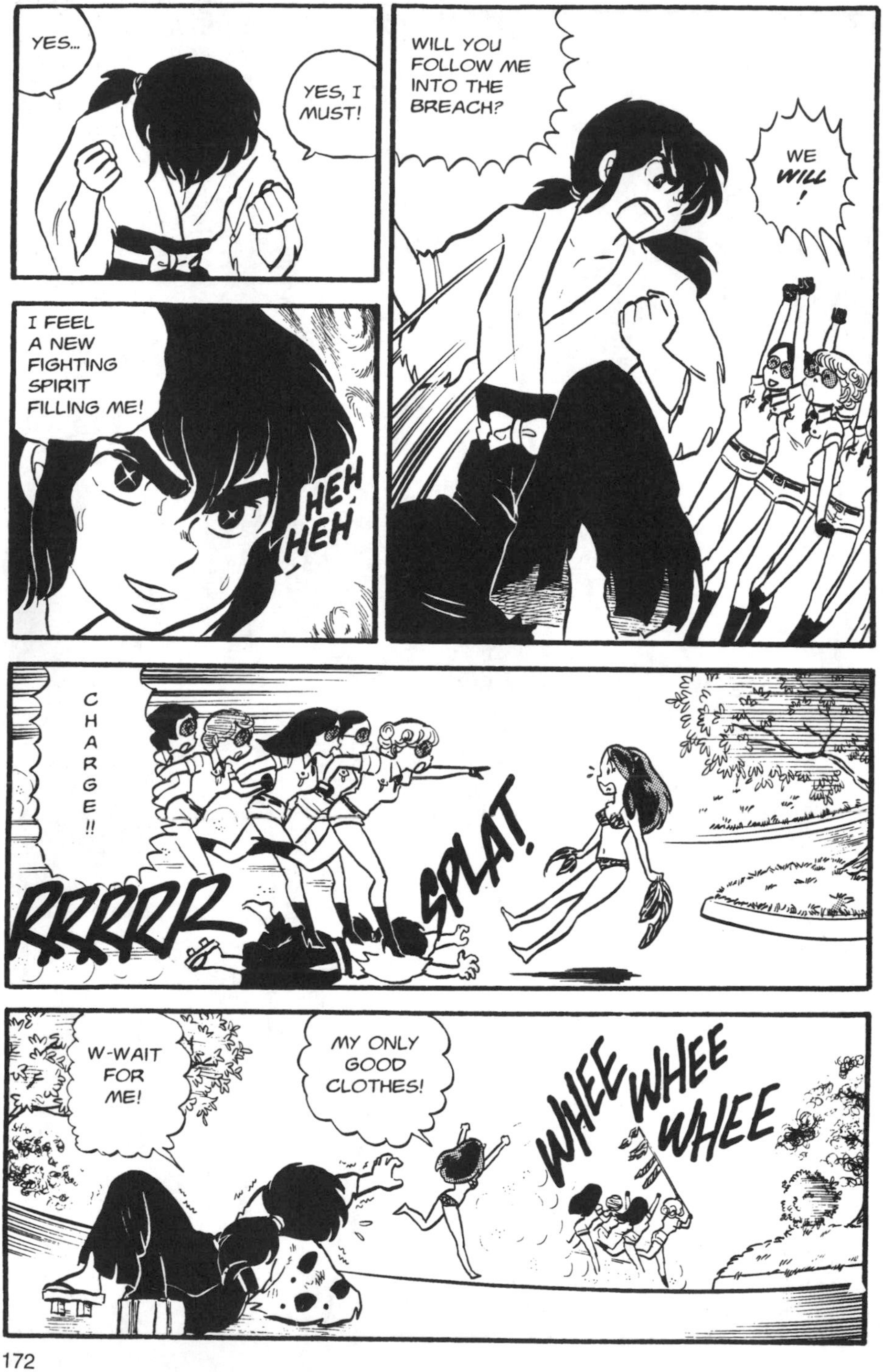
YES...
YES, I MUST!
I FEEL A NEW FIGHTING SPIRIT FILLING ME!
HEH HEH
WILL YOU FOLLOW ME INTO THE BREACH?
WE WILL!
CHARGE!!
RRRRRR
SPLAT!
W-WAIT FOR ME!
MY ONLY GOOD CLOTHES!
WHEE WHEE WHEE

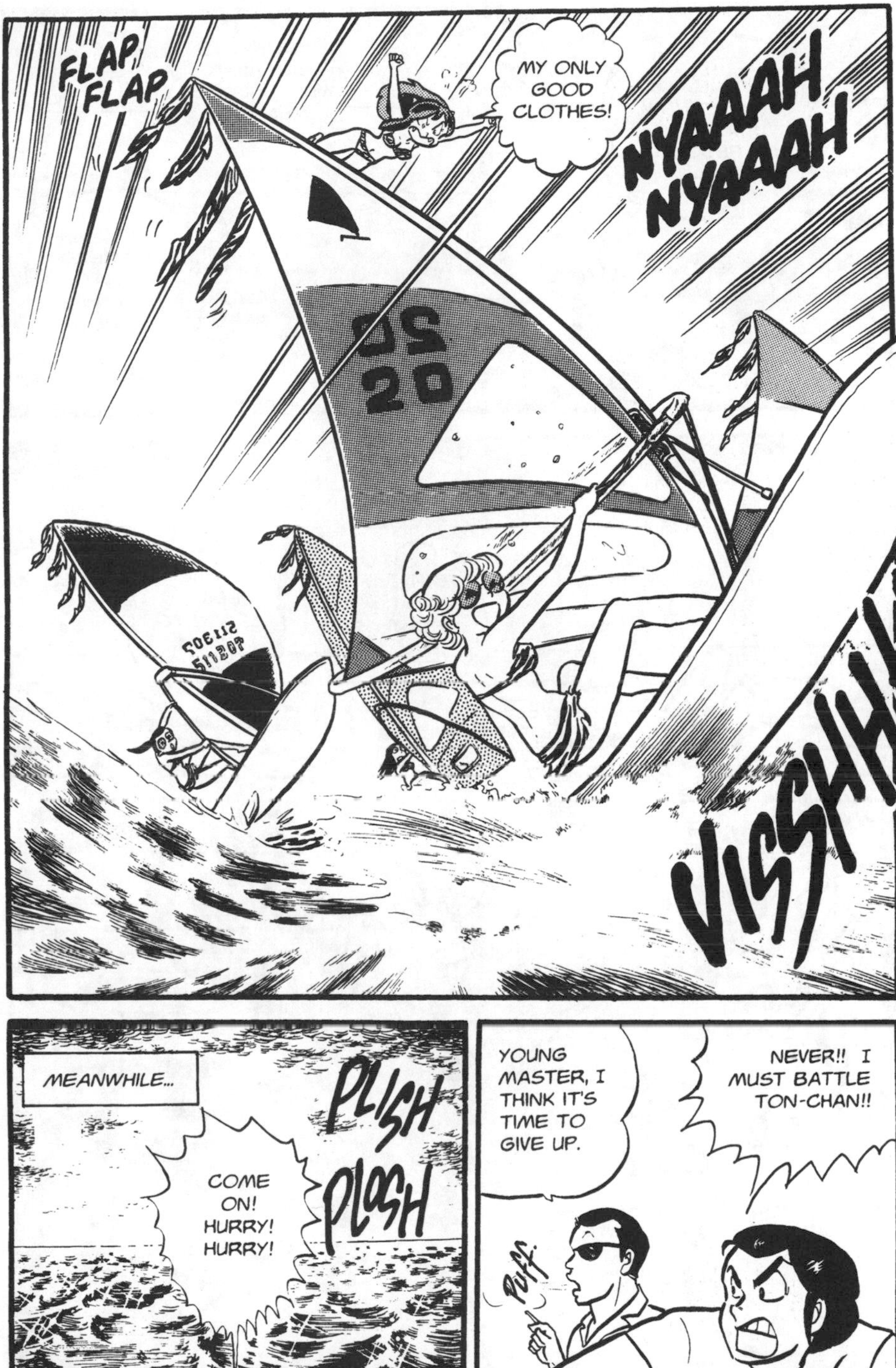

FLAP FLAP
MY ONLY GOOD CLOTHES!
NYAAAH NYAAAH
VISSHHH
MEANWHILE...
COME ON! HURRY! HURRY!
PLISH PLOSH
YOUNG MASTER, I THINK IT'S TIME TO GIVE UP.
PUFF
NEVER!! I MUST BATTLE TON-CHAN!!

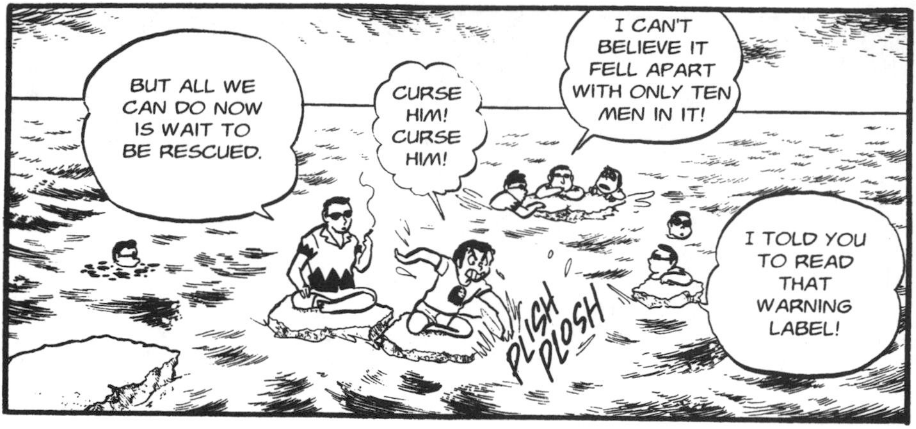
BUT ALL WE CAN DO NOW IS WAIT TO BE RESCUED.
CURSE HIM! CURSE HIM!
I CAN'T BELIEVE IT FELL APART WITH ONLY TEN MEN IN IT!
PLISH PLOSH
I TOLD YOU TO READ THAT WARNING LABEL!

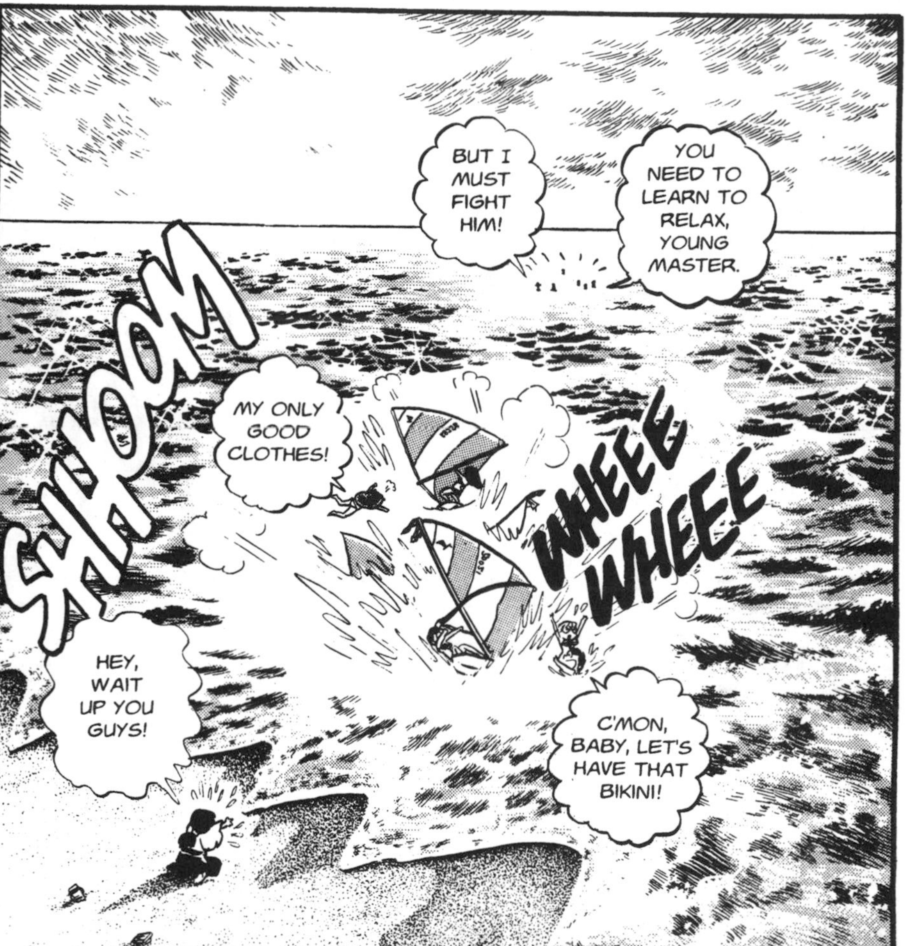
BUT I MUST FIGHT HIM!
YOU NEED TO LEARN TO RELAX, YOUNG MASTER.
SHOOM
MY ONLY GOOD CLOTHES!
WHEEE WHEEE
HEY, WAIT UP YOU GUYS!
C'MON, BABY, LET'S HAVE THAT BIKINI!

PART ELEVEN
FOOD FIGHT

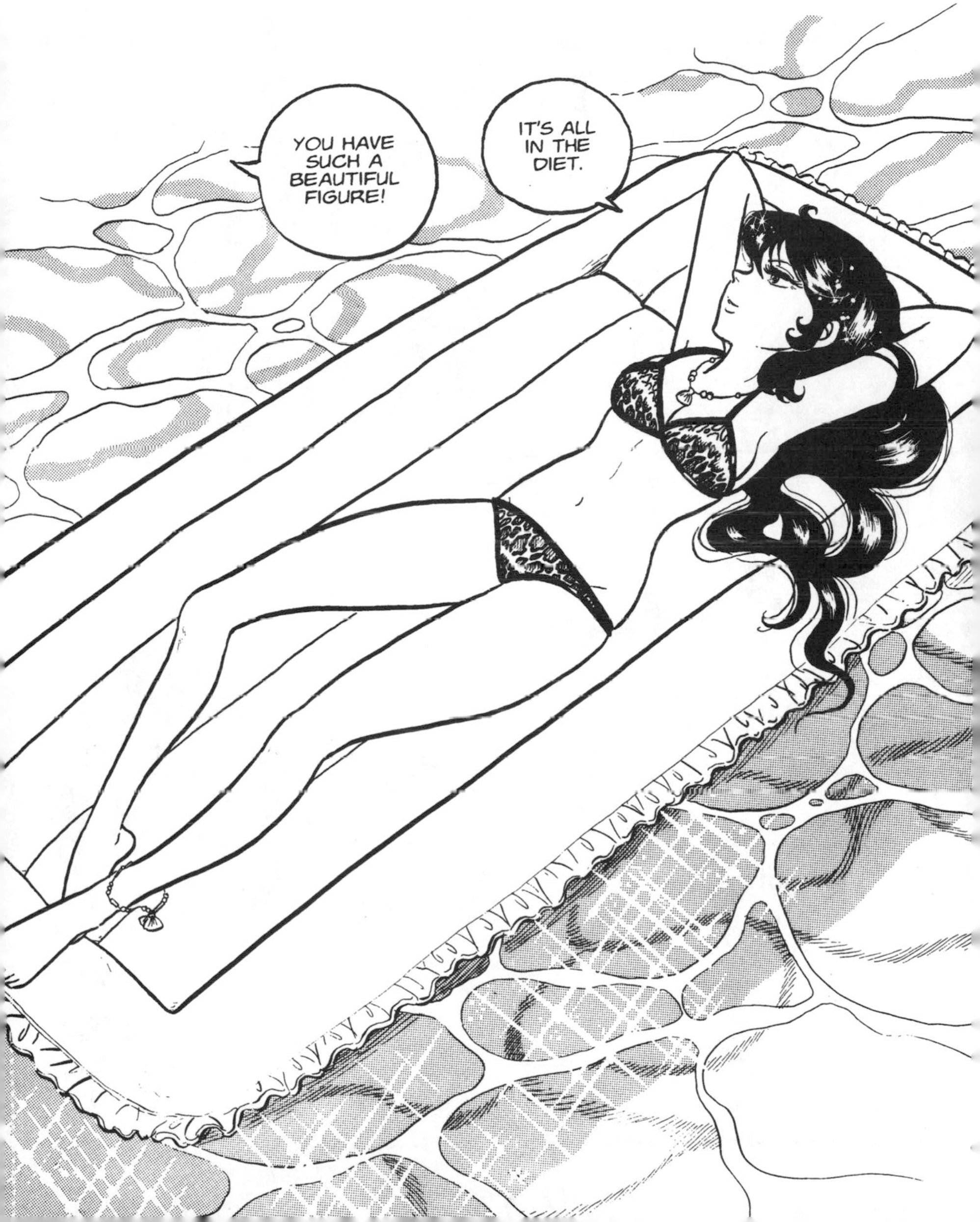
YOU HAVE SUCH A BEAUTIFUL FIGURE!
IT'S ALL IN THE DIET.

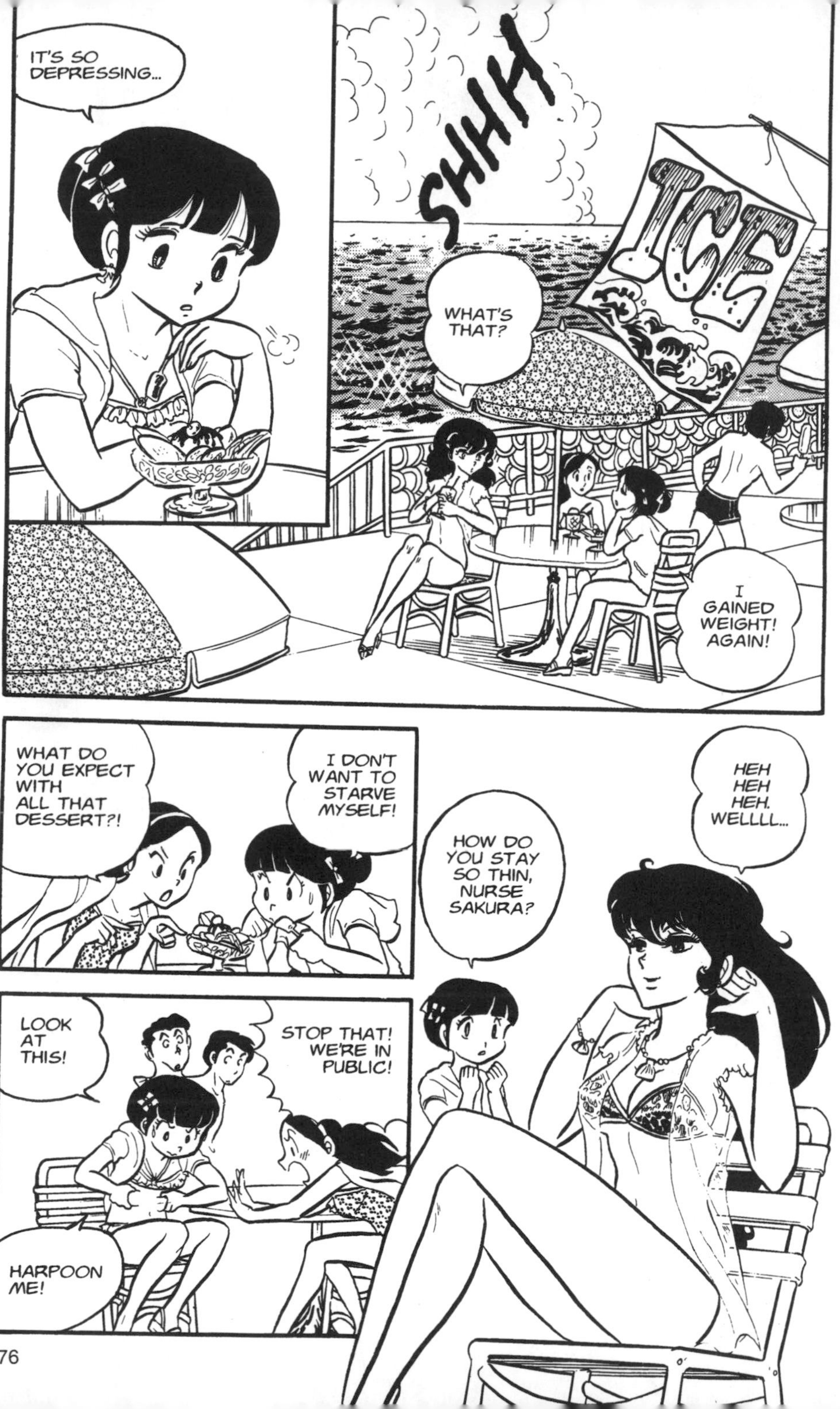
IT'S SO DEPRESSING...
SHHH
ICE
WHAT'S THAT?
I GAINED WEIGHT! AGAIN!
WHAT DO YOU EXPECT WITH ALL THAT DESSERT?!
I DON'T WANT TO STARVE MYSELF!
LOOK AT THIS!
STOP THAT! WE'RE IN PUBLIC!
HARPOON ME!
HOW DO YOU STAY SO THIN, NURSE SAKURA?
HEH HEH HEH. WELLLL...

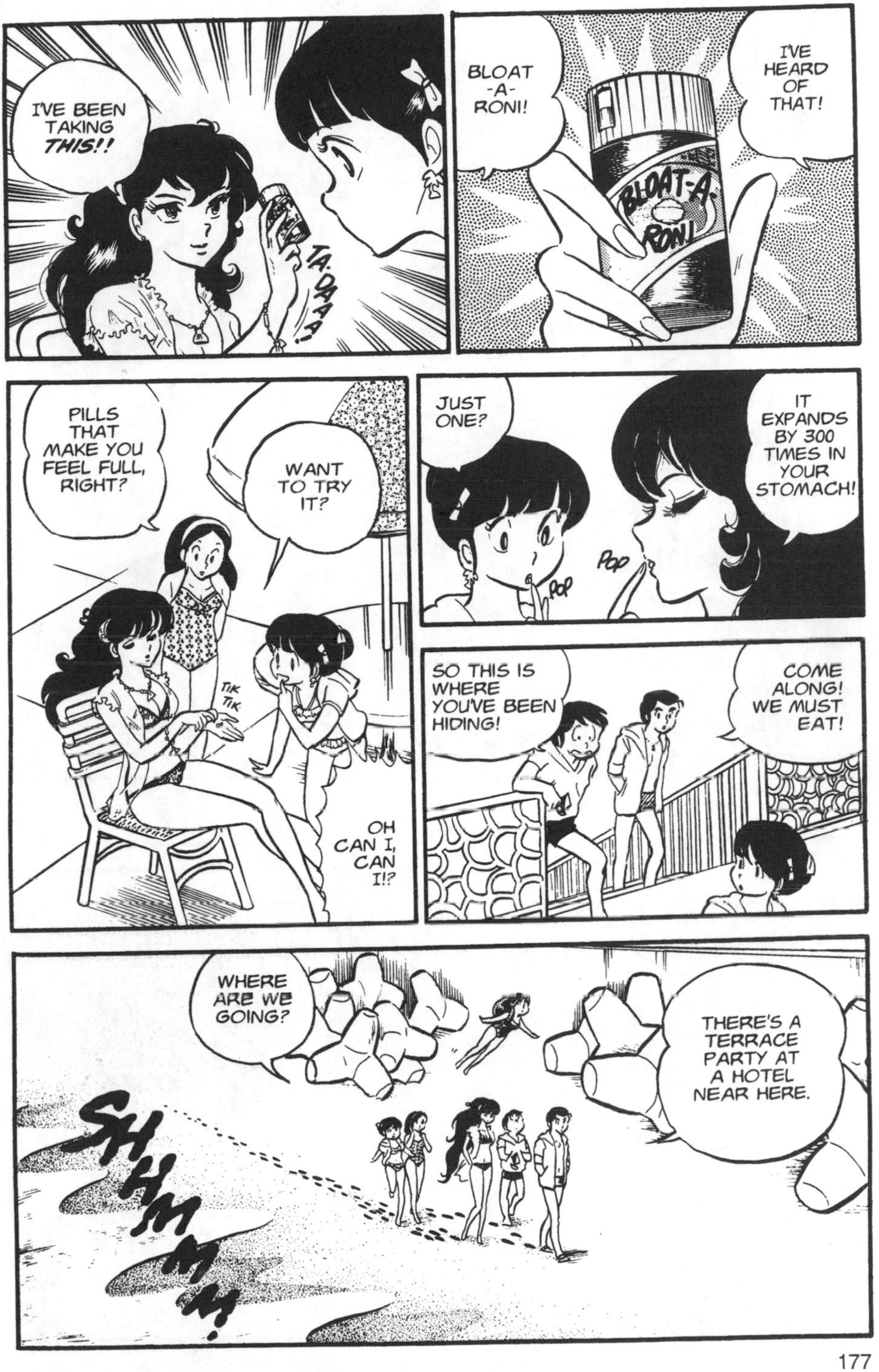
I'VE BEEN TAKING THIS!!
TA-DAAAA!
BLOAT-A-RONI!
BLOAT-A-RONI
I'VE HEARD OF THAT!
PILLS THAT MAKE YOU FEEL FULL, RIGHT?
WANT TO TRY IT?
TIK TIK
OH CAN I, CAN I!?
JUST ONE?
IT EXPANDS BY 300 TIMES IN YOUR STOMACH!
POP POP
SO THIS IS WHERE YOU'VE BEEN HIDING!
COME ALONG! WE MUST EAT!
WHERE ARE WE GOING?
THERE'S A TERRACE PARTY AT A HOTEL NEAR HERE.
SHHMMM!

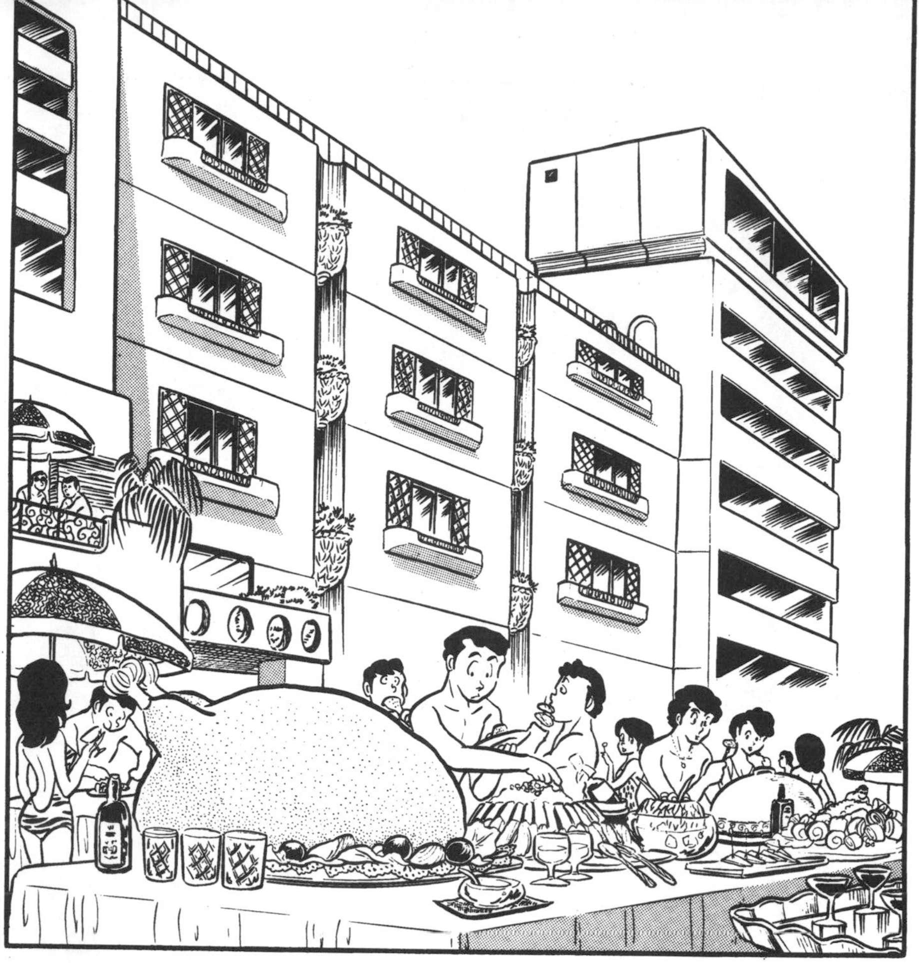

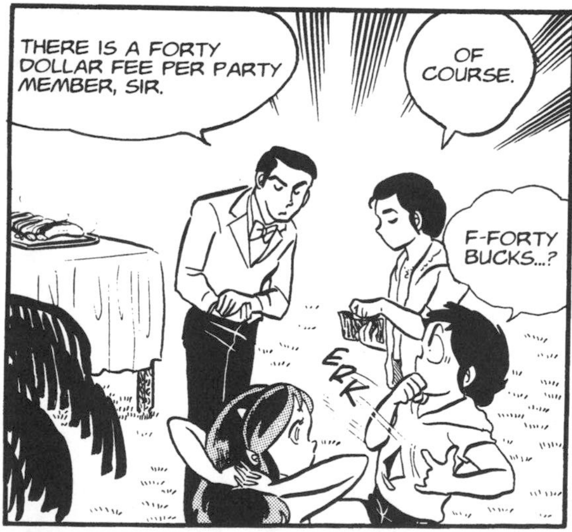
THERE IS A FORTY DOLLAR FEE PER PARTY MEMBER, SIR.
OF COURSE.
F-FORTY BUCKS...?
ERK

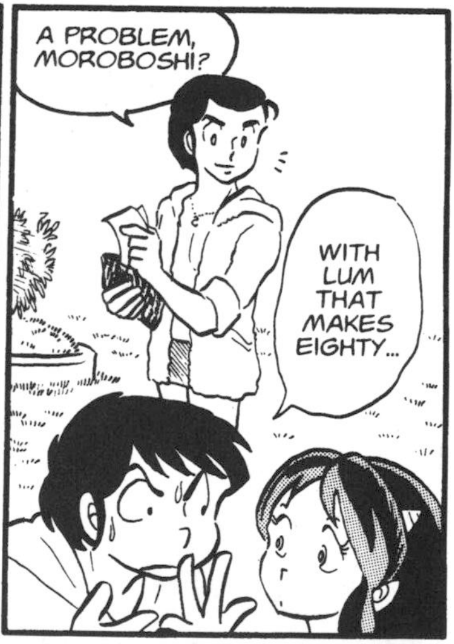
A PROBLEM, MOROBOSHI?
WITH LUM THAT MAKES EIGHTY...

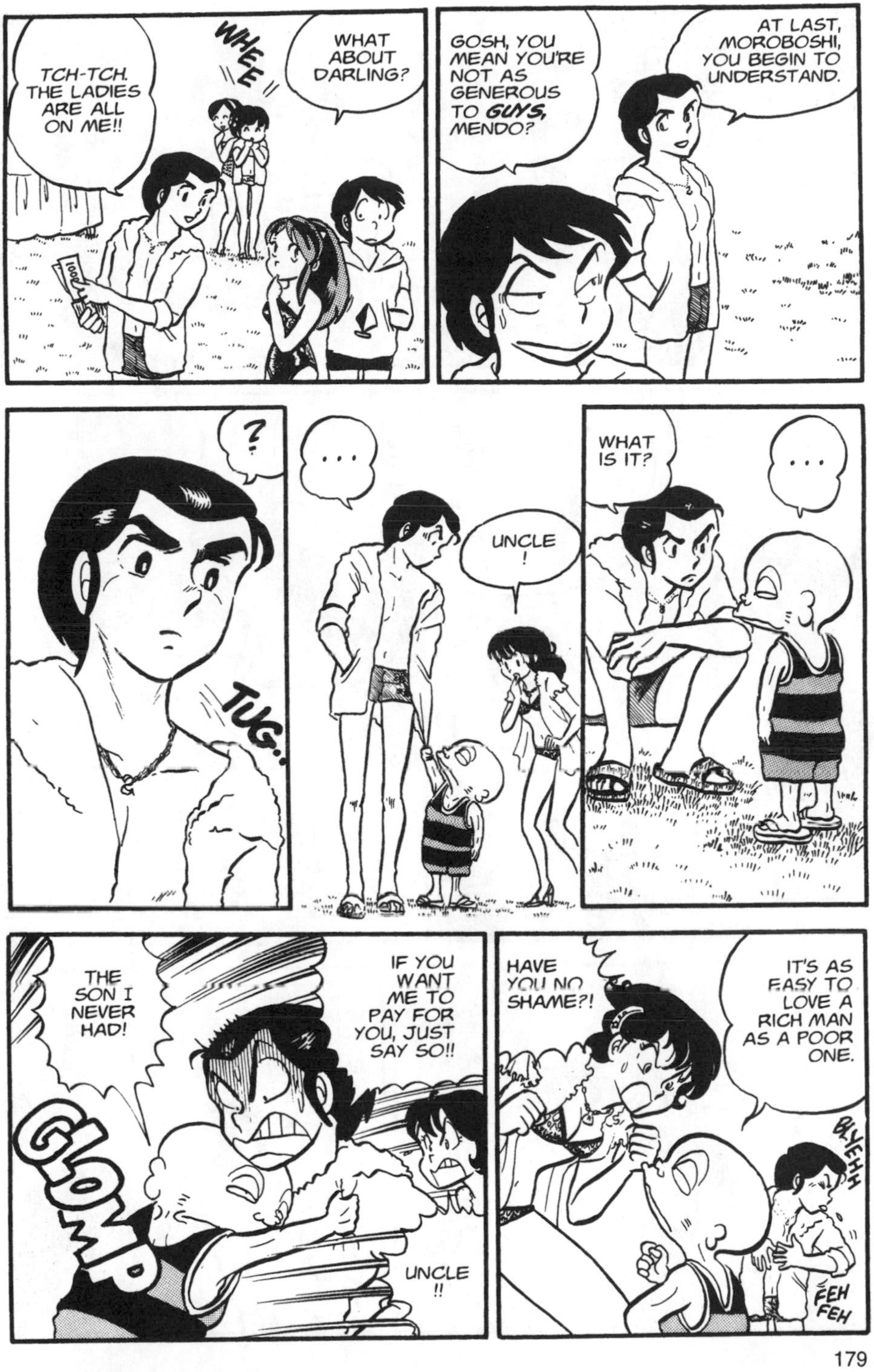
TCH-TCH. THE LADIES ARE ALL ON ME!!
WHEE
WHAT ABOUT DARLING?
GOSH, YOU MEAN YOU'RE NOT AS GENEROUS TO GUYS, MENDO?
AT LAST, MOROBOSHI, YOU BEGIN TO UNDERSTAND.
?
TUG..
...
UNCLE !
WHAT IS IT?
...
THE SON I NEVER HAD!
GLOMP
IF YOU WANT ME TO PAY FOR YOU, JUST SAY SO!!
UNCLE !!
HAVE YOU NO SHAME?!
IT'S AS EASY TO LOVE A RICH MAN AS A POOR ONE.
BLYEHH
FEH FEH

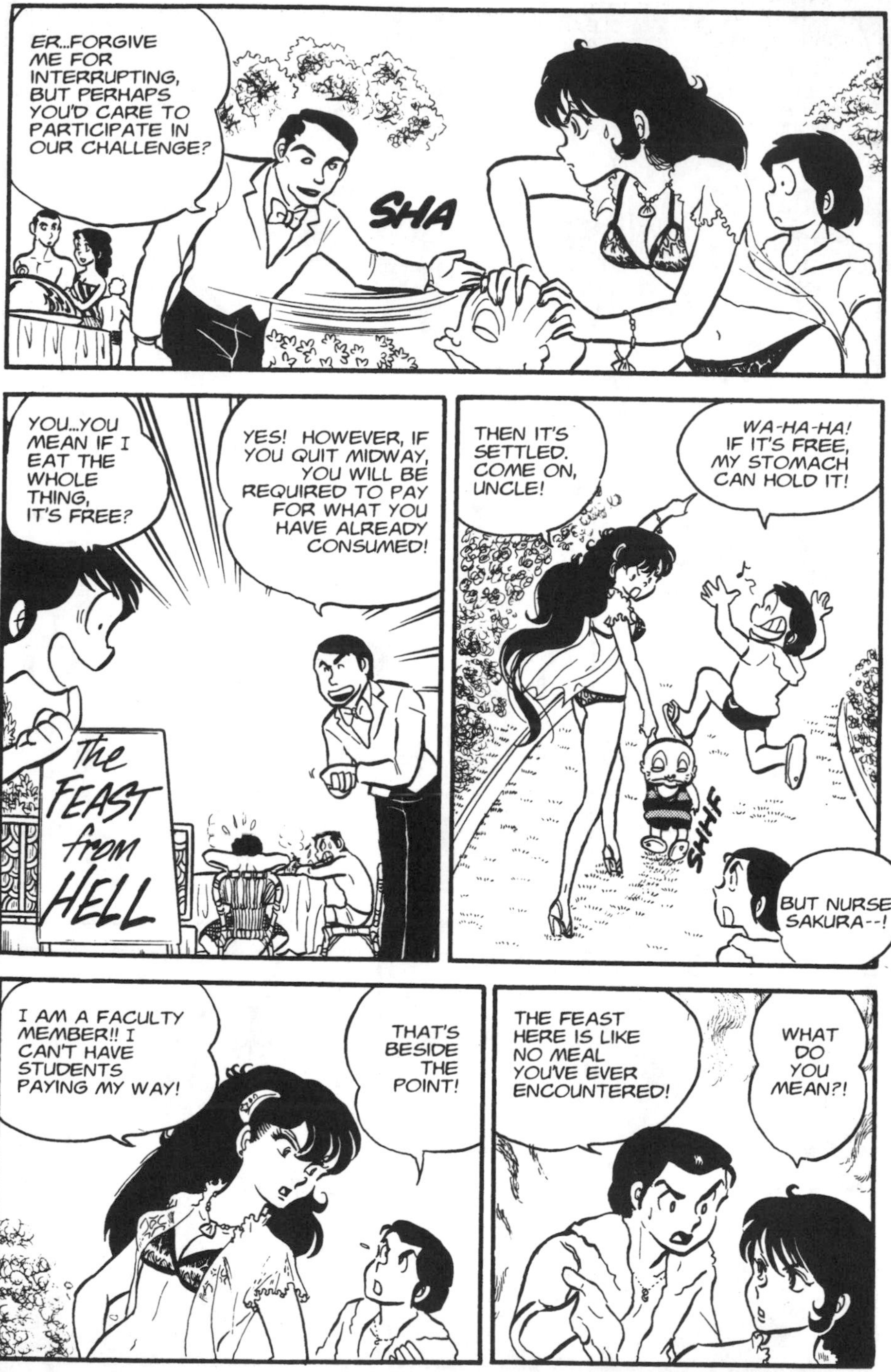
ER...FORGIVE ME FOR INTERRUPTING, BUT PERHAPS YOU'D CARE TO PARTICIPATE IN OUR CHALLENGE?
SHA
YOU...YOU MEAN IF I EAT THE WHOLE THING, IT'S FREE?
YES! HOWEVER, IF YOU QUIT MIDWAY, YOU WILL BE REQUIRED TO PAY FOR WHAT YOU HAVE ALREADY CONSUMED!
The FEAST from HELL
THEN IT'S SETTLED. COME ON, UNCLE!
WA-HA-HA! IF IT'S FREE, MY STOMACH CAN HOLD IT!
SHHF
BUT NURSE SAKURA--!
I AM A FACULTY MEMBER!! I CAN'T HAVE STUDENTS PAYING MY WAY!
THAT'S BESIDE THE POINT!
THE FEAST HERE IS LIKE NO MEAL YOU'VE EVER ENCOUNTERED!
WHAT DO YOU MEAN?!

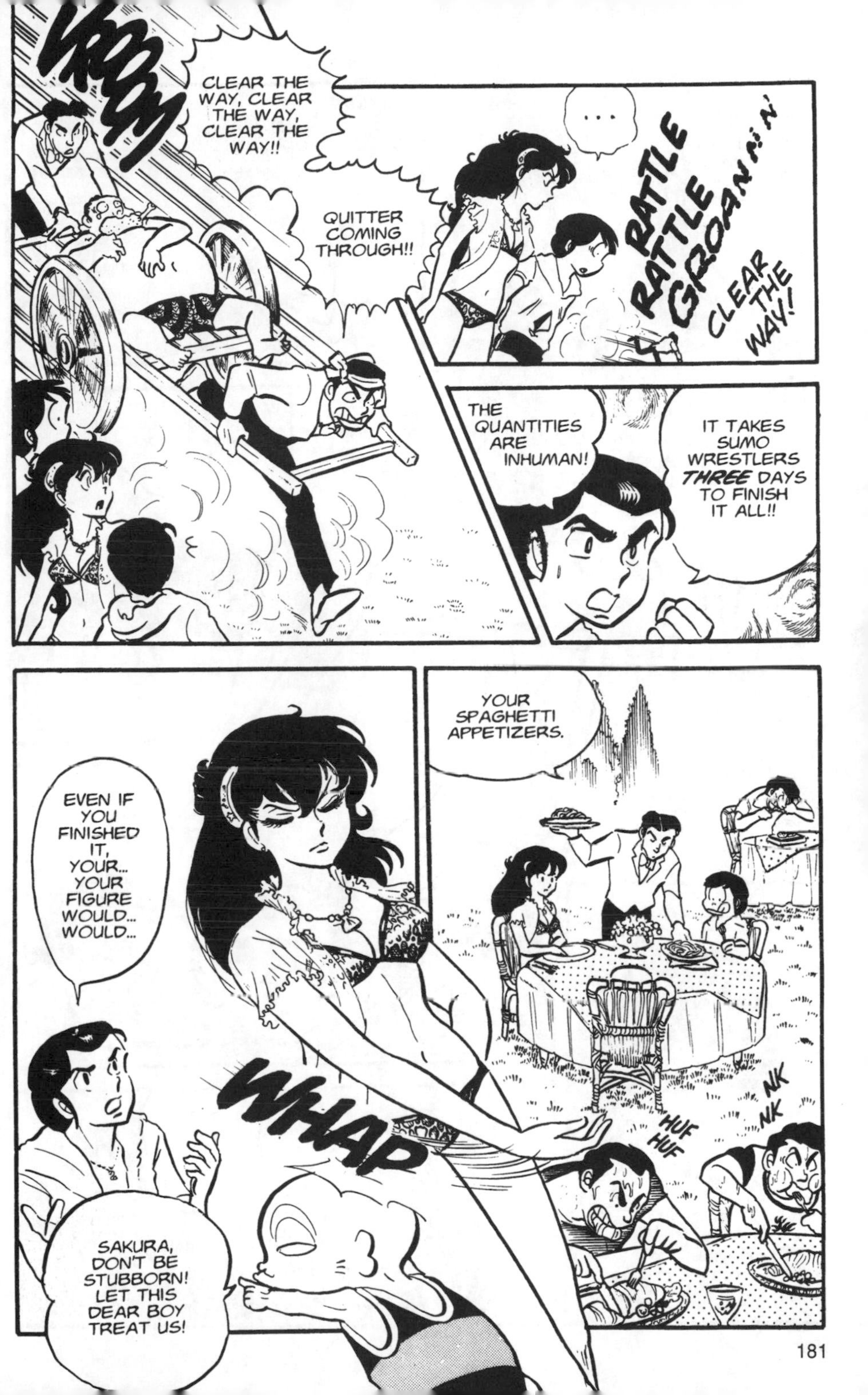
VROOOM
CLEAR THE WAY, CLEAR THE WAY, CLEAR THE WAY!!
QUITTER COMING THROUGH!!
...
RATTLE RATTLE GROAN N N N
CLEAR THE WAY!
THE QUANTITIES ARE INHUMAN!
IT TAKES SUMO WRESTLERS THREE DAYS TO FINISH IT ALL!!
EVEN IF YOU FINISHED IT, YOUR... YOUR FIGURE WOULD... WOULD...
YOUR SPAGHETTI APPETIZERS.
WHAP
HUF HUF
NK NK
SAKURA, DON'T BE STUBBORN! LET THIS DEAR BOY TREAT US!

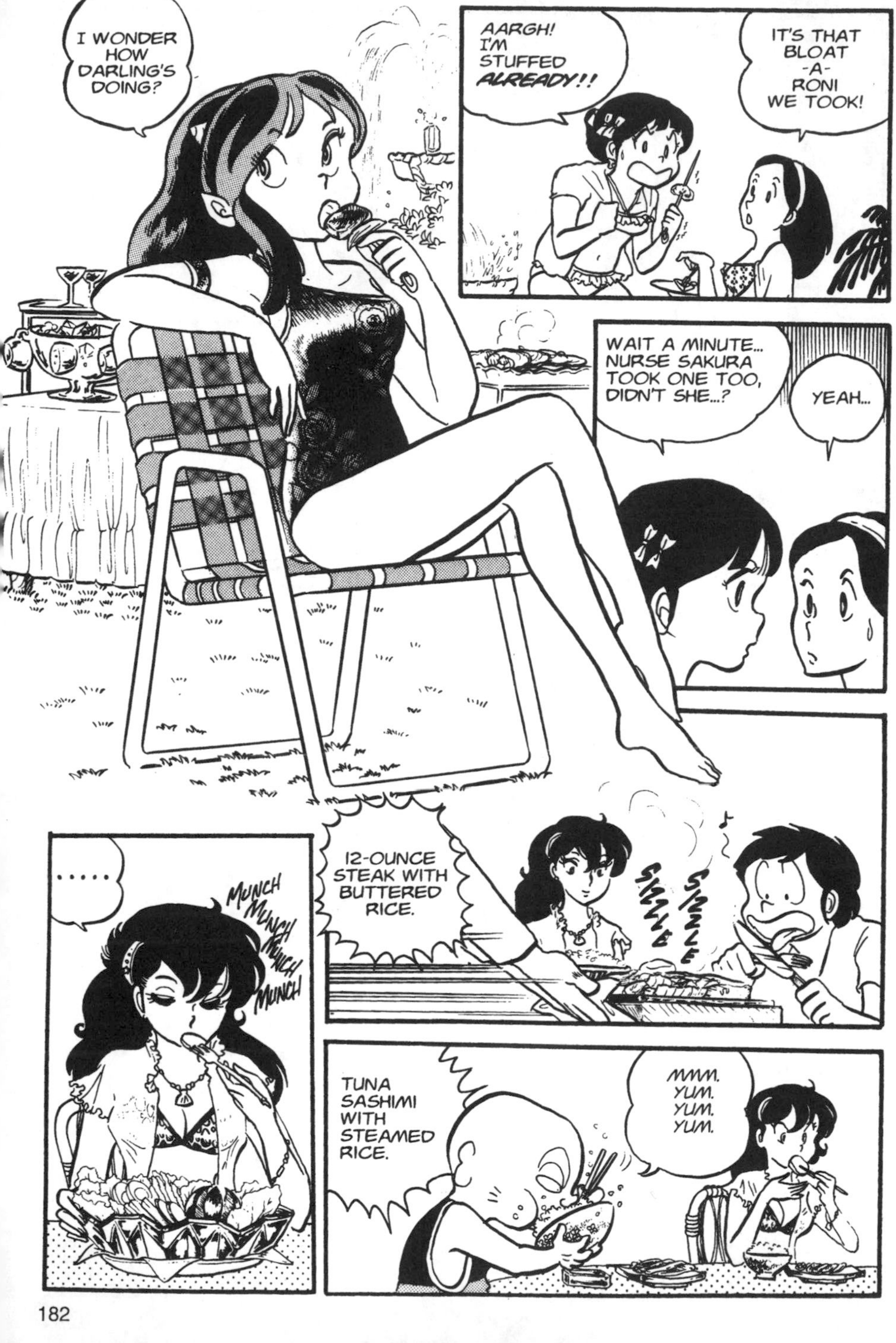
I WONDER HOW DARLING'S DOING?
AARGH! I'M STUFFED ALREADY!!
IT'S THAT BLOAT -A- RONI WE TOOK!
WAIT A MINUTE... NURSE SAKURA TOOK ONE TOO, DIDN'T SHE...?
YEAH...
12-OUNCE STEAK WITH BUTTERED RICE.
SIZZLE
SIZZLE
......
MUNCH MUNCH MUNCH MUNCH
TUNA SASHIMI WITH STEAMED RICE.
MMM. YUM. YUM. YUM.

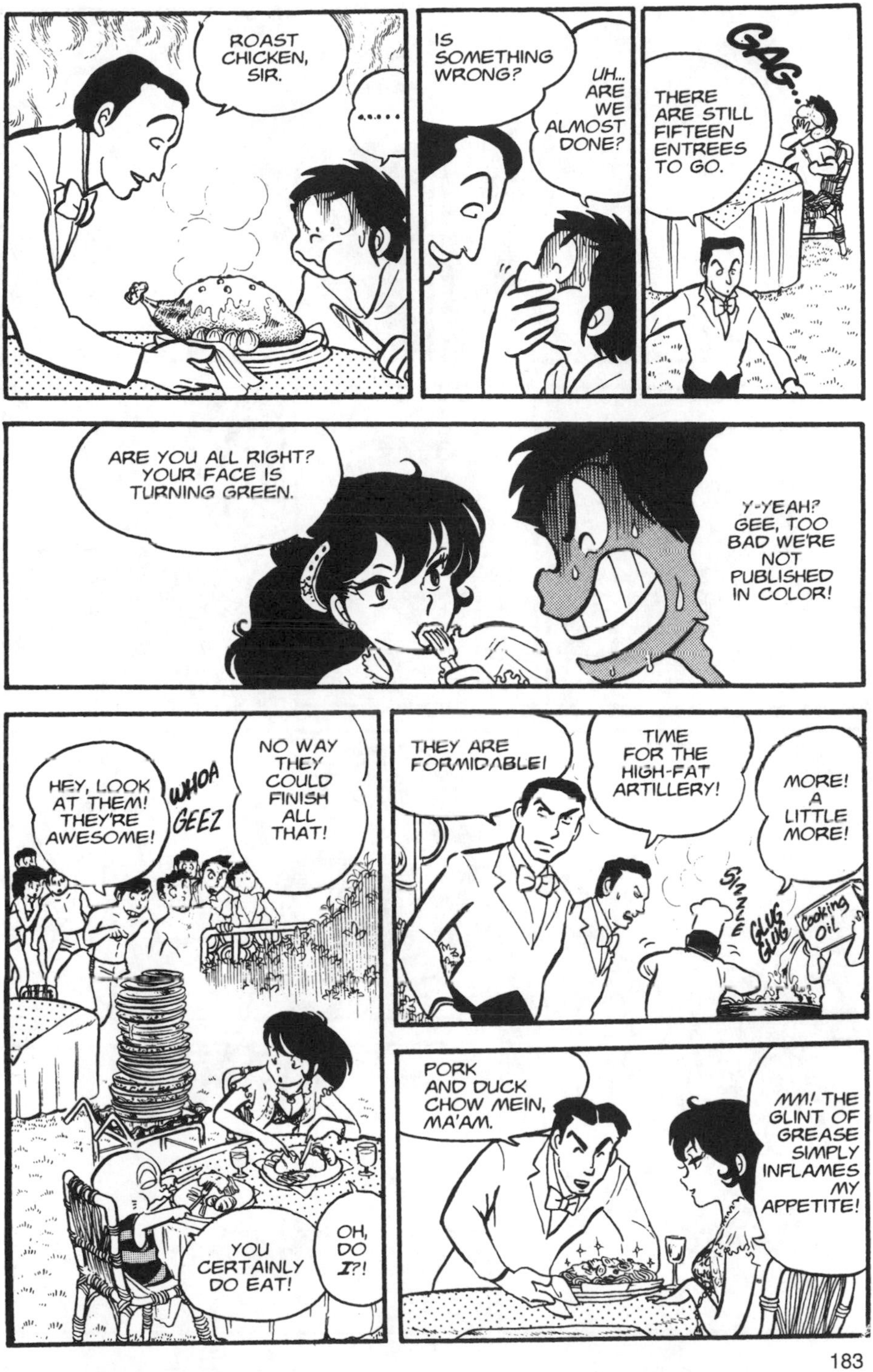
ROAST CHICKEN, SIR.
......
IS SOMETHING WRONG?
UH... ARE WE ALMOST DONE?
GAG...
THERE ARE STILL FIFTEEN ENTREES TO GO.
ARE YOU ALL RIGHT? YOUR FACE IS TURNING GREEN.
Y-YEAH? GEE, TOO BAD WE'RE NOT PUBLISHED IN COLOR!
HEY, LOOK AT THEM! THEY'RE AWESOME!
WHOA
GEEZ
NO WAY THEY COULD FINISH ALL THAT!
YOU CERTAINLY DO EAT!
OH, DO I?!
THEY ARE FORMIDABLE!
TIME FOR THE HIGH-FAT ARTILLERY!
MORE! A LITTLE MORE!
SIZZLE
GLUG GLUG
Cooking Oil
PORK AND DUCK CHOW MEIN, MA'AM.
MM! THE GLINT OF GREASE SIMPLY INFLAMES MY APPETITE!

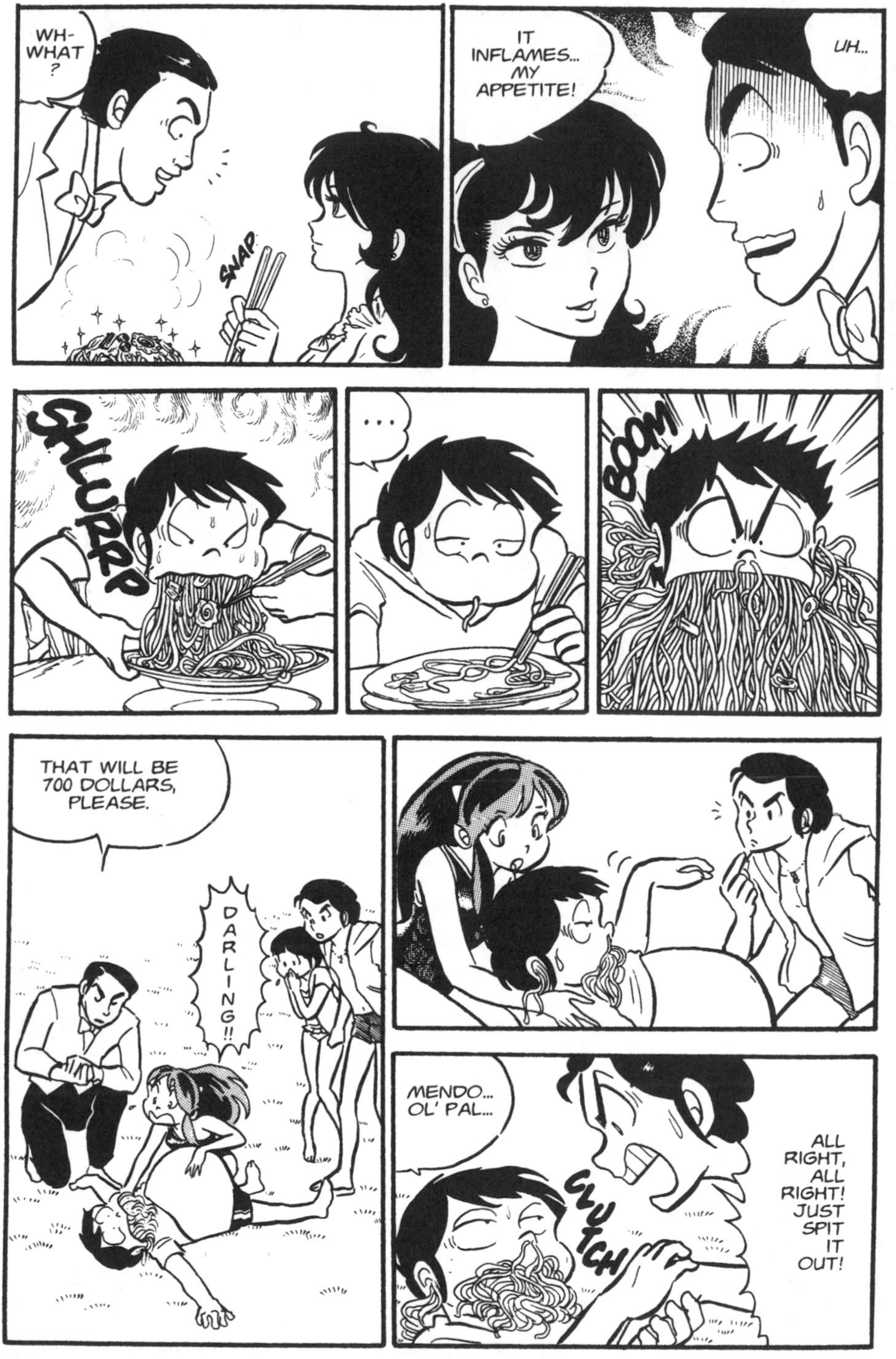
WH- WHAT ?
SNAP
IT INFLAMES... MY APPETITE!
UH...
SHLURRP
...
BOOM
THAT WILL BE 700 DOLLARS, PLEASE.
DARLING!!
MENDO... OL' PAL...
CLUTCH
ALL RIGHT, ALL RIGHT! JUST SPIT IT OUT!

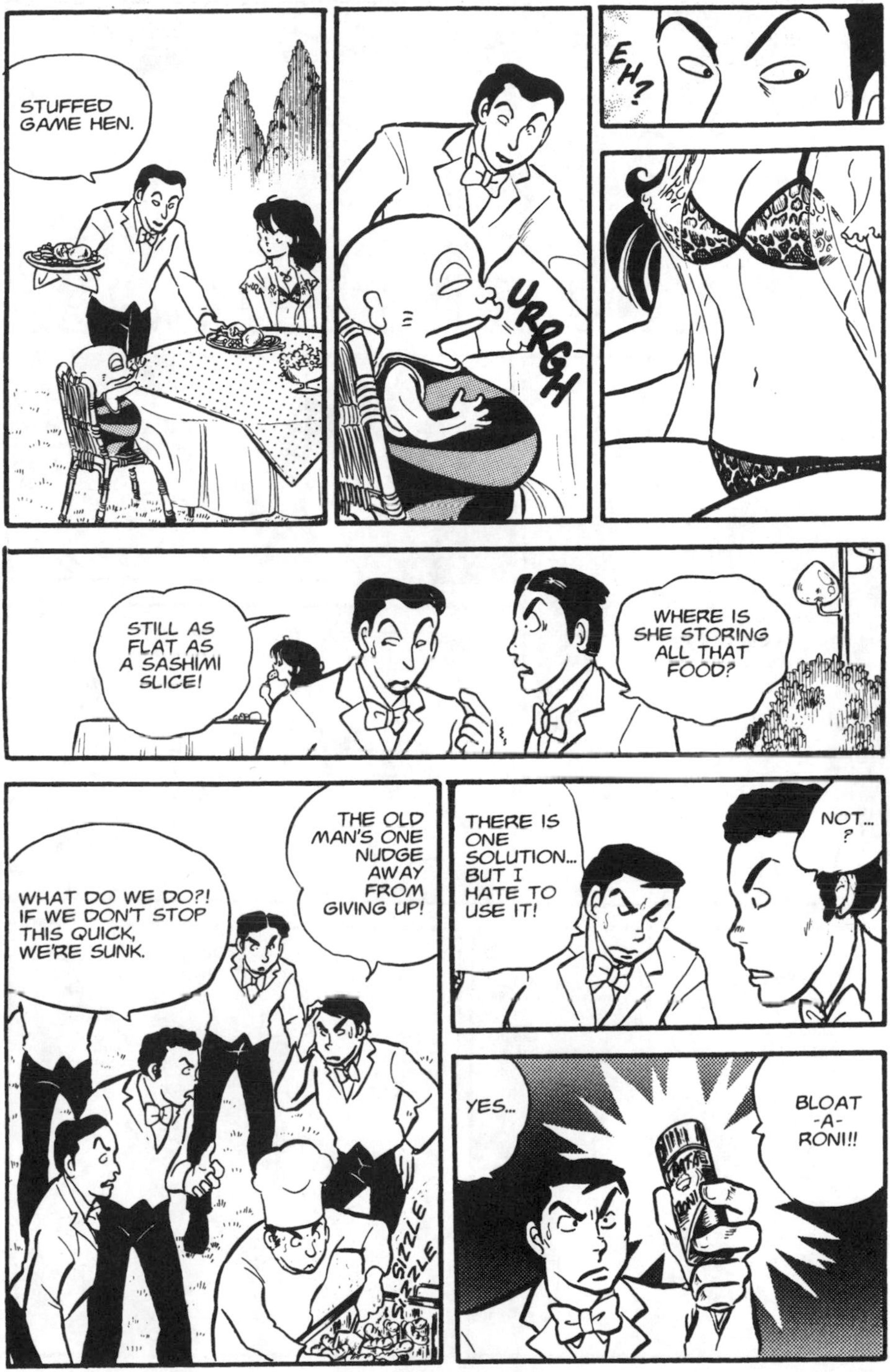
STUFFED GAME HEN.
URRGH
EH?
STILL AS FLAT AS A SASHIMI SLICE!
WHERE IS SHE STORING ALL THAT FOOD?
WHAT DO WE DO?! IF WE DON'T STOP THIS QUICK, WE'RE SUNK.
THE OLD MAN'S ONE NUDGE AWAY FROM GIVING UP!
SIZZLE SIZZLE
THERE IS ONE SOLUTION... BUT I HATE TO USE IT!
NOT...?
YES...
BLOAT-A-RONI!!

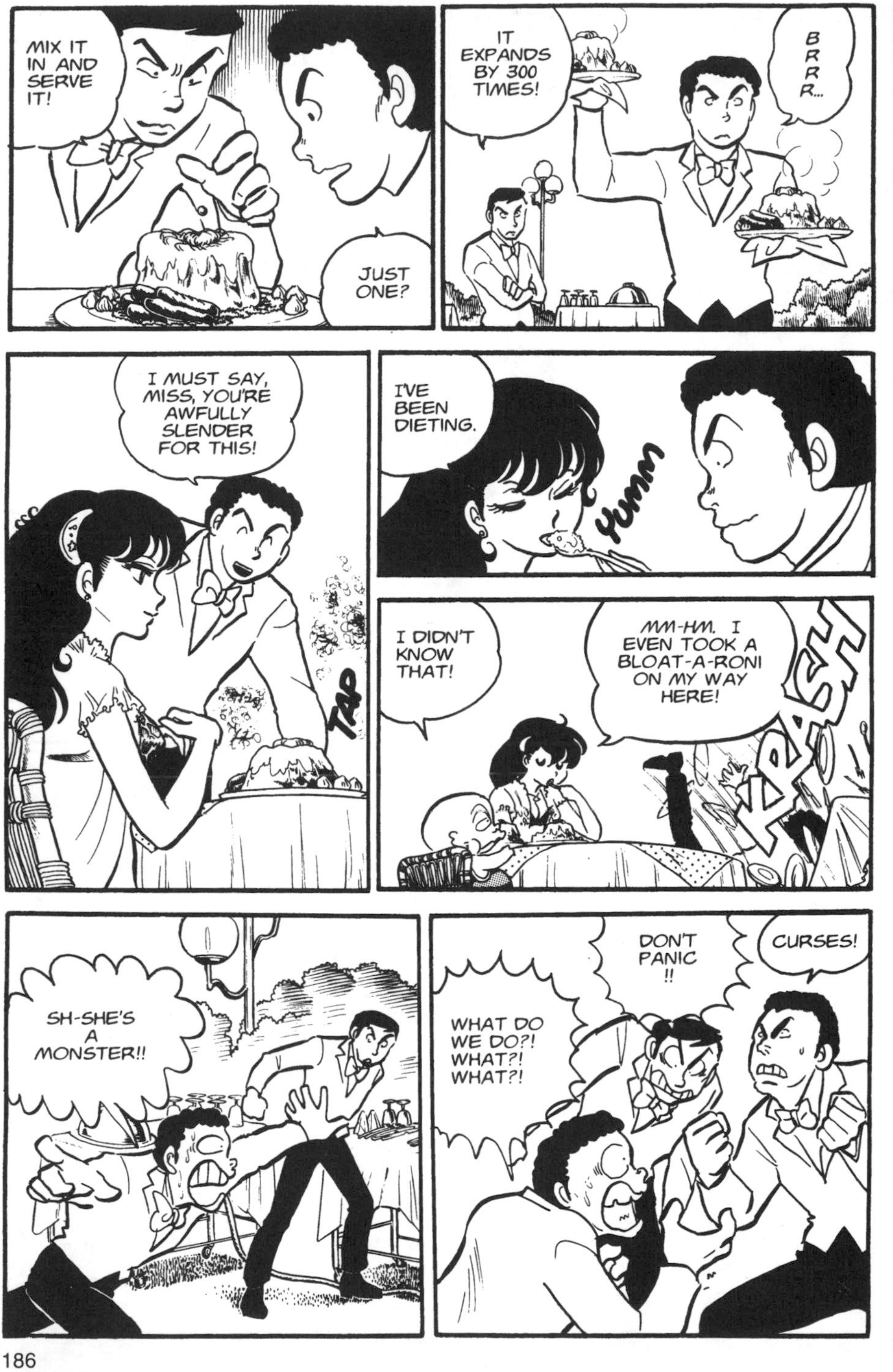
MIX IT IN AND SERVE IT!
JUST ONE?
IT EXPANDS BY 300 TIMES!
BRRR...
I MUST SAY, MISS, YOU'RE AWFULLY SLENDER FOR THIS!
TAP
I'VE BEEN DIETING.
YUMM
I DIDN'T KNOW THAT!
MM-HM. I EVEN TOOK A BLOAT-A-RONI ON MY WAY HERE!
KRASH
SH-SHE'S A MONSTER!!
WHAT DO WE DO?! WHAT?! WHAT?!
DON'T PANIC !!
CURSES!

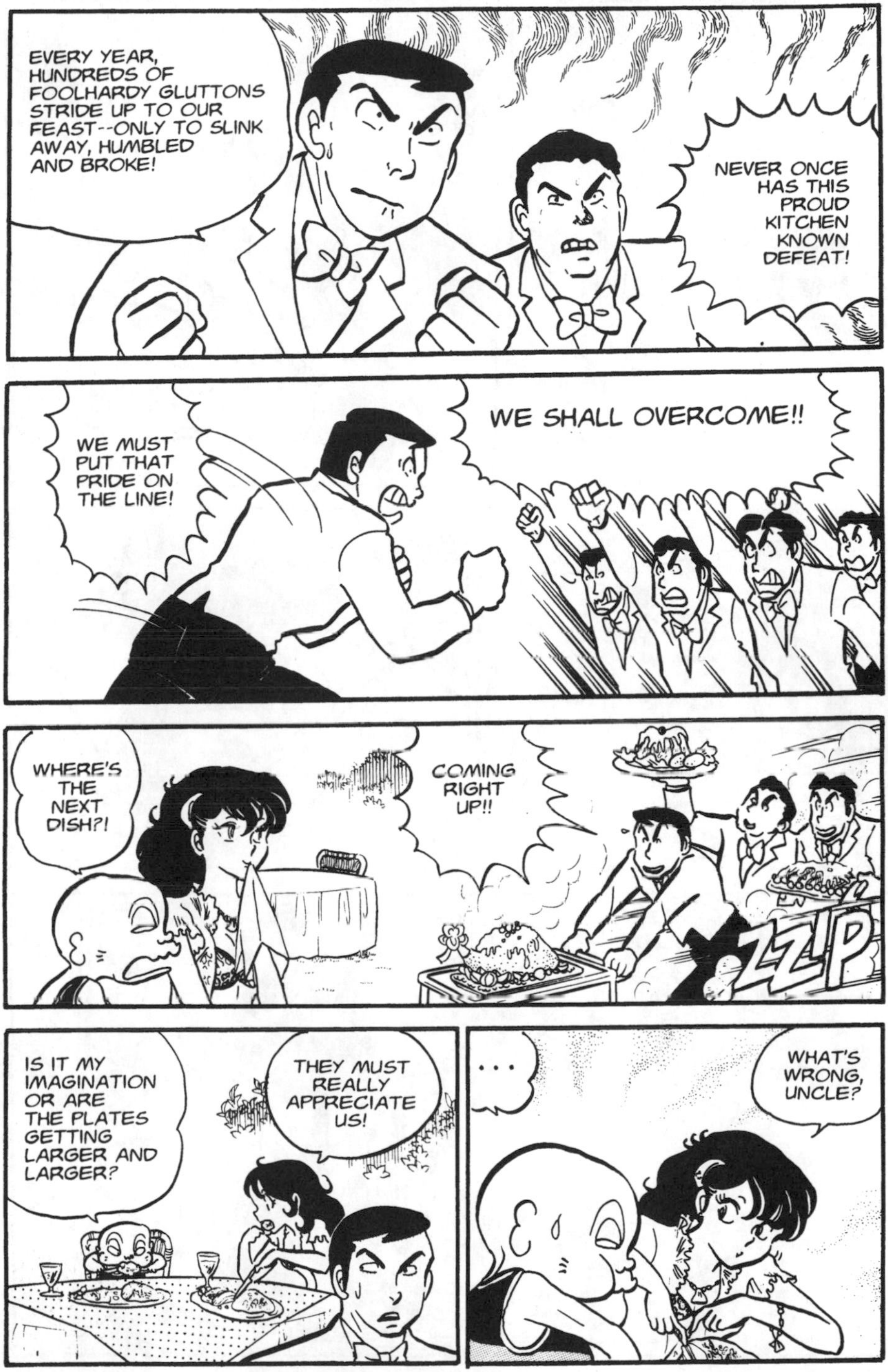
EVERY YEAR, HUNDREDS OF FOOLHARDY GLUTTONS STRIDE UP TO OUR FEAST--ONLY TO SLINK AWAY, HUMBLED AND BROKE!
NEVER ONCE HAS THIS PROUD KITCHEN KNOWN DEFEAT!
WE MUST PUT THAT PRIDE ON THE LINE!
WE SHALL OVERCOME!!
WHERE'S THE NEXT DISH?!
COMING RIGHT UP!!
ZZIP
IS IT MY IMAGINATION OR ARE THE PLATES GETTING LARGER AND LARGER?
THEY MUST REALLY APPRECIATE US!
...
WHAT'S WRONG, UNCLE?

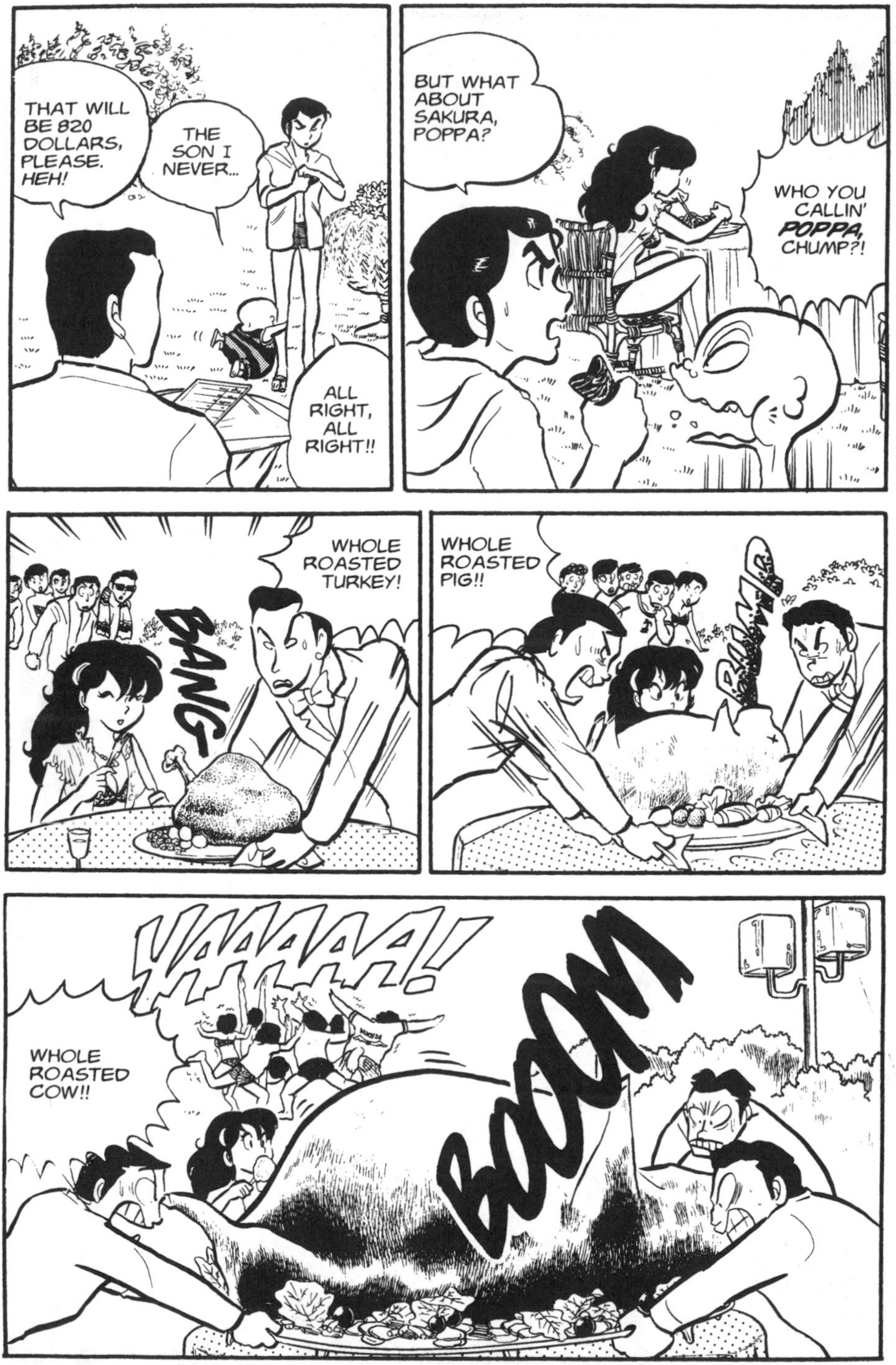

THAT WILL BE 820 DOLLARS, PLEASE. HEH!
THE SON I NEVER...
ALL RIGHT, ALL RIGHT!!
BUT WHAT ABOUT SAKURA, POPPA?
WHO YOU CALLIN' POPPA, CHUMP?!
BANG
WHOLE ROASTED TURKEY!
WHOLE ROASTED PIG!!
YAAAAA!
WHOLE ROASTED COW!!
BOOM

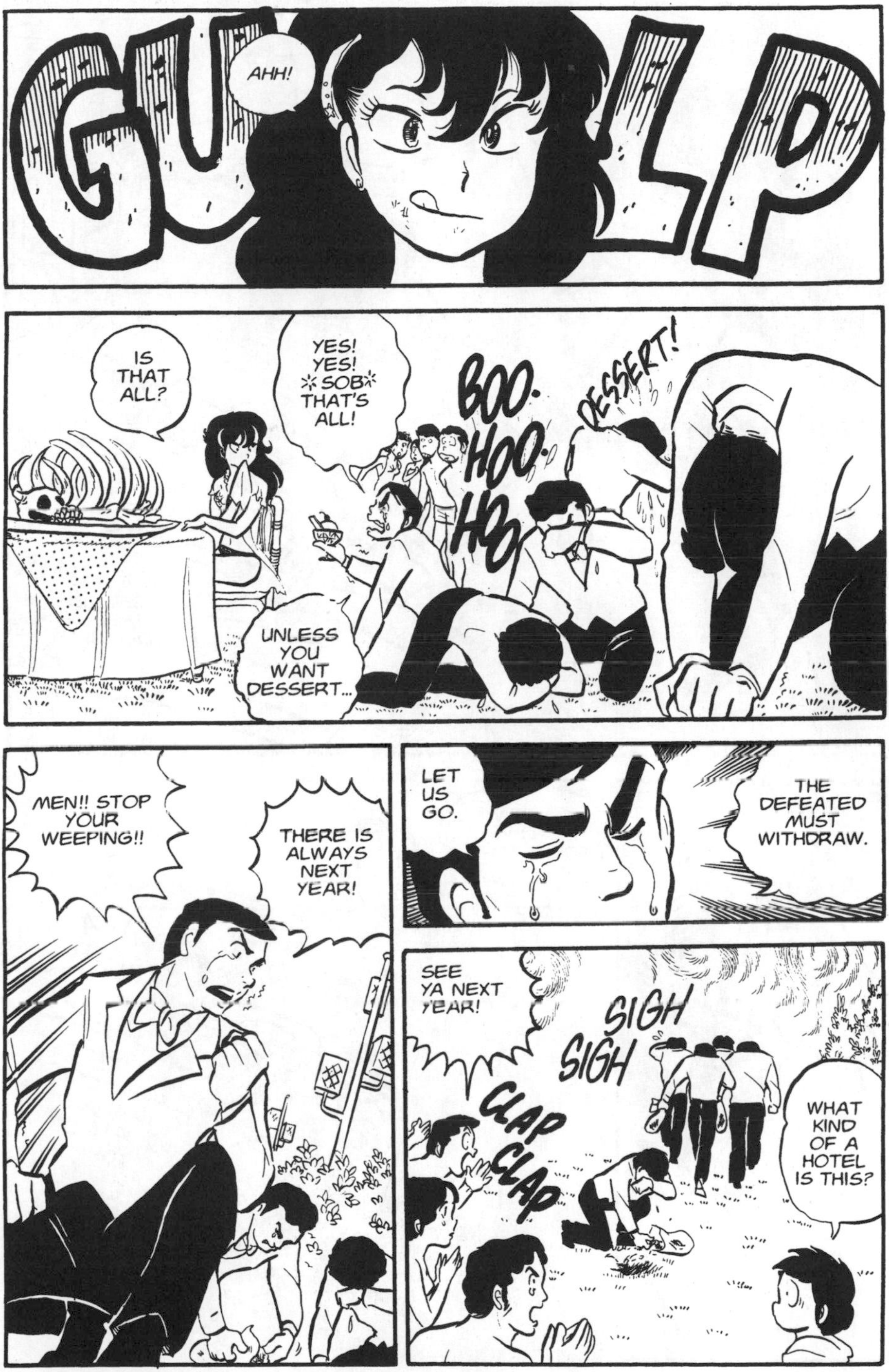
AHH!
GULP
IS THAT ALL?
YES! YES! *SOB* THAT'S ALL!
BOO-HOO-HOO
DESSERT!
UNLESS YOU WANT DESSERT...
MEN!! STOP YOUR WEEPING!!
THERE IS ALWAYS NEXT YEAR!
LET US GO.
THE DEFEATED MUST WITHDRAW.
SEE YA NEXT YEAR!
SIGH SIGH
CLAP CLAP
WHAT KIND OF A HOTEL IS THIS?

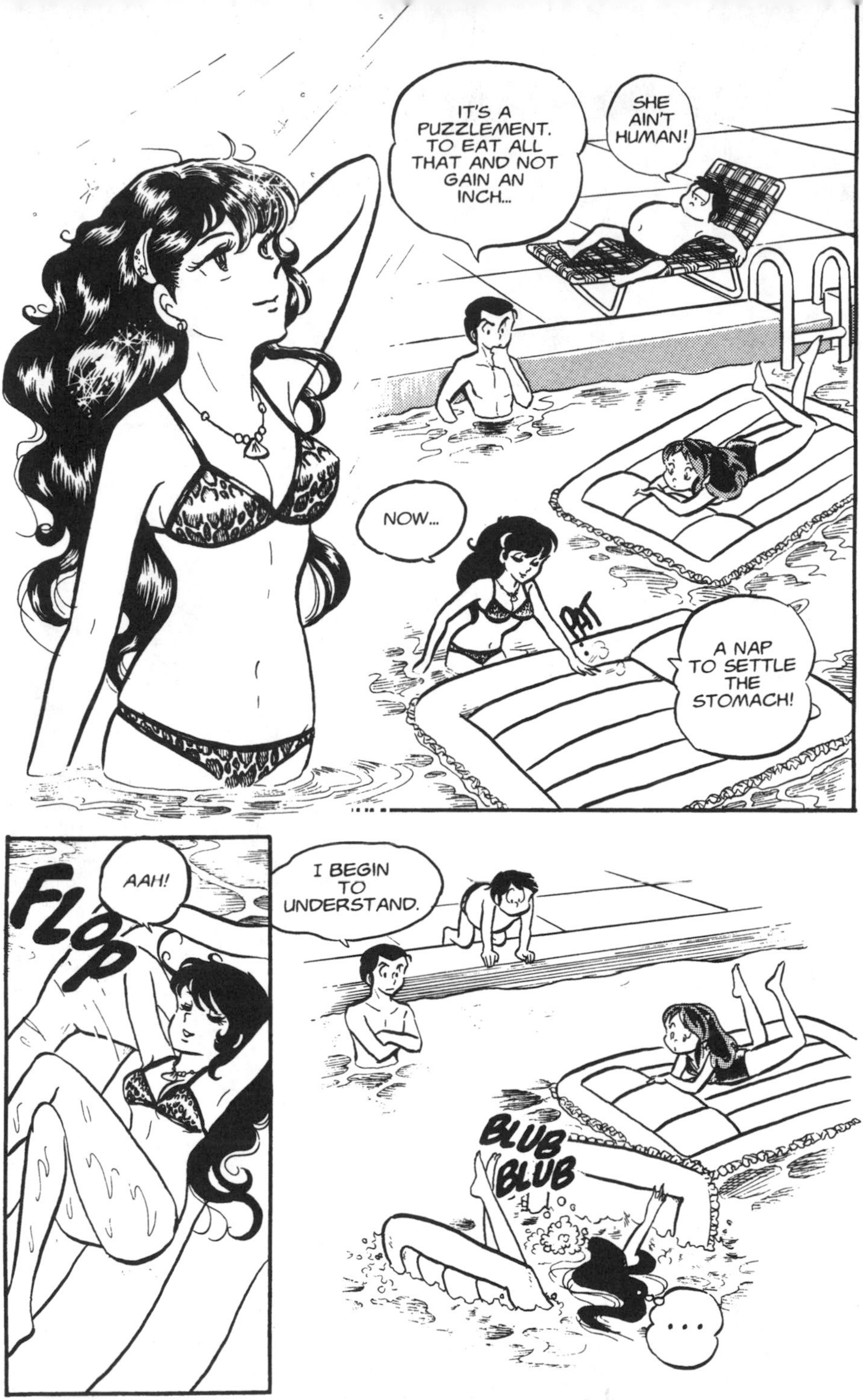
IT'S A PUZZLEMENT. TO EAT ALL THAT AND NOT GAIN AN INCH...
SHE AIN'T HUMAN!
NOW...
PAT
A NAP TO SETTLE THE STOMACH!
FLOP
AAH!
I BEGIN TO UNDERSTAND.
BLUB
BLUB
...

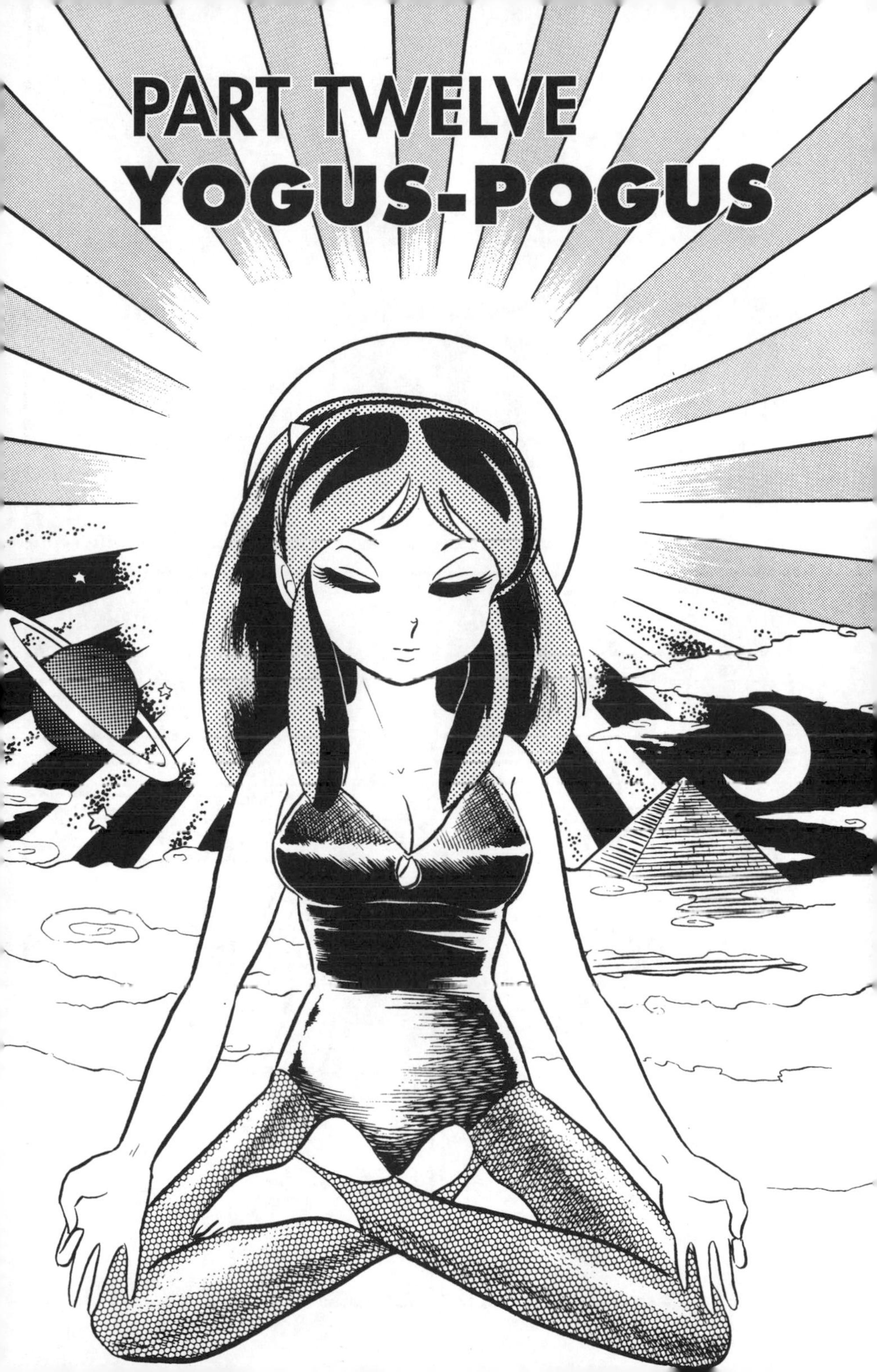
PART TWELVE
YOGUS-POGUS

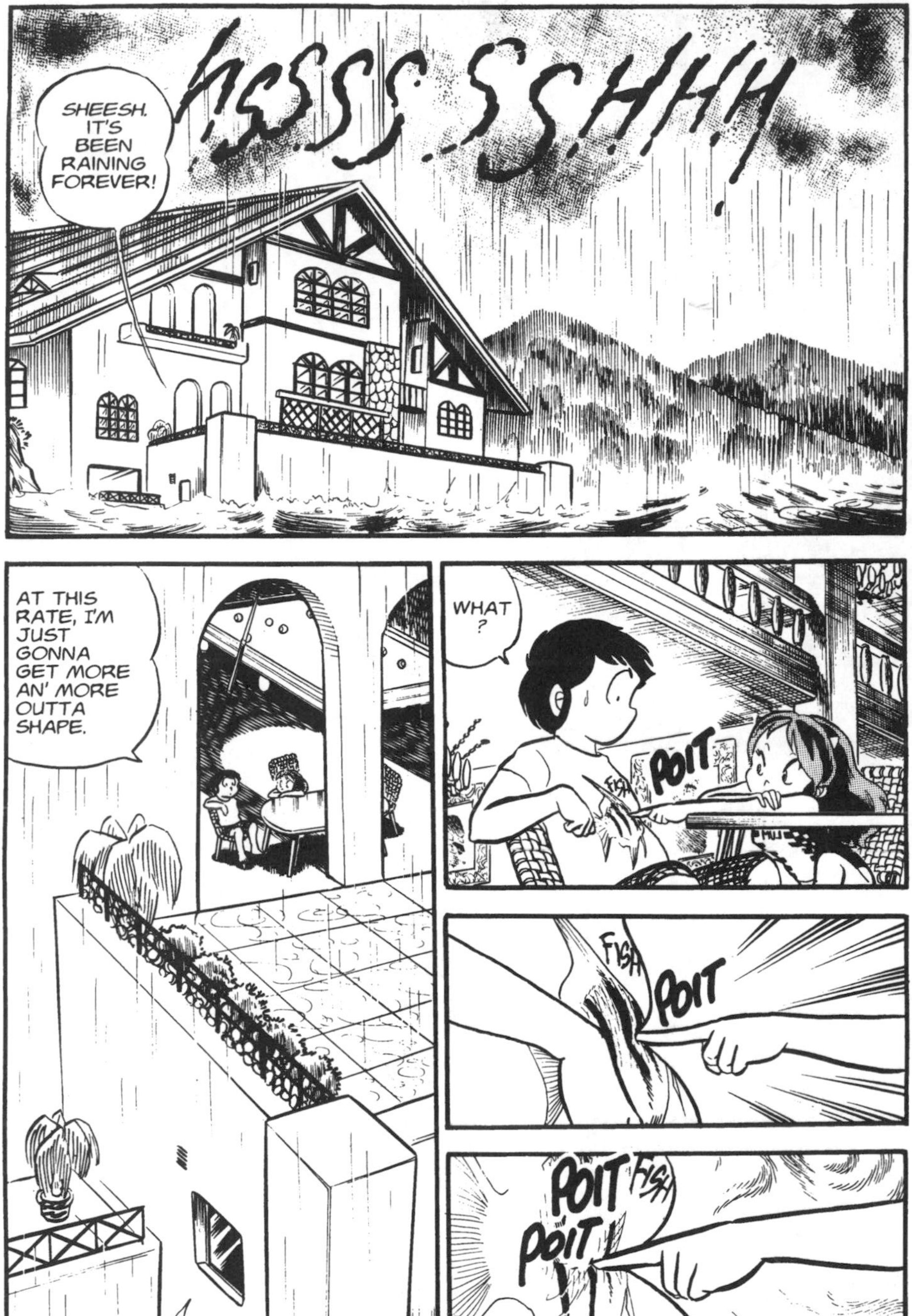
HSSSSSHHH
SHEESH. IT'S BEEN RAINING FOREVER!
AT THIS RATE, I'M JUST GONNA GET MORE AN' MORE OUTTA SHAPE.
WHAT?
FISH
POIT
FISH
POIT
POIT
FISH
POIT

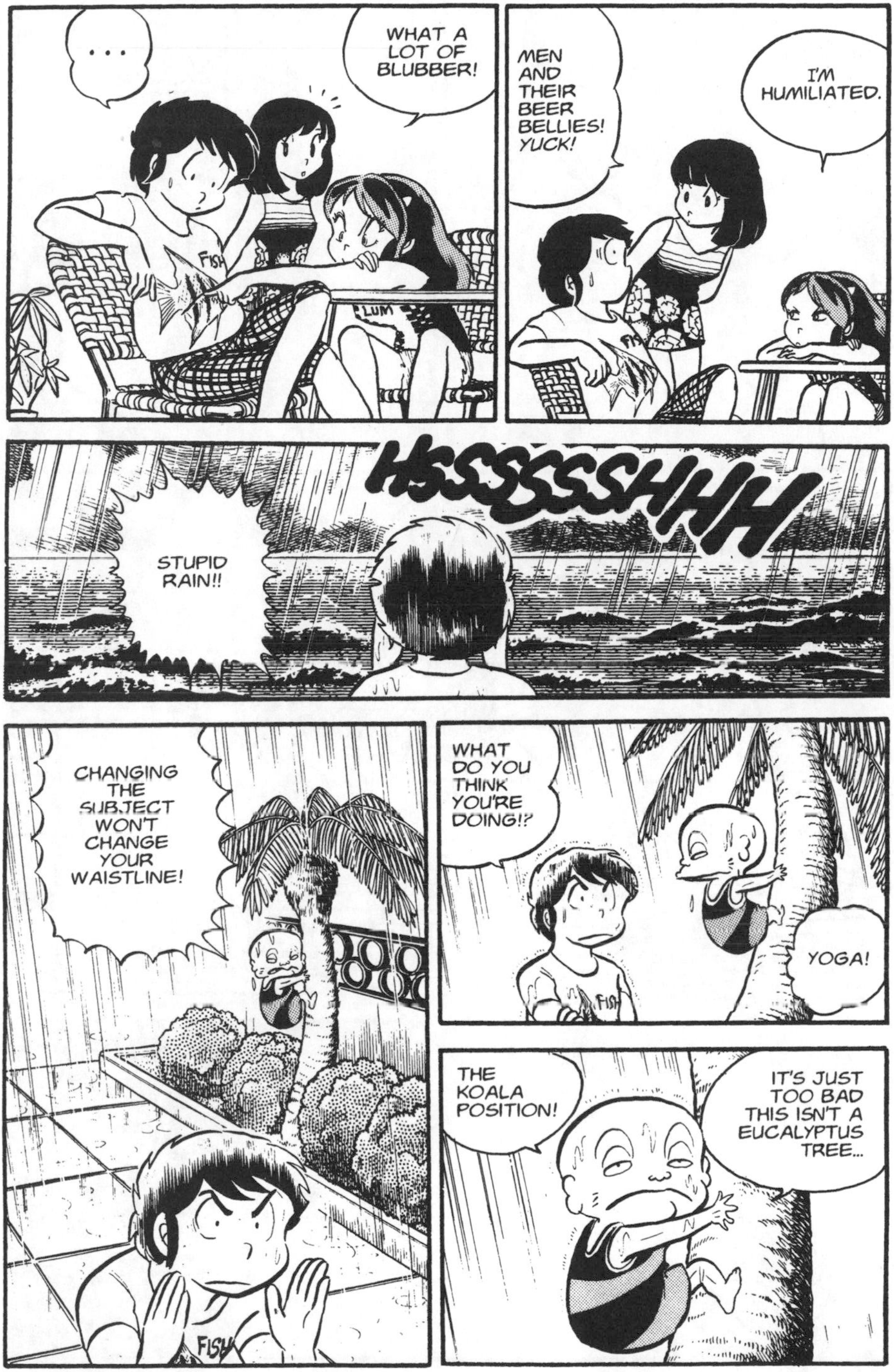
. . .
WHAT A LOT OF BLUBBER!
MEN AND THEIR BEER BELLIES! YUCK!
I'M HUMILIATED.
HSSSSSSHHH
STUPID RAIN!!
CHANGING THE SUBJECT WON'T CHANGE YOUR WAISTLINE!
WHAT DO YOU THINK YOU'RE DOING!?
YOGA!
THE KOALA POSITION!
IT'S JUST TOO BAD THIS ISN'T A EUCALYPTUS TREE...

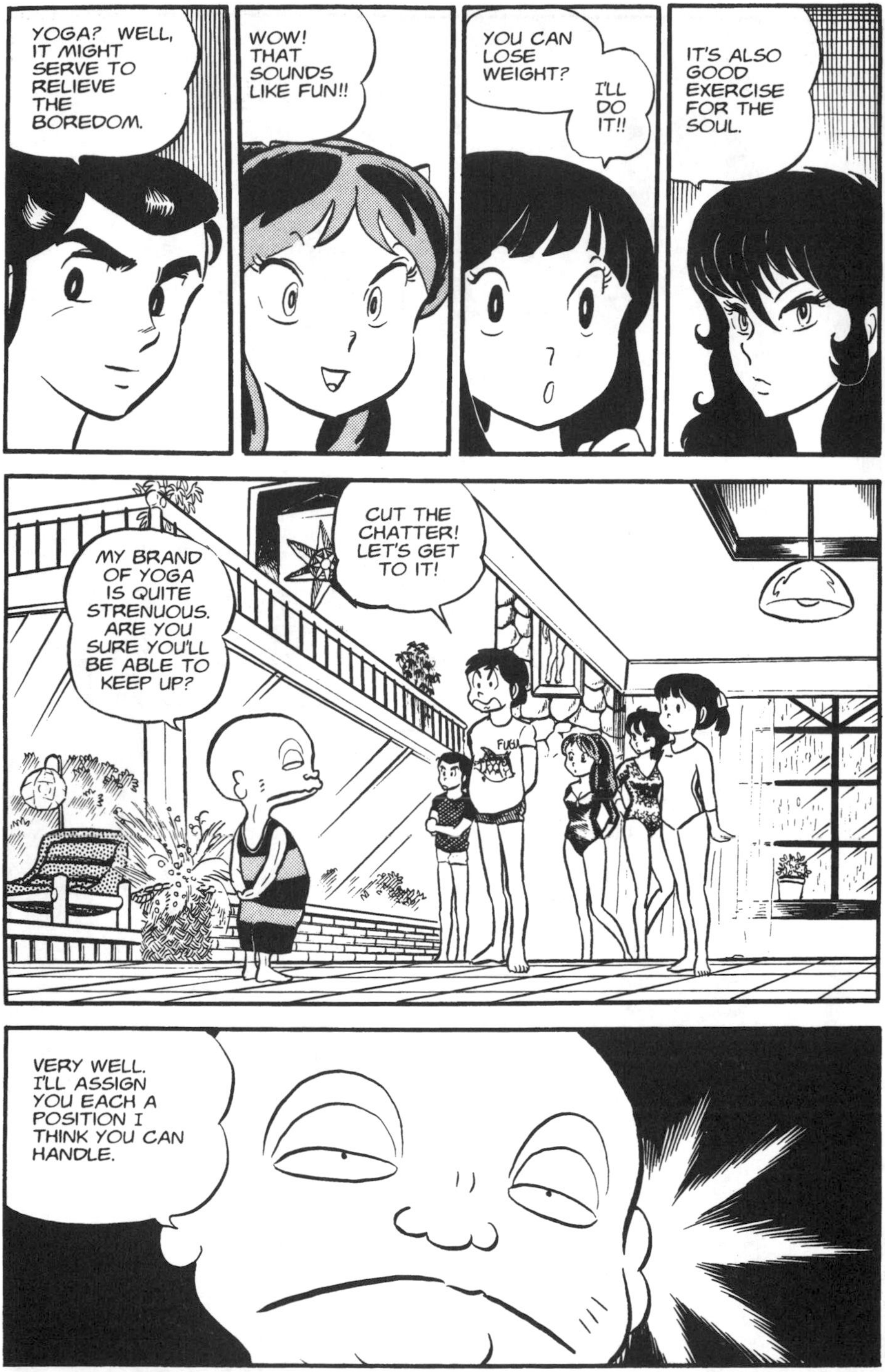
YOGA? WELL, IT MIGHT SERVE TO RELIEVE THE BOREDOM.
WOW! THAT SOUNDS LIKE FUN!!
YOU CAN LOSE WEIGHT?
I'LL DO IT!!
IT'S ALSO GOOD EXERCISE FOR THE SOUL.
MY BRAND OF YOGA IS QUITE STRENUOUS. ARE YOU SURE YOU'LL BE ABLE TO KEEP UP?
CUT THE CHATTER! LET'S GET TO IT!
FUGU
VERY WELL. I'LL ASSIGN YOU EACH A POSITION I THINK YOU CAN HANDLE.

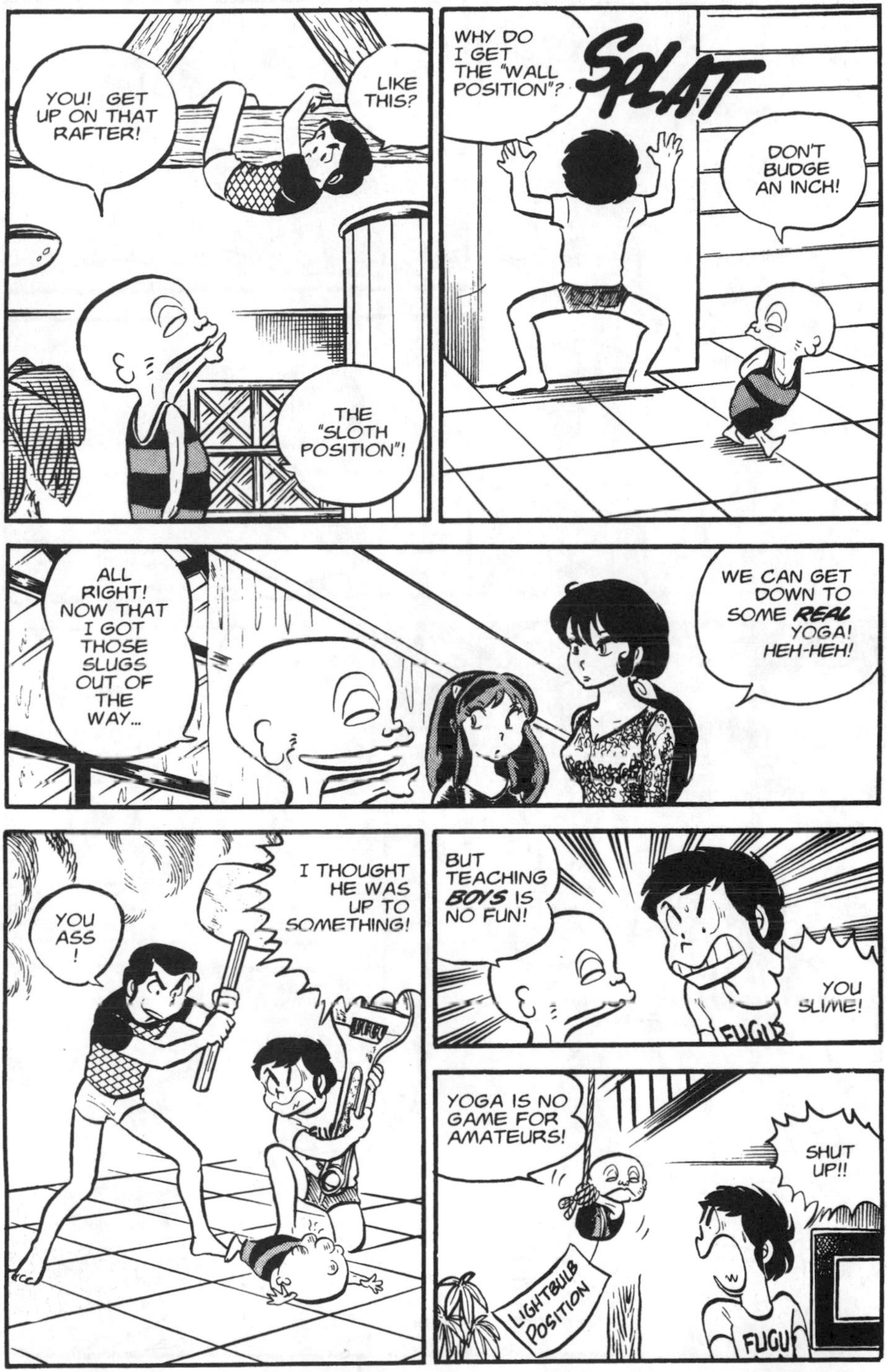
YOU! GET UP ON THAT RAFTER!
LIKE THIS?
THE "SLOTH POSITION"!
WHY DO I GET THE "WALL POSITION"?
SPLAT
DON'T BUDGE AN INCH!
ALL RIGHT! NOW THAT I GOT THOSE SLUGS OUT OF THE WAY...
WE CAN GET DOWN TO SOME REAL YOGA! HEH-HEH!
YOU ASS!
I THOUGHT HE WAS UP TO SOMETHING!
BUT TEACHING BOYS IS NO FUN!
YOU SLIME!
FUGU
YOGA IS NO GAME FOR AMATEURS!
LIGHTBULB POSITION
SHUT UP!!
FUGU

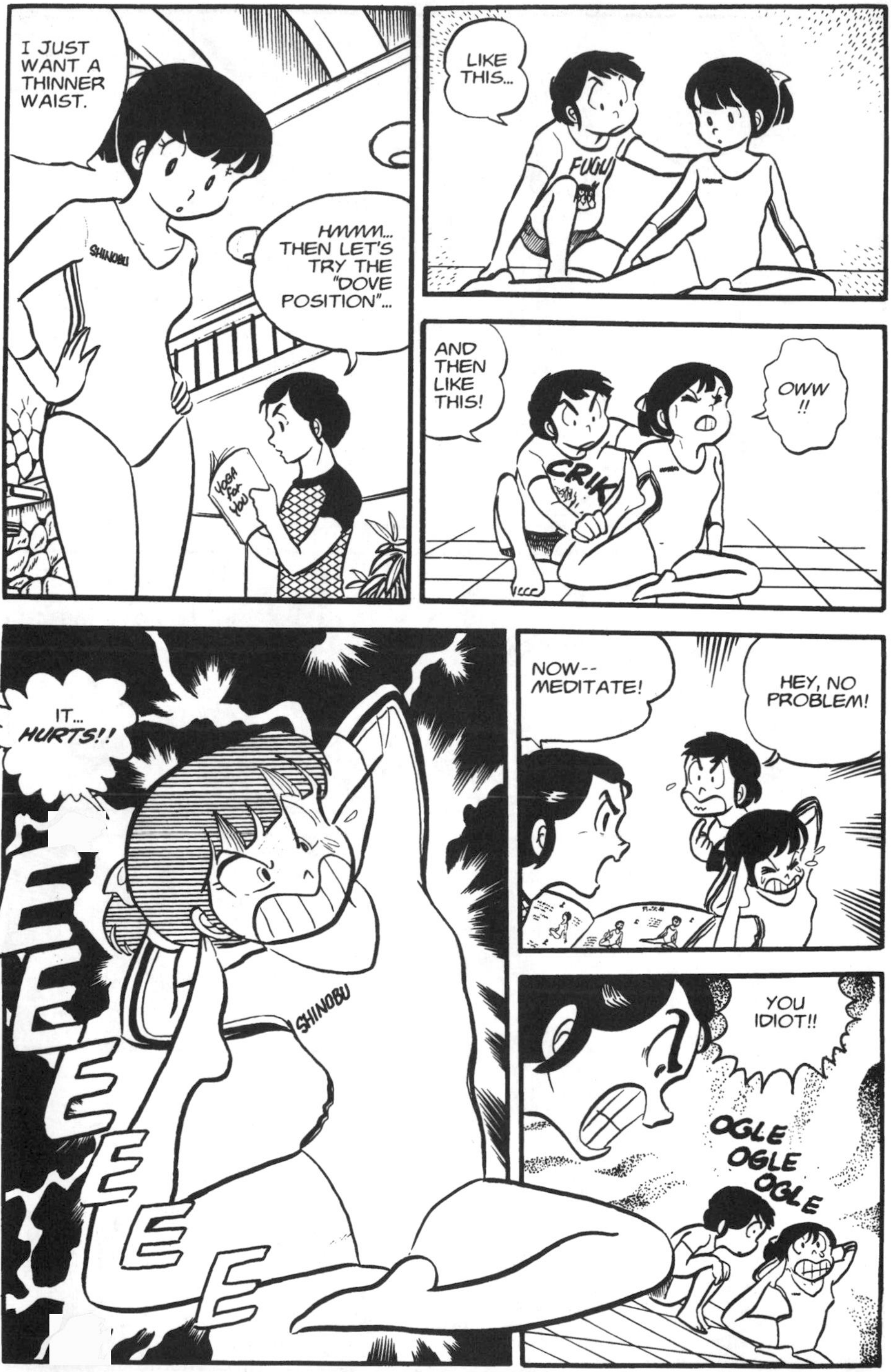
I JUST WANT A THINNER WAIST.
SHINOBU
HMMM... THEN LET'S TRY THE "DOVE POSITION"...
YOGA for YOU
LIKE THIS...
FUGU
AND THEN LIKE THIS!
CRIK
OWW!!
IT... HURTS!!
EEEEEEEE
SHINOBU
NOW-- MEDITATE!
HEY, NO PROBLEM!
YOU IDIOT!!
OGLE OGLE OGLE

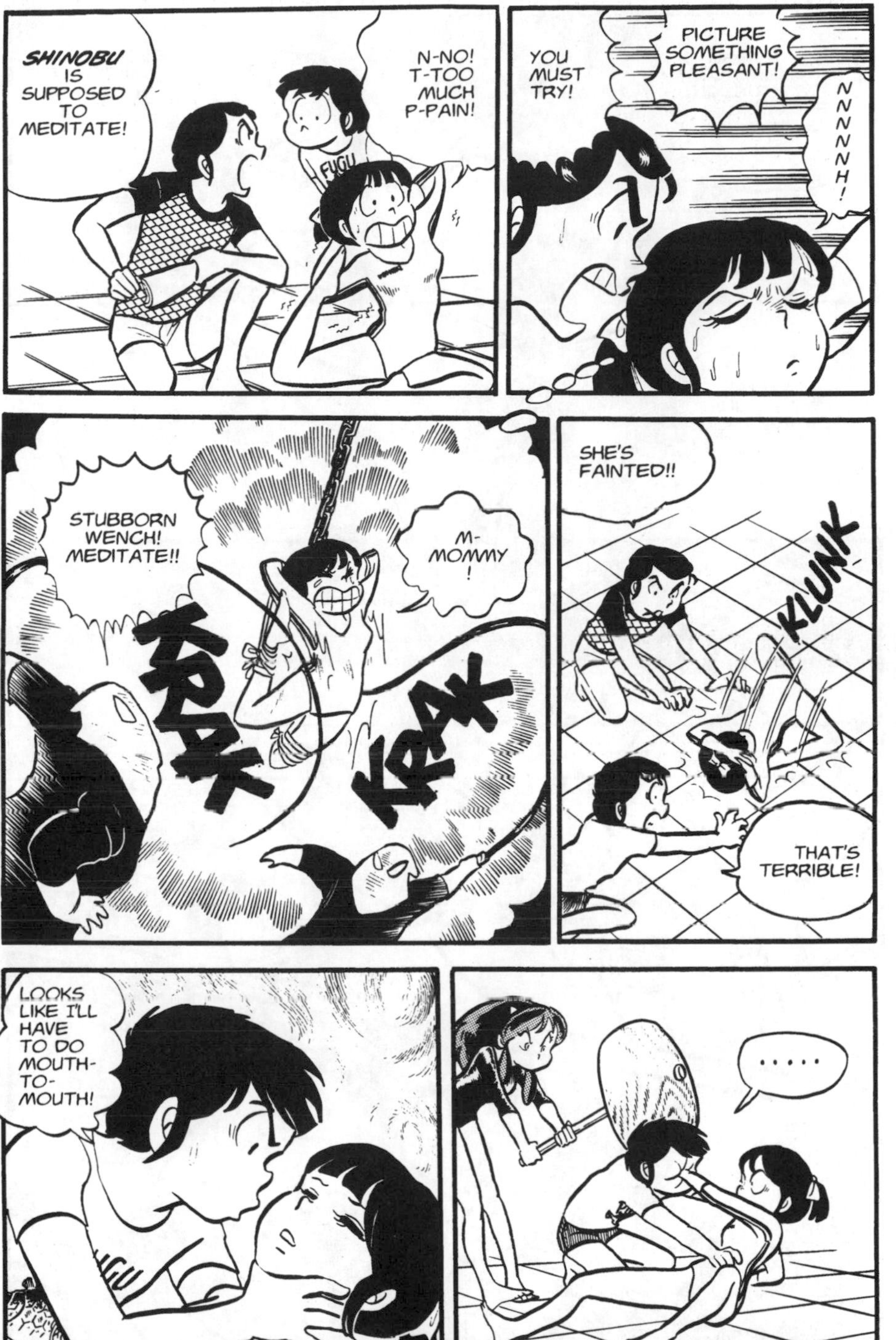
SHINOBU IS SUPPOSED TO MEDITATE!
N-NO! T-TOO MUCH P-PAIN!
YOU MUST TRY!
PICTURE SOMETHING PLEASANT!
NNNNNNH!
STUBBORN WENCH! MEDITATE!!
M-MOMMY!
KRAK
KRAK
SHE'S FAINTED!!
KLUNK
THAT'S TERRIBLE!
LOOKS LIKE I'LL HAVE TO DO MOUTH-TO-MOUTH!
.....

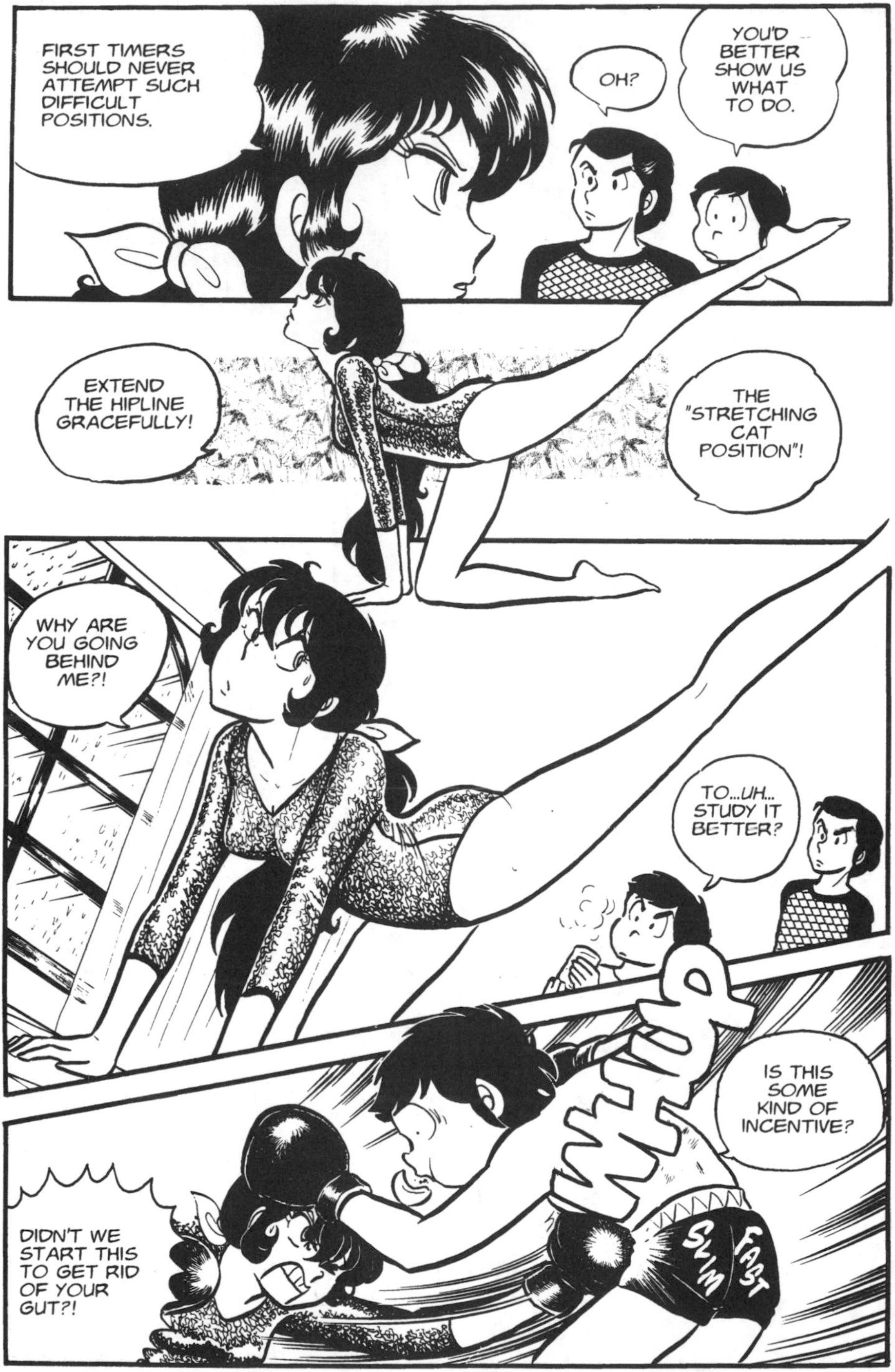
FIRST TIMERS SHOULD NEVER ATTEMPT SUCH DIFFICULT POSITIONS.
OH?
YOU'D BETTER SHOW US WHAT TO DO.
EXTEND THE HIPLINE GRACEFULLY!
THE "STRETCHING CAT POSITION"!
WHY ARE YOU GOING BEHIND ME?!
TO...UH... STUDY IT BETTER?
IS THIS SOME KIND OF INCENTIVE?
WHUD
DIDN'T WE START THIS TO GET RID OF YOUR GUT?!
SLIM FAST

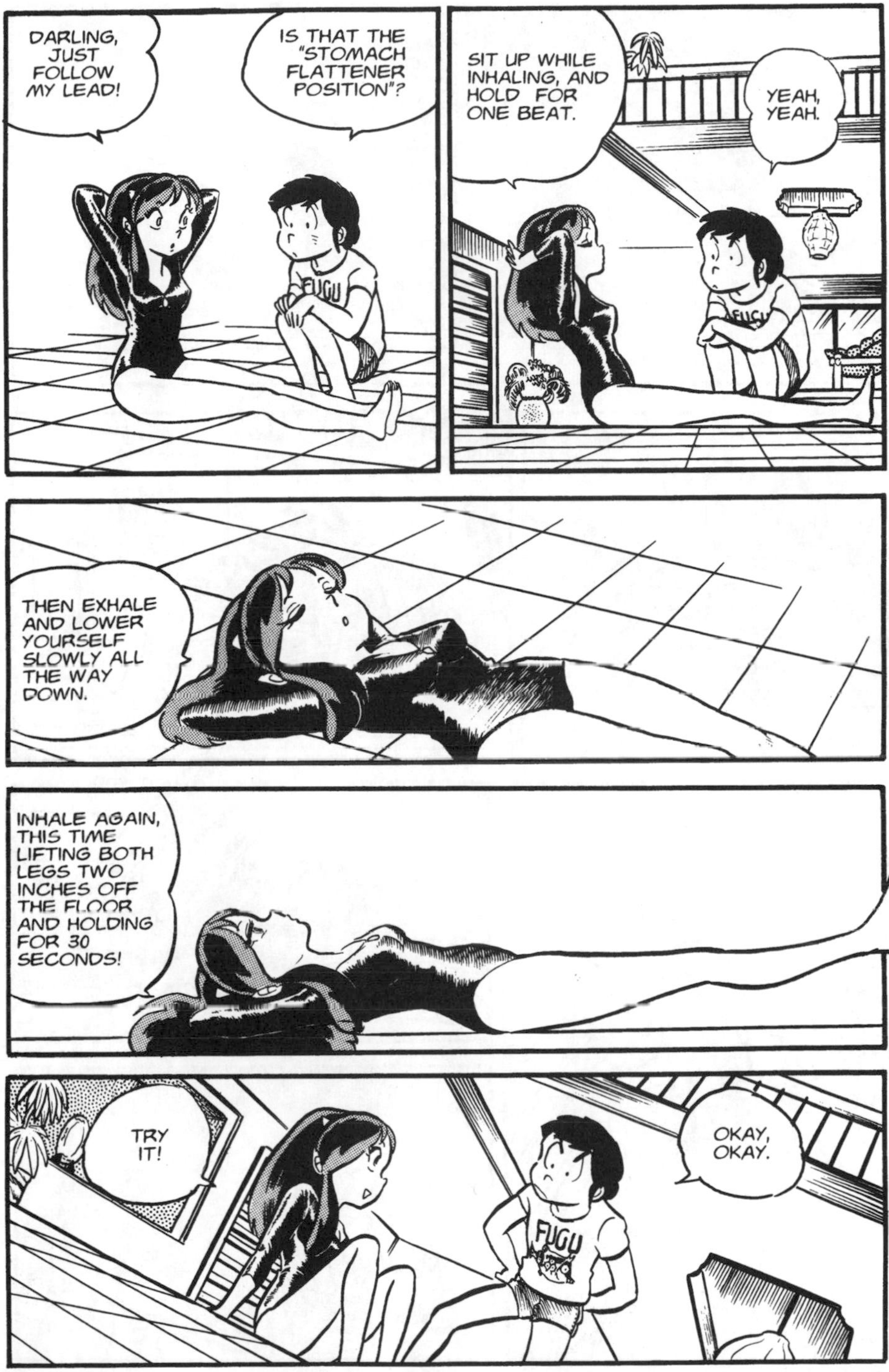
DARLING, JUST FOLLOW MY LEAD!
IS THAT THE "STOMACH FLATTENER POSITION"?
SIT UP WHILE INHALING, AND HOLD FOR ONE BEAT.
YEAH, YEAH.
FUGU
THEN EXHALE AND LOWER YOURSELF SLOWLY ALL THE WAY DOWN.
INHALE AGAIN, THIS TIME LIFTING BOTH LEGS TWO INCHES OFF THE FLOOR AND HOLDING FOR 30 SECONDS!
TRY IT!
OKAY, OKAY.
FUGU

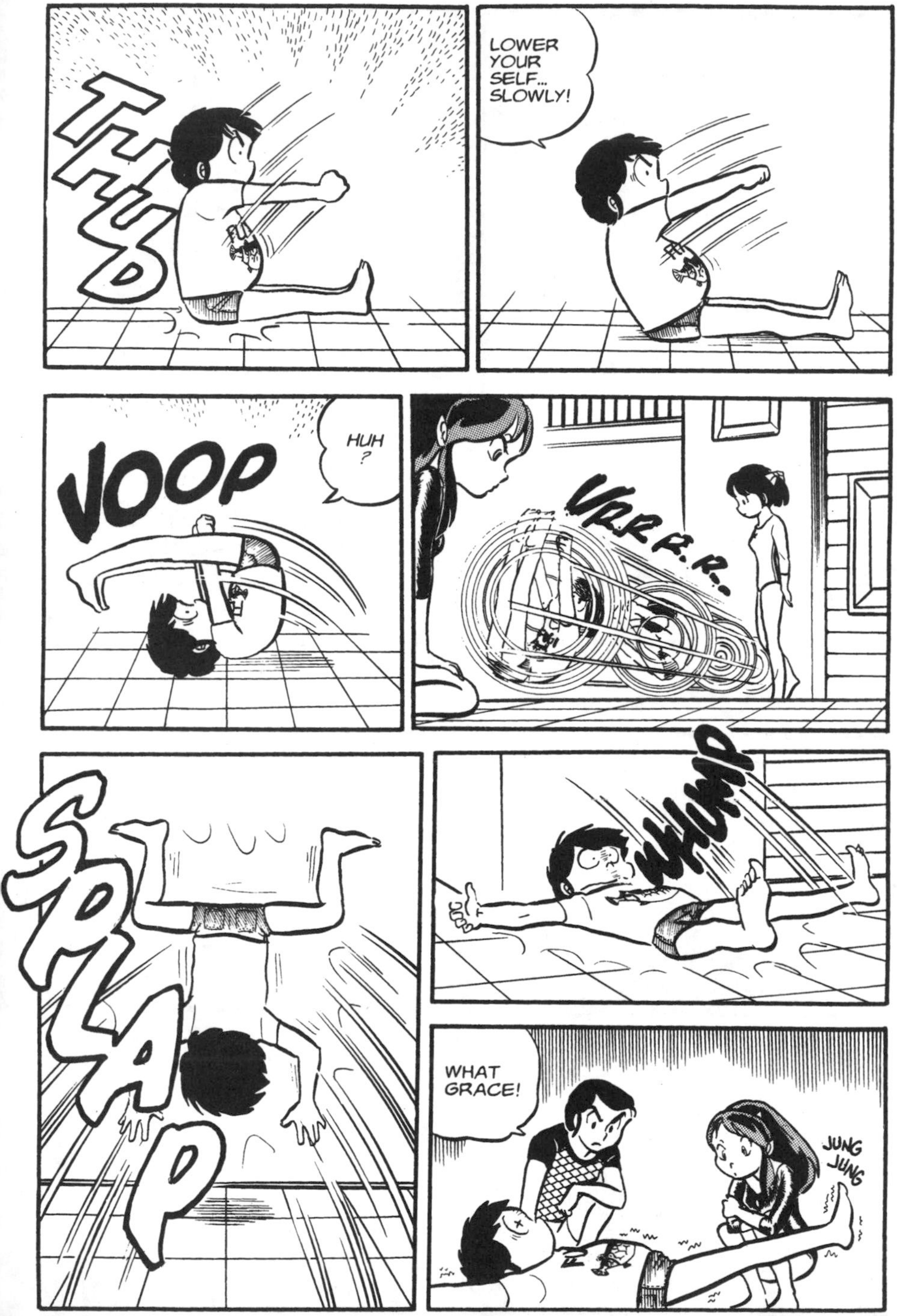
THUD
LOWER YOUR SELF... SLOWLY!
VOOP
HUH ?
VRRRR...
SPLAP
WHUMP
WHAT GRACE!
JUNG JUNG

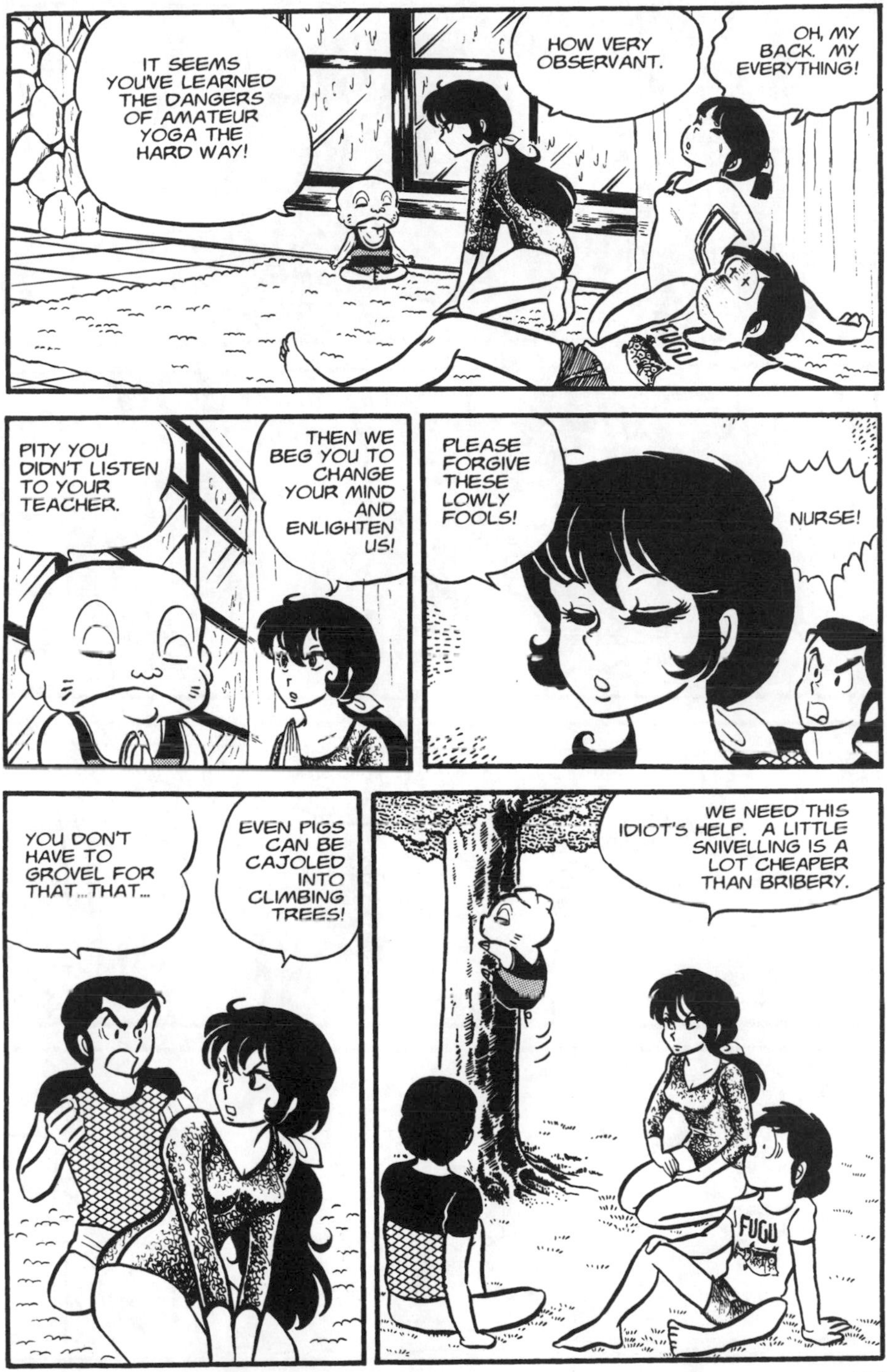
IT SEEMS YOU'VE LEARNED THE DANGERS OF AMATEUR YOGA THE HARD WAY!
HOW VERY OBSERVANT.
OH, MY BACK. MY EVERYTHING!
FUGU
PITY YOU DIDN'T LISTEN TO YOUR TEACHER.
THEN WE BEG YOU TO CHANGE YOUR MIND AND ENLIGHTEN US!
PLEASE FORGIVE THESE LOWLY FOOLS!
NURSE!
YOU DON'T HAVE TO GROVEL FOR THAT...THAT...
EVEN PIGS CAN BE CAJOLED INTO CLIMBING TREES!
WE NEED THIS IDIOT'S HELP. A LITTLE SNIVELLING IS A LOT CHEAPER THAN BRIBERY.
FUGU

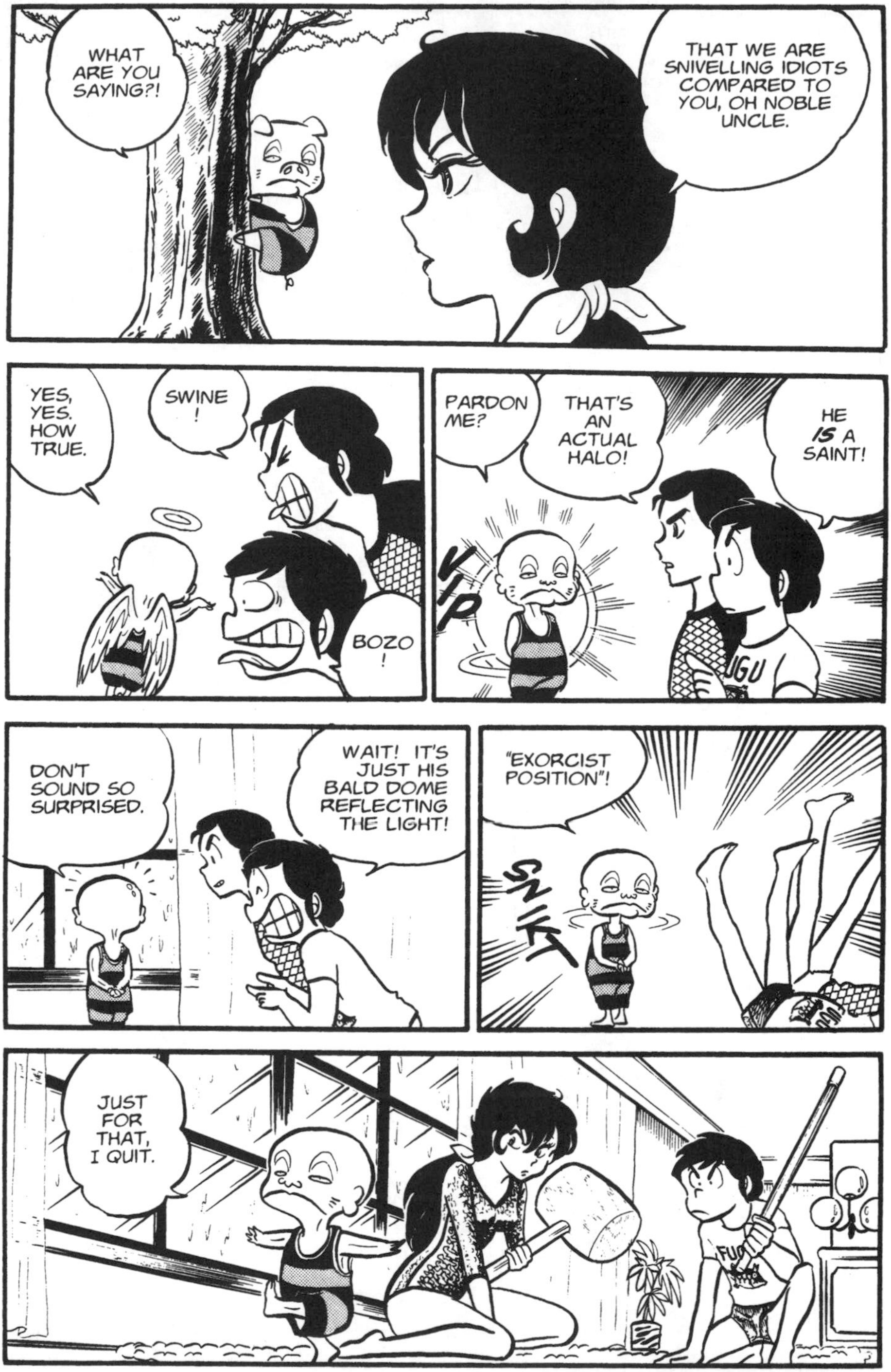
WHAT ARE YOU SAYING?!
THAT WE ARE SNIVELLING IDIOTS COMPARED TO YOU, OH NOBLE UNCLE.
YES, YES. HOW TRUE.
SWINE!
BOZO!
PARDON ME?
THAT'S AN ACTUAL HALO!
HE IS A SAINT!
VIP
DON'T SOUND SO SURPRISED.
WAIT! IT'S JUST HIS BALD DOME REFLECTING THE LIGHT!
"EXORCIST POSITION"!
SNIKT
JUST FOR THAT, I QUIT.

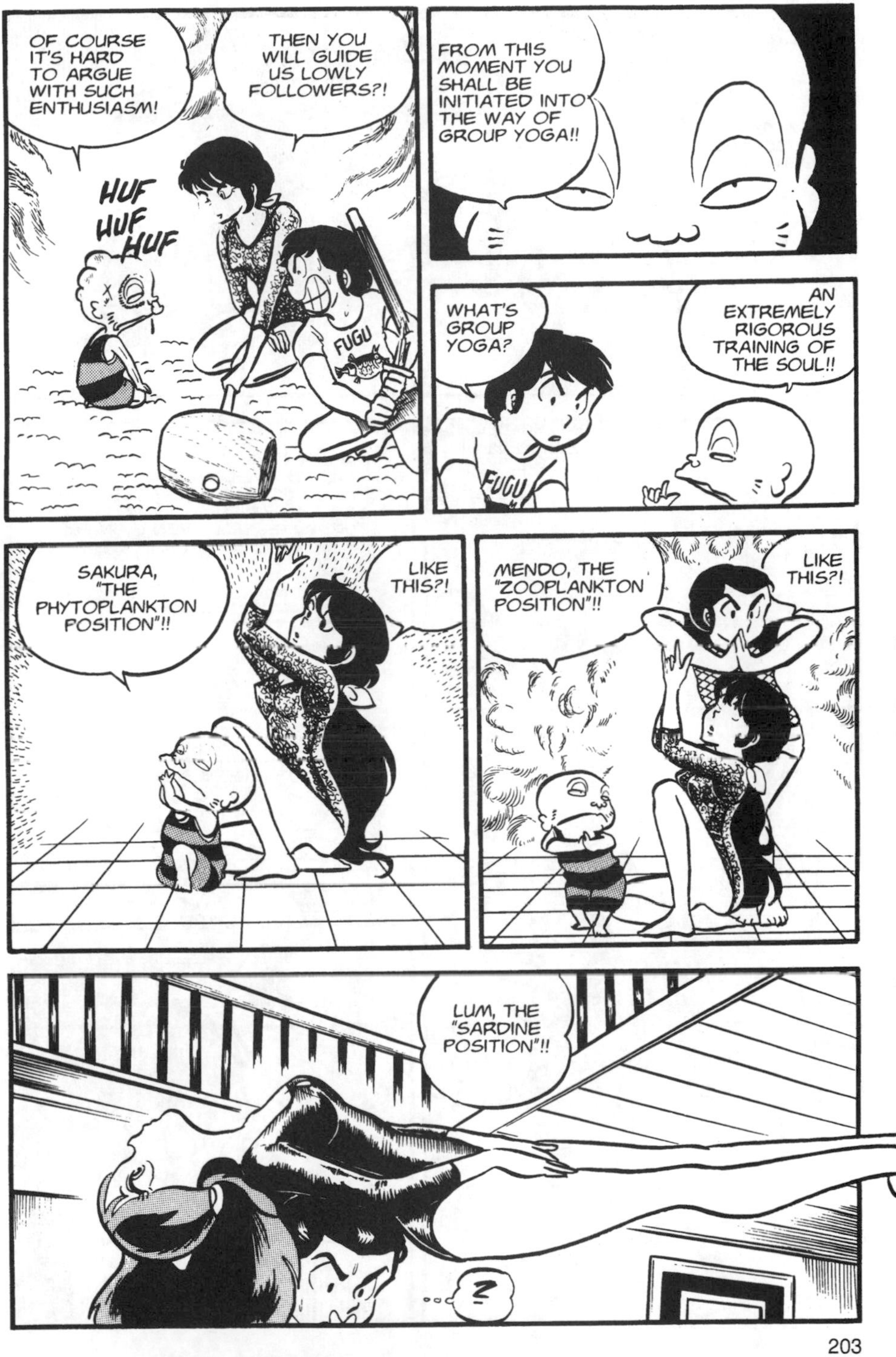
OF COURSE IT'S HARD TO ARGUE WITH SUCH ENTHUSIASM!
THEN YOU WILL GUIDE US LOWLY FOLLOWERS?!
HUF HUF HUF
FUGU
FROM THIS MOMENT YOU SHALL BE INITIATED INTO THE WAY OF GROUP YOGA!!
WHAT'S GROUP YOGA?
AN EXTREMELY RIGOROUS TRAINING OF THE SOUL!!
FUGU
SAKURA, "THE PHYTOPLANKTON POSITION"!!
LIKE THIS?!
MENDO, THE "ZOOPLANKTON POSITION"!!
LIKE THIS?!
LUM, THE "SARDINE POSITION"!!
?

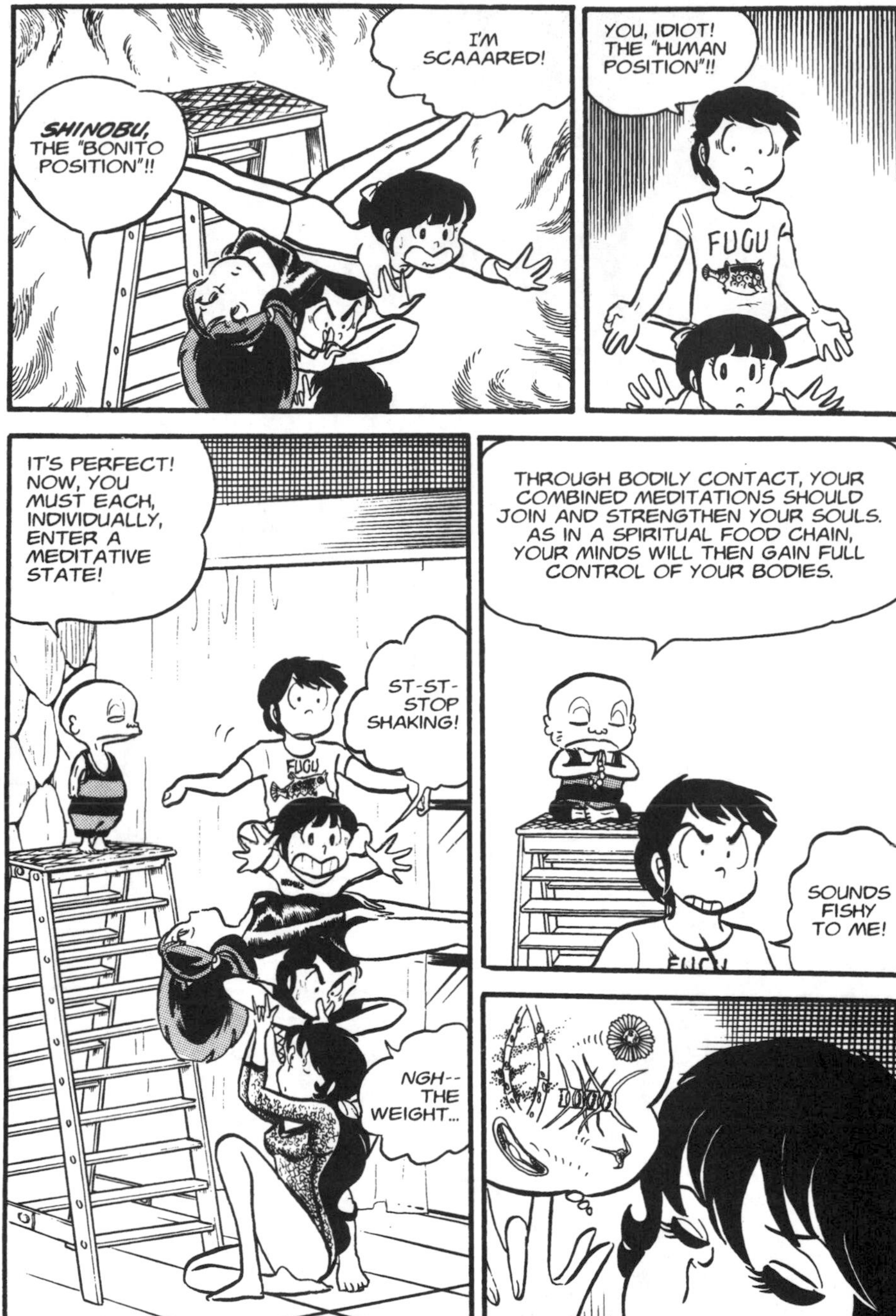
I'M SCAAARED!
SHINOBU, THE "BONITO POSITION"!!
YOU, IDIOT! THE "HUMAN POSITION"!!
FUGU
IT'S PERFECT! NOW, YOU MUST EACH, INDIVIDUALLY, ENTER A MEDITATIVE STATE!
ST-ST-STOP SHAKING!
FUGU
NGH-- THE WEIGHT...
THROUGH BODILY CONTACT, YOUR COMBINED MEDITATIONS SHOULD JOIN AND STRENGTHEN YOUR SOULS. AS IN A SPIRITUAL FOOD CHAIN, YOUR MINDS WILL THEN GAIN FULL CONTROL OF YOUR BODIES.
SOUNDS FISHY TO ME!

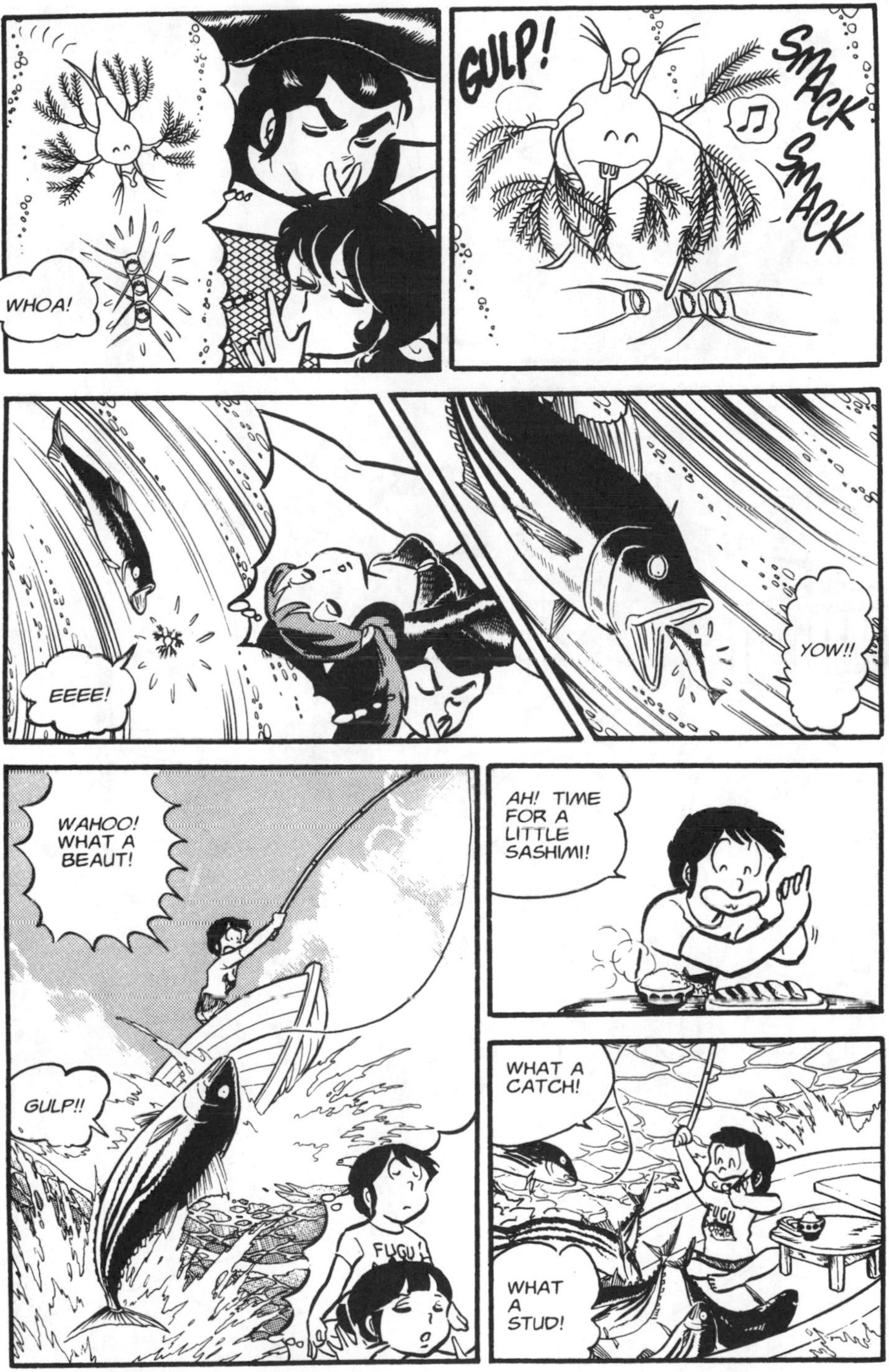
WHOA!
GULP!
SMACK
SMACK
EEEE!
YOW!!
WAHOO! WHAT A BEAUT!
GULP!!
FUGU!
AH! TIME FOR A LITTLE SASHIMI!
WHAT A CATCH!
WHAT A STUD!
FUGU

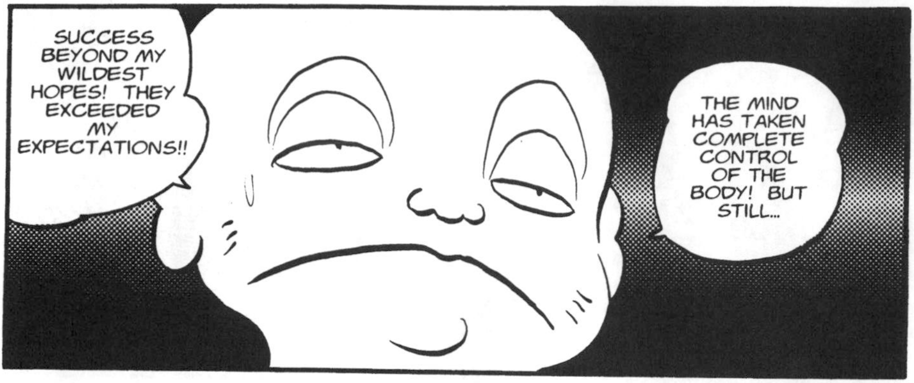
SUCCESS BEYOND MY WILDEST HOPES! THEY EXCEEDED MY EXPECTATIONS!!
THE MIND HAS TAKEN COMPLETE CONTROL OF THE BODY! BUT STILL...

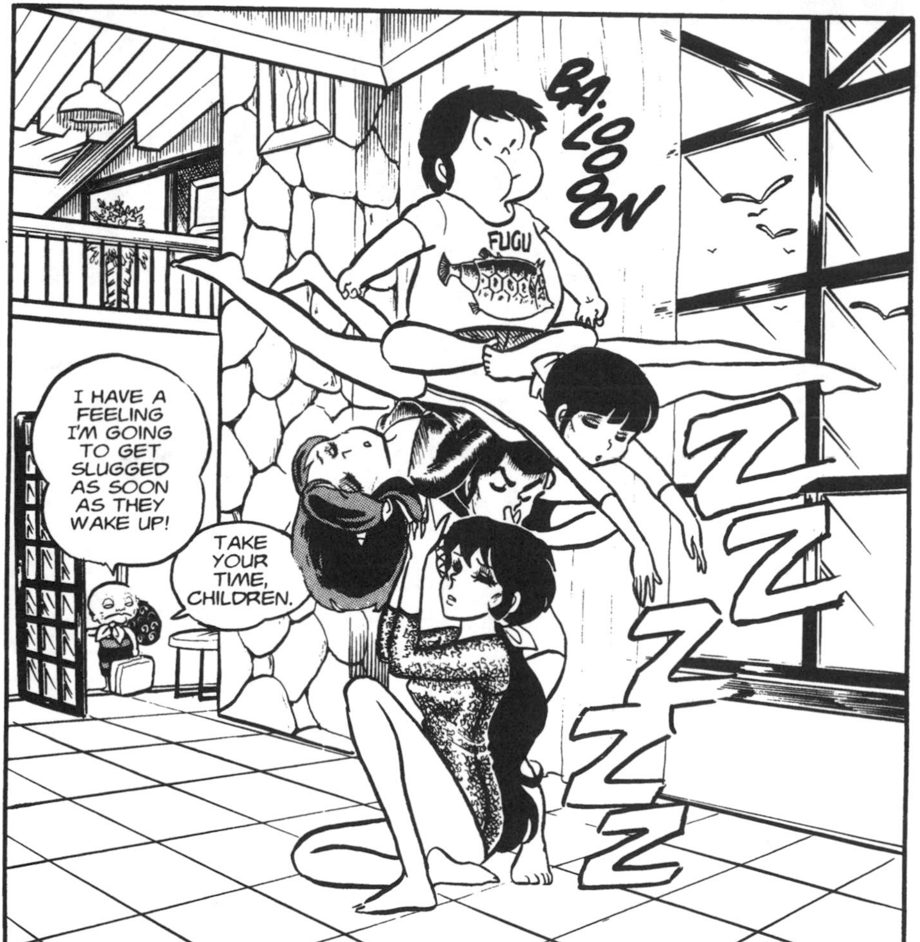
BA-LOOOON
I HAVE A FEELING I'M GOING TO GET SLUGGED AS SOON AS THEY WAKE UP!
TAKE YOUR TIME, CHILDREN.
FUGU
ZZZZZ

PART THIRTEEN
OCEAN OF TEARS

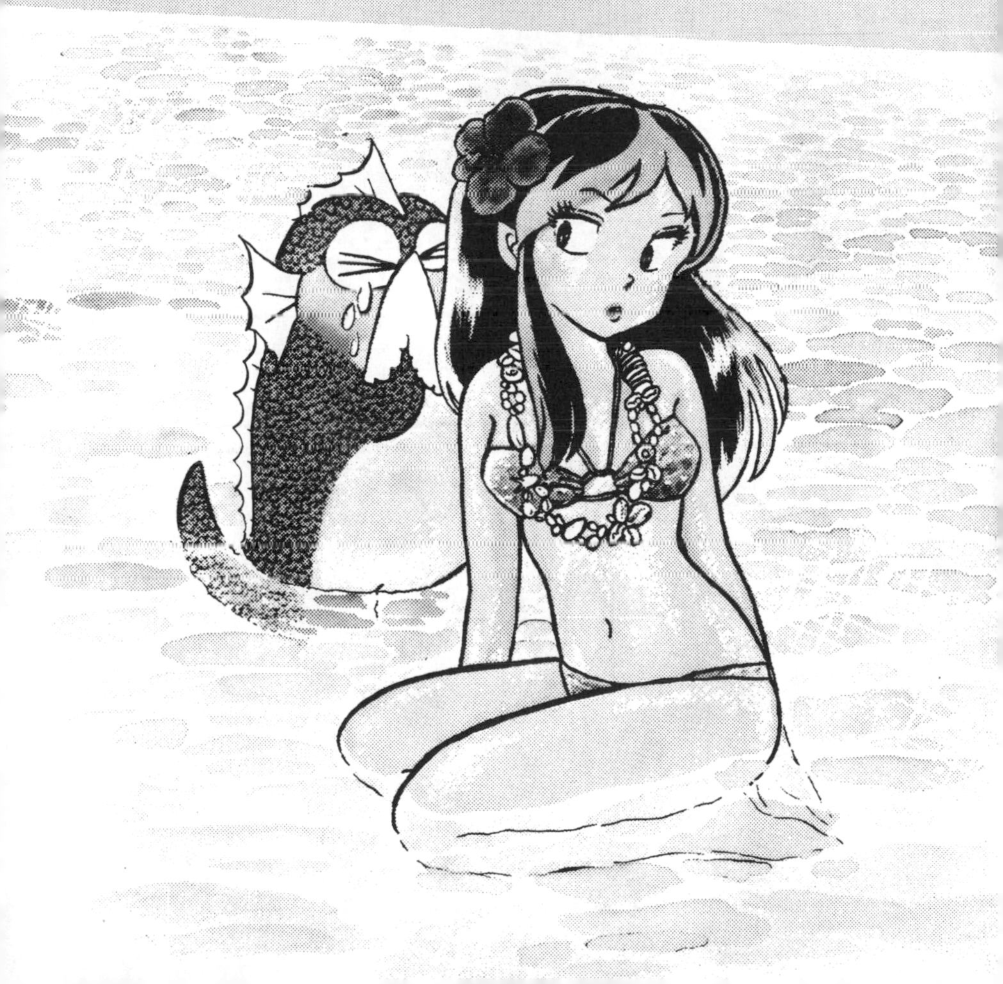

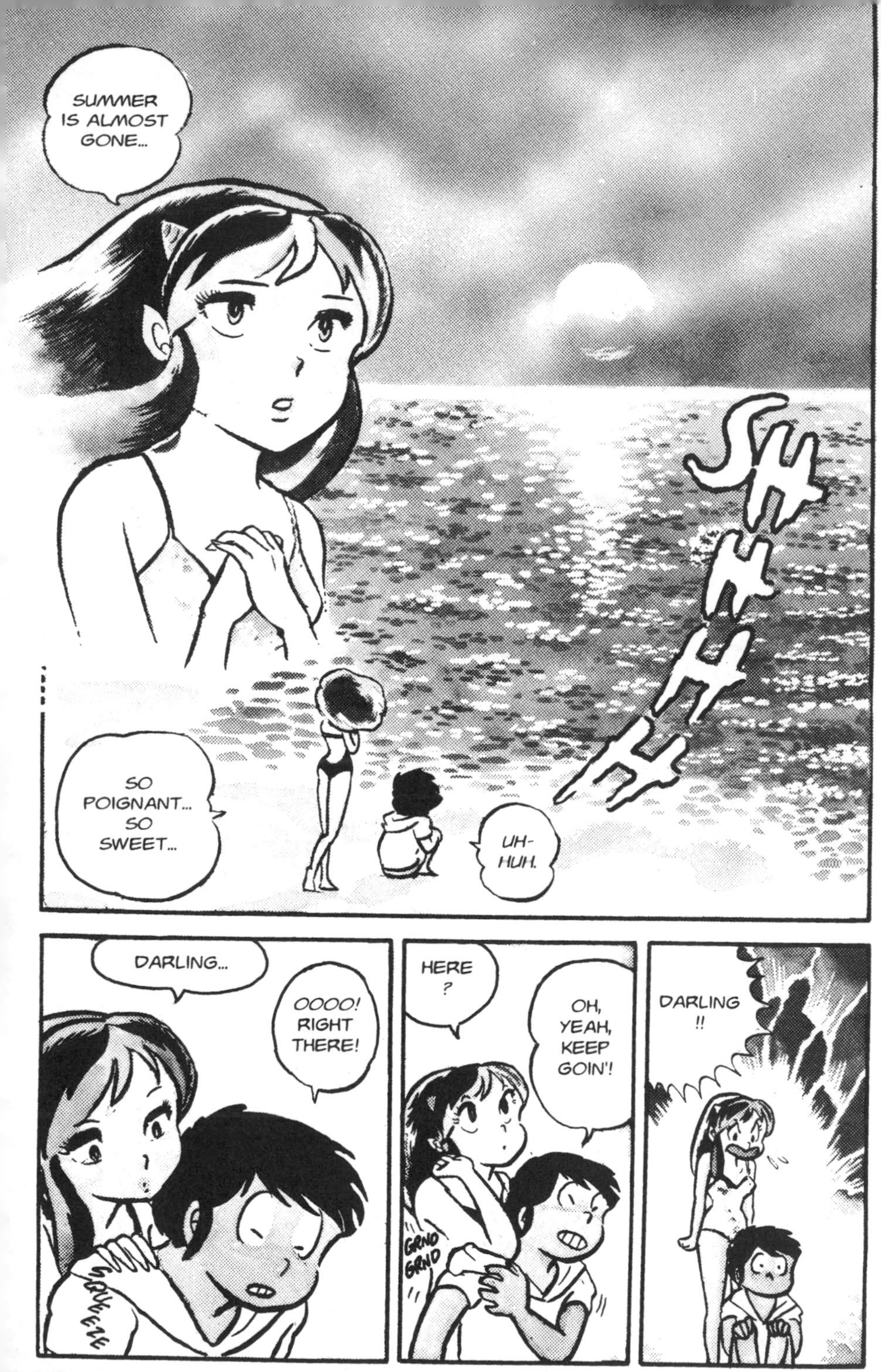
SUMMER IS ALMOST GONE...
SO POIGNANT... SO SWEET...
UH-HUH.
SHHHHH
DARLING...
OOOO! RIGHT THERE!
SQUEEZE
HERE?
OH, YEAH, KEEP GOIN'!
GRND GRND
DARLING!!

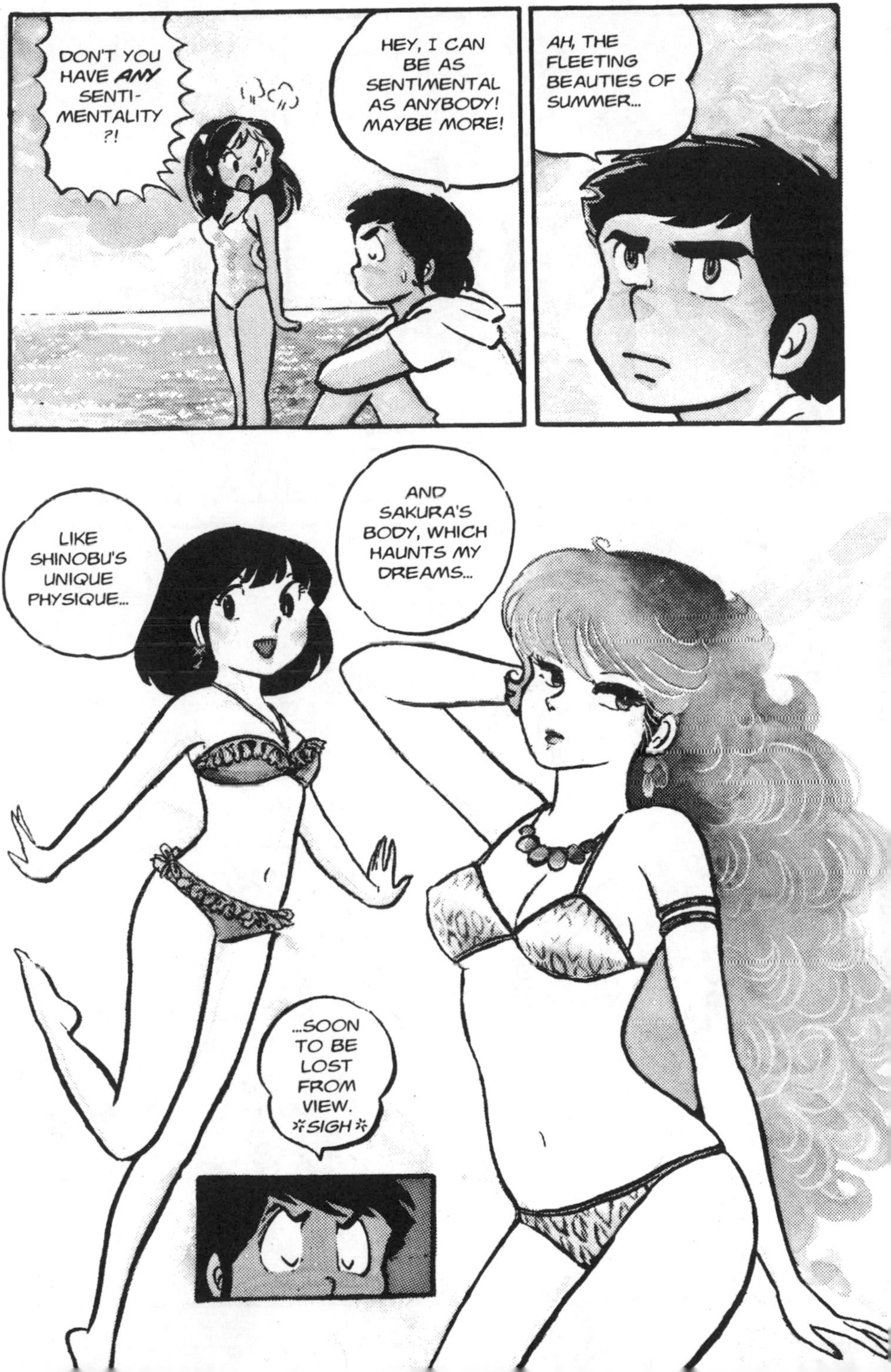
DON'T YOU HAVE ANY SENTI-MENTALITY ?!
HEY, I CAN BE AS SENTIMENTAL AS ANYBODY! MAYBE MORE!
AH, THE FLEETING BEAUTIES OF SUMMER...
LIKE SHINOBU'S UNIQUE PHYSIQUE...
AND SAKURA'S BODY, WHICH HAUNTS MY DREAMS...
...SOON TO BE LOST FROM VIEW. *SIGH*

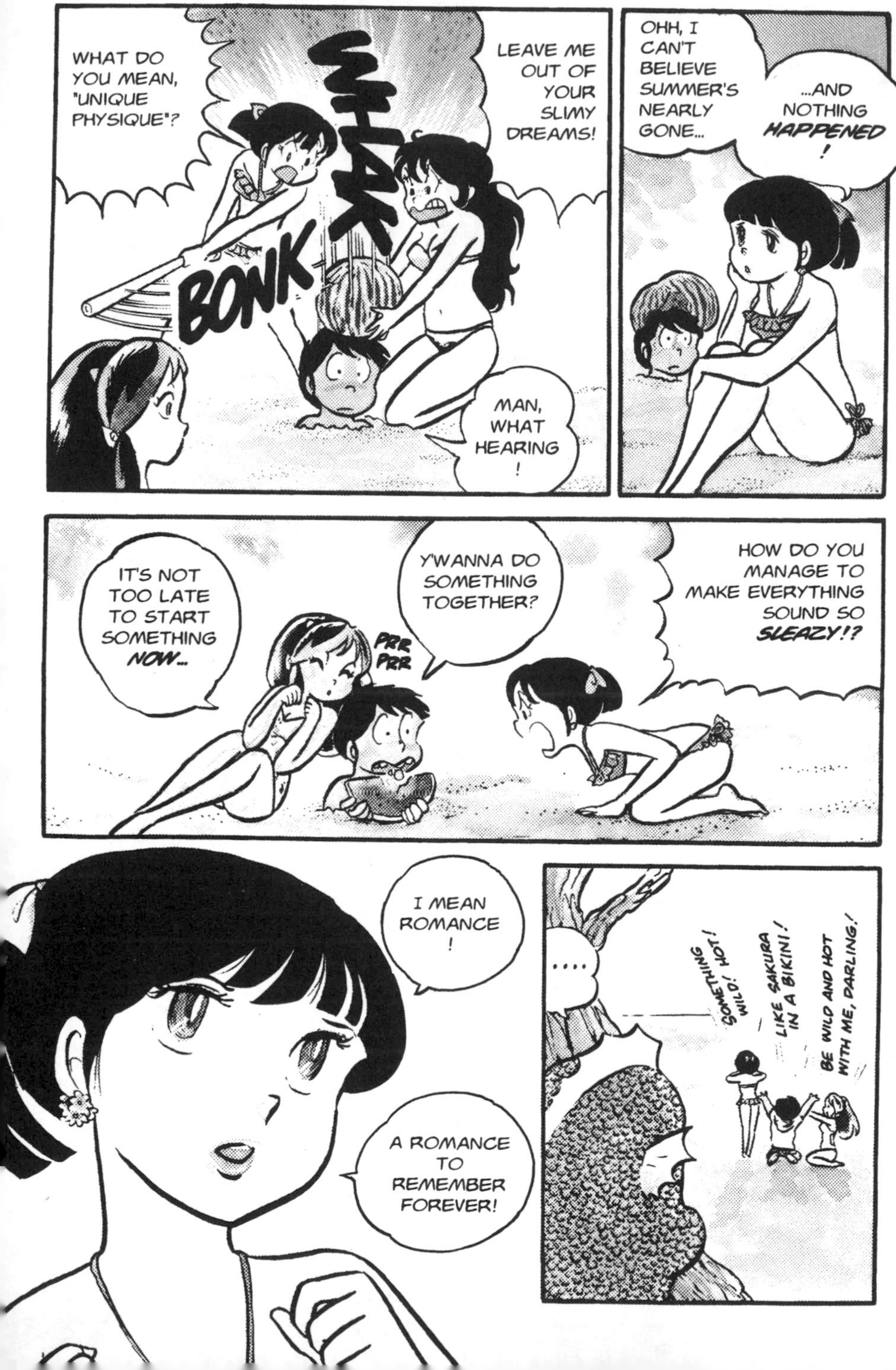
WHAT DO YOU MEAN, "UNIQUE PHYSIQUE"?
LEAVE ME OUT OF YOUR SLIMY DREAMS!
BONK
MAN, WHAT HEARING!
OHH, I CAN'T BELIEVE SUMMER'S NEARLY GONE...
...AND NOTHING HAPPENED!
IT'S NOT TOO LATE TO START SOMETHING NOW...
Y'WANNA DO SOMETHING TOGETHER?
PRR PRR
HOW DO YOU MANAGE TO MAKE EVERYTHING SOUND SO SLEAZY!?
I MEAN ROMANCE!
A ROMANCE TO REMEMBER FOREVER!
....
SOMETHING WILD! HOT!
LIKE SAKURA IN A BIKINI!
BE WILD AND HOT WITH ME, DARLING!

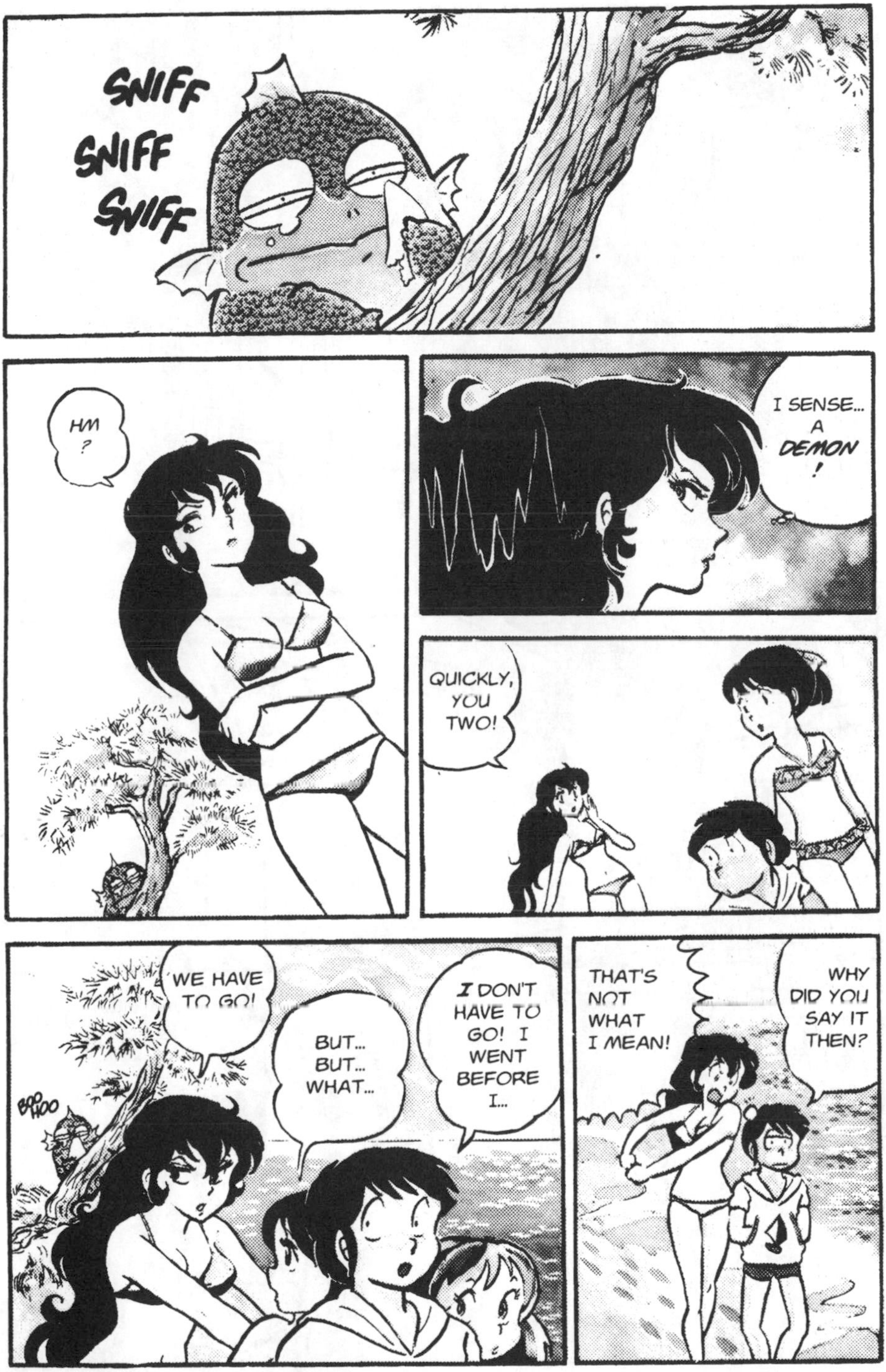
SNIFF SNIFF SNIFF
HM ?
I SENSE... A DEMON !
QUICKLY, YOU TWO!
WE HAVE TO GO!
BOO HOO
BUT... BUT... WHAT...
I DON'T HAVE TO GO! I WENT BEFORE I...
THAT'S NOT WHAT I MEAN!
WHY DID YOU SAY IT THEN?

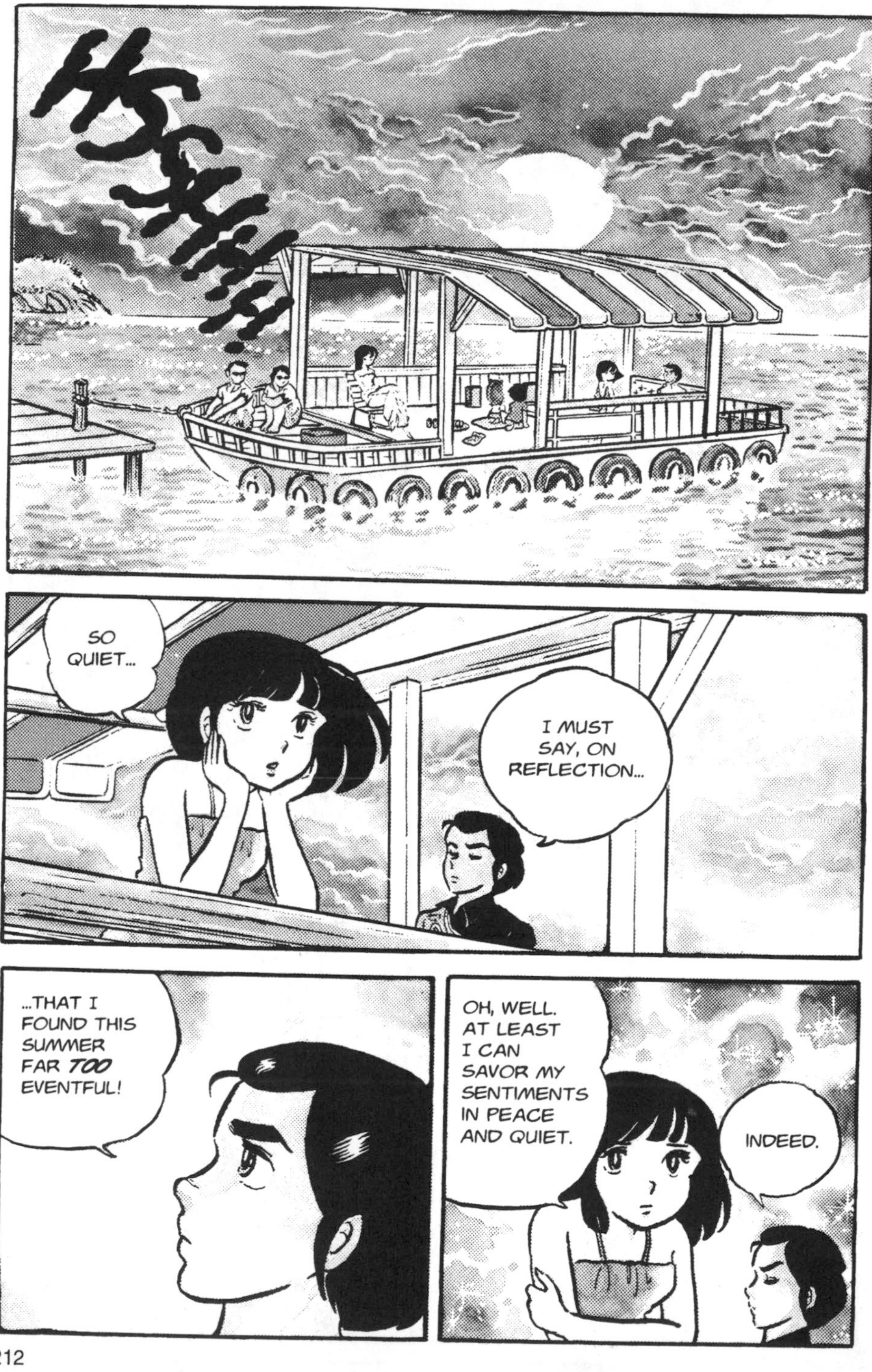
SO QUIET...
I MUST SAY, ON REFLECTION...
...THAT I FOUND THIS SUMMER FAR *TOO* EVENTFUL!
OH, WELL. AT LEAST I CAN SAVOR MY SENTIMENTS IN PEACE AND QUIET.
INDEED.

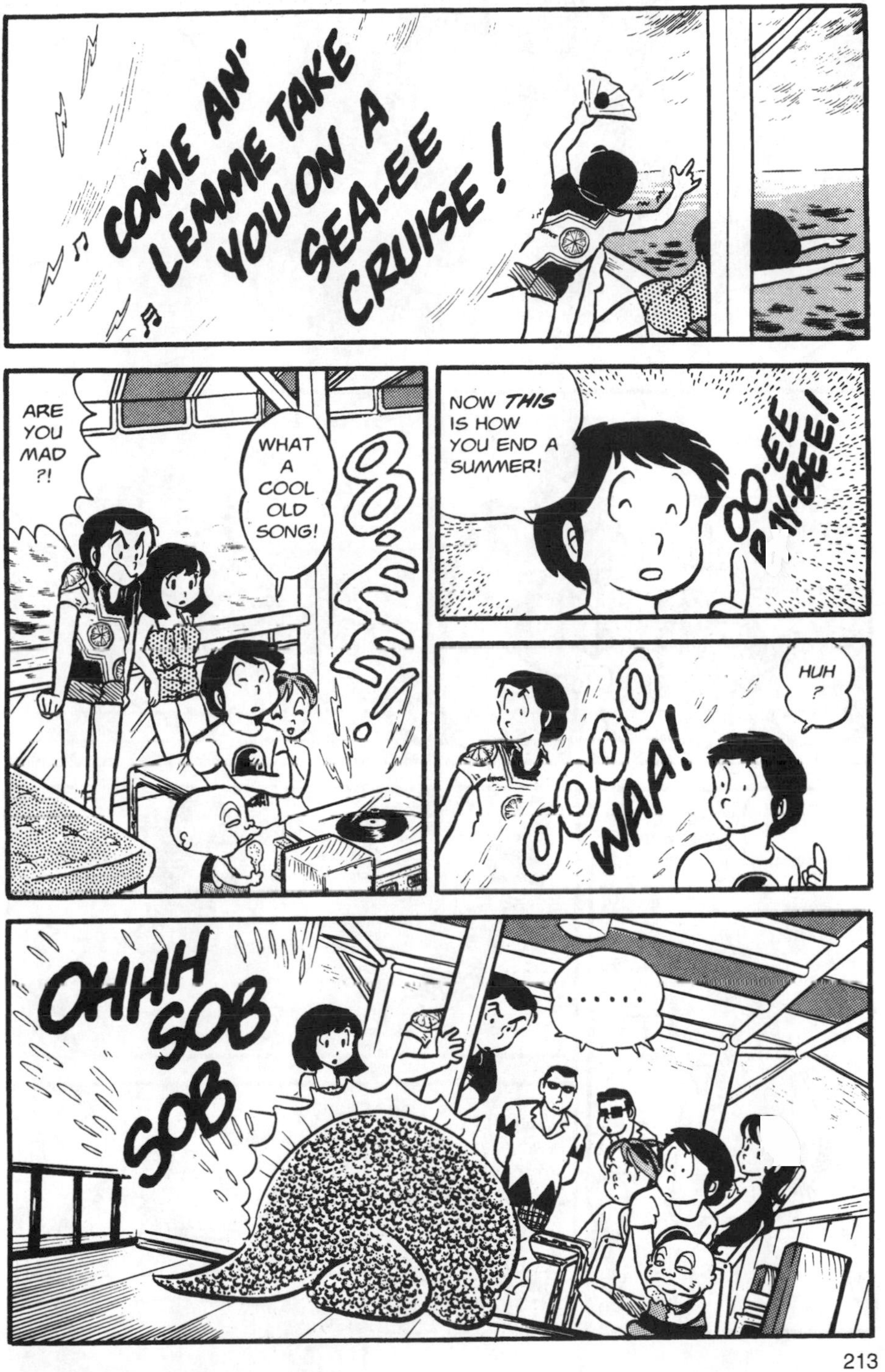
COME AN' LEMME TAKE YOU ON A SEA-EE CRUISE!
ARE YOU MAD ?!
WHAT A COOL OLD SONG!
NOW THIS IS HOW YOU END A SUMMER!
OO-EE
Y-BEE!
OOOOO WAA!
HUH ?
OHHH SOB SOB
......

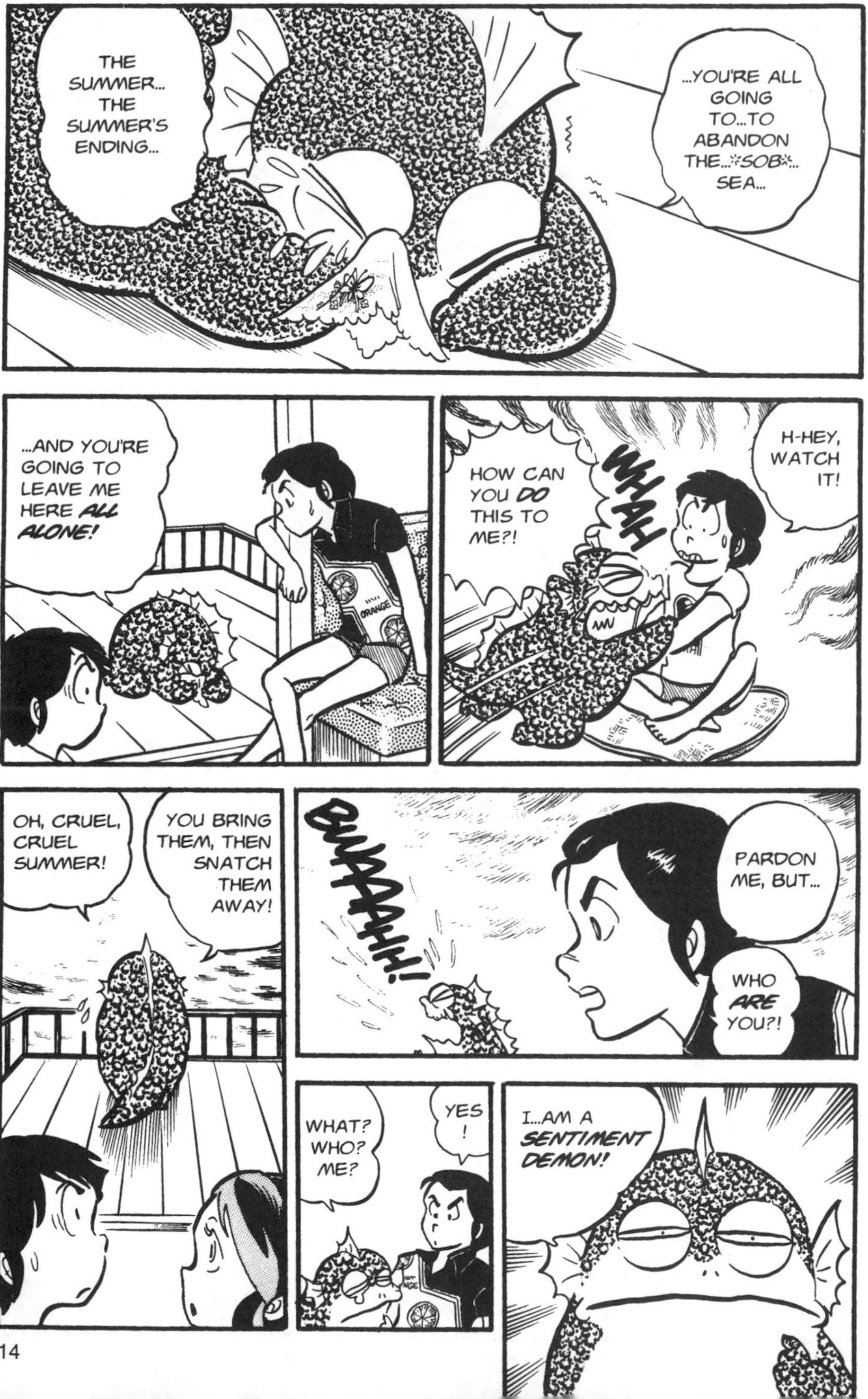
THE SUMMER... THE SUMMER'S ENDING...
...YOU'RE ALL GOING TO...TO ABANDON THE...*SOB*... SEA...
...AND YOU'RE GOING TO LEAVE ME HERE ALL ALONE!
HOW CAN YOU DO THIS TO ME?!
WHAH
H-HEY, WATCH IT!
OH, CRUEL, CRUEL SUMMER!
YOU BRING THEM, THEN SNATCH THEM AWAY!
BWAAAAHH!
PARDON ME, BUT...
WHO ARE YOU?!
WHAT? WHO? ME?
YES!
I...AM A SENTIMENT DEMON!

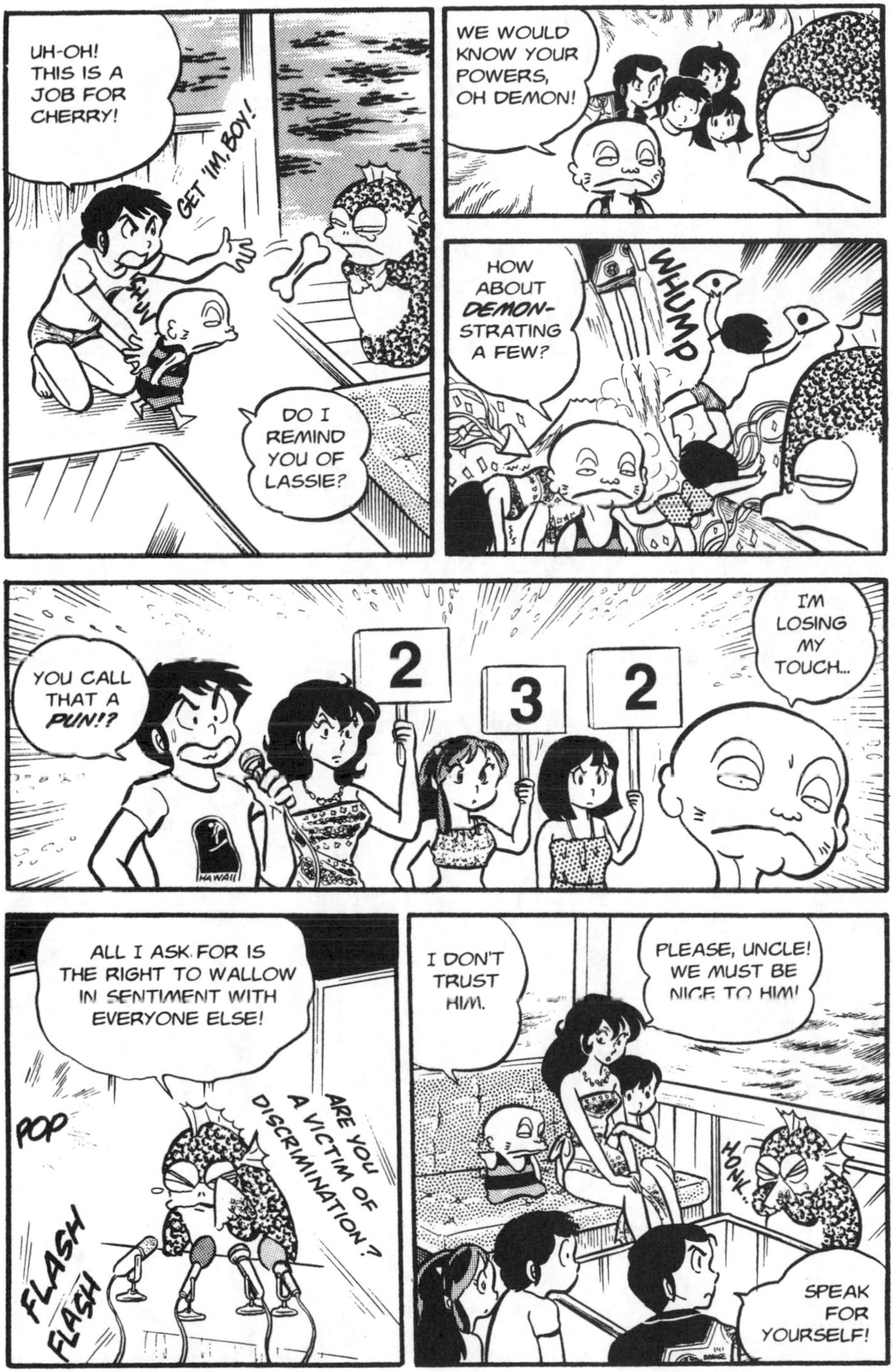
UH-OH! THIS IS A JOB FOR CHERRY!
GET 'IM, BOY!
CHUN
DO I REMIND YOU OF LASSIE?
WE WOULD KNOW YOUR POWERS, OH DEMON!
HOW ABOUT DEMON-STRATING A FEW?
WHUMP
YOU CALL THAT A PUN!?
2
3
2
I'M LOSING MY TOUCH...
HAWAII
ALL I ASK FOR IS THE RIGHT TO WALLOW IN SENTIMENT WITH EVERYONE ELSE!
POP
ARE YOU A VICTIM OF DISCRIMINATION?
FLASH
FLASH
I DON'T TRUST HIM.
PLEASE, UNCLE! WE MUST BE NICE TO HIM!
HONK..
SPEAK FOR YOURSELF!

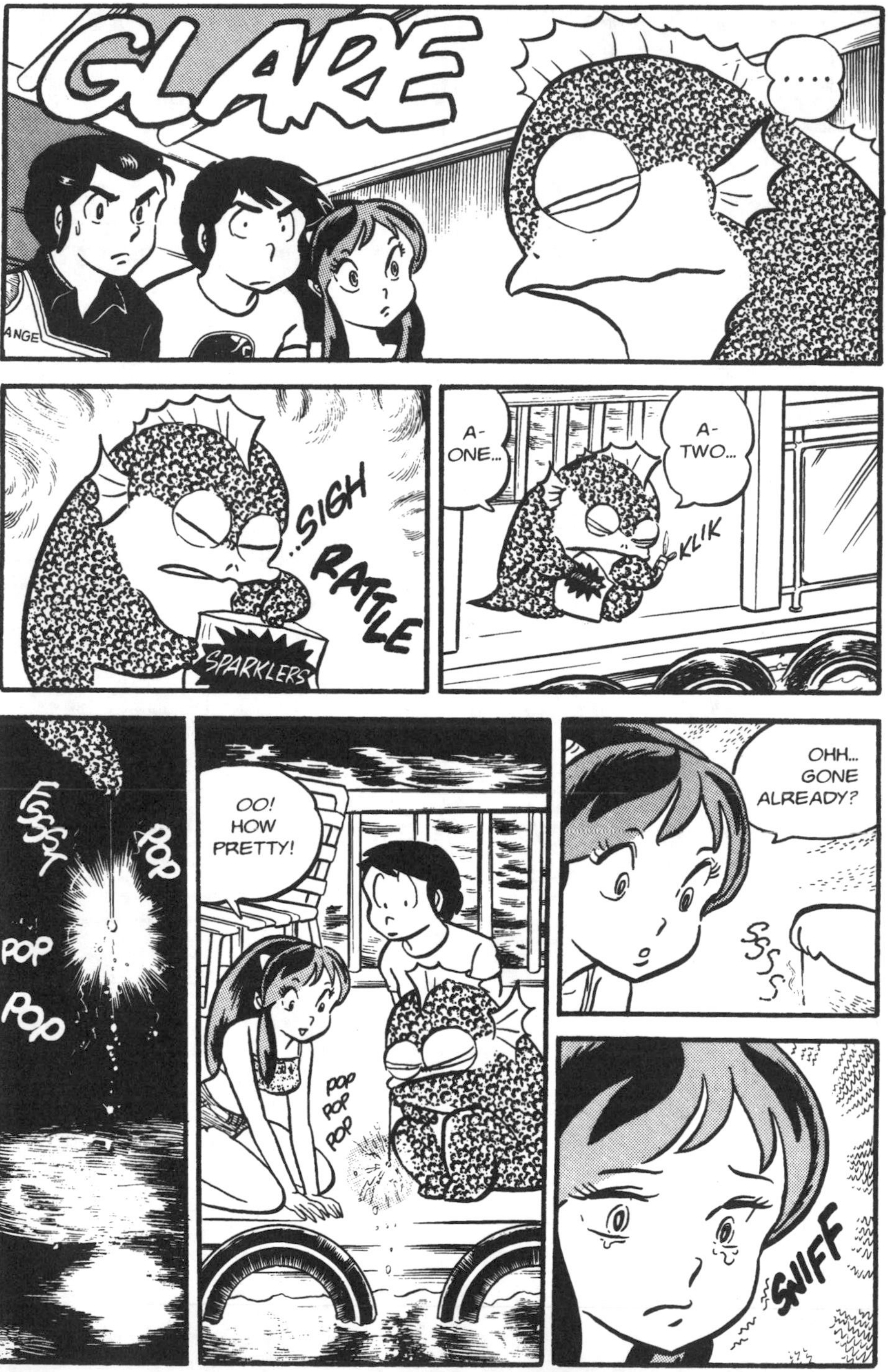
GLARE
....
ANGE
...SIGH
RATTLE
SPARKLERS
A-
ONE...
A-
TWO...
KLIK
FSSSSH
POP
POP
POP
OO!
HOW
PRETTY!
POP
POP
POP
OHH...
GONE
ALREADY?
SSSS
SNIFF

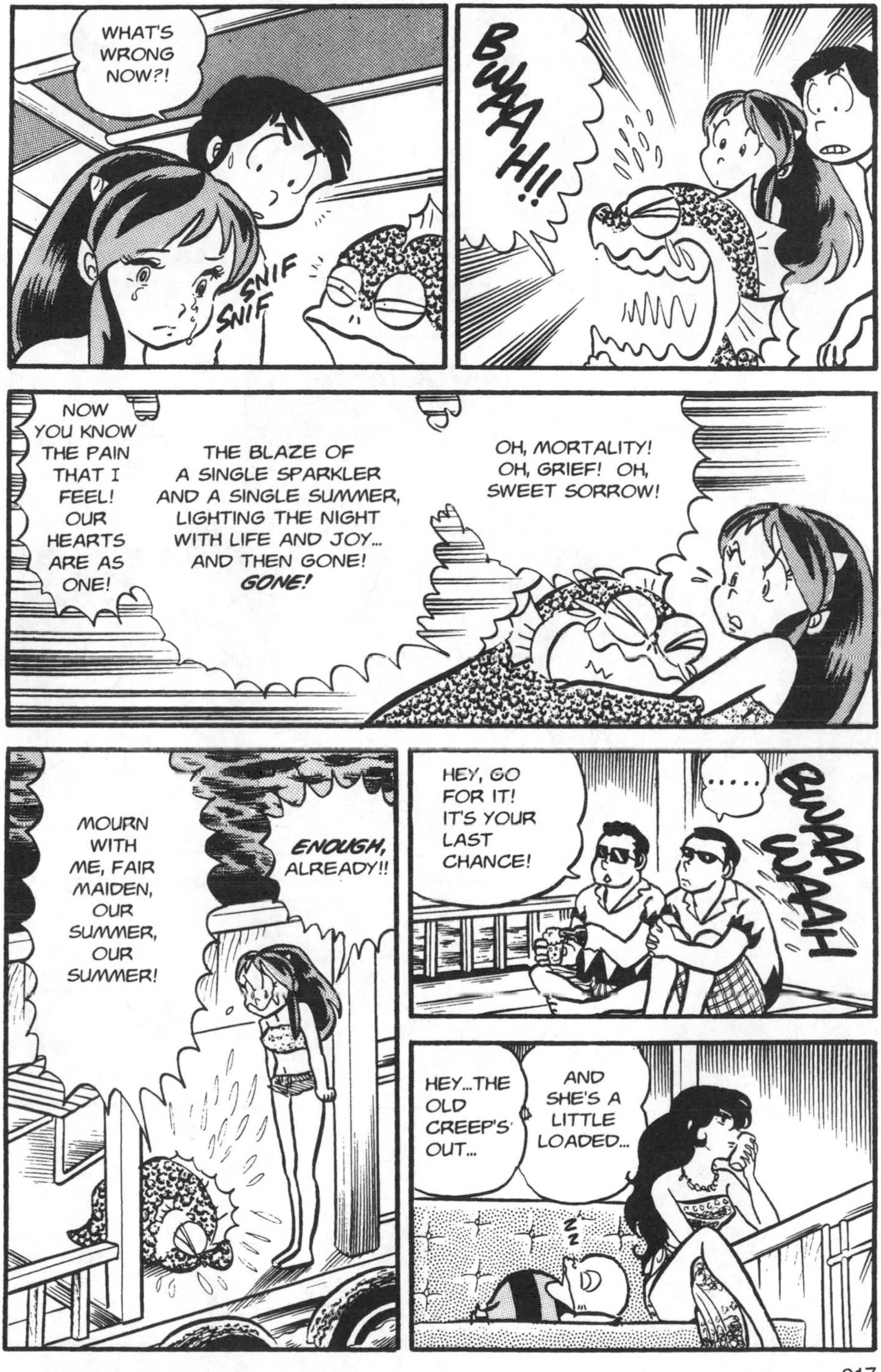
WHAT'S WRONG NOW?!
SNIF SNIF
BWAAH!!
NOW YOU KNOW THE PAIN THAT I FEEL! OUR HEARTS ARE AS ONE!
THE BLAZE OF A SINGLE SPARKLER AND A SINGLE SUMMER, LIGHTING THE NIGHT WITH LIFE AND JOY... AND THEN GONE! GONE!
OH, MORTALITY! OH, GRIEF! OH, SWEET SORROW!
MOURN WITH ME, FAIR MAIDEN, OUR SUMMER, OUR SUMMER!
ENOUGH, ALREADY!!
HEY, GO FOR IT! IT'S YOUR LAST CHANCE!
.....
BWAA WAAH
HEY...THE OLD CREEP'S OUT...
AND SHE'S A LITTLE LOADED...

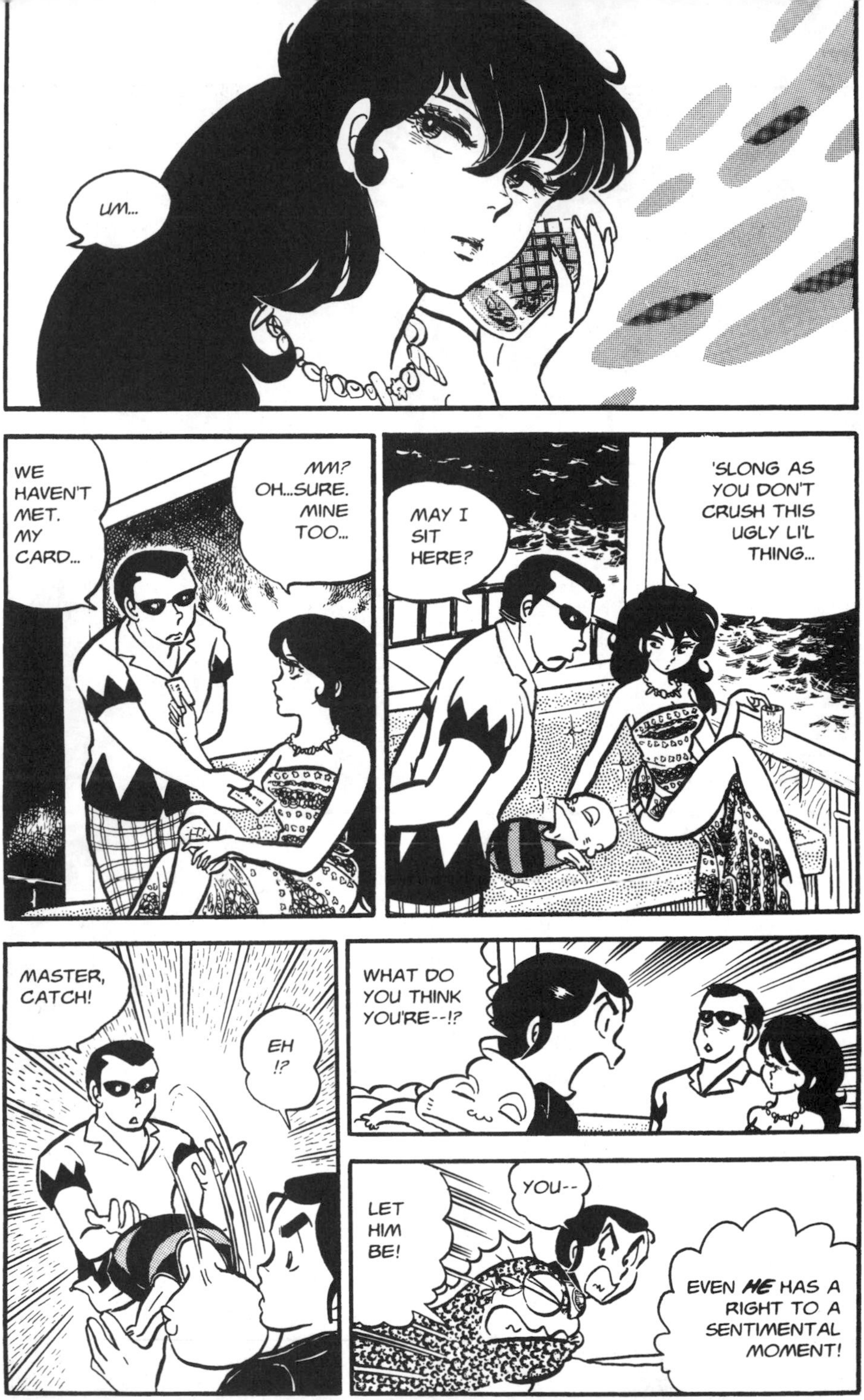
UM...
WE HAVEN'T MET. MY CARD...
MM? OH...SURE. MINE TOO...
MAY I SIT HERE?
'SLONG AS YOU DON'T CRUSH THIS UGLY LI'L THING...
MASTER, CATCH!
EH !?
WHAT DO YOU THINK YOU'RE--!?
LET HIM BE!
YOU--
EVEN ME HAS A RIGHT TO A SENTIMENTAL MOMENT!

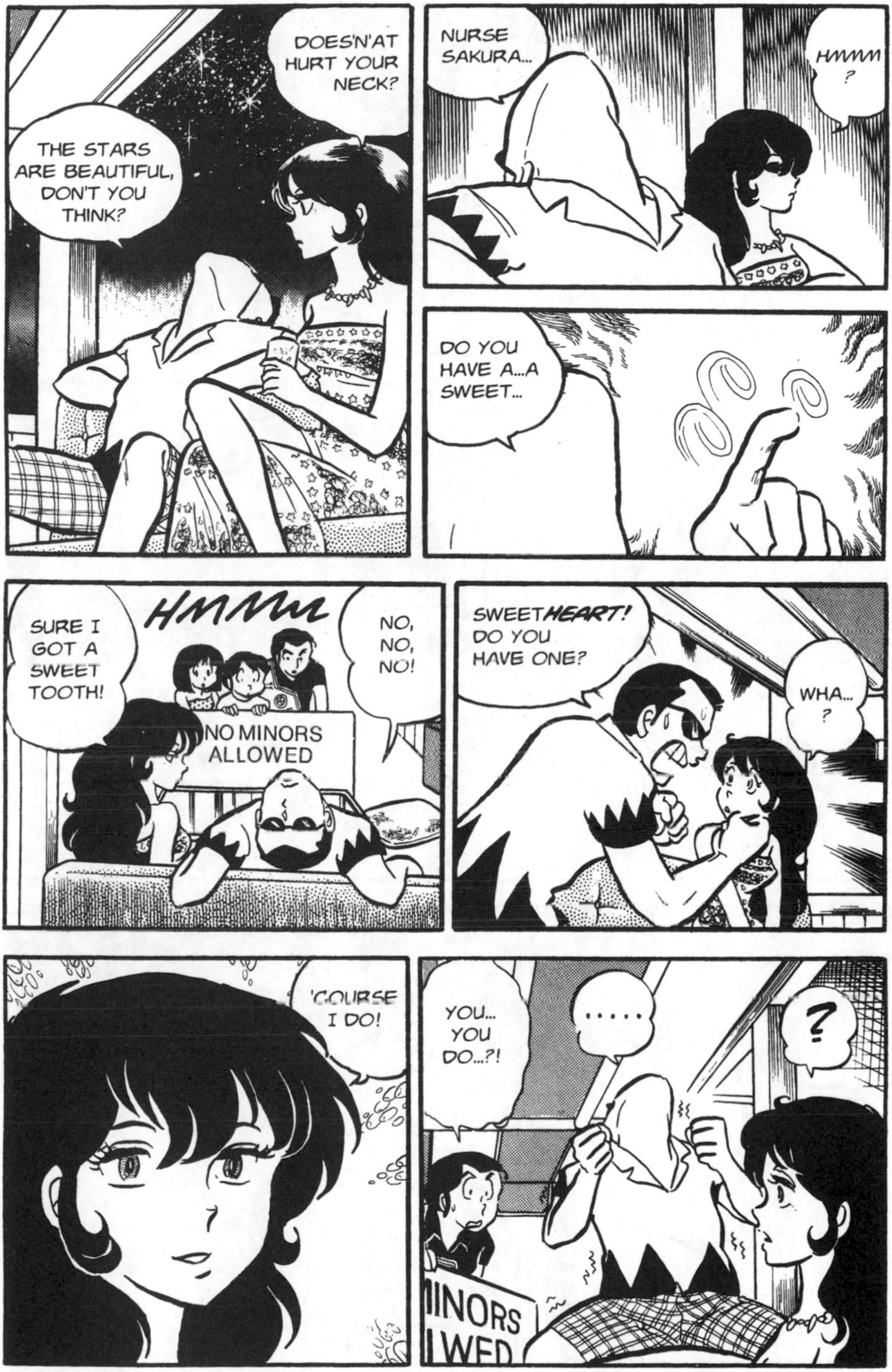
THE STARS ARE BEAUTIFUL, DON'T YOU THINK?
DOES'N'AT HURT YOUR NECK?
NURSE SAKURA...
HMMM ?
DO YOU HAVE A...A SWEET...
SURE I GOT A SWEET TOOTH!
HMMM
NO MINORS ALLOWED
NO, NO, NO!
SWEETHEART! DO YOU HAVE ONE?
WHA... ?
'COURSE I DO!
YOU... YOU DO...?!
.....
?

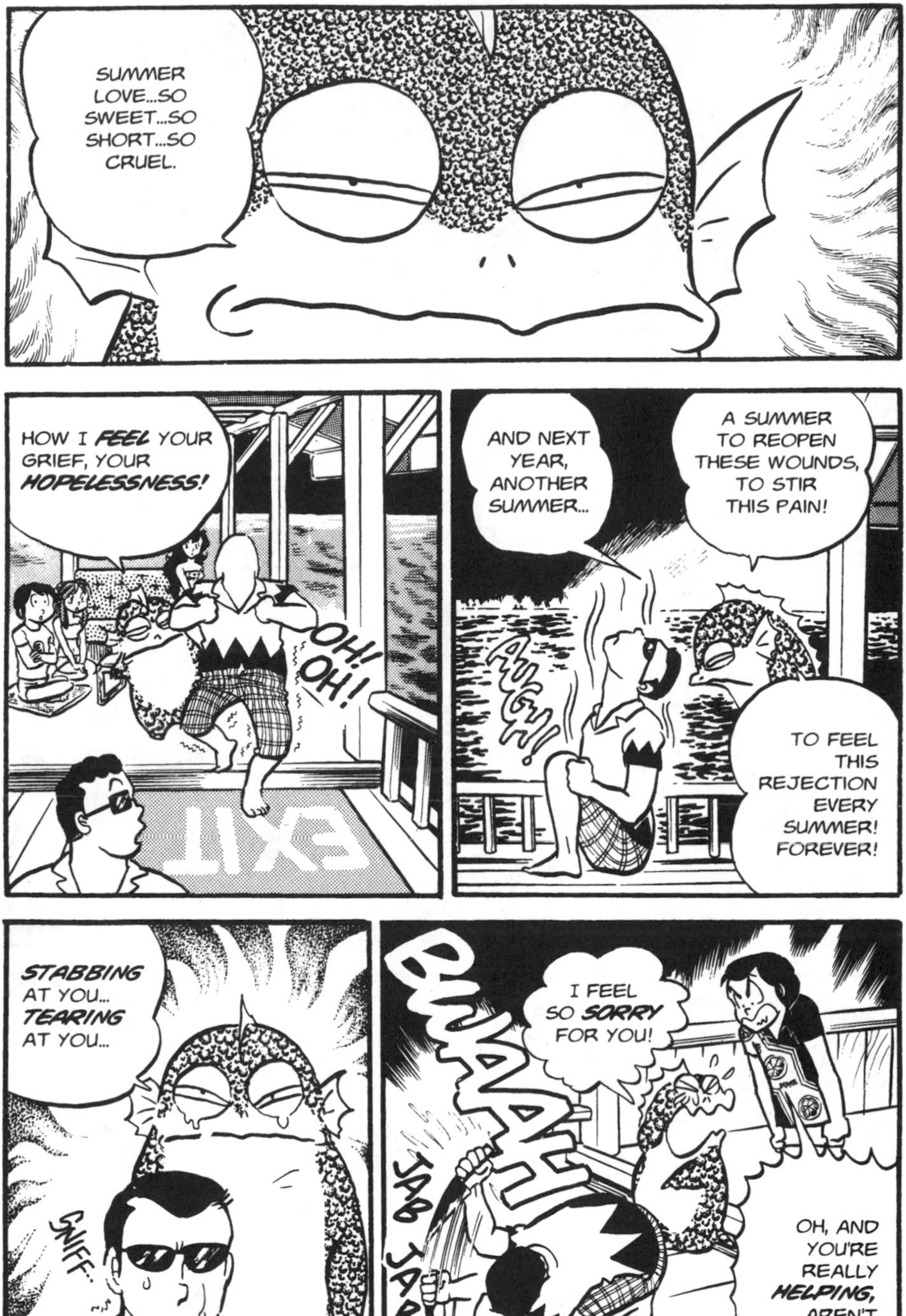
SUMMER LOVE...SO SWEET...SO SHORT...SO CRUEL.
HOW I FEEL YOUR GRIEF, YOUR HOPELESSNESS!
OH! OH!
AND NEXT YEAR, ANOTHER SUMMER...
A SUMMER TO REOPEN THESE WOUNDS, TO STIR THIS PAIN!
AUGH!!
TO FEEL THIS REJECTION EVERY SUMMER! FOREVER!
STABBING AT YOU... TEARING AT YOU...
SNIFF...
I FEEL SO SORRY FOR YOU!
JAB JAB
OH, AND YOU'RE REALLY HELPING, AREN'T YOU?!

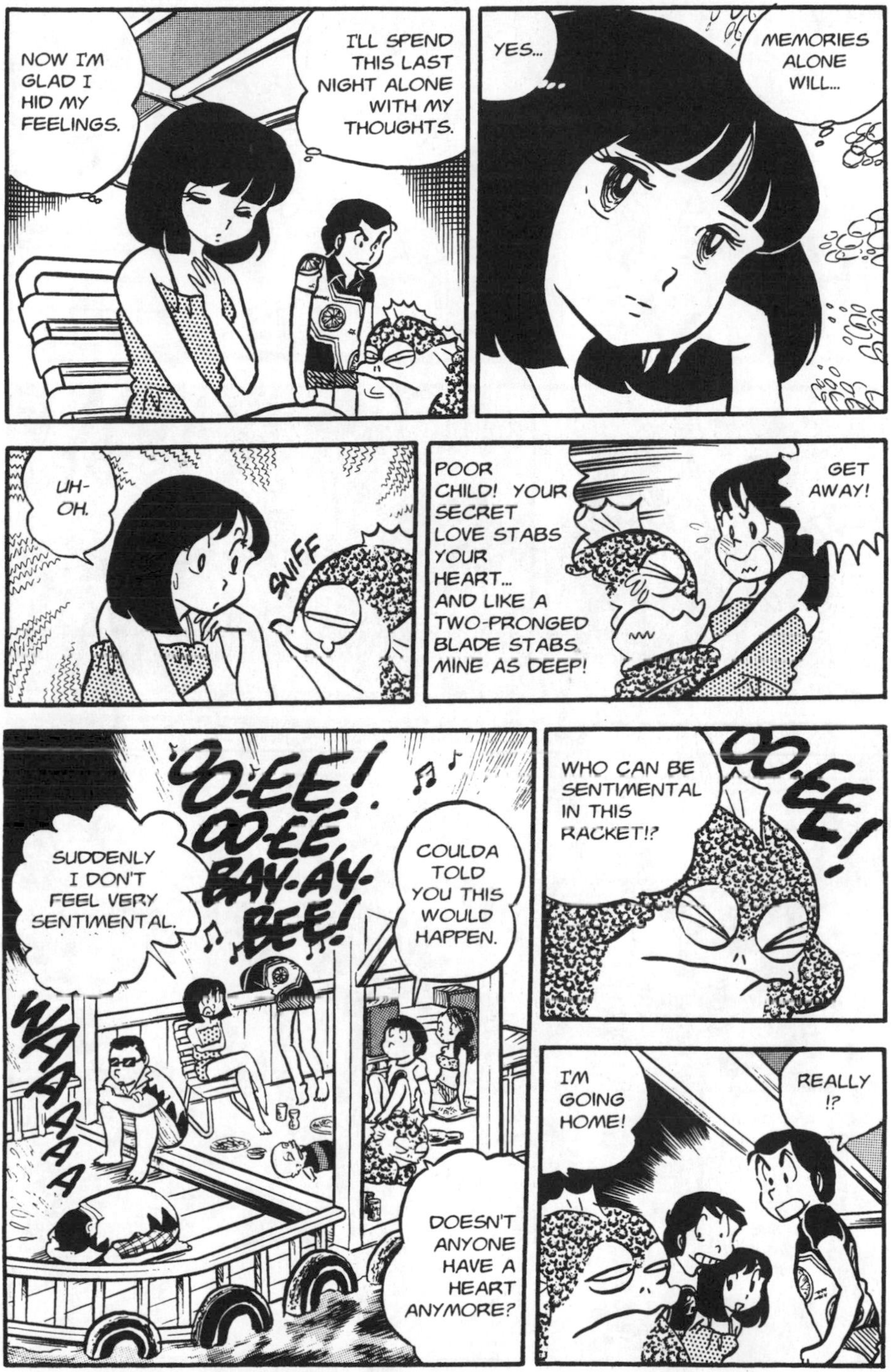
NOW I'M GLAD I HID MY FEELINGS.
I'LL SPEND THIS LAST NIGHT ALONE WITH MY THOUGHTS.
YES...
MEMORIES ALONE WILL...
UH-OH.
SNIFF
POOR CHILD! YOUR SECRET LOVE STABS YOUR HEART... AND LIKE A TWO-PRONGED BLADE STABS MINE AS DEEP!
GET AWAY!
OO-EE! OO-EE BAY-AY-BEE!
SUDDENLY I DON'T FEEL VERY SENTIMENTAL.
COULDA TOLD YOU THIS WOULD HAPPEN.
WAAAAAA
DOESN'T ANYONE HAVE A HEART ANYMORE?
WHO CAN BE SENTIMENTAL IN THIS RACKET!?
OO-EE!
I'M GOING HOME!
REALLY !?

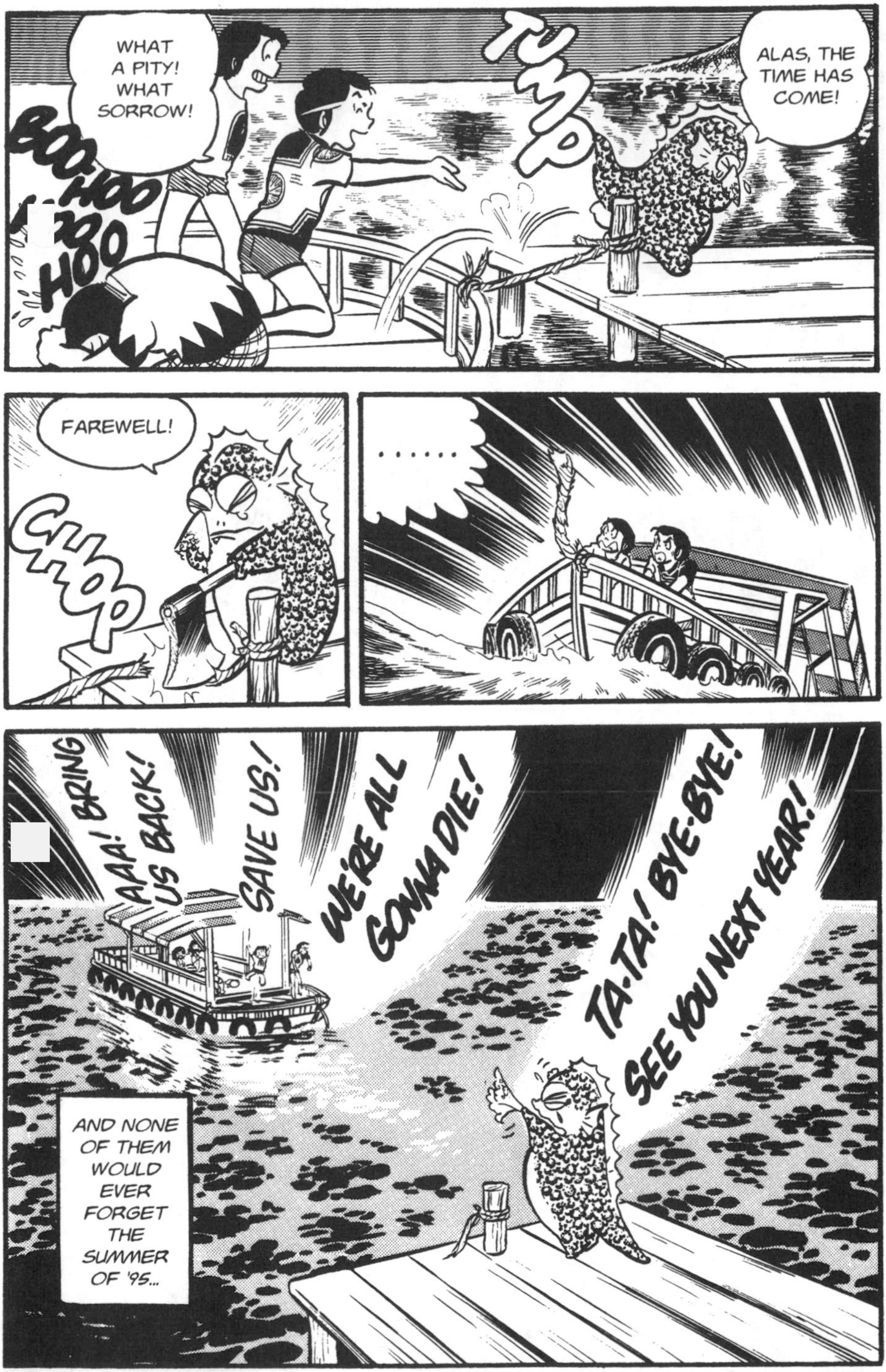
WHAT A PITY! WHAT SORROW!
BOO-HOO BOO HOO
TUMP
ALAS, THE TIME HAS COME!
FAREWELL!
CHOP
......
AAA! BRING US BACK!
SAVE US!
WE'RE ALL GONNA DIE!
TA-TA! BYE-BYE! SEE YOU NEXT YEAR!
AND NONE OF THEM WOULD EVER FORGET THE SUMMER OF '95...

END OF LUM IN THE SUN